A Century of Conflict

Communist Techniques of World Revolution

A CENTURY OF CONFLICT

Communist Techniques of World Revolution

STEFAN T. POSSONY

Professor of International Politics
Georgetown University

Chicago • HENRY REGNERY COMPANY • 1953

H X 40
P 85

TO THE

NATIONAL SECURITY COUNCIL OF THE UNITED STATES

WHICH IS FACING UP TO THE INSPIRING

RESPONSIBILITY OF BUILDING

A FUTURE FOR THE

FREE WORLD

Preface

THE PURPOSE of this book is to present the soviet pattern of conquest.

The method of this book is to trace the development of the communist doctrine of conflict management. A synthesis of the bolshevik "science of victory" concludes the volume.

Communist techniques of usurpation and expansion represent the culmination of a co-ordinated effort by several generations of skilled revolutionaries and soldiers. These methods, which reflect the political, social, and military experience of previous conquerors, are based upon elaborate studies in the humanities and social sciences as well as upon extensive pragmatic tests.

So far, communist conflict management—poorly imitated by the nazis—has stood the test of victory as well as that of defeat and catastrophe. The writer submits that the successful soviet encroachment on the free world is due largely to the operational know-how of the communists.

Marxian communism has been an important political movement since 1848. The procedures and plans of the Soviet Union have been a major, if not the most important, source of international friction since 1917. But, while great attention has been paid to the more theoretical aspects of communism, soviet strategy and tactics have been neither fully studied nor clearly understood.[1]

Kinetic communism often is termed an "ideology," as if the com-

[1] Some of the few major studies devoted to this subject are: Curzio Malaparte, *Tecnica del Colpo di Stato* (originally 1931, reprinted at Milan, Bompiani, 1948); Fedotoff White, "Soviet Philosophy of War," *Political Science Quarterly*, LI (1936), 321–53; Henry Rollin, *La Révolution Russe* (2 vols., especially Vol. II, *Le Parti Bolcheviste* [Paris, Delagrave, 1931]); Timothy Taracouzio, *War and Peace in Soviet Diplomacy* (New York, Macmillan, 1940), Chap. 2; Sigmund Neumann, "Engels and Marx: Military Concepts of the Social Revolutionaries" and Edward Mead Earle, "Lenin, Trotsky, Stalin: Soviet Concepts of War," both in *Makers of Modern Strategy: Military Thought from Machiavelli to Hitler*, ed. by E. M. Earle (Princeton, N. J.,

munist movement were held together by a bond of idealism, with individuals succumbing to communism because of its ideological attraction. Exponents of this thesis, when discussing ideas and ideologies, usually do not have in mind Marx's theoretical analysis of capitalist economics or his materialistic philosophy of history but rather the stated platform of the communist party.

Actually, the communists themselves do not preoccupy themselves unduly with their program. In their very voluminous writings they devote a minimum of space to the society of the future. There are but three basic programmatic statements in all the classical communist literature. The first of these is contained in Section II of the *Communist Manifesto* (1848). This original platform was scrapped in part when Marx and Engels, in an introduction to the 1872 edition of the *Manifesto,* described it as "antiquated . . . in some details." Second, programmatic statements are found in Marx's *The Civil War in France* (1871). Third and last, the Sixth World Congress of the Communist International (1928) built a platform which has been allowed to stand and must be considered as still the officially sanctioned one. If the ideological orientation of communists were as strong as is so often assumed, they hardly would content themselves with a program drafted a generation ago.[2]

For the most part, the communist plan as laid down in these documents is neither original nor can it be distinguished easily from other projects for social reform.

Princeton University Press, 1943); William R. Kintner, *The Front is Everywhere, Militant Communism in Action* (Norman, Okla., University of Oklahoma Press, 1950); and Nathan Leites, *The Operational Code of the Politburo* (New York, McGraw-Hill, 1951). There are also numerous studies on the Russian armed forces, communist party procedures, front organizations, propaganda, and so forth. The books by Kintner and Leites are particularly important. See also, *The Soviet Union, Background, Ideology, Reality,* a symposium ed. by Waldemar Gurian (Notre Dame, Ind., University of Notre Dame Press, 1951).

[2] The Russian social democratic party adopted a program in 1903 which Lenin, in 1917, described as "utterly antiquated." According to him, it had been antiquated long before World War I. Lenin and a few other bolsheviks, during May 1917, prepared a draft for a revision of the program, but this draft was never accepted as the official program. See V. I. Lenin, *Selected Works* (New York, International Publishers, 1943), VI, 105–24 and explanatory notes, 540–44. The program adopted in 1919 by the Russian communist party never assumed any importance and admittedly has been under revision for many years.

In its advocacy of progressive taxation, free education, wasteland cultivation, and abolition of child labor, it has, in general, been overtaken by events. One plan, for example, demands "the establishment of institutions that will gradually relieve the burden of house drudgery." Certainly the "institution" of the American dishwasher has relieved house drudgery more successfully than has the communist movement.

In other instances, the Soviet Union clearly has neglected or departed from the platform. Marx called for the closing of pawnshops, the abolition of nightwork for bakers, and the establishment of cooperative societies; and the Sixth World Congress came out against nightwork and overtime. Yet there still is nightwork and overtime in Russia.

The promised radical reform of marital and family laws was carried out, but very soon the reform measures were withdrawn: government-sponsored free love and military strength hardly are compatible.

Surely, the Soviet Union follows Marx's exhortation to burn the guillotine only in a figurative sense: it uses more modern tools of punishment.

All this is quite in line with Engels's remark: "The irony of history willed—as is usual when doctrinaires come to power—that [the parties of the commune] did the opposite of what the doctrine of their school prescribed."[3]

There remains the communist program in the strict sense of the term. It consists of three main points: (1) the abolition of private ownership; (2) the dictatorship of the proletariat; and (3) the setting up of labor armies.[4] This is not the place to take issue with these three proposals. But since, in their propaganda, the communists constantly invert this program to mean "land reform," "welfare,"[5] "de-

---

[3] Introduction to Karl Marx's *The Civil War in France, 1871* (New York, International Publishers, 1940), p. 18.

[4] The *Communist Manifesto* called for: "Equal liability of all labor. Establishment of industrial armies, especially for agriculture." "Industrial armies," of course, is a circumlocution for "forced labor." This is a point which in the early twenties was admitted quite frankly by Trotsky but which since has been dropped from public discussion. See Samuel Gompers, *Out of Their Own Mouths* (New York, Dutton, 1921).

[5] The concept of planned economy figures in the communist program only by implication. It was conceived in its modern form, not by communists, but

mocracy," and "free labor," their reluctance to push their own product is demonstrated. Truly, the last word on the matter was said by
Edmund Burke: "The people never give up their liberties but under
some delusion."

The fact of the matter is that the communists gain popular support not through pushing their own platform but by espousing non-
communist ideas. Like proper pirates, they sail under false flags.
Bolshevik propaganda strives to make people believe that communism stands for the abolition of things that are bad. Whatever may
be worrying a nation, the communists promise that they will abolish
the trouble. Whenever a country is finding its own solutions, the
communists work to undermine confidence in existing institutions. It
is true the communists have an ideology, but it is strictly a creed for
small militant and power-hungry groups.

Hence, communism is *not* a modern version of Islam. In many respects the communists are the heirs of the Mongols who conquered,
not because they had an attractive ideology, but because they out-
performed their opponents in the fields of strategy and tactics. Winston Churchill pointed out rightly: "Communism is not only a creed,
it is a plan of campaign. A communist is not only the holder of
certain opinions, he is the pledged adept of a well-thought-out means
of enforcing them."[6]

Lenin admitted this state of affairs quite frankly. "Our party has
not written a new program and the old one is worthless," he exclaimed on July 5, 1918. And, anticipating the worthlessness of
future programs, he added this remarkable statement: "Socialism

---

by Walter Rathenau, president of the German General Electric Company, for
the purpose of supporting the German army during World War I. In 1920,
Lenin, who had been impressed by the German war economy, copied the idea
and asked one of his assistants to "produce a plan (not a technical but a political scheme) which would be understood by the proletariat. For instance,
in 10 years (or 5?) we shall build 20 (or 30 or 50?) power stations. . . . We
need such a plan at once to give the masses a shining unimpeded prospect to
work for." Thus, planning is a political scheme. As to its pretended "scientific"
nature, Lenin's words are self-revealing. Even as an embryo this child of communism was characterized by "political cynicism, slapdash economics and ob-
sessions with the spectacular." See John Jewkes, *Ordeal by Planning* (New
York, Macmillan, 1948), pp. 2 f.

[6] Winston Churchill, *The Great Contemporaries* (New York, Putnam,
1938), p. 168.

has ceased to be a dogma just as it has ceased to be a program."[7]

If it is true that communist successes largely stem from the effective application of their operational techniques, do we at least have a proper appreciation of these methods? Unfortunately, examples of a lack of understanding of communist procedures are as common as they are, only too often, basic.

In the opinion of Senator Wayne Morse, "the Russian pattern is never to move from the outside in until it thinks it is also in a position to move from the inside out." Senator Morse failed to elaborate on this perplexing idea.[8]

Former Secretary of Defense Louis A. Johnson stated that Americans did not read *Mein Kampf* very intelligently, although that book presaged "anything that Hitler did, or tried to do." Mr. Johnson intimated that he was studying Stalin's works. According to his interpretation Stalin "does not look to a clash of arms" but "expects America to spend itself into bankruptcy."[9]

If Stalin believed in the economics of the classical school, this interpretation, which Mr. Johnson failed to document, might be acceptable. However, since Stalin is an economic "planner" of some prominence and proceeds from non-classical premises, it would seem more logical to argue that he expects the United States to become stronger through armament-induced government management of the economy. Russia has carried out what are relatively larger armament programs than the United States while gaining strength, economic-

---

[7] "Proceedings of the Fifth All-Russian Congress of Soviets, July 5, 1918," reprinted in James Bunyan, *Intervention, Civil War, and Communism in Russia, April–December 1918, Documents and Materials* (Baltimore, Johns Hopkins Press, 1936), p. 210.

[8] *Hearings before the Committee on Armed Services and the Committee on Foreign Relations, Military Situation in the Far East, Part I* [U.S. Congress, 82nd, 1st sess., Senate. (Washington, D.C., Govt. Print. Off., 1951), p. 227]. (Hereafter referred to as *Far East Hearings*.)

[9] *Ibid., Part IV*, pp. 26 f. John Maynard Keynes appears to be the original source of this interpretation, although his version does not refer to spending or bankruptcy. "Lenin is said to have declared that the best way to destroy the capitalist system was to debauch the currency." See *The Economic Consequences of the Peace* (New York, Harcourt, Brace, 1920), p. 235. *If* Lenin said it, he probably was discussing communist tactics applied in Russia against the financial resources of the White armies during the civil war. He dealt with a situation where the communists already had seized power, not with a tactic of power conquest.

ally. The United States can lay on a far better performance, and
Stalin knows it. If anything, Stalin would view the American armament program as a most undesirable safeguard against an economic
crisis and as an obstacle to Russia's catching up in the race for industrial output.

According to Senator Taft, the soviets intend to take over Europe
by "infiltration and persuasion." If Russia took Germany, the soviets
"would rely on France turning communist by itself."

I doubt very much if Russia would attack France or Britain in a military
war. . . . I do not believe it is at all clear that the Russians contemplate
the military conquest of the world. . . . I believe they know it is impossible. It would take them at least 100 years to build up their sea power to
enable them to get across the seas. I do not believe that they even contemplate a military aggression with their own soldiers against the other
nations.[10]

Nor was Admiral Sherman convinced that the Russians wanted
"a general war, largely because the industrial potential of the United
States would act as a great deterrent against such a Russian plan."[11]

Both General Marshall[12] and General Bradley[13] expressed the belief that the soviets aim to dominate the whole world. But how?

Admiral Sherman stated: "I am not convinced that they do not
see a way to achieve domination without general war." But General
Bradley apparently cannot concur with this cautious, triple-negative
estimate. He said: "I wish we could feel sure that Russia realized the
destructiveness of these [atomic] bombs, . . . and would consent to
a period of peace. Apparently, they are not willing to do so."

These conflicting estimates reveal a most dangerous confusion. Is
it really so difficult to solve the Churchillian riddle wrapped up in an
enigma inside a mystery?

It is my hope that this book may contribute to a better understanding of the nature of the beast. More than ever before, *knowledge is
power.*

STEFAN T. POSSONY

November 1952

[10] *Congressional Record*, January 5, 1951, p. 68.
[11] *Far East Hearings, Part II, op. cit.*, p. 1658.
[12] *Ibid., Part I*, p. 384.
[13] *Ibid., Part II*, p. 945.

Acknowledgments

M Y THANKS go to Leon Gouré who led me through problems of primary sources and over difficulties with the Russian language; to Joseph Z. Kornfeder who taught me how to decipher communist double-talk; to Benjamin Mandel who provided me with otherwise unobtainable documentation and who also gave me the benefit of his experienced counsel; to Herschel Williams whose moral and intellectual support carried me through many weary moments; to D. S. W., without whose stubborn criticism and stylistic skill I could not have overcome the difficulties posed by the confusing context of the book; to Lee Coker who made it possible for me to collect my thoughts and start on an otherwise forbidding task; and above all to Vally Possony, without whose infinite patience, indomitable endurance, and exceptional talent at unraveling illegible manuscripts this volume never could have been completed.

STEFAN T. POSSONY

Table of Contents

"Our cruel and unrelenting enemy leaves us only the choice of a brave resistance, or the most abject submission. We have, therefore, to resolve to conquer or to die."

GEORGE WASHINGTON

August 1776

Introduction

Violence Is the Father of All Things

VIOLENCE is the focus of bolshevik operational thinking. The communists believe that class war is the essence of history and that old social orders die and new social orders emerge only through violence. Specifically, they do not believe that fundamental social transformations can take place in a gradual or evolutionary fashion. The historical process must carry through convulsion and crisis, revolution and war. The communist millennium will be prepared by a profound and long-lasting crisis of the capitalist system, but it can be ushered in only after the preceding social order has been destroyed by force.[1]

[1] The communists express their thoughts through the use of terms which are not habitually employed in the English language. Some of these terms are propaganda clichés, such as, "progressive," "forward-looking," "peace-loving," and so forth. Quite a few terms are "false-flag expressions," elements of the "Aesopian language" used among professional communists. For example, the term "proletariat" usually is a circumlocution for communists; "vanguard of the proletariat" simply means communist party. Whenever the communists talk about the "mass of the people," they really mean communist sympathizers. In English, the term "democracy" means government by the people, or a form of government in which the supreme power is vested in the people and is exercised by them or their elected agents. (*The American College Dictionary* [New York, Random House, 1947].) In soviet terminology, the word "democracy" means a government in which members of the communist party participate and which appoints communist agents to key positions. It also means a type of government preceding full control of the state by the communists. Similarly, the term "peace" means, in English, freedom from war and hostilities and, in a broader sense, absence of strife or dissension. To the communists, peace is a condition in which national or international struggle is waged without the employment of regular armed forces. Terms such as "class" and its various derivatives, "bourgeoisie," "proletariat," "capitalist," and so forth, reputedly have scientific meaning but in reality cannot be defined properly. Marx stopped writing *Das Kapital* when he found himself incapable of defining the class concept.

The importance ascribed by the communists to violence is a matter of dogmatic belief. This belief is not held arguable and never has been questioned by any orthodox communist. It permeates all their thinking and most of their actions. Communist behavior cannot be comprehended unless this dogmatic belief in violence is accepted as the key.

The communist dogma does not preach that violence must be employed always and everywhere. Violence is merely the method by which great historical crises are finding their ultimate solutions. According to Marx, the capitalist system is cleft by its inherent contradictions. With the passing of time, these contradictions become ever more acute. They render the downfall of capitalism inevitable but not automatic. The supreme crisis produced by these contradictions will lead to a revolutionary situation, but the rule of capitalism can be ended only through a revolutionary act, through the application of violence.

Marx, himself, clarified his position through the simile of the midwife: while the new order may grow within the womb of the capitalist mother, revolution is required for the act of birth. This position was re-emphasized by Lenin who insisted upon the "inevitability of a violent revolution." The bourgeois state "cannot be replaced by the proletarian state . . . through withering away, but as a general rule only through a violent revolution."[2]

According to Stalin,

Capitalism is decaying, but it must not be compared simply with a tree which has decayed to such an extent that it must fall to the ground of its own accord. No, revolution, the substitution of one social system for another, has always been a struggle, a painful and cruel struggle, a life and death struggle, and every time the people of the new world came into power they had to defend themselves against the attempts of the old world to restore the old order by force. . . . The communists regard the substitution of one special system for another, not simply as a spontaneous and peaceful process, but as a complicated, long and violent process.[3]

At another place Stalin wrote:

The dictatorship of the proletariat cannot come about as a result of the peaceful development of bourgeois society and of bourgeois democracy;

[2] Lenin, *State and Revolution* (New York, International Publishers, 1935), pp. 18–20, 43, 73.

[3] H. G. Wells, *Marxism versus Liberalism—An Interview of Joseph Stalin* (New York, International Publishers, 1935), pp. 16 f.

it can come only as the result of the destruction of the bourgeois state machine, of the bourgeois army, of the bourgeois civil administration, and of the bourgeois police.[4]

It is an error to assume that the communists equate violence with armed uprising. At its Sixth World Congress in 1928, the Communist International proclaimed specifically: "The overthrow of capitalism is impossible without force, without armed uprising and *proletarian wars* against the bourgeoisie."[5]

The erroneous assumption that armed uprisings are the chief bolshevik technique of violence is due to a misunderstanding of the term "revolution." The soviets, of course, are committed to "revolution." They want to liquidate the upper classes, abolish the democratic form of government, destroy the free enterprise system of production, and take away power from their political opponents. The communists have the firm intention of remaking society, a process of social "re-structuration" which is often described as revolution.

However, the communists are *not* committed to armed uprising as their one and only method of social and political change. Armed uprisings and revolutions are not identical. Armed uprising simply is one of the methods by which a revolution, the remaking of a society, can be initiated. The communists feel free to select any method of seizing power that may be practical and advantageous at a given time and place.

The dogma of violence does not stand in isolation but depends upon the thesis that non-violent means of struggle must be employed together with techniques of violence. The communists have accepted Clausewitz's statement that no strong power *not* in the throes of internal discord can be defeated. They insist that uprisings cannot succeed without the existence of crucial dissensions within the ranks of the government. Hence, non-violence techniques of struggle must precede, accompany, and follow the application of violence whether violence takes the form of insurrection, partisan warfare, or war.

As a first approximation to the identification of the bolshevik concept of operation, we may accept General MacArthur's description

[4] J. V. Stalin, *Foundations of Leninism* (New York, International Publishers, 1934), p. 52.

[5] *The Struggle Against Imperialist War and the Tasks of the Communists,* Resolution of the Sixth World Congress of the Communist International, July–August 1928 (New York, Workers Library Publishers, 1932), p. 10. [Italics added.]

of communist tactics. Replying to a statement by Senator James W. Fulbright that the "combination of communism with the great military strength of Russia," the "extension of the physical power of Russia over so many satellites," and the "imbalance in the power potential among nations" are the main concern of American security, the general answered:

That would be one of the threats of communism but I do not believe for a minute that you should discount the enormous attempts at internal sabotage, the fact that the various cells that they feed out don't practice military force, but they practice the tremendous psychological factors of propaganda, of creating confusion, of bewilderment, of belittling and assassinating characters of the people that are opposed to them, of all the methods of the fifth column, which have so undermined the confidence of free peoples in their own institutions—those things are raging every day in almost every country of the world. They have nothing to do with military force but they are allied with it.[6]

[6] *Hearings before the Committee on Armed Services and the Committee on Foreign Relations, Military Situation in the Far East, Part I* [U.S. Congress, 82nd, 1st sess., Senate. (Washington, D. C., Govt. Print. Off., 1951), p. 277].

A Century of Conflict

1. Origins · 1848–1916

MARX AND ENGELS AS WORLD STRATEGISTS

A GREAT deal of early socialist writing was based on the usually unstated premise that there is a close interrelationship between war and revolution. This idea was part and parcel of the political thinking in the nineteenth century. (It appears frequently in Bismarck's papers.) Hence, many nineteenth-century revolutionaries concerned themselves with matters of war. Wilhelm Weitling, a friend of Marx and Engels, called for a new messiah who would realize the teachings of the first Messiah through revolutionary war. J. P. Proudhon wrote a two-volume book,[1] perhaps the most radical glorification of war ever penned, which went further than even the celebrated passage on the "divine character" of war written by Joseph de Maistre.

Marx and Engels did not produce a systematic theory of war, but they showed much interest in military matters. Engels served as an active participant in the Baden insurrection during the 1848 German revolution and devoted a great deal of time to the study of military problems. He became quite an expert in military technology and maintained personal contacts with some of the foremost military writers of his time, particularly with Wilhelm Rüstow, a Prussian staff officer who served as chief of staff to Garibaldi. Appropriately, his corevolutionaries nicknamed Engels the "general."

If the scattered writings of Engels on military problems were collected, they would make up several large volumes. In fact, his writings in the field of military science "are more numerous than the rest of his literary work."[2] If such a collection ever had been made, this

---

[1] *La Guerre et la paix* (2 vols., Paris, Dentu, 1861).

[2] Sigmund Neumann, "Engels and Marx: Military Concepts of the Social Revolutionaries," in *Makers of Modern Strategy: Military Thought from Machiavelli to Hitler,* ed. by Edward Mead Earle (Princeton, Princeton University Press, 1943), p. 158.

side of the Marxist doctrine probably would have drawn as much attention as the economic analyses set forth in *Das Kapital*.[3]

In action and theory, both Marx and Engels consistently opposed pacifism. To them, war was an instrument of revolution and progress. They usually called, and worked, for support of those countries whose victory could further the cause of revolution, even to the point of plain warmongering.

Since there is a close interrelationship between internal and external politics, they reasoned, the fight for revolution must be waged both on the national and on the international front.[4]

As early as 1848, Marx and Engels advocated revolutionary war by Germany against Denmark. Such a war might have pitted the weak democratic German states against the crushingly superior power of Prussia, England, and Russia. Yet, they argued that war would stimulate the waning revolutionary movement in Germany.

In another variant of this same concept, Marx thought that victory of revolution in Germany would lead to a preventive attack by Russia. The revolution could not be secured without a defeat of the tsarist regime. Hence, he called for a war of revolutionary Europe against European reaction.

If Germany could be brought into war against Russia, it would be all over with Habsburg and Hohenzollern, and the revolution would win everywhere.

Marx and Engels advocated a German alliance with Poland, which at that time was a province of Russia, and they envisaged a war for the liberation of Italy. They wanted to fight for every "revolutionary people."[5]

Marx also considered the role of England. He believed, for example, that the Hungarian revolution could not survive without a concurrent successful insurrection of the French proletariat. A successful rising in France would provoke British intervention. A world war

---

[3] Some of his military writings were collected in Friedrich Engels, *Notes on the War. Sixty articles reprinted from the "Pall Mall Gazette," 1870–1871* (Vienna, Volksbuchhandlung, 1923). Note: An English book published in Austria.

[4] G. Sinowjew (Sinovyev), *Der Krieg und die Krise des Sozialismus* (Vienna, Verlag fuer Literatur und Politik, 1924), pp. 98, 164.

[5] *Ibid.,* pp. 98–100.

would follow; Britain would be defeated; and the British revolutionaries, the chartists, would have a chance to seize power.

The chartists at the head of the English government—only at that moment will the social revolution cross from the realm of utopia into the realm of reality.[6]

Marx often talked of violence as the "midwife" of a future society. But he conceived of violence not merely in insurrectionist terms. War is the highest form of violence; hence, it would be the preferred midwife at the birth of communism. "Surely the fact is evident," wrote Friedrich Engels to Karl Marx on September 26, 1851, "that a disorganized army and a complete breakdown of discipline have been the condition as well as the result of every victorious revolution." Trotsky added: "The whole history of humanity proves this simple and indubitable law."[7]

In 1853, Marx stated to the central committee of the communist league:

You have to go through fifteen, twenty, fifty years of civil wars and wars between nations, not only to alter conditions, but to change yourselves and make yourselves fit for political rule.

During the Crimean war, Engels advocated a "war of principle," as he called it, uniting the revolutionary forces of Germany, Poland, Finland, Hungary, and Italy against counterrevolutionary Russia. Marx published numerous articles in the New York *Tribune* in which he showed himself both a "Russophobe" of large dimensions and a radical warmonger.[8] He rooted for British victory because the defeat of Russia would weaken and possibly destroy the world's foremost "reactionary" power and hence facilitate the revolutionary movement.

---

[6] Marx, quoted from Sinovyev, *op. cit.,* p. 105.

[7] Earle, "Lenin, Trotsky, Stalin: Soviet Concepts of War," in *Makers of Modern Strategy, op. cit.,* p. 337.

[8] These articles were collected under the title *The Eastern Question* (London, Sonnenschein, 1897). On Marx's motivations and his contempt for pacifists, see *Karl Marx und Friedrich Engels, Briefwechsel,* issued by D. Ryazanov and V. Adoratski (4 vols., Berlin and Moscow, Marx-Engels Archiv, 1929–31).

In 1859, at the time of the Franco-Austrian war, Engels wrote to Ferdinand Lassalle:

Long live the war, if the French and the Russians attack us at the same time. When we are about to go down, then in that desperate situation, all parties will wear themselves out, and for its salvation, the nation will have to turn to the most energetic party.

This was the early version of the theory of "revolutionary defeatism": the crisis would impose a "people's government" in which the revolutionaries must participate. In order to win, resistance would be reorganized through revolution.

The revolutionaries favored the unification of Italy and Germany even if it were achieved by Napoleon III or Bismarck. Marx and Engels called upon Germany to enter the war of 1859 against Napoleon III—the Rhine must be defended on the Po, said Engels. Russian intervention against Germany would follow. Then, the nationalist war could be transformed into revolutionary war. At the same time, the exigencies of the war against Russia would lead to the overthrow of reaction in Germany.[9]

Marx and Engels paid great attention to the American Civil War. When Engels became doubtful about the victory of the North, Marx warned him not to give excessive weight to the purely military aspects of conflict.[10] Engels concluded that force and economics are the key factors of historic change.

In his preface to the first edition of *Das Kapital* (1867), Marx wrote:

As in the 18th century the American war of independence sounded the tocsin for the European middle class, so in the 19th century the American civil war sounded it for the European working class.

This statement describing the relationship between war and revolution became, in variations, perhaps the single most frequent soviet utterance.[11] It is often phrased in this form: World War I brought

---

[9] Sinovyev, *op. cit.,* pp. 110–14.

[10] Neumann in Earle, *op. cit.,* p. 167.

[11] Pacifists and the Philistines "go on evading the question of how to combat imperialist wars. . . . *The first bolshevik revolution has wrested the first hundred million people* of this earth from imperialist war and from imperialist peace. Subsequent revolutions will wrest the whole of humanity from such

communism to Russia; World War II brought communism to eastern Europe and China. As to what World War III can be expected to bring, the reader is not left in any doubt.

For example, Malenkov, celebrating the thirty-second anniversary of the communist revolution, asserted that World War II

led to the establishment of peoples' democratic regimes in a number of countries of central and southeast Europe, led to the victory of the great Chinese people. Can there be any doubt whatever, . . . [that] a third world war . . . will be the grave not only for individual capitalist states, but for the whole world capitalism?[12]

During the Austro-Prussian war of 1866, Engels expected a defeat of Prussia and a resulting revolutionary upheaval. His hopes were in vain.

During the Franco-Prussian war of 1870, Marx and Engels took the position that Prussia fought a defensive war. They believed that Napoleon's victory would hurt the revolutionary cause by delaying the unification of Germany and reducing the *élan* of the "democratic" movement. In the case of a Prussian victory, Bismarck's sword would create favorable circumstances for revolution by changing, through the resultant unification, the internal force relationship in Germany to the advantage of the proletariat. Engels wrote in August 1870: "Bismarck accomplishes part of our work, in his fashion and against his will, but he does so." The German revolution required national unification which could not be achieved without war. However, the war also should enhance the cause of internationalism directly—Germans and Frenchmen should fraternize.

The war had yet another advantage: it was training the French proletariat in the use of weapons. "This is the best guarantee of the

wars and from such peace." Lenin, *Selected Works* (New York, International Publishers, 1943), VI, 506. (The italics are Lenin's.) Stalin (*Sochineniya* [Moscow, Ogis, 1948], IX, 108) explained that World War I cost capitalism the Russian revolution and undermined the position of capitalism in the colonial areas. A second attempt at the redivision of the world would cost capitalism even more. "These prospects lead directly to the possibility of socialist victory in some capitalist countries in the period of imperialism." For similar quotes, see Robert Strausz-Hupé and Stefan T. Possony, *International Relations in the Age of the Conflict between Democracy and Dictatorship* (New York, McGraw-Hill, 1950), pp. 777, 779, 795.

[12] *New York Times,* November 7, 1948, p. 15.

future."[13] Marx realized that the war would sound the death knell for Louis Napoleon and destroy the Second Empire. To him, this constituted progress.

By contrast, he feared that the revolutionary movement in Germany would be endangered if Prussia and Russia were to conclude an alliance—Russia being still the chief enemy of revolution. He believed that Tsar Alexander was betting on the mutual exhaustion of France and Germany, making Russia the arbiter of Europe. With uncommon insight, he predicted that the annexation of Alsace-Lorraine would ultimately drive France into Russia's hands and render war between Germany and Russia inevitable. This war would be the midwife of the unavoidable social revolution in Russia.[14]

The Paris commune which resulted from the defeat of France by Prussia attracted the strongest attention of the communist founding fathers. The commune was to set a tradition. The interpretation of this event by Marx and Engels became the starting point of Lenin's operational thinking.[15]

THE FATHERS OF MODERN WAR

MARX and Engels were called "the fathers of modern total war." Modern strategists discovered that warfare is of a fourfold nature—diplomatic, economic, psychological, and, as a last resort, military. This was common knowledge to Engels and Marx:

They were fully aware that military campaigns could be lost long before the first bullet was shot, that they would, in fact, be decided beforehand on the preliminary battle fronts of economic and psychological warfare. They certainly recognized that the many-fronted war was one and undivided and thus could be won or lost on the international battle line as well as by a nation's civil strife or within each citizen's faltering soul.

[13] Sinovyev, *op. cit.,* pp. 118, 150.

[14] This remarkable prophecy is contained in a letter to Adolf Sorge, September 1, 1870, see, Sinovyev, *op. cit.,* p. 151.

[15] Lenin made a close study of the military achievements and policies of the commune, paying particular attention to the writings of the revolutionary military leader Cluseret. He also consulted Lissagaray's *Histoire de la Commune de 1871*; a recent edition of this rare work came out in Buenos Aires, Editions du Triolent, 1944. See further, Frank Jellinek, *The Paris Commune of 1871* (London, Gollancz, 1937).

War and revolution—unmistakably established as twin movements in our time—were at that early period seen in their fundamental and continuous inter-relationship by these keen strategists of the world revolution.[16]

Actually, Engels even saw the fifth element of modern war: technology. According to him, armaments, composition of armed forces, organization, tactics, and strategy depend, above all, on the level of production and the development of the means of transportation.

It is not the free creation of the commander's intellect or genius which revolutionizes the art of war, but the invention of a better weapon and changes in the human material. The influence even of the greatest military genius is restricted to the adaptations of fighting methods to new weapons and to a new type of fighter.[17]

For a long while Engels played with the idea that the army could serve as "the major channel through which a democratic society might emerge."[18] This thought was re-emphasized in 1922 by Bukharin[19] and later characteristically amended by Stalin, who considered that the army of the proletarian dictatorship is a great social and educational force where both workers and peasants meet together and with the party.

The army is the only all-Russian, all-federal assembly where people of all areas meet, learn and get used to political life. *The army is a gigantic transmission belt.*[20]

Engels's idea presupposed that in a democratic country conscription must break down the traditions built by previous class armies officered by the upper classes and, therefore, deprive the bourgeois government of its usual instrument of repression. The conscript

[16] Neumann in Earle, *op. cit.,* p. 156.

[17] This summary of Engels' foresighted doctrine was given by D. B. Ryazanov, "Voyennoye delo i Marksism," speech of March 1926, reprinted in *Voina i voyennoye iskusstvo v svete istoricheskoye materializma,* ed. by M. N. Gorev, Sbornik statei (Moscow-Leningrad, 1927). See also, Colonel Théodore A. Makhine, *L'Armée rouge, La puissance militaire de l'URSS* (Paris, Payot, 1938), pp. 64 f.

[18] Neumann in Earle, *op. cit.,* p. 168. See also, Engels, "The Military Question and the German Working Class," 1865.

[19] N. Bukharin and E. Preobrazhensky, *The ABC of Communism* (Communist Party of Great Britain, 1924), pp. 212–15.

[20] Stalin, *op. cit.,* V, 204 f. [Italics added.]

army would change the class structure of the army and set up the lower classes as the main military striking force. It also would arm the proletariat, thus creating the main prerequisite of revolution and, directly or indirectly, bring about a different type of society.

Old socialist ideas never die. They may fade away, but they are bound to return. In 1928, the Sixth World Congress of the Comintern told the communist parties to

follow the precepts of Marx and Engels who, in the epoch of great national wars, opposed the petty bourgeois democratic utopia of militia and advocated universal military service, the democratization of existing armies and their conversion into revolutionary armies. After the Paris commune, Marx and Engels advocated . . . the dissolution of standing bourgeois armies and their substitution by the armed nation.[21]

In 1895, shortly before his death, Engels, in an introduction to a new edition of an old work by Marx, took a critical attitude toward the conventional doctrine of the uprising.[22] He pointed out that barricades no longer could have material effect on street battles and that, generally speaking, the fighting methods of 1848 had become obsolete "in every respect." In the early part of the nineteenth century, he continued, the worker was capable of making weapons and ammunition by his own hands. Large numbers of workers armed with homemade weapons could and did engage the bourgeois army on equal or better terms. Given substantial equality in armament, the workers could rely on their larger numbers, mobility, and camouflage to counteract the better training and discipline of the army. By the end of the nineteenth century, however, workers no longer were able to produce effective weapons at home. The bourgeois armies had acquired vastly superior equipment and, through railroads, superior mobility: they now possessed a greater "war potential" than the revolutionaries.

In former times, political life had been concentrated in the capital city. By paralyzing the capital's garrison, a revolutionary minority could often gain control of the entire country. But capital cities no

21 *The Struggle against Imperialist War and the Tasks of the Communists.* Resolution of the Sixth World Congress of the Communist International, July–August 1928 (New York, Workers Library Publishers, 1932), p. 37.

22 Engels, Preface to Marx's "Class Struggles in France, 1848–1850," reprinted in *The Revolutionary Act* (New York, 1922).

longer held the monopoly of political power. Since entire nations were becoming politically conscious, power had to be seized in many cities. Numerous garrisons had to be won over or defeated. The conditions that made possible uprisings by minorities had ceased to exist. Modern revolution required large masses. Therefore, preparatory work for revolution had to be accomplished by legal means rather than by conspiracy.

Engels's thesis was shared by many socialists. It was used by the reformist elements of the social democratic parties to develop the doctrine that socialism would come to power by the ballot rather than by the bullet.

For a long while the more radical socialists denied the authority of Engels's paper.[23] On second thought, they realized that Engels had been speaking the truth: the conditions of revolution had changed. Unlike the reformists, the revolutionaries under Lenin's leadership concluded that given the continued validity of the belief that capitalism must be overthrown by violence, new revolutionary tactics had to be worked out: the state apparatus had to be destroyed by means different from conventional uprising.

SPADE WORK

IN SUMMING up the lessons of the Moscow uprising of 1905, Lenin reminded the communists that Engels had dinned into their ears the plain truth that "military attacks depend on the level of mili-

[23] See, for example, the editorial footnote to Lenin, *The Revolution of 1905* (London, Lawrence and Wishart, 1942 [a reprint]), p. 37, according to which the paper, "as has been proven, was revised in an opportunist sense by the executive committee of the social-democratic party of Germany without Engels' knowledge." It is true that the German socialist paper *Vorwaerts,* to influence legislation, produced extracts from Engels's remarks which did some violence to his thoughts. Engels admitted that he had used careful language in order to avoid political complications for the German socialists: The German *Reichstag* was discussing a bill against revolutionary activities (early 1895). However, he left no doubt that he had written the text, including the analysis of modern revolutionary methods, and that the text of his Introduction to the new edition of Marx's *Class Struggles* had been printed as written by him. On the other hand, Engels had not forsaken his revolutionary tradition and had not become a proponent of "legal means" only and always. See Karl Kautsky, *Der Weg zur Macht, Politische Betrachtungen ueber das Hineinwachsen in die Revolution* (3rd ed., Berlin, Vorwaerts, 1920), pp. 54 f.

tary technique." This technique had changed since the middle of the nineteenth century. Hence:

It would be folly for crowds to contend against artillery and defend barricades with revolvers. Kautsky was right when he wrote that . . . Moscow had inaugurated new "barricade tactics."[24]

Lenin added that the new tactics were those of guerrilla warfare, making use of mobile and exceedingly small units of ten or only two or three men.[25] Of course, this was only one aspect of the new tactics as developed by the more advanced communist tacticians. Lenin hinted that modern military technique had imposed the requirement for entirely new tactics and organizations. Since violent revolution was posed as a necessity, the question arose: how can the revolutionaries defeat the government forces in battle? Although Lenin's idea of the "small detachment" was valid, nobody quite knew how to apply it in practice.

Lenin understood that the arming of the proletariat was the most important problem of revolution.

An oppressed class which does not strive to learn how to use arms, to acquire arms, deserves to be treated as slaves. . . . Our slogan must be arming of the proletariat in order to vanquish, to expropriate, and to disarm the bourgeoisie.[26]

Yet how to get arms? Arms-smuggling as organized by Maksim Litvinov was not a success. The financing of armaments through "expropriations" (bank holdups)—a tactic invented by Stalin on the theoretical ground that the bourgeoisie should pay for its own destruction—hurt the communists politically.

Lenin stuck firmly to one idea: revolution would not come "spontaneously" but must be prepared and organized by a specially trained party of professional revolutionaries.

The significance of this idea lay not only in its importance to revolutionary tactical planning but also in its strategic denial of the democratic concept of revolution: the revolution was not to spring

[24] *Selected Works, op. cit.,* III, 351.

[25] Lenin preceded Ludendorff's invention of "infiltration tactics" by about twelve years.

[26] Lenin, *Collected Works, 1916–17* (New York, International Publishers, 1942), XIX, 365.

directly from the people but was to be the work of an elite. It was not to be a missionary effort at persuasion, but conquest. The pre-bolshevik communists

were fond of ridiculing the idea of technical preparations for an armed insurrection. According to their conception the center of gravity would be in the sphere of propaganda, of arming the minds of the workers. To this Lenin's reply was: "He who refuses technically to prepare for the insurrection ultimately rejects the insurrection itself, and transforms the program of the revolution into an empty phrase."[27]

This statement should be read carefully by those who think that propaganda is the main communist weapon.

The conquest must not be achieved by the majority over the minority but by the minority over the majority. The elite must not be simply a group of people with exceptional combative instincts; it must be organized as a "party" to provide leadership and disciplined cadres. Not an organ of democratic policies or electioneering, it must be an instrument of combat because, as Lenin re-emphasized *ad nauseam,* "at present, power can no longer be seized peacefully."[28]

Yet all of this neither told the bolsheviks how to make a revolution nor did it help them in political tactics. It merely defined those tactics that no longer could be used effectively. It did clear away much nineteenth-century underbrush which had been impeding progress toward solutions of the revolutionary problem in the twentieth century.

KARL KAUTSKY

THE CONFUSION in socialist ranks about revolutionary strategy and tactics was so great that Karl Kautsky, the theoretical leader

[27] A. Losovsky, *Lenin, the Great Strategist of the Class War* (Chicago, Trade Union Educational League, 1924), p. 17. In the current phase of bolshevik thinking, the importance of "class consciousness" is again being emphasized. See Otto Grotewohl, *La rivoluzione del 1918 in Germania, Insegnamenti della Storia del Movimento Operaio Tedesco* (Rome, Rinascita, 1952), pp. 136, 145. (This German key book was available to the author only in an Italian translation.)

[28] *Collected Works, op. cit.,* XXI, Book 1, 45. See also, *Lenin and Stalin on the Party* (London, Little Lenin Library, 1949).

of the Second International and spiritual heir to Marx and Engels, saw himself compelled to take up the matter and discuss it *in extenso*.[29]

Kautsky contended that the social democrats were a revolutionary party but not a party which makes revolution.[30] The social democrats know, he said, that they can reach their objectives only through revolution and not by any lesser means. But, Kautsky believed, it was not in the power of the socialists to *produce* that revolution, just as it was not in the power of their opponents to *prevent* revolution.

No one can predict the nature of the decisive battles of the "social war." Hence, it is not known whether these battles will be fought partly with physical and violent weapons or exclusively with means of economic, legislative, and moral pressure. Kautsky stated that socialists were neither for legality at any price nor for violent revolution at any price.[31]

Kautsky thought it probable that non-military weapons would prove more important than those of violence. Why? Because modern governments were stronger militarily than were the governments of the eighteenth century and because the modern revolutionaries had far better non-military weapons than had their predecessors. Governments had acquired machine guns and other effective firearms, but the proletariat possessed newspapers, class organizations, the capability to demonstrate and strike, and many other political means of pressure.[32] Only in Russia was the situation different: against tsarism, violent weapons would have to be used in preference to political and economic means.

Revolution would be inevitable if four conditions were to occur simultaneously:

(1) The mass of the people must be strongly opposed to the government;

(2) There must be a strong party in organizational control of the masses, maintaining uncompromising opposition to the government;

29 Kautsky, *op. cit.*, 1st ed., 1909.

30 *Ibid.*, p. 57. "Die Sozialdemokratie ist eine revolutionäre, nicht aber eine Revolutionen machende Partei." This statement was originally made in Engels's lifetime and had not been disavowed by him.

31 *Ibid.*, p. 65.

32 *Ibid.*, pp. 58 f.

(3) This party must represent the interests of the people and have its confidence;

(4) Bureaucracy and army must have lost confidence in the government.

Kautsky granted that these four conditions had not occurred together recently. He did not say how these simultaneous conditions could be created. With the exception of a casual remark on "mass strikes" he failed to point out how the actual seizure of power could be accomplished once the revolutionary situation had brought itself into existence.[33]

Kautsky thought that the class struggle would become ever more intense. The continuing concentration of capital and the numerical growth and increasing power of the proletariat would lead to crisis situations. The proletariat should not become impatient and nervous if this process took a long time but should forestall repressive action by refraining from violent action and avoiding provocation of the bourgeoisie. Since socialism can be realized only through democracy,[34] it is in the interest of the proletariat to avoid bloody conflict.

The proletariat should accumulate its power silently and imperceptibly, avoid strong opposition, and build up its organization so that when the time comes it would be more powerful than its opponents. Implied was the idea that the growth of the working class and its professional and propaganda organizations would propel the socialists into power.

Yet Kautsky's construction ran into a few difficulties. He denied that a bourgeois-socialist coalition government could be a substitute for revolution. He quoted approvingly a statement by Engels according to which the bourgeoisie would not look on passively while socialism was building up its strength. It was inevitable that one day the bourgeoisie would shoot and would shoot first. Since the socialists believed that the belligerent shooting first would be at a disadvantage,[35] why, then, should it not be in the interest of the socialists to provoke the bourgeoisie?

[33] *Ibid.*, p. 66.

[34] *Ibid.*, pp. 6, 57.

[35] *Ibid.*, p. 56. It will be remembered that at certain periods of military history, the firing of the first salvo entailed tactical disadvantages. During the battle of Fontenoy (1745), for example, the opponents invited each other to fire first, for very practical technical reasons, not because of chivalry as contemporary propaganda was asserting.

Kautsky noted that the proletariat could not reach a popular majority position without support of the petty bourgeoisie. Yet the petty bourgeoisie would not join the proletariat except in a crisis. Even in a crisis it would not desert the bourgeoisie unless the bankruptcy of the ruling classes became obvious, for everyone to see. This would happen only in the case of a "catastrophe," such as the Russo-Japanese war.[36]

Kautsky was uneasy about the causal relationship between war and revolution. He asserted that the "growing strength" of the proletariat had prevented war for more than thirty years, since the governments were so afraid of internal revolution that they were eager to keep external peace. But now, in 1909, war was becoming inevitable.[37]

According to Kautsky there are three relationships between war and revolution:

(1) A nation in the throes of defeat wants to avoid disaster. Hence, it calls upon its strongest and most energetic class, the proletariat, to mount a rejuvenated war against the enemy: revolution for victory;

(2) A nation may want to end the sufferings of war and, for this purpose, overthrows the government: revolution to make peace;

(3) A government concludes a dishonorable peace and is overthrown by the nation and army who do not want to live in infamy: revolution to negate defeat.

However, to the revolutionary strategist of the Kautsky variety, war is of doubtful value. According to Kautsky, no one can predict whether a revolution caused by war will be either socialist or successful; and no one can predict whether there will be war. By contrast, the trends of the class struggle are predictable, or so Kautsky thought. The revolutionary movement which emerges from this struggle may suffer temporary setbacks. But ultimately it must win.[38]

Kautsky talked about war as a "means of revolution" but he did not "desire" war. In his opinion, making revolution through war would imperil the future of the revolution. The war would cause destruction, moral and intellectual degradation, and perhaps bring the proletariat into power prematurely. Hence, it would "enormously

[36] *Ibid.*, pp. 108 f.
[37] *Ibid.*, p. 101.
[38] *Ibid.*, p. 36.

increase the tasks of the revolutionary regime and at the same time weaken its strength."[39]

Was Kautsky opposed to the use of war as a means of revolution? The bolsheviks, specifically Lenin and Rosa Luxemburg, interpreted the book differently. They approved Kautsky's opinions. Since they were hardly opponents of war,[40] they must have thought that Kautsky wanted to exploit war for revolution and that his pacifist remarks were mere double talk. Lenin wrote that *Der Weg zur Macht* predicted the approach of a revolutionary period and analyzed the relation between war and revolution. Kautsky, he added, "signed the Basel Manifesto on revolutionary utilization of the coming war."[41] He also agreed "clearly and definitely," Lenin said, "that a European war would create a revolutionary situation."[42]

In 1920, Kautsky stated that events had decided the question of whether socialism would come peacefully and imperceptibly or through catastrophes, wars and revolutions. History, he asserted, had borne out his analysis.[43] But what did he really mean?

In 1932 he scolded those who considered the French Revolution as the only model of revolutionary policy. Too many socialists, he thought, were impressed by the war policies of the Jacobins who appear to them to be the only true masters of revolution.[44] Kautsky reaffirmed the close interrelationship between war and revolution: the democratic revolutions in Europe which occurred between 1815 and 1848 resulted from a state of peace and led to military action. After 1848, he thought, the sequence had been reversed: with the exception of the Spanish revolution of 1870, there was no major war in Europe which did not produce fundamental political changes and often revolutions in the defeated as well as in the victorious country. "War no longer is a consequence of a democratic revolution but revolution has become a consequence of war."[45]

[39] *Ibid.*, p. 11.

[40] See the following section, "Congresses and Confusion," and Chap. 3 *passim.*

[41] Lenin, *The Proletarian Revolution and Renegade Kautsky* (New York, Marxist Library, International Publishers, 1934), p. 12.

[42] *Ibid.*, p. 67.

[43] Kautsky, *op. cit.*, p. 4.

[44] Karl Kautsky, *Krieg und Demokratie, Eine historische Untersuchung und Darstellung ihrer Wechselwirkung in der Neuzeit. Erstes Buch, Revolutionskriege* (Berlin, Dietz, 1932), p. 203.

[45] *Ibid.*, p. 452.

But this, according to Kautsky, was not a reason to adopt a policy of revolution through war. While revolutionary wars often increased the powers of the new regimes and saved the revolutions from military defeat, he more than ever believed that such wars nullify the revolutionary achievements. Kautsky's thinking could be paraphrased like this: war produces the revolution *as well as the counterrevolution*. War and democratic socialism cannot coexist. Hence, Kautsky called upon the socialist movement to desist from a policy of violence, militarism, and war.

Kautsky himself, of course, remained committed to his old revolutionary ideas. An inconsistency? Kautsky was caught in a moral quandary. He wanted to combine socialism with democracy and human, liberal ideals. Ethically motivated to bring about the betterment of mankind, he realized that there was but one road to true revolutionary power: violence and war. He recoiled from the conclusion that oceans of blood are the price of revolution. It was left to more ruthless men to face this issue squarely.

CONGRESSES AND CONFUSION

THE MOST SIGNIFICANT disagreements among pre-1914 international socialists centered on finding the proper policy with respect to war. Believing that the time for revolution had not yet come, the right-wing socialists were inclined to favor national defense. The left-wing socialists wanted to prevent war and, in case of failure, to exploit the conflict to bring about a revolutionary crisis.

As early as 1868 the First International had called upon workers to prevent war through industrial strikes. At the congress of the Second International at Zürich (1893), the Dutch socialist Domela Nieuwenhuis proposed that, in case of war, the soldiers should refuse to fight and the reservists should refuse to enter the army. This "military strike" should be supported by an industrial general strike, particularly in the defense industries. Women should launch appeals to the effect that they did not want to lose their husbands and sons.[46]

This idea was criticized, particularly by the Russian Marxist Georgi Plekhanov, who stated that such a tactic exceeded the capa-

[46] Sinovyev, *op. cit.*, p. 600.

bility of the proletariat. "If we would be capable of carrying out a general strike, economic power already would be in the hands of the proletariat and then the general strike would be superfluous."[47] The military strike, Plekhanov continued, would disarm the more civilized nations of Europe and turn them over to the Cossacks. The Dutch program, therefore, would inaugurate the world regime of the "Russian knout."

Nevertheless, the Second International accepted the general strike as one of the three weapons of the proletariat supplementing the ballot and the uprising.

During the congress of Stuttgart in 1907 the socialists refused to endorse national defense even against unprovoked aggression but acknowledged that they could not prevent war. Rosa Luxemburg came out with the new idea that agitation should aim at the termination of the conflict and, at the same time, utilize the war for the overthrow of class rule.[48] The crisis produced by the war was to contribute to the political awakening of the people and to pave the way for the destruction of capitalism. Rosa Luxemburg's resolution was signed by Lenin and adopted by the Stuttgart congress. It linked war and revolution in a novel, though as yet undeveloped, fashion. It became a milestone in communist thinking.

At the Copenhagen congress of 1910 the Stuttgart resolution was confirmed. Earlier resolutions, of Zürich (1893) and Paris (1901), according to which socialists should refuse to vote for armament budgets, were reiterated.

The Basel congress, which took place at the time of the Balkan wars (1912), decided that socialists would have to fight to prevent general war. If war should come despite socialist opposition, it would be the duty of the socialists "with all their powers to utilize the economic and political crisis created by the war, to arouse the people and hasten the downfall of capitalist class rule."[49]

The Basel congress threatened the European bourgeoisie with revolution as the socialist answer to war: "The governments should not forget that the Franco-German war led to the commune and that the Russo-Japanese war put in motion the revolutionary forces of the peoples in the Russian Empire." However, since it was not based

[47] *Ibid.*, p. 602.
[48] *Ibid.*, p. 618.
[49] *Collected Works*, 1930, *op. cit.*, XVIII, 469.

upon a concept of effective revolutionary tactics, this threat was an empty one.

Many socialists recognized the possibility of a just and defensive war: Jean Jaurès's famous book *L'Armée nouvelle* was based essentially on the idea that a people's army would provide France with a maximum of security. Others recognized that if war should break out, passions would be stimulated to such a point that no one would dare oppose it by words or deeds. This view, presented by Marcel Sembat, was confirmed by the events of 1914.[50] The war came and the socialists were powerless to stop it, let alone make a revolution. Socialist strategy and tactics were bankrupt.

CLAUSEWITZ, COMMUNIST MENTOR

SOMETIME between 1913 and 1915, Lenin studied the works of Karl von Clausewitz, the foremost theoretician of war. It is not entirely certain whether this study was provoked by the outbreak of World War I or was undertaken earlier, but it is certain that Lenin was influenced greatly by Clausewitz. To simplify: Marx gave Lenin a doctrine of intelligence, a method of analyzing political situations. Clausewitz taught the bolsheviks the secret of operations.

Lenin valued Clausewitz so highly that when he went into hiding after the July uprising of 1917, he took with him two books—Marx's *The Civil War in France* and Clausewitz's *On War*.[51] The first taught Lenin what to do *with* power; Clausewitz showed him how to *conquer* power.

Lenin's ideas on Clausewitz were never put down in a systematic fashion, but he left voluminous annotated extracts from Clausewitz's classic[52] which illuminate the train of his thinking.

The greatest emphasis was laid on the connection between war and politics, and specifically on the allegedly "dialectic rule," enunciated by Clausewitz, that war is the continuation of politics by other means. Lenin's notes emphasize that war is not only a political act but *the ultimate instrument of politics*. Lenin learned that political

---

[50] *Faites un roi, sinon faites la paix* (Paris, Fiquière, 1913), pp. 109–21.

[51] Jellinek, *op. cit.*, p. 390.

[52] "Vypiski i zamechaniya na knigu Klauzevitsa 'o voina i vedenii voin,'" in *Leninsky Sbornik* (Moscow, 1931), XII, 389–452.

and military tactics are closely related to each other. War is simply politics in which the saber has been exchanged for the pen.

Lenin extracted statements to the effect that in addition to the hostile military force and his territory, the *will* of the enemy is the principal objective of war. A convinced "materialist," he jotted down many remarks on morale, leadership, hatred in war, courage, prudence, cowardice, tenacity, and other "spiritual" factors.

Lenin devoted some attention to Clausewitz's discussion of the relationship of forces and adopted the idea that the defeated country must put its hope in moral superiority and courage. He added: "The right to insurrection of the defeated."

Clausewitz's statement that the conqueror always pretends to be peace-loving because he would like to attain his objectives in a bloodless fashion and that, therefore, aggression must be presented as a defensive reaction of the attacking nation was considered by Lenin to be a good idea. So it is: This idea still is at the bottom of communist pacifist propaganda.

Clausewitz wrote a strong criticism of the eighteenth-century idea, originated by Lloyd, a prominent military writer of his time, that there are "keys" to a country. He took pains to point out that geographic position is not quite as important as is usually thought. However, Clausewitz stressed that there is one key to every country, the enemy army. Lenin commented: "clever and intelligent." According to another definition the key is that element "without the possession of which we may not dare to force our way into a country." It is probable that the communist doctrine of the life force, which will be discussed later, had its origin in Clausewitz's chapter on the "Key of the Country."[53]

Clausewitz discussed the differences between the offensive and defensive, and he underscored that an offensive often requires subsidiary defensive action and vice versa. Lenin found in this discussion an excellent example of dialectics. It is probable that this is the source of the communist infatuation with "active defense."[54]

Another example of dialectics was found by Lenin in Clausewitz's

[53] Karl von Clausewitz, *On War* (New York, Modern Library, 1943), Book VI, Chap. 23, pp. 432–35.

[54] *Leninsky Sbornik, op. cit.,* p. 418. Modern proponents of the theory of games will be interested to learn that Lenin wrote down this equation, "war equals game" *(voina=igra).*

discussion of the gradations of war. Clausewitz asserted that there is sometimes more, sometimes less, war. It is probably from this remark that communist theories of cold, limited, civil, national, and revolutionary wars originally were derived. Lenin also accepted Clausewitz's idea that there are wars which have the only objective of menacing the opponent and supporting diplomatic negotiations: bloodless wars.

Lenin showed interest in Clausewitz's sociology of war. Each historical epoch has its own type of war. The social and political structure of a nation must be considered if its military art is to be understood. The enthusiasm of the people and the participation of the entire nation are factors of great importance. For example, the military successes of the French Revolution were ascribed by Clausewitz to the awakening by revolution of new social forces. Lenin agreed.

In 1920, Lenin amplified on this idea: "In the last analysis victory in war depends on the morale of the masses which are shedding their blood on the battlefield. The conviction of fighting a just war and the willingness to give one's own life for one's brothers, therein lies the morale of the soldier. This is his readiness to bring enormous sacrifices. The tsarist generals stated that the men of the Red army were able to endure things which the tsarist soldiers never could have withstood." This statement was reproduced in *Pravda* on February 1, 1942.

According to Lenin, the most important chapter in Clausewitz is the one entitled "War as an Instrument of Politics."[55] Lenin remarked: "War is part of a whole. The whole is politics."[56] But what is politics? Clausewitz defined it as the objective interests of the government and of the citizens as modified by ambitions, personal interests, and vanities. Clausewitz also described politics as the representation of all the interests of the society as a whole. In these arguments Lenin found many similarities with Marx.

When Lenin's notes were published in 1931, the editor, A. Bubnov, appended a few interesting remarks. For example, he stated that war cannot be reduced to a short shock. Because the military means cannot all be put into operation at once, wars must be conducted by successive action. The military art should not only consider weapons but also the means of their skillful employment. Ac-

[55] Clausewitz, *op. cit.*, Book VIII, Chapt. 6-b.
[56] *Ibid.*, p. 444.

cording to Clausewitz, Bubnov said, it is in no way impossible to fight a war with a weaker army. On the contrary, war is possible with *any* given relationship of strength. The inhabitants of a country, even when deprived of their weapons and of the possibility of revolting, have an influence on military events by their attitude and by the way in which they can serve as a free force. Hence, while defeat often has purely military causes, it is more usually the result of weak or deficient policies. This, of course, is quite true: improper military preparation almost always is the outcome of political and not military decisions.

Clausewitz is no longer considered *the* military prophet of the communists. However, soviet military writers have produced only one really important criticism of the old Prussian. They objected to his idea that the offensive is the weaker form of war. Clausewitz arrived at this conclusion because he assumed a conflict between socially homogeneous belligerents. Soviet military science, however, is based on the idea that *conflict is likely to take place between socially heterogeneous nations.* In addition to the pure arithmetics of material and man-power strength, social and political factors must be taken into account. In a war between two bourgeois societies the offensive may be the weaker form of war but not in a war between a bourgeois and a proletarian society. The society which suffers less from class conflict has a greater capability to fight war offensively.[57] It would follow that the communists believe they can wage offensive warfare more readily than their opponents.

This may be the key to understanding Lenin's dictum: "It is the military science, the military means, and the revolutionary army which in practice will decide the future battles of the Russian people, and which also will decide the most important question, the question of freedom."

THE THEORY OF REVOLUTIONARY DEFEATISM

THE BREAK between the Second International and the bolsheviks was caused largely by disagreements on antiwar tactics. The bolsheviks took the 1907 Stuttgart resolution seriously, but they did

[57] Berthold C. Friedl, *Les Fondements théoriques de la guerre et de la paix en URSS; Lénine sur Clausewitz* (Paris, Medicis, 1945), p. 115.

not know how to implement their own program. After the start of World War I, it took some time before they were intellectually ready to resume action.

On November 1, 1914, Lenin came out with the formula that the imperialist war should be transformed into civil war. How was this to be done? Lenin did not know yet. He had realistically opposed the idea that socialists should refuse to do military service. He considered military strikes "stupid" and said that it was a sad and cowardly dream to think of unarmed battle against the armed bourgeoisie. Socialists should not vote for military budgets but, more important, they should begin using illegal forms of combat. Lenin admitted that the transformation of the imperialist war into a civil war would not be easy and could not be carried out according to a rigid plan.[58] He had no better advice to offer.

In February 1915, Sinovyev proposed that the bolsheviks should work toward the defeat of Russian tsarism.[59] In July 1915, eleven months after the outbreak of World War I, Lenin outlined the doctrine of revolutionary defeatism for the first time.[60] His basic conclusion was this: the correct policy for the proletariat was "to take advantage of the embarrassment of its governments and its bourgeoisie in order to overthrow them. This, however, cannot be achieved, it cannot be striven for, without desiring the defeat of one's own government, without facilitating this defeat."[61]

Lenin anticipated the following sequence of events: defeat—revolution—civil war: "The defeat of the governmental army weakens the government, aids the liberation of the nationalities oppressed by it and makes civil war against the ruling classes easier."[62] Military defeat of capitalist states was beginning to become the fulcrum of communist strategy.

The Second International, objecting to this policy of ubiquitous

[58] Lenin and G. Sinovyev, *Gegen den Strom, Aufsaetze aus den Jahren 1914–1916* (Hamburg, Verlag der Kommunistischen Internationale, 1921), pp. 5 f.

[59] *Ibid.,* p. 52.

[60] *Ibid.,* pp. 105–9; also *Selected Works, op. cit.,* V, 142–48.

[61] *Selected Works, op. cit.,* V, 146. The expression, "facilitating this defeat," reads in the original German "wenn man . . . diese Niederlage nicht fördert," and should be translated more correctly by "without working toward this defeat."

[62] *Collected Works, op. cit.,* XVIII, 149.

high treason, clung to a policy of disarmament and advocated ending the war through compromise peace. While the bolsheviks wanted to use war as a weapon of revolution and as a preparation for uprising, the Second International took the line of humanitarianism, welfare, and peaceful evolution.[63] This conflict between liberalism and revolutionism was discussed at the conferences of Kienthal, Zimmerwald, and Stockholm. Never resolved, it ultimately led to the founding of the Third International.[64]

In October 1916, Sinovyev wrote an article on the history of defeatism. Defeatism existed in Russia—*avant le mot*—as a strong movement during the Russo-Japanese war.[65] Plekhanov was quoted to the effect that in the case of a tsarist victory over Japan the vanquished would have been no other than the Russian people. There was a relationship between the fall of Port Arthur and the destruction of Russian absolutism. He quoted a comment by Marx that the Turks by their victory over the Russians in 1877 hastened the revolution. "The modern history of Russia is an excellent illustration of the principle that external defeat of a reactionary government helps the democratic movement within the nation."[66] Jaurès was approvingly described as a "retroactive defeatist" because he acknowledged that the Third Republic could not have been established without the defeat of Napoleon III.[67] Even the German historian Hans Delbrück was called as witness on the intimate relationship between defeat and revolution.

Sinovyev bluntly favored "pan-defeatism": it really did not matter which "despicable" imperialist colossus would be knocked down. Wherever defeat might occur, there the proletarian revolution would accomplish its break-through.[68]

[63] In 1920, Lenin declared that "the masses will starve until the Red Army triumphs." *Selected Works, op. cit.,* VIII, 95.

[64] Details on these conferences can be found in Merle Fainsod, *International Socialism and the World War* (Cambridge, Harvard University Press, 1935), Chaps. 4–6.

[65] Lenin and Sinovyev, *op. cit.,* p. 428.

[66] *Ibid.,* p. 438.

[67] *Ibid.,* p. 445.

[68] *Ibid.,* p. 411. It is interesting to note that Sinovyev rather than Lenin seems to have been the originator of revolutionary defeatism. There is evidence from his writings that he worked out the idea of defeatism in all its details. He made a more elaborate study on the relationship between war, defeat,

About twenty years later, Stalin endorsed the principle of active defeatism:

The bolsheviks maintained that the lesser evil for the people would be the military defeat of the tsarist government in the imperialist war, for this would facilitate the victory of the people over tsardom. . . . Lenin held that the policy of working for the defeat of one's own imperialist government must be pursued not only by the Russian revolutionaries, but by the revolutionary parties of the working class in all the belligerent countries.[69]

Post-World War II declarations of the leaders of the communist parties in Italy, France, the United States, and many other countries made it clear that the principle still stands, with this modification: communists will work for the defeat of every belligerent except that of the Soviet Union and its satellites.

---

and revolution than did Lenin. However, Sinovyev's writings on the subject were published either with Lenin as a coauthor or with Lenin's approval. The theory was tried out for the first time in Germany where Karl Liebknecht stated in May 1915: "The chief enemy stands in our own country." See Grotewohl, *op. cit.*, p. 74.

[69] *History of the Communist Party of the Soviet Union (Bolsheviks), Short Course* (New York, International Publishers, 1939), p. 167. Stalin has acknowledged or assumed authorship of this book.

2. The First Round of World Revolution: Russia · 1917–1921

> *"The October revolution in Russia serves as a model for the whole world proletariat. . . . The October revolution is a brilliant example of the conversion of imperialist war into civil war . . . into a war for the revolutionary way out of catastrophe, which grew into the victorious proletarian revolution."*
>
> *International Press Correspondence*
> *October 20, 1932, page 997*

THE REVOLUTIONARY SITUATION IN RUSSIA

THE HISTORY of the Russian "Red October" is not well known, and a great deal of what is accepted as known is more communist legend than fact.

The term "October Revolution" is in itself somewhat of a misnomer. In its literal sense, "revolution" denotes a change of government by violent means, and the events of October 1917[1] certainly fit within this definition. However, the word also carries the connotation of forceful liberation from tyranny, and in this sense the changes of October must be described rather as a counterrevolution.[2]

The October revolt was directed not against a tsarist regime but against a democratic government which had been given a mandate to administer the state until a constituent assembly could determine the permanent form of the Russian democracy. When the communists found they could not prevent the convocation of this assembly—in which they had polled a minority of seats—they dispersed it

---

[1] According to the western calendar, the uprising took place in November 1917.

[2] *Verdict of Three Decades, From the Literature of Individual Revolt against Soviet Communism in 1917–1950,* ed. by Julien Steinberg (New York, Duell, Sloan and Pearce, 1950), pp. 21–46.

CALENDAR OF RUSSIAN REVOLUTION, 1917

Mar. 12	Petrograd soviet formed. Provisional duma committee begins constituting itself as governmental authority.
Mar. 14	First provisional government formed. Petrograd soviet issues Order No. 1.
Mar. 15	Tsar Nicholas II abdicates.
Apr. 16	Lenin reaches Petrograd.
May 18	Second provisional government formed (a coalition government).
June 16	All-Russian congress of soviets. Russian military offensive.
July 10–17	Russian military reverses.
July 16–18	Bolshevik-inspired uprising in Petrograd.
July 18	Bolsheviks accused of being German agents.
July 19	Break of Russian front. Arrest of bolshevik leaders.
July 20	Kerensky prime minister.
Aug. 1	Kornilov appointed commander-in-chief.
Aug. 6	Third provisional government.
Sept. 3	Riga falls.
Sept. 8–12	Kornilov affair.
Sept. 27	All-Russian democratic conference.
Oct. 4	Democratic conference forms pre-parliament.
Oct. 7	Fourth provisional government, also known as third coalition government.
Oct. 8	Trotsky elected chairman of Petrograd soviet.
Oct. 18	Government decides to transfer capital to Moscow.
Oct. 20	Pre-parliament opens.
Oct. 23	Bolsheviks decide on uprising.
Oct. 25	Formation of revolutionary military committee.
Oct. 30	Opening of second All-Russian congress of soviets postponed to November 7.
Nov. 3	Petrograd garrison acknowledges military revolutionary committee.
Nov. 5	Revolutionary military committee appoints commissars to military units.
Nov. 7	Uprising. Government deposed.
Nov. 8	Congress of soviets proclaims soviet government. Kerensky tries to organize expedition against Petrograd.
Nov. 12–13	Kerensky's forces defeated.
Nov. 22	Krylenko commander-in-chief.
Nov. 25	Elections for constituent assembly begin.
Dec. 5	Suspension of military hostilities.
Dec. 15	Armistice signed at Brest-Litovsk.
Dec. 20	Forming of Cheka (political police and terror machine).

1918

Jan. 18	Constituent assembly opens.
Jan. 19	Constituent assembly dispersed.
Jan. 28	Creation of Red army.

by force,[3] thus establishing the counterrevolutionary character of their regime.

Many authors have laid great emphasis on the fact that Russia was captured by a mere 70,000 communists—a tiny minority.[4] The truth is that the bolshevik party had a membership of 240,000 men,[5] or one communist for about every 666 persons in Russia. In the elections to the constituent assembly, held a few days after the bolshevik seizure of power, they polled close to ten million votes,[6] to which must be added another estimated two million votes for the left social revolutionaries. This means that there was one communist-left social revolutionary vote for every thirteen Russians, or one communist-left social revolutionary voter for every eight adults in Russia. Hence the communists possessed very substantial strength.

The record shows that the bolsheviks were the second strongest party in Russia and far stronger than any of the other minority parties. In a number of places, for instance in Petrograd, Petrograd province, Vitebsk, Minsk, Smolensk, Tver, Moscow province, Tula, Vladimir, and Moscow, the bolsheviks polled a majority.

At the same time, many persons who did not vote for the bolsheviks were not strongly opposed to them. No less than two-thirds of the total vote was socialist; there was 1 socialist voter[7] for about every 3.5 adult Russians. These socialist voters may have had tacti-

---

[3] The bolsheviks polled about 24 per cent of the total vote and had 168 out of 703 deputies in the assembly. Together with the left social revolutionaries, they controlled 29 per cent of the vote. The social revolutionaries (minus their left wing) accounted for almost 55 per cent. See Oliver Henry Radkey, *The Election to the Russian Constituent Assembly of 1917* (Cambridge, Harvard University Press, 1950), pp. 16 f., 21.

[4] A variant of this theory occurred in a statement by J. Edgar Hoover: "In 1917 when the communists overthrew the Russian government, there was one communist for every 2,277 persons in Russia. In the United States today there is one communist for every 1,814 persons in the country." *Hearings before the Committee on Un-American Activities, Testimony of J. Edgar Hoover, Director, Federal Bureau of Investigation,* March 26, 1947 [U. S. Congress, 80th, 1st sess., House. (Washington, D. C., Govt. Print. Off., 1947), pp. 37 f.].

[5] Lenin, *Selected Works* (New York, International Publishers, 1943), VI, 271. According to communist sources, the party had a membership of 20,000 to 23,000 by April 1917. This corresponds to one hard-core communist for about every 8,000 persons. *International Press Correspondence* (London, August 11, 1933), p. 770.

[6] Radkey, *op. cit.,* p. 80.

[7] For clarification: This includes the bolsheviks.

cal differences with the bolsheviks, but there was no difference in principle. Certainly there was no correct identification of the threat which the bolsheviks posed both to Russia and to their "comrades."

Among the Russian electorate of 1917, there was only a small group of people who were hostile to socialism in all its shades and shapes. These antisocialists possessed but one-third of the bolshevik and about one-ninth of the total socialist voting strength.

Not a few writers were greatly impressed by the novel technique of insurrection which the communists employed to seize the Russian state. This insurrectional technique was indeed quite original and contributed to the success of the bolsheviks. But it was *not* of decisive importance to the final outcome. As will be seen, the main features of the bolshevik uprising are to be found in the transfer of the allegiance of the army from the government to the indirect control of the bolshevik party; the neutralization of the high command; and the inactivity of the government and the democratic and moderate socialist parties.

Other authors held that the bolshevik coup was the result of thorough prior planning. Yet most of the crucial events which culminated in the bolshevik success originated outside the ranks of Lenin's party. Far from being long-range planners, the bolsheviks succeeded through flexibility and *expertise* in handling the unforeseen.

With these corrections in mind, let us see how the revolutionary situation developed in the Russia of 1917. Who set the stage on which the bolsheviks acted out their drama?

THE DECENTRALIZATION OF POWER

ONE OF THE tsar's last acts was the dissolution of the duma, as the parliament of the period was called. The duma refused to comply with the decree and set up a provisional government. Following the overthrow of the tsar in March 1917, this government of doubtful standing became the *de facto* ruling body of Russia. While its authority was accepted by the population at large, the socialists, who held no posts in the provisional government and who found its radicalism wanting, took advantage of the tangled legal situation and organized the Petrograd soviet (or council). Thus emerged a second, competing, paragovernmental authority which considered it as its mission to stimulate the "progress" of the revolution.

During the revolution of 1905, the soviets had been committees of strikers, with each factory electing one soviet. In 1917, the revived and enlarged institution embraced both workers and soldiers. Elected on the basis of one deputy for every company of soldiers or every one thousand workers, local soviets soon covered all of Russia. These local councils elected regional soviets which in turn elected those on higher echelons, and so on. In the army, the hierarchy of soviets similarly pyramided from the company to the army group level. The All-Russian soviet became the highest, though not the most important, council.

The first soviet was created at Petrograd and, by virtue of its location at the seat of government, achieved very early a commanding position. While the other councils exerted influence and the All-Russian soviet was able to push itself into the foreground whenever it was in session, the Petrograd organization played the dominating role. Within its unwieldy full body of 778 deputies, the executive committee of the Petrograd soviet exercised control, preparing and issuing crucial orders, frequently without reference to the floor.

The government failed to challenge the power of the soviets and accommodated itself to a system of "dual power." Since there was fundamental disagreement on most vital issues, co-operation between the government and the soviet was obtained but rarely. The government pledged itself to continue the war. By contrast, the soviet favored an early "democratic peace" and an immediate army reform. The government proclaimed a program of land reform and, on March 30, confiscated the imperial and monasterial lands. It announced that the distribution of land to the peasants was to be decided upon by the constituent assembly. By contrast, the soviet was in favor of immediate land distribution.[8] The provisional government followed a moderate and long-range policy. The soviet fought for radical and immediate measures. Given the temper of the Russian people, it was almost a foregone conclusion that the soviet would win the popularity contest.

---

[8] Originally the mensheviks and social revolutionaries had 68, and the bolsheviks 13, per cent of the seats in the Petrograd soviet.

One of the most consequential steps was taken on March 21, 1917, when the Petrograd soviet decided that the garrison of the capital would be placed at its disposal. The significance of this measure was not immediately obvious because the cleavage between soviet and government was as yet in its infancy, and the resolution which placed the Petrograd garrison in charge of defending the new regime against counterrevolution was thought to protect both soviet and government. Ultimately, however, this resolution provided the soviet with military strength while denying it to the government, and it thus created the main prerequisite of the bolshevik uprising. Like the Praetorian Guard of ancient Rome, the Petrograd garrison emerged as the king-maker of Russia.

Yet the soviet was not the only competitor for government authority. The remnants of the duma, various paralegislative bodies organized by the government to precede the constituent assembly, the *zemstvo* municipalities, peasant organizations, regional and national minority bodies, and so forth, they all insisted on participation in important decisions. Some of these organizations achieved considerable prominence, such as the railroad trade unions and the Cossack councils.

Under the circumstances, the government had to negotiate every step with dozens of committees. Few orders, but innumerable counterorders, were issued, and organizational chaos resulted on a scale rarely, if ever, paralleled in history.

Naturally, these multitudinous suborganizations competed with each other for power. Continuous elections not only kept political passions at fever pitch but also brought individual organizations under different political party control at various times. Government became a practical impossibility, and the election returns went from bad to worse.

The whole situation can be summarized by saying that Russia was trying an experiment in total and direct democracy. Every interest was to have a voice, the people were to influence decisions directly, and the elected bodies were to reflect the latest fluctuations in political opinion. The need for full authority and public discipline was denied. The problem of representative government was not comprehended. Progress was identified with uninterrupted radicalization, and government was confused with speech-making. The experiment failed as it inevitably had to fail.

ILLUSIONS OF THE NON-COMMUNIST GROUPS

THE VARIOUS non-bolshevik groups could have acted more effectively against the movement which, within a few short months, was to engulf them all. The non-communist parties, from the right social revolutionaries via the moderate socialists to the national minority groups, possessed fully seventy per cent of the popular vote. Bolshevik successes were based on the inability and unwillingness of the non-communist parties to undertake joint, or even coordinated, defensive action.

The provisional government also failed to take proper precautions against bolshevik activities. Although the bolsheviks provoked an uprising in July 1917 and were not hiding their intention to launch another uprising, the government played the role of a passive onlooker. Its attitude toward the bolshevik insurrection was revealed by Kerensky in his last speech as prime minister. Voicing resentment over the accusation that the government had not acted in time, he stated that his regime was compelled to follow a moderate policy in order to protect itself against any reproach of cruelty or oppression. Russian democracy was the freest in the world, and the government had to be careful before deciding to use its power for the quelling of insurrectionary movements.[9]

The non-communist left generally favored the suppression of the insurrection by pacific means only. The bolsheviks neutralized this group by contending that they had not started the uprising; and provided certain concessions were made, they stated that they would be willing to help terminate it. Through these negotiations, the bolsheviks gained considerable tactical advantages. Above all, the fighting forces of the social revolutionaries and mensheviks were not mobilized in time.[10] When bolshevik bad faith finally was recognized, it was too late.

One segment of the mensheviks and social revolutionaries conditioned its support of the government on the prior introduction of

[9] Serge Oldenbourg, *Le coup d'état bolchéviste, 20 octobre–3 décembre 1917, Recueil de documents relatifs à la prise du pouvoir par les bolshévistes* (Paris, Payot, 1929), p. 113.

[10] Alexander S. Kerensky, *The Catastrophe* (New York, Appleton, 1927), p. 328.

certain social reforms designed to remove the basic causes of mass unrest. Although their house was burning, they wanted to clean it before helping to put out the fire. Other socialists felt that while they wanted to suppress the bolshevik danger, they should not become instruments of the counterrevolution. A civil war against the bolsheviks, they reasoned, would jeopardize the concepts of revolution and socialism. Therefore, they favored compromise and opposed active resistance against the bolsheviks.[11]

According to another version of the same thought, a civil war would lead neither to a victory of the provisional government nor to that of the bolsheviks but to the victory of a reactionary third force which would brush away not only the bolsheviks and the provisional government but also Russian democracy.[12]

Several Marxists who had known Lenin and his comrades for many years and who considered him slightly insane did not believe that he would be able to stay in power. Quite a few liberals voiced the same belief on the grounds that the bolsheviks were a hopeless minority and did not represent the will of the people. Many soldiers felt the same way. Scarcely anybody took the bolsheviks seriously.

The conservative forces were unorganized and without a clear political concept of their own. On the one hand, they were happy that the provisional government was in trouble; on the other, they estimated that a bolshevik experiment would become the *reductio ad absurdum,* hence the terminal point of the revolution, and would send Russia back on the road to normalcy. Like the parties of the left, they overrated their ability to maintain their organizations intact under bolshevik rule. The conservatives did not participate in the political contest and were content to let events take their course.

Various national minorities took the attitude that a bolshevik regime would weaken the Great Russians to such an extent that they could obtain total independence for their groups. Fearing that other Russian parties might re-establish the national *status quo ante,* they supported chaos in order to further separatist interests.

Thus, everybody had a reason not to fight and defend Russian democracy. Abdication is not only a monarch's privilege. Democratic forces also abdicate.

[11] Oldenbourg, *op. cit.,* p. 391.
[12] *Ibid.,* p. 140.

The Revolutonary Situation in the Russian Army

"Conscription may prove to be a costly experience for Russia."

ENGELS IN 1893

FROM the beginning of World War I the Russian army suffered serious defeats. Sent into combat with inadequate armaments and poor logistics, it was far too large to be supported by the economic and industrial structure of the country. Its weaknesses were accentuated by poor leadership, widespread illiteracy, and the failure of the western allies to provide adequate support.

For more than three years heavy casualties were constantly inflicted on the Russian forces.[13] Millions of young recruits were pulled into the army, but few of them received adequate military training. Regimental cadres changed nine or ten times between 1914 and 1917, with only a handful of enlisted men, noncommissioned officers, and officers remaining in the original formations. Replacements were seldom properly integrated into the military organization. The old symbols of loyalty had disappeared, and there was no indoctrination concerning the military obligations of the defenders of a young democracy. All these conditions combined with the fear of heavy losses and the deplorable supply situation quite naturally caused very poor morale among the enlisted men of the Russian army.

The situation among the officers, also, was most unsatisfactory. The Russian army had lost most of its experienced officers. A large portion of the new officers was deficient in professional know-how

---

[13] These losses are, however, often exaggerated. If measured in per cent of the total numbers mobilized, the casualty rate including fatalities of the Russian army was 76 per cent, as contrasted with the Austro-Hungarian rate of 90 per cent, the highest of all belligerents. The ratio between killed and other casualties was smaller in Russia than in Germany and France, but higher than in Austria, indicating that Russian morale in the early stages must have been fairly high. If measured against the total population, Russian fatalities were only one-quarter of those suffered by France and less than one-half of those suffered by Germany or Austria. In total *casualties,* as measured against the over-all population, Russia suffered about as much as Italy and far less than France, Austria, or Germany (6 per cent as against 16, 14, and 11 per cent respectively).

and, in many instances, lacked the political motivation to maintain discipline.

There is a widespread opinion that the Russian officers corps was almost exclusively pro-tsar and reactionary. In reality, it embraced many progressive elements. General Brusilov, commander-in-chief during the summer of 1917, supported the democratic revolution and later adhered to the Red regime. So did Serge Kamenyev, Boris Shaposhnikov, and many other erstwhile tsarist officers. Even officers like General Mikhail V. Alexeyev, longtime commander-in-chief, and General Lavr G. Kornilov, both of whom ultimately opposed the communists as leaders of White armies, were not monarchists but originally adopted an attitude of wait-and-see, vis-à-vis the revolution.[14]

General Alexander I. Verkhovsky, war minister in the fourth provisional government, was a "non-partisan socialist." Formerly a personal page to the tsar, he was reduced to the ranks for political activity but was reinstated. In 1919 he joined the Red army and eventually became a professor at the Military Academy. Admiral Dimitri V. Verderevsky, navy minister during October 1917, also was a socialist. So was General Mikhail D. Bonch-Bruyevich, and so were quite a few others.

The following story may illustrate conditions in the Russian armed forces. Admiral Andrei S. Maksimov, an officer of extreme ambitions, used the revolution to further his career. He donned immense red ties, proudly called himself the "first revolutionary admiral,"[15] and got himself elected by a sailors' committee to become commander of the Baltic fleet. When the legally appointed commander, Admiral Nepenin, refused to acknowledge this "election," he was murdered in the midst of a sailors' demonstration by an assassin. Maksimov assumed command and was confirmed by the government. Later, he was promoted to the post of chief of the naval staff.[16]

According to General Anton I. Denikin, of forty commanding

[14] See Robert Goudima, *L'Armée rouge dans la paix et la guerre* (Paris, Editions Défense de la France, 1947), p. 20.

[15] H. Graf, *The Russian Navy in War and Revolution from 1914 up to 1918* (Munich, Oldenbourg, 1923), pp. 120 f.

[16] *The Testimony of Kolchak and other Siberian Materials*, ed. by Elena Varneck and H. H. Fisher (Stanford, Calif., Stanford University Press, 1935), p. 225.

generals and admirals, only fourteen opposed the "democratization" of the army; fifteen approved of it; and eleven went along; that is, 65 per cent were in favor of the more radical aspects of the revolution or did not oppose, even intellectually, measures designed to reduce discipline as well as command authority (summer 1917). Of the approving group, six subsequently joined the bolsheviks, as did one member of the opposing group, but only nineteen of these commanding officers ended up fighting in the White armies. Less than half of the commanding generals felt strongly about the bolsheviks; more than half apparently found it possible to accommodate themselves to the new regime. Of course, it must be remembered that between March and April 1917, no less than 150 senior officers of more conservative persuasion were placed on the retired list.[17]

The deterioration of the Russian army was, in part, the inevitable result of war and defeat. But its utter disintegration was a function of mistaken and avoidable political measures. The prime example is contained in the notorious Order No. 1, issued on March 14, 1917, by the Petrograd soviet, calling for the immediate establishment of military soviets. These committees were to be elected by the soldiers in order to represent their interests and control all arms (which were not to be handed over to the officers). Order No. 1, which, to the surprise of its originators, was applied throughout the army and navy, reduced the authority of the officers and stipulated that the army was to obey the orders of the government only if such orders did not contradict those issued by the Petrograd soviet.[18]

Promulgated in the midst of war, this devastating order was the handiwork of liberal and socialist reformers but not of the bolsheviks. The stated purpose of the order was to close the gap between officers and men and thus make possible a more effective prosecution of the war.[19] The order's true purpose was to deprive officers who had not joined the revolution of their command authority.[20]

[17] See Denikin, *The Russian Turmoil, Memoirs: Military, Social and Political* (London, Hutchison, 1922), pp. 145 ff.

[18] Kerensky is reported to have said that he would have given ten years of his life to prevent this order from being signed. *Ibid.*, p. 62.

[19] James Mavor, *The Russian Revolution* (London, Allen and Unwin, 1928), p. 66.

[20] According to M. I. Skobelev, vice-president of the Petrograd soviet and, in 1922, member of the communist party. From the transcript of a conference between high command and government reproduced by Denikin, *op. cit.*, p. 115.

Order No. 1 was followed by the *Declaration of the Rights of the Soldiers and Committees,* issued on May 22 by the war ministry. The declaration gave to the soldiers many obvious rights enjoyed in any democratic country, but it also introduced politics and political discussion into the army and weakened the system of military justice. Interminable discussions and innumerable meetings transformed the army into a debating society.[21]

Demoralization was accentuated by still additional developments. As a result of various promises for land reform, the weakening of governmental authority, and the dissolution of the police, the peasants spontaneously began redistributing land. The government tried to stop the movement but, lacking executive force, achieved nothing. The land grab led to a great deal of unrest among the peasant-soldiers who were afraid that in their absence the land would be divided among those right there on the spot. Many soldiers deserted in order to stake their claims.[22] Ultimately, there were no fewer than two million deserters.[23]

On top of this, the provisional government granted a broad amnesty to criminals, who were sent to serve out their sentences in the army. Allegedly, the criminals had strayed because of the nature of the tsarist regime! These types, quite naturally, contributed their share to the lowering of morale and started the Russian soldier on the road of plunder and terror.[24]

Since only five million soldiers were armed with rifles,[25] a partial demobilization might have been the solution to some of the difficulties. The front commanders resisted this measure, pointing out that no staff machinery existed by which a partial and orderly demobilization could be carried out.

One particular form of demobilization backfired badly. Mutinous elements were broken up, prompting many units to mutiny in order to be disbanded. Individual mutineers were assigned to new units, and the circle began again. Responsibility for this policy lay jointly with the high command, the war ministry, and the political commissars.

[21] Text of the *Declaration* is reproduced in Denikin, *op. cit.,* p. 174.
[22] Mavor, *op. cit.,* p. 113.
[23] Oldenbourg, *op. cit.,* p. 96.
[24] Denikin, *op. cit.,* p. 157.
[25] Oldenbourg, *op. cit.,* p. 93.

Of greatest importance was the dispersal of the command structure. The army legalized the military soviets and tolerated the establishment of political commissars, jointly appointed by government and soviet. Orders required three-way concurrence, and commanders no longer could make even purely military decisions alone. Officers were compelled to plead with their men to keep the trenches secure. The high command and the government resorted to speechmaking and written appeals to influence their soldiers. No order was carried out which the common soldiers did not like, and they liked neither to work nor to fight.

This situation reached the height of absurdity when, during October, revolutionary military committees were established in all major units at the front. These committees constituted a fourth chain of command and eliminated the last vestiges of military authority.[26]

Under the circumstances, one should have expected the Russian army to stay on the defensive. However, the provisional government, to prove its contention that the revolution had strengthened Russian morale, launched an offensive (July 1917).[27] Some minor successes were achieved against the even more highly demoralized Austrians, but the Germans held fast and greatly weakened the few remaining fighting units of the Russian army. Morale took a new dip.

Still, not all would have been lost if at that point there had not arisen a fatal conflict between government and high command.

Kerensky, the most influential member of the provisional government, dismissed General Brusilov from his post as commander-in-chief and in his place appointed General Kornilov. Brusilov was loyal to the revolution, and his dismissal signified that, even in the opinion of Kerensky, the military reforms had been a disastrous failure. Kornilov was the strongest advocate of the re-creation of strict discipline. He insisted that the government must eliminate command by committee. Kerensky was not at all happy about Kornilov, but he had little choice.

Kerensky and Kornilov had an informal agreement covering the measures needed to re-establish discipline and authority. Yet the

[26] On these committees which co-ordinated revolutionary and subversive activities throughout the army, see sections on "The Bolsheviks Prepare to Strike" and "The Bolsheviks Strike."

[27] Russian morale at that time was so low that perhaps as much as three-quarters of the wounded were fakers or self-mutilators. See Denikin, *op. cit.*, p. 288.

personalities of these two men proved incompatible. Kerensky continually reverted to his illusions and failed to act. Exasperated, Kornilov considered carrying out his plans without support of the bungling provisional government.[28]

Suddenly, a crisis arose: the general sent Kerensky an ultimatum for the establishment of a dictatorship under the former's direction but with Kerensky's participation. In reply, Kerensky dismissed the general.

This conflict may have been due to misunderstanding and misinterpretation on the part of the intermediary between the two men. Kornilov later maintained that he had not sent an ultimatum but had simply a suggested plan for action. Kerensky failed to examine or determine Kornilov's real position. Apparently, he jumped at the opportunity to get rid of the prospective military savior.

In any event, Kornilov refused to comply with the dismissal order and prepared to seize power. Kerensky appealed to the soldiers' soviets, instructing them to disobey the orders from the military high command. The railroad unions were told not to transport military units to Petrograd. The telegraphers were instructed to hold up Kornilov's messages. Red guards were formed from among the civilian population to defend Petrograd. Kornilov's forces never moved.[29]

This incident had far-reaching consequences. The least important was that the Red guards retained their arms, although the government repeatedly invited them to return the weapons. More important was the new purge instituted by the provisional government among high-ranking Russian officers. Officers considered friendly to Kornilov were dismissed and replaced by others whom the government considered loyal.

Kerensky found no suitable commander-in-chief who would accept his commission. Hence, he appointed himself "generalissimo." The irresolute and weak General Nikolai N. Dukhonin became his chief of staff in charge of technical matters.[30] Kerensky was compelled to retain a large number of officers who, because of the Kornilov affair, were in opposition to the generalissimo and his group.

[28] *Ibid.*, p. 307. Be it noted that Kornilov, a Cossack of modest circumstances, opposed all schemes to restore the monarchy.

[29] Kerensky, *op. cit.*, p. 321.

[30] When called upon by Kornilov to set up a reliable guard unit and a weapons depot for the use of officer-volunteers in case of emergency, Dukhonin remarked: "This might lead to excesses." Denikin, *op. cit.*, p. 238.

Some of these officers felt that the Kerensky government was an evil greater even than the bolsheviks. The garrison commander of Petrograd who, during the crucial hours of the October insurrection, displayed a great deal of studied inactivity, reputedly shared this belief.

Perhaps the most fundamental result of the Kornilov affair was that, according to Kerensky's own testimony, it "succeeded in destroying the confidence of the rank and file of the army in the provisional government." It also "destroyed the entire work of the restoration of discipline in the army, achieved after almost superhuman efforts."[31]

During October 1917 the supply crisis in the Russian army reached a climax. According to the minister of war, General Verkhovsky, the Russian army comprised 9,500,000 men, with food available for but 7,000,000. Many military bakeries were closing. Winter clothing and shoes were all but unobtainable. The distribution system, heavily harassed by transportation shortages, plunder, and hoarding, was breaking down.[32]

While the Russian army was falling to pieces, the Germans launched a new offensive. Riga was taken. By October the German army posed a direct threat to Petrograd. Demoralization degenerated into near panic.

The demand for immediate peace became almost irresistible. The civilian population in the Petrograd area did not cherish the idea of a German occupation. The soldiers at the front did not care to fight in a hopeless cause. The Petrograd garrison, which did not want to go to the front, did not like the prospect of the front coming to Petrograd.

The politicians had become convinced that the war against Germany could no longer be continued. Yet the provisional government could not bring itself to renege on Russia's commitments to the West and sue for a separate peace. The bolsheviks, virtually alone among the Russian parties, promised immediate peace.

Aware that German terms would be onerous, most Russian politicians recoiled from surrender, preferring to "pass the buck" to the bolsheviks. They reasoned that the bolsheviks would assume respon-

---

[31] Kerensky, *op. cit.,* p. 321.

[32] James Bunyan and H. H. Fisher, *The Bolshevik Revolution 1917–18, Documents and Materials* (Stanford, Calif., Stanford University Press, 1934), pp. 46–49.

sibility for the capitulation and the peace terms and thereby destroy
their own chances of political survival. After the bolsheviks had discredited themselves, they would be kicked out by the loyal troops,
rendering possible the return to power of the politicians of more
moderate convictions. Then, Russian democracy, liberated from the
yoke of the war as well as from the danger of bolshevism, could face
the future with confidence. A wonderful plot; too bad the actors refused to play their roles.

The German-Bolshevik Conspiracy

The destruction of the Russian army from above was accompanied by burrowing from below.

Bolshevik antimilitarist work dates back to 1905,[33] but their early
successes were small, with the exception of the much publicized mutiny on the battle cruiser *Potëmkin* (which cannot be considered bolshevik in nature and origin). The first mutiny of World War I occurred in October 1915 on the battleship *Gangut,* but it is not too
well established whether or not this was bolshevik handiwork. Gradually, however, the bolsheviks and other socialist organizations set
up nuclei within the Russian armed forces. They were helped by
large-scale German propaganda along the Russian front.

German leaders decided to wage psychological warfare against
Russia and apparently hit early on the idea of utilizing Russian revolutionaries. The exact transactions have never been revealed in full,
and the story must be reconstructed from scattered documents and
circumstantial evidence. The most important documentary source is
a U.S. government publication entitled *The German-Bolshevik Conspiracy*.[34] The documents reprinted in this publication, for the most
part, are reproductions of letters exchanged between an agency of
the German secret service (and other German agencies) and bolshevik leaders. Edgar Sisson, representative of the Committee on Public

---

[33] E. Jaroslavski, *El Trabajo de los Bolcheviques en el Ejército antes de la
Revolución de Octubre* (Barcelona, Edeya, no year). Jaroslavski was the first
bolshevik arrested for antimilitarist work and presumably was the originator
of this technique.

[34] This collection of documents was issued by George Creel's Committee
on Public Information as No. 20 of the *War Information Series*. It is dated
October 1918.

Information, was employed in Russia during the revolutionary days. During his stay, he obtained photographs of part of this correspondence and brought them, as well as some of the originals, to the United States. The final report also contains an appendix including a smaller number of documents, the originals of which had not been examined by Sisson. These documents had been circulated by antibolsheviks in Petrograd and purport to be copies of documents secured by officials who vacated their offices after the *coup d'état*.[35]

The authenticity of the documents was challenged, and Creel submitted them to J. Franklin Jameson, editor of the *American Historical Review* and director of the department of historical research, Carnegie Institution; and to Samuel N. Harper, professor of Russian language and institutions, University of Chicago, for an opinion on their genuineness. These experts concluded that the first group of documents, numbered 1–53, were authentic.[36]

[35] Edgar Sisson, *100 Red Days* (New Haven, Conn., Yale University Press, 1931), pp. 357–86, tells the story of the documents and the subsequent disputes about them. See also, S. P. Melgunov, *Zolotoi nemetskii klyuch bolshevikov* (Paris, Maison du livre étranger, 1940).

[36] The originals and photographs were "subjected . . . with great care to all the applicable tests to which historical students are accustomed to subject documents of the kind. . . . Besides studying whatever internal evidences could be derived from the pages themselves, we have, so far as we could, compared their versions of what went on with the actual facts. Upon the basis of these investigations, we have no hesitation in declaring that we see no reason to doubt the genuineness or authenticity of these fifty-three documents." *Report of the Special Committee on the Genuineness of the Documents,* in *The German-Bolshevik Conspiracy,* p. 29. There is no question that antibolshevik organizations frequently resorted to fabrication of documents and provocation. Classical cases are the Sinovyev letter, the Reichstag fire, the accusation that the German communist party planned an insurrection in February 1933, and the more recent "protocol M." Sufficient evidence was procured to disprove the nazi falsifications and the authenticity of "protocol M." There is considerable documentation to question the authenticity of the Sinovyev letter. The case of the Sisson documents is entirely different: Not one shred of direct or indirect evidence was ever adduced to disprove their genuineness. Statements occurring frequently in the literature to the effect that these documents were "proven" to be falsifications are entirely without foundation. It is true that there was a dispute between Harper and Sisson as to what the documents showed, namely, whether or not "Lenin not only had contacts with the German general staff when he journeyed across Germany but had been and still was a German agent." This obviously is a matter of interpretation. The fact remains that even late in his life Harper did not retract his earlier findings concerning the authenticity of the documents as such. See Samuel N. Harper, *The Russia I Believe In,* ed. by Paul V. Harper (Chicago, University of Chicago Press, 1949), p. 112.

With respect to the second group of documents, numbered 54, 55, 57, 59–68, the experts made "no confident declaration," but, on the strength of internal evidence, they saw "in these texts nothing that positively excludes the notion of their being genuine, little in any one of them that makes it doubtful. . . ."

Corroboration was furnished later by Kerensky who, in his capacity as former war minister and prime minister of the provisional government, asserted it to be a "positive and irrefutable fact" that Lenin returned to Russia "with the knowledge and consent and at the desire of the German government, but even in Russia . . . worked with the mighty financial backing of the enemies of his country, coordinating his attacks against the provisional government with the military plans of Ludendorff and Hindenburg."[37]

On his part, General Denikin stated that the Russian war ministry had "evidential material" concerning the treason of the bolsheviks and other socialists. The military, officially and in writing, had called upon the government to take measures against these men.[38] During the July uprising, 1917, the ministry of justice, "exasperated by the laxity of the leaders of the government, decided, with the knowledge of their minister," to publish the official correspondence and "other documents exposing Lenin's treason to his country."[39] The documents were printed by two non-bolshevik socialists, Alexinsky and Pankratov, collaborators of Georgi V. Plekhanov, the founder of Russian Marxism.

In the wake of the public resentment aroused by the July uprising, the bolsheviks were indicted by the procurator of the Petrograd high court of justice. According to the indictment, Lenin's organization, aimed "at assisting the states warring against Russia in their hostile actions against her, entered into an agreement with the agents of the said states to forward the disorganization of the Russian army and

[37] Alexander S. Kerensky, *The Crucifixion of Liberty* (New York, Day, 1934), p. 314.

[38] Denikin, *op. cit.*, p. 196. First evidence was obtained from a Russian prisoner of war sent by the Germans behind the Russian lines. It would seem as though the German authorities had directed him to Lenin. *The Crucifixion of Liberty, op. cit.*, p. 321.

[39] *Ibid.*, p. 198. According to Kerensky, p. 323, the disclosure was premature, and prevented the arrest of "a very prominent German agent." The chief offenders and the most damning documents slipped from the hands of the provisional government.

the Russian rear, for which purpose it used the financial means received from these states to organize a propaganda among the population and the troops . . . and also, for the same purpose, organized in Petrograd, from July 3rd to 5th, an armed insurrection against the supreme power existing in the state."[40]

While an exile in Germany, Kerensky secured additional proof for the treason of the bolsheviks. The well-known German social democrat and prominent Marxist theoretician, Eduard Bernstein, confirmed the collaboration between the German army and the bolsheviks before the October uprising. According to him, the bolsheviks received fifty million marks.[41]

On the authority of Kerensky, the French minister of munitions, socialist Albert Thomas, passed on to the provisional government "very confidential information . . . about Lenin's treachery."[42]

Furthermore, Kerensky quoted a letter by Leonid Krasin to his wife, in which this close friend of Lenin's, and subsequently member of the soviet government, clearly linked the bolsheviks with "German headquarters."[43]

Thus, we have as main crown witnesses the former Russian prime minister and war minister, the Russian ministry of justice, a commanding general of the Russian army, a highly placed German socialist, a French socialist and cabinet minister, and a representative of the American government. In addition, we have original documents and photographs of documents, authenticated by a panel of American experts; and we have the undenied fact of bolshevik deal-

---

[40] Denikin, *op. cit.*, p. 196. The dates are given in the old style, that is, thirteen days early. Kerensky reproduces the indictment in *The Crucifixion of Liberty, op. cit.*, p. 323.

[41] Kerensky wrote: "He gave me the whole story of Lenin's connection with the German government and also related how President Ebert himself and other high officials of the Reich had persuaded, or rather forced, him . . . to put an end to his disclosures of the Lenin-Ludendorff alliance and to withdraw his demand for a Reichstag inquiry. . . . In personal conversation with Bernstein I established the final link which we lacked in the chain that connected Lenin with the German government." *Ibid.*, p. 325.

[42] *Ibid.*, p. 321. The investigation of the affair by the provisional government was lax. When the first shock had subsided, the bolsheviks went over to the counteroffensive and announced that they were establishing a committee for the investigation of the accusation that their party had taken German money. Nobody ever heard of the results of this investigation. Melgunov, *op. cit.*, p. 121.

[43] *The Crucifixion of Liberty, op. cit.*, p. 327.

ings with the Germans concerning Lenin's trip from Switzerland to Russia.

Hence, our evidence is quite voluminous. What is more, this evidence is in full accord with logic.

It would indeed be against all logic to assume that the Germans, who showed enough imagination to ship the comrades into Russia, would not have driven a more ambitious bargain fully satisfactory to themselves.

And it would be even more contrary to logic to assume that Lenin and his friends, who had written that the "defeat of Russia will be the least of all evils" and who were preaching the concept of revolutionary defeatism as well as the doctrine of "right is what helps the revolution," would have hesitated to live up to their own principles. Transactions of this kind are practical applications of the bolshevik theory that it is the duty of the revolutionary to take advantage of the contradictions in the capitalist camp. The German-bolshevik deal was nothing but a consummation of communist convictions.

At the beginning of the war, Lenin lived in Austrian Galicia. Immediately upon the outbreak of hostilities he was arrested, but within two weeks he was released upon the intervention of Viktor Adler, prominent Austrian social democrat. Lenin was permitted to move to Switzerland where he was joined by Sinovyev. From his correspondence, Lenin possessed very little money.[44] Shortly after arrival, he made strenuous efforts to bring some of his manuscripts into print, with little success. By early October 1914 he could raise but 170 francs.

By the end of October, however, he was thinking of reviving the official party magazine *Sotsial Demokrat,* and announced that the magazine would be issued shortly.[45] On November 14 he wrote a letter indicating that the *Sotsial Demokrat* had come out, and in another letter of the same day he stated: "I am not hard up for money at the moment."[46]

[44] *The Letters of Lenin,* trans. and ed. by Elisabeth Hill and Doris Mudie (London, Chapman and Hall, 1937), p. 334. In using Lenin's letter, it is well to keep in mind that the "conspirational" letters were written in invisible ink and always destroyed upon receipt. The really significant letters will probably never be found. Kerensky stated that Lenin's lack of funds at that time "has been definitely established." *The Crucifixion of Liberty, op. cit.,* p. 319.

[45] *Ibid.,* pp. 336, 344.

[46] *Ibid.,* p. 346.

On November 28 he wrote a letter to Stockholm asking for a receipt for money which he had repaid on a loan. He added: "If you have not received any money and you cannot find any, we shall probably be able to send you a little."[47]

From whence this new-found prosperity? The puzzle may be solved if we look up Mr. Sisson's document No. 57.[48] This document, dated November 2, 1914, purports to be a circular of the German Reichsbank to various German bank organizations. It reads in part as follows:

At the present time there have been concluded conversations between the authorized agents of the Imperial Bank and the Russian revolutionaries, Messrs. Sinovyev and Lunacharsky.[49] Both the mentioned persons addressed themselves to several financial men, who for their part addressed themselves to our representatives. We are ready to support the agitation and propaganda projected by them in Russia on the one condition that the agitation and propaganda noted by the above-mentioned Messrs. Sinovyev and Lunacharsky will touch the active armies at the front. In case the agents of the Imperial Bank should address themselves to your banks we beg you to open them the necessary credit which will be covered completely as soon as you make demand on Berlin.

This document would indicate that the bolsheviks took the initiative in the matter, as indeed they must have.

It is doubtful whether the exact nature of the transaction will ever be determined, but it is a fact that the bolsheviks, between 1914 and early 1917, issued twenty-four numbers of the *Sotsial Demokrat,* including two double numbers of a supplement, a variety of other pamphlets, and several large books—all this with no visible source of income.[50] It also seems to be a fact that the transportation of this illegal literature into Russia, despite obvious difficulties, was "fairly successful."[51] It is a third fact that the bolsheviks were allowed by

[47] *Ibid.,* p. 352.

[48] *The German-Bolshevik Conspiracy,* p. 26. This is a document of the second type, that is, one whose original was not examined by Mr. Sisson. German World War I documents presently available in a practically unusable form at the National Archives at Washington, D. C., contain evidence of similar transactions.

[49] Sinovyev was at that time Lenin's closest collaborator. Lunacharsky was a prominent bolshevik.

[50] Olga Hess Gankin and H. H. Fisher, *The Bolsheviks and the World War, The Origin of the Third International* (Stanford, Calif., Stanford University Press, 1940), pp. 137 f.

[51] *Ibid.* Further information of the distribution of these materials will be found in *ibid.,* p. 144.

the Germans to circulate their literature, in fairly substantial quantity, among Russian prisoners of war in German camps.[52] General Denikin, of the Russian high command, later commented that the revolutionaries began their work "with a widespread revolutionary and separatist (Ukrainian) propaganda among the prisoners of war." Denikin quoted Karl Liebknecht, the most prominent German communist of the time, to the effect "that the German government not only helped this propaganda, but carried it on itself."[53]

Nothing is known about the German-bolshevik co-operation during 1916, although there is evidence in Lenin's correspondence that his source of money had dried up. By February 1917, Lenin had become so poor that he wanted his wife to write a *Pedagogic Encyclopedia,* which "will bring in some money *which is arch important for us.*"[54]

Upon the outbreak of the revolution in Russia, Julius Martov,[55] a menshevik but then a close friend of Lenin's, suggested that Lenin seek the assistance of the Germans to enable him and his comrades to travel to Russia.[56] Contact with the German government was accordingly made, and the matter was settled within so short a time (less than ten days) that one is forced to conclude that relations must have existed previously. There is evidence that at one point the negotiations hit a snag, but apparently the Germans accepted Lenin's conditions, whatever they were.[57] Lenin traveled to Russia in the company of 32 bolsheviks and socialists, and at a later date the

[52] *Ibid.,* p. 214. This is confirmed by Kerensky, *The Crucifixion of Liberty, op. cit.,* p. 319, according to whom Lenin founded at Bern a "committee of intellectual assistance for the Russian prisoners of war."

[53] Denikin, *op. cit.,* p. 194. There are indications that the Germans later released indoctrinated prisoners to have them participate in bolshevik riots and in Red army operations.

[54] Italics in original. Hill and Mudie, *op. cit.,* p. 408. Other evidences for the utter poverty of the bolsheviks can be found *ibid.,* pp. 329, 385, 392, 400, 407.

[55] *Ibid.,* p. 416.

[56] It has often been asserted that the Entente powers did not let Lenin pass through their territory. But the Russian foreign minister, Paul Milyukov, insisted that all Russian emigrés should be permitted to return, and he intervened to secure the return of Trotsky. In Lenin's letters we find no allusion to any intention to ask the Entente power for passage. We do hear about a plan to travel under a false name with a wig (*ibid.*). This plan was dropped within two or three days.

[57] *Ibid.,* p. 320.

Germans permitted yet another 127 revolutionaries to proceed to Russia. Virtually every one of these persons was carried on an "international control list" issued by the Entente to identify those suspected of relations with an enemy government.

How was the liaison with the Germans organized? There was in Copenhagen a former member of the Saint Petersburg soviet (1905), Alexander L. Parvus-Helphand. Parvus had become a German citizen and member of the German social democratic party. Shortly after the beginning of the war he set up in Denmark an intelligence and propaganda center working against Russia. Together with the German minister at Copenhagen, Count Brockdorff-Rantzau, subsequently ambassador at Moscow and protagonist of a German-Russian alliance, he invented the scheme of the "sealed carriage," this modern replica of the Trojan horse. Upon intercession by the leading deputy of the center party and subsequently German foreign minister, Erzberger, Reich Chancellor Bethmann-Hollweg was won for the idea of sending revolutionaries to Russia.[58] He, in turn, suggested the operation to the military. This was confirmed by General Ludendorff who, in 1936 as well as at other times, indicated that the idea was given to Bethmann-Hollweg by the social democrat Scheidemann and by Erzberger, on a suggestion by Parvus.[59]

In Bern, Lenin negotiated with the German Minister von Ramberg through the Swiss left-wing socialist Fritz Platten. From Petrograd, Lenin communicated with the German diplomat Lucius through Jacob Ganetsky-Fürstenberg, member of the bolshevik party's central committee; both Lucius and Fürstenberg were stationed at Stockholm, yet after the uprising Lucius, as well as members of the German intelligence service, moved to Petrograd.[60] So much for the liaison arrangements.

[58] *The Crucifixion of Liberty, op. cit.,* pp. 324 f.

[59] G. R. Treviranus, *Revolutions in Russia, their Lessons for the Western World* (New York, Harper, 1944), p. 92. Ludendorff's reference to Scheidemann is supported by document No. 4, *The German-Bolshevik Conspiracy,* according to which "Fürstenberg and Radek are in correspondence with Messrs. Scheidemann and Parvus regarding the destruction of the traces of the business relations of the party with the Imperial government. . . . This correspondence was caused by the demand of leading groups of German socialists, who saw in the said communications a danger to the cause of world socialism."

[60] *The Crucifixion of Liberty, op. cit.,* p. 325.

The most significant question is whether the bolsheviks and the Germans reached an agreement on long-term collaboration. The existence of an agreement of sorts has been admitted officially by the bolsheviks, although, according to the official version, the exiles committed themselves only "to agitate for the release of an equal number of Austrians and Germans who were interned in Russia."[61]

However, upon Lenin's return to Russia, the bolsheviks embarked on a large-scale, and therefore costly, propaganda campaign which, as Kerensky pointed out, closely paralleled the themes of German propaganda. Again: where did the money come from? On April 12, 1917, Lenin wrote to Fürstenberg and Radek in Stockholm: "So far nothing has come . . . we have received neither letters, parcels nor money from you."[62] Since the bolshevik party had hardly any funds left, the question must be asked: what money did they expect from Stockholm? And in turn: if they had been so broke in Switzerland that they were waiting anxiously for a few francs, how could they finance their propaganda so shortly afterwards? What were their Russian sources of income? No communist historian has ever tackled this fairly obvious question.

Fortunately, the facts are well known, at least in their broad outline. Document No. 1 of *The German-Bolshevik Conspiracy* indicates that on March 15, 1917, there may have been an agreement reached between Lenin and other bolsheviks and the German Reichsbank. This agreement called "for the propaganda of peace in Russia."[63]

The provisional government established the fact that the Germans paid their money to the Nia Bank at Stockholm which transferred it to the Siberian Bank at Petrograd, where it was credited to the ac-

[61] *Lenin Biography,* prepared by the Marx-Engels-Lenin Institute (Moscow, London, Hutchinson, 1943), p. 112.

[62] Hill and Mudie, *op. cit.,* p. 424. It should not go unnoticed that this letter linking Lenin to Fürstenberg and Radek in this fashion was published much later than document No. 4, referred to above; thus, it serves to authenticate that document. Radek subsequently conducted many negotiations with the Reichswehr. Another of Lenin's representatives in Stockholm was Alexandra Kollontay, who was ambassador to Sweden during World War II, and in that capacity participated in secret peace negotiations. In other words, these persons repeatedly served as contacts with German authorities. On the German side, too, personnel implicated in this affair participated in Soviet-German relations and secret arrangements right down to the post-World War II period.

[63] Sisson secured photostats of both documents No. 1 and No. 4.

counts of a Mrs. Sumenson, a relative of Fürstenberg's, and to a bolshevik party member by the name of Kozlovsky. At the time of her arrest in July 1917, Mrs. Sumenson had withdrawn from her account the sum of 750,000 rubles, with 180,000 rubles remaining.[64] The sums handled by Kozlovsky are not known.

As soon as Lenin had set foot on Russian soil, he gave highest priority to defeatist propaganda in the army. Strongly opposing "defensism" (the view that Russia should continue to fight against Germany), he emphasized the need "to explain the indissoluble connection between capital and the imperialist war, and to prove that it is impossible to end the war by a truly democratic, noncoercive peace without the overthrow of capital. The widespread propaganda of this view *among the army on active service* must be organized."[65]

The appearances indicate that the Germans were highly satisfied with Lenin's work. Originally, they had supported revolutionaries of all hues, and there are indications that even Maksim Gorki may have drunk at the well. Yet it must soon have become evident to the Germans that Lenin's group was the most likely to deliver the goods. Hence, according to Document No. 5,[66] a new agreement was negotiated in July at Kronshtadt between "officials" of the German general staff and "leaders of the Russian revolutionary army and democracy, Messrs. Lenin, Trotsky, Raskolnikov and Dybenko."[67] Nothing is known about the terms of this agreement except that it coincided approximately with the July uprising. One non-certified document shows that in September 1917, Fürstenberg opened an account "for the undertaking of comrade Trotsky," and that this account was used for the purchase of arms and their delivery to the

[64] *The Crucifixion of Liberty, op. cit.,* p. 326. According to Kerensky, this was approximately $375,000 and $90,000. Kozlovsky was also a member of Pilsudski's Polish socialist party. The dealings between Pilsudski and the Austrian and German governments are a matter of admitted public record. They offer indirect confirmation for the parallel transactions between the Germans and the bolsheviks. Compare also the dealings between the Germans and the Irish revolutionaries under Sir Roger Casement.

[65] *Selected Works, op. cit.,* April theses, VI, 22. [Italics added.] Compare the wording of the last sentence with the purported Reichsbank circular quoted above.

[66] Photostat available.

[67] Documents No. 62, 63, and 68, of which originals were not available, indicate that money was transferred to the bolsheviks from the Germans during June and July 1917.

Finno-Swedish border. Also in September, Lenin received a new sum of money. By that time, according to the evidence contained in the documents, he had obtained a minimum of half a million marks from the Germans.[68]

According to authenticated Documents 8 and 9, the Germans made two additional payments of fifty million and five million gold rubles during January 1918. Most of this money was to be used for the payment of Red guardsmen, who received twelve to sixteen rubles a day, while the soldiers were paid only a few kopeks.[69] Sisson believes that the payments of January 1918 were the last payments received by the bolsheviks from the Germans; from that time on, the bolsheviks controlled the financial resources of a large nation.[70]

THE DISAFFECTION OF THE ARMY

How SUCCESSFUL was the defeatist work of the bolsheviks? According to Lenin, the bolsheviks obtained the support of "almost half the army, which numbered at least 10,000,000."[71] Is this true?

Fortunately, we are in a position to check Lenin's estimate through an examination of the election returns to the constituent assembly. While neither complete nor fully accurate, these figures nevertheless provide the basis for a reliable inference.

[68] Document No. 65. Approximately $120,000. Presumably this would have to be added to the sums transmitted through Mrs. Sumenson.

[69] According to Sisson, "the bolshevik government also required factory owners to pay regular wages to their workers while they served in the red guard." This was a transitory arrangement during the period of early consolidation. Simultaneously, the bolsheviks destroyed the Russian banking system, "a maneuver that deprived all opponents of bolshevism of their financial means of warfare." See *The German-Bolshevik Conspiracy,* p. 9.

[70] This story would not be complete without mentioning that the cynicism of the Germans backfired badly. After infecting the Russian army, the German army in turn became infected through revolutionary propaganda and fraternization. The German navy showed itself especially vulnerable. One naval mutiny in 1917 was followed by numerous cases of desertion, self-mutilation, breaches of discipline, and strikes in key industries. A second naval mutiny, in November 1918, unleashed the German revolution and sealed the military fate of imperial Germany. It also liberated Russia from the shackles of the Brest-Litovsk treaty.

[71] *Selected Works, op. cit.,* X, 282. This statement was made on July 1, 1921.

The returns from the army and navy elections show that about 1.6 million soldiers voted the bolshevik ticket. This figure does not reflect the vote in the Caucasian army, the returns of which are not available. Since the bolsheviks, however, made their poorest showing in the Caucasus, it is obvious that the bolsheviks did not have five million votes as Lenin asserted.[72]

Of the votes counted, the bolsheviks polled over one hundred thousand more votes than did the social revolutionaries, their main competitors. Percentage-wise, the bolsheviks polled 45 per cent and the social revolutionaries 43 per cent of the military vote (minus the Caucasus).

This seems impressive; yet a large part of the armed forces did not vote. Assuming the total military strength to have been 9.5 million, as stated by the minister of war, vote participation was about 42 per cent.[73]

Accordingly, the bolshevik vote accounted for 18 per cent of the soldiers under arms and the social revolutionary vote for 16 per cent, in round figures.

The two main socialist parties together polled about one-third of the military strength and about 88 per cent of the total vote. There was a fairly substantial vote for the various Ukrainian, national minority, and socialist splinter parties. The constitutional democrats (cadets), who occupied the right wing, polled less than 2 per cent, drawing their strength almost exclusively from the officers.

However, while about one-fifth of the army was clearly bolshevik and two-fifths were demonstrated socialists of one complexion or another, three-fifths failed to vote, apparently holding no firm opinions. These non-voters cannot be classed either as convinced socialists or as revolutionaries, or as antisocialists.

Overall figures, however, do not tell the whole story; the influence of the bolsheviks was the stronger, the closer the units were stationed to the metropolitan centers. The western front was strongly infected, while on the Rumanian front bolshevik influence was small, albeit greater than in the Caucasus. While the bolsheviks were strong in the Baltic fleet, they made a poor showing in the Black Sea fleet, where, incidentally, the Ukrainian parties made a rather impressive record.

[72] Radkey, op. cit., p. 37.
[73] Bunyan and Fisher, op. cit., p. 46.

The following table does not purport to show accurate figures but probably indicates correct orders of magnitude:

Voting in Russian army and navy, November–December 1917[74]

	PER CENT OF VOTE	VOTES IN PER CENT OF THE ESTIMATED TOTAL MILITARY STRENGTH
Western Front:		
bolsheviks	70	29
social revolutionaries	18	8
Northern Front:		
bolsheviks	56	23
social revolutionaries	29	12
Southwestern Front:		
bolsheviks	30	13
social revolutionaries	40	17
Rumanian Front:		
bolsheviks	15	6
social revolutionaries	60	26
Black Sea Fleet:		
bolsheviks	20	?
social revolutionaries	42	
Baltic Fleet:		
bolsheviks	62	?
social revolutionaries	23	
All units:		
bolsheviks	45	18
social revolutionaries	43	16

These figures show that the bolsheviks had not been quite so successful as Lenin suggested—but the vote was decisive enough. There is no doubt that the Russian army had been destroyed as an instrument of state security.

[74] Calculated from Radkey's figures, *op. cit.*, p. 80, and based on an assumed total military strength of 9,500,000. In the absence of information on the strength of the various army groups, a total vote participation of 42 per cent was assumed uniformly for all army groups.

BOLSHEVIK MOBILIZATION

IN MARCH the bolsheviks began their participation in the revolution while their leader was still in Switzerland; Lenin arranged with the German government for his return to Russia. Upon arrival in Petrograd, he laid down the basis for bolshevik tactics.[75] His most important point was that the events of February simply represented the first stage of the revolution. This was to be followed by a second, "which must place power into the hands of the proletariat and the poor strata of the peasantry."[76] To carry the revolution into its second stage, Lenin called for the transfer of the entire power of state to the soviet, opposing the idea that Russia should become a parliamentary republic.

Lenin proceeded to explain the great significance of "dual power," which he described as "the striking feature of our revolution."[77] This fact, he stated, "must be grasped first and foremost." "Unless it is understood, we cannot advance. . . . *Nobody* hitherto thought, or could have thought, of dual power."

How should dual power be exploited? The slogan "all power to the soviets" was to deprive the provisional government of its authority and to transfer control of the state to the soviet. Lenin not only grasped the true revolutionary potentiality of the soviet but also understood how the split power situation could be exploited best for revolutionary purposes. Lenin decided that, at that time, it was correct tactics for the bolsheviks to gain a majority in the soviet.

In May, the situation developed further, as a reorganization of the government shifted the center of the political gravity to the left. Centrist elements were displaced by socialists, unrest continued, and bolshevik propaganda efforts against the army increased. However, the intensity of the revolution seemed to have abated, and military discipline and morale appeared to be improving.

At this point the government committed a very serious error. Partly to show good will vis-à-vis the allies, and partly because it overrated the improvement in the army, the regime determined to mount a major offensive against the Germans. News of the impend-

[75] The famous "April theses," dated April 20, 1917, *Selected Works, op. cit.,* VI, 21–26.
[76] *Ibid.,* p. 22.
[77] *Ibid.,* p. 27.

ing resumption of active operations provoked mass disorders during June, and the announcement of the commencement of the offensive was greeted by a big demonstration in Petrograd on July 1. When it became clear that the offensive would fail, an uprising took place in the capital (July 16–18).

The origins of this uprising have not been fully clarified. Whether the bolsheviks planned a full-scale insurrection or simply an operation with limited objectives has not been determined.

While the uprising might have been a more or less spontaneous event, it quite possibly was a bolshevik improvisation. Lenin explained that the July uprising was "an outburst of indignation, which the bolsheviks attempted to restrain, but which they were, of course, bound to endeavor to lend the most organized form possible."[78]

According to an official soviet version, a machine-gun regiment from the Petrograd garrison sent delegates to the bolshevik party announcing that it wanted action and desired support.[79] The bolsheviks, thinking that the time was premature (or afterwards stating that they thought so), issued a call for a peaceful demonstration which, however, degenerated into armed clashes. But who influenced and guided the behavior of the regiment?

The government suppressed the uprising without difficulty, and Kerensky became prime minister. At this inopportune moment for the bolsheviks, documents showing Lenin's connections with the Germans were widely published. Since the uprising did coincide and interfere with a Russian offensive, there was prima-facie evidence of a German-bolshevik conspiracy to sabotage Russian military operations. Public pressure became strong, and the provisional government issued orders for the arrest of the bolsheviks, most of whom were put in prison. Lenin and Sinovyev escaped to Finland.

But within a few weeks the Kerensky government, seeking allies against the generals and eager to live up to its reputation as the most democratic of all governments, amnestied the arrested bolsheviks. This measure enormously enhanced the self-confidence of the bolsheviks and greatly reduced the willingness of loyal troops to carry out orders for the suppression of unrest. Why should they risk their lives in combat against an opponent who would neither be punished

[78] *Selected Works, op. cit.*, VI, 202. See also, Bunyan and Fisher, *op. cit.*, pp. 13, 17.
[79] *Ibid.*, p. 563.

nor rendered harmless but rather released to foment further unrest? The bolshevik organization was left intact. No precautions were taken by the government against a renewed threat.

Following the July uprising, two genuine courses were open to the government: it could adopt a policy of early peace and compromise with the radical revolutionary elements, or it could continue the war and suppress all subversive organizations.

The government determined upon a third course: continue the war and appease the revolutionaries. The government was strongly influenced in this decision by Arthur Henderson and Albert Thomas, British and French socialists who had been sent by their governments as representatives of European labor to establish close liaison with the Russian revolution. Thomas and Henderson minimized the dangers of the revolutionary movement and gave the easy advice of patience and moderation.[80]

Even more portentous was the deterioration of the financial position of the state. At the beginning of the war, the fiscal condition of Russia had been relatively favorable, and as late as early 1917 the situation was still fairly well in hand. But the provisional government greatly increased expenditures to maintain food prices, pay increased wages, and grant enormous subsidies to soldiers' wives. At the same time, the state experienced a drying up of its tax revenues: city people as well as peasants stopped paying taxes.[81] To postpone bankruptcy, the printing press was resorted to, and within four months, during the summer of 1917, the amount of money in circulation was more than tripled. During the weeks preceding the July uprising, inflation continued at an accelerated pace, accentuating food shortages as well as other manifold scarcities. The temper of the workers and peasants became quite unmanageable.[82]

In an attempt to consolidate governmental authority after the July uprising, Kerensky resorted to the Kornilov appointment. Within a few weeks, however, the Kornilov crisis threw the country into a new turmoil.

Insofar as the bolsheviks were concerned, the Kornilov affair necessitated a change in tactics. Some bolsheviks suggested that Kerensky be supported in his fight, but Lenin decided upon a more dia-

[80] Mavor, *op. cit.,* p. 94.
[81] Denikin, *op. cit.,* pp. 117–25.
[82] Mavor, *op. cit.,* p. 84.

lectic solution. While supporting Kerensky against Kornilov, the bolsheviks also were to oppose the government in order to drive it into
an ever more revolutionary course. "Partial demands" were to be
presented to Kerensky, such as: "arm the Petrograd workers; sum-
mon the Kronstadt, Viborg, and Helsingfors troops to Petrograd,
disperse the state duma; . . . legalize the transfer of the landlords'
estates to the peasants," and so forth.[83]

In Lenin's mind, the Kornilov affair had brought the conquest
of power by the proletariat much nearer, "only not *directly* but
obliquely. And at *this very minute* we must conduct our agitation
against Kerensky not so much directly as indirectly, that is, by demanding a most active energetic and truly revolutionary war against
Kornilov. The development of that war alone may put *us* in power,
but of this we must speak as little as possible in our agitation."[84]

Lenin elaborated his thought in a short dissertation on compromise.[85] He pointed out that it was absurd to oppose compromises
which are nothing but stops "at intermediate stations." The task, he
said, "of a truly revolutionary party is not to renounce compromises
once and for all, but to be able *throughout all compromises,* when
they are unavoidable, to remain true to its principles, to its class, to
its revolutionary purpose, to its task of preparing the way for the
revolution and of educating the masses for victory in the revolution."[86]

The Kornilov affair had set the stage for a compromise between
the bolsheviks on the one hand and the social revolutionaries and
mensheviks on the other. The compromise was to call for a united-
front government of these three parties which would be responsible
to the soviets alone. During a very brief period it might be possible
to organize such a government, guaranteeing "the peaceful advance
of the whole Russian revolution."[87] Since the possibility of such a
peaceful advance is *"extremely* rare in history and *extremely* valuable, a possibility that comes only in exceptionally rare cases," Lenin
planned to take advantage of the situation.[88]

[83] *Selected Works, op. cit.,* VI, 206.
[84] Lenin to the central committee, September 12, 1917, *ibid.,* p. 207. [Ital-
ics in original.]
[85] *Ibid.,* pp. 208–14.
[86] *Ibid.,* p. 208. [Italics in original.]
[87] *Ibid.,* p. 209.
[88] *Ibid.,* p. 210. [Italics in original.]

But Lenin's proposal was not published in time. Kerensky overcame Kornilov before the communists budged. The end of the Kornilov incident meant that Lenin's concept of peaceful revolution through temporary compromise fell into the category of what he himself called "belated thoughts." But these thoughts are illustrative of the flexibility of bolshevik tactics.

THE BOLSHEVIKS PREPARE TO STRIKE

SHORTLY after the Kornilov affair, elections were held which demonstrated considerable bolshevik strength. In the Moscow municipal contest, bolshevik representation jumped from 12 per cent in June to 51 per cent in September, and in Petrograd they increased their strength in similar fashion.[89] A few weeks after the bolsheviks gained their majority, Trotsky was elected chairman of the Petrograd soviet. In the strategic urban centers, there was a clear trend in favor of the bolsheviks.

Lenin, still in Finland, realized that events had taken another turn. Again, new tactics were required. He was worried by rumors of an impending peace between Britain and Germany, and he was even more perturbed by the danger that Petrograd would be taken by the Germans.[90] He felt that an armed uprising could be successful and that the international situation favored such a coup. The bolsheviks were in possession of an apparatus through which they could act: the soviets and the "democratic" organizations. He suggested that revolt be placed "on the order of the day."[91]

Once Lenin had made this fundamental decision, probably on September 25, 1917, he proceeded to explain it. The situation was different from that of July, he maintained, when the bolsheviks could not have retained power, because "before the Kornilov affair the army and provinces might, and would, have marched against Petrograd. The picture is now entirely different." Furthermore, in July the soldiers and workers did not hate Kerensky and his people as

[89] Radkey, *op. cit.*, p. 53.

[90] According to Kerensky, *The Crucifixion of Liberty, op. cit.*, pp. 384–86, the Germans told Lenin about their negotiations through the Spanish minister in Belgium with the English minister at The Hague.

[91] *Selected Works, op. cit.*, VI, 217.

they did in September. The ranks of the non-bolsheviks had not been split sufficiently. Now, the government did not know what policy to adopt: whether to continue the war or conclude a separate peace. The socialists and the other non-bolshevik revolutionary parties had broken with the liberal groups, thereby losing political power.[92] Lenin went one step further and outlined the tactics and objectives of insurrection.[93]

Lenin's new ideas were received skeptically by the comrades at Petrograd, who apparently thought that Lenin was willing to risk his followers while hiding in safety himself. Lenin became increasingly impatient, especially when he found out that a non-bolshevik officer, on October 5, had told the Petrograd soviet that the soldiers would not fight any longer and wanted the war stopped immediately. As Lenin phrased it, the army and the government had "parted ways." He also insisted that the peasant uprisings were getting out of hand.[94]

On October 12, Lenin reiterated his position in an article entitled "The Crisis Has Matured." When he sent the article for publication, he appended a letter to the central committee expressing the belief that further delay would be "utter idiocy or sheer treachery" and would lead to the destruction of the bolshevik party.[95]

But the Petrograd bolsheviks suggested that the uprising be postponed till the congress of the All-Russian soviet convened. Lenin replied that the congress "will give nothing and can give nothing," not even moral support. Waiting for the congress would therefore mean losing an opportunity which might never return. Lenin stated that the bolsheviks had enough military power to seize Petrograd and Moscow and suggested that the revolt be started in Moscow "so as to catch the enemy unawares." He "guaranteed" success for the uprising if the attack were launched simultaneously in Petrograd, Moscow, and the Baltic fleet.

But, he complained, the party had done nothing to study the situa-

[92] *Ibid.,* pp. 219 ff.

[93] "Marxism and Insurrection," *ibid.,* pp. 218–24; see also, *ibid.,* pp. 291, 321 f.

[94] Peasant unrest and uprisings were not new, but, according to the statistical evidence, a peak had been reached in summer at harvest time. The government was increasingly unable to maintain order. See Bunyan and Fisher, *op. cit.,* p. 33.

[95] *Selected Works, op. cit.,* VI, 230.

tion of the troops, nor had it concerned itself with developing the art of insurrection. Since the central committee had left unanswered his demands and apparently was eager to adopt an entirely different tactic involving co-operation with other parties, Lenin tendered his resignation from the central committee.

Despite his resignation, Lenin continued to agitate for the armed uprising. He produced an entire brochure in which he argued that the bolsheviks could seize and retain state power. In this booklet, finished on October 14, he made the point that the bolsheviks could stay in power simply because they would not take over the existing state apparatus but, rather, would smash it and replace it by a new soviet apparatus.[96] This idea was sharpened tactically a few days later when Lenin exhumed the slogan "all power to the soviets," stating that it had become "equivalent to a call for insurrection."[97]

This was not simply a repetition of words uttered often before. While the words remained identical, an entirely new meaning emerged. In April and May, as already pointed out, this slogan had served as a means of creating a competition for the power of the provisional government. By July 1917, Lenin discovered that the slogan "has patently ceased to be true."[98] As Lenin pointed out at that time, this slogan would have furthered the peaceful development of the revolution: with control over the soviets in non-bolshevik hands, a transfer of power to the soviets would have made little difference.[99] But, by October, the soviets had come under bolshevik control, while retaining in full measure the confidence of the Petrograd garrison. Hence, the old slogan resumed its importance and became "a call for revolt."[100] Why?

Lenin realized that very few people were inclined to follow bolshevik leadership, let alone accept the bolshevik program. There were only a few bolsheviks in the true sense of the word. Yet a large number of people followed the *soviet* (as distinct from the bolshevik) authority because they considered that institution, regardless of its party composition, as the supreme arbiter of Russian democ-

[96] *Ibid.*, p. 262.
[97] *Ibid.*, p. 300.
[98] "On Slogans," *Selected Works, op. cit.*, VI, 167.
[99] *Ibid.*, p. 174.
[100] *Ibid.*, p. 300.

racy. This was true especially of the soldiers who were willing to obey soviet directives but would not accept instructions from any political party. Since it was impossible to rise without the support of the soldiers, there was no choice but to act through the soviets.

Thus came into being the device of the "transmission belt" or, as it is called frequently, the "front organization." Trotsky gave the most cogent description of the tool. "The party sets the soviet in motion, the soviet sets in motion the workers, soldiers and to some extent the peasantry." The organization was constructed like a system of interconnected cogwheels. "The impatient attempt to connect the party wheel directly with the gigantic wheel of the masses—omitting the medium-sized wheel of the soviets—would have given rise to the danger of breaking the teeth of the party wheel and nevertheless not setting sufficiently large masses in motion."[101]

The revolutionary trend took a new upswing on October 21, when the bolsheviks achieved considerable success in yet another election at Moscow. But a new problem arose: should the uprising be waged defensively or offensively? Lenin demolished the argument of the defensive uprising, stating that "if you revolt, assume the offensive while the forces of your enemy are still scattered—catch your enemy unawares."[102] Nevertheless, the opposition against an openly offensive strategy, as well as the course of events, modified Lenin's view in this respect. In the words of Trotsky, "although an insurrection can win only on the offensive, it develops better the more it looks like self-defense."[103]

While the bolsheviks were discussing the strategy of the armed uprising, Trotsky participated in a meeting of the soldiers' section of the Petrograd soviet. He learned that one-third of the Petrograd garrison had been ordered to the front. He and his comrades immediately inferred that this directive was designed "to remove the bolshevik and the more revolutionary troops from the capital."

Suddenly, "it occurred to some of us we might use the occasion to bring about the armed uprising." As president of the Petrograd soviet, he suggested that the soviet should concur in the removal of the

[101] Leon Trotsky, *The Triumph of the Soviet* ("The History of the Russian Revolution," Vol. III [New York, Simon and Schuster, 1932]), p. 284.

[102] *Ibid.,* p. 294.

[103] *Ibid.,* p. 207.

troops only if it were proved to be a military necessity. It should not concur if the order proved to be simply a Kornilov move. "We decided to call for some kind of an organization to investigate the matter."[104]

In order not to be too obvious, the bolsheviks persuaded a member of the left social revolutionary party to demand the establishment of a revolutionary military committee. "Whether he perceived that this was a question of a conspiracy or simply expressed the formless revolutionary mood of the left s. r.'s, I don't know. . . . At any rate he agreed to it, while other left s. r.'s were suspicious. . . . When he produced his project we polished it up, masking as much as possible the revolutionary insurrectionist nature of the plan. Next evening the plan was put before the Petersburg soviet and accepted."

Thus, on October 22, the Petrograd soviet resolved to form a "collegium of representatives" from its own ranks and from other organizations "to function alongside the commander of troops of the Petrograd military district. No part of the garrison is to be moved without first notifying this collegium." The revolutionary military committee was instructed to study the defense of Petrograd and its approaches and work out "a plan for the protection of the city . . . with the active support of the working class."[105] We shall see how the committee contrived to develop the offensive under the guise of a defensive.

By October 23, Lenin finally convinced the central committee that armed insurrection had become "inevitable." Yet, on October 24, Sinovyev and Kamenyev precipitated a new crisis in the party by opposing the decision to launch an armed insurrection on the ground that the chances of seizing power through elections were excellent. The insurrection was described as a grave and unnecessary risk. According to Kamenyev and Sinovyev, the antibolsheviks were militarily strong. They had "5,000 military cadets *excellently* armed, *organized, anxious* . . . and able to fight, also the staff, shock troops, Cossacks, a substantial part of the garrison, and very considerable artillery, which has taken up a position in fan-like formation around

[104] Bunyan and Fisher, *op. cit.,* p. 68, quoted from Trotsky's "Vospominaniya ob oktyabrskom perevorote," in *Proletarskaya Revolutsiya,* 1922, No. 10, pp. 52 ff.

[105] Bunyan and Fisher, *op. cit.,* p. 69.

Petrograd."[106] Lenin stood by his guns, and the two "deviationists" were silenced.

The revolutionary military committee was established formally on October 25 and was given the broad powers of arming and provisioning the garrison of the capital, assuring its defenses, maintaining revolutionary discipline, and subduing "pogroms," that is, counter-revolutionary attacks.[107]

On October 27 the soviets of the regions of the North called upon the peasants to seize the property of landowners. The agrarian revolution was put into high gear. Accordingly, the central committee of the bolshevik party held a meeting on October 29 and confirmed its decision to launch the uprising. The central committee called "upon all organizations, workers and soldiers to undertake comprehensive and intensive preparation for armed insurrection." The resolution expressed its confidence that the central committee, together with the soviet, would "in good time indicate the favorable moment and the most suitable method of action."[108] The stage was set for the climax of the drama.

THE BOLSHEVIKS STRIKE

THE REVOLUTIONARY military committee functioned as a front organization for the Petrograd soviet, which, in turn, was acting as a bolshevik front. This trick of the double transmission belt might not have worked had the moderate parties in the Petrograd soviet not boycotted the committee, leaving it in the hands of the bolsheviks and of inconsequential left social revolutionaries. The committee was allowed to hold just one session. Thereafter, the bolshevik members, free to use its name, dispensed with formalities and concentrated on organizing their revolt.

In Stalin's words, the committee became the "legally functioning headquarters of the uprising."[109] Its most active members were Vla-

---

[106] Kamenyev's and Sinovyev's letter is reproduced in *ibid.*, pp. 59–62. [Italics in original.]

[107] Mavor, *op. cit.*, p. 145.

[108] *Selected Works, op. cit.*, VI, explanatory notes, 595.

[109] *History of the Communist Party of the Soviet Union (Bolsheviks), Short Course* (New York, International Publishers, 1939), p. 206. This history is not a bona fide description of events but a guide to future action and a handbook in communist tactics.

dimir Antonov-Ovseyenko, who issued most of the operational and tactical orders; Nikolai Podvoisky, who devoted most of his time to controlling the Red guard and the commissars sent in the name of the committee to the various military units; and Jacob Sverdlov, who co-ordinated the committee's activities with those of the bolshevik party. Leon Trotsky was in charge of over-all operational decisions, while Lenin, who had secretly returned from Finland, exerted political leadership.[110] The revolutionary activities of the bolshevik party were directed by a military and political center consisting of Stalin, Sverdlov, Bubnov, Uritsky, and Dzerzhinsky. Stalin later claimed that this center was headed by himself and that it had "practical direction of the whole uprising." However, documentation for this contention is entirely lacking, and there is no proof that Stalin took a very active, let alone a decisive, part in the insurrection.

One of the first acts of the revolutionary military committee was to establish full command authority over the Petrograd garrison. Commissars were appointed to the various units within the city and to all important military establishments, arsenals and weapon depots within the entire area. Selected from the ranks of the bolshevik party, these new commissars superseded the commissars previously nominated by the soviet.[111]

While preparations for the uprising were going on full blast, the government split over the war issue. The situation in the army had become virtually untenable, but Foreign Minister Mikhail S. Tereshchenko came out for a continuation of the war, stating that "no one in Russia could agree to peace which would humiliate her or adversely affect her vital interests...."[112] This statement further undermined the popularity of the Kerensky government.

By November 3, the revolutionary military committee's commissars were installed safely and successfully in their units. At a meeting of the Petrograd soviet, representatives of the garrison adopted a resolution welcoming the formation of the committee and pledging support to it in all its undertakings. The resolution stated that the time for words had passed. The coalition government, it continued,

---

[110] Total membership of the committee was ten, with the president of the soviet, Trotsky, as ex officio member.

[111] Mavor, *op. cit.,* p. 146. Allegedly the future Marshal Vasilyevski was one of the commissars.

[112] Bunyan and Fisher, *op. cit.,* pp. 40 f.

"is against the people. It became the tool of the enemies of the people. . . . The all-Russian congress of the soviet must take the power into its own hands in order to give to the people peace, land, and bread. Only thus can the safety of the revolution and of the people be insured." And then came the famous four slogans: "All power to the soviets; an immediate armistice on all fronts; the land to the peasants; an honest and prompt convocation of the constituent assembly."[113] Thus, these slogans were not promulgated by the bolshevik party, or by the captive Petrograd soviet, but by the military garrison of the Russian capital. The deception was complete.

This defiant attitude openly challenged constituted authority. On October 30, Colonel Polkovnikov, commander in chief of the Petrograd military district, had exhorted his troops to be on guard against irresponsible undertakings and had issued the somewhat strange order "not to allow themselves to become involved in uprising."[114] The military command was convinced that the majority of the garrison would disapprove of an uprising and that there was sufficient force available to suppress an insurrection should one break out.[115] The command was still confident; it was sure that the Cossacks would remain loyal.

This estimate, of course, was known to the revolutionaries. Hence, following the resolutions of November 3, the Petrograd soviet addressed an eloquent appeal to the Cossacks, inviting them "to take their destiny into their own hands."[116] When this appeal was well received, the committee informed the Petrograd command that, as of then, it (the committee) would control all military decisions. Polkovnikov refused to comply. Thereupon, on November 4, the committee declared to the garrison that the military command had broken off relations with the soviet and had become the tool of the counter-revolution. The document continued: "Soldiers of Petrograd, it is up to you, under the direction of the revolutionary military committee, to defend the revolutionary order against counter-revolution. Orders not signed by this committee are void. Every soldier should be on

113 *Ibid.*, p. 79.
114 *Ibid.*, p. 76.
115 *Ibid.*, p. 77.
116 This appeal written by Trotsky will be found in *ibid.*, pp. 80 f. On the special role of the Cossacks and their gradual adherence to the revolution, despite the extraordinary privileges enjoyed by them, see Denikin, *op. cit.*, pp. 239 ff.

guard and maintain strict discipline. The revolution is in danger: Long live the revolutionary garrison."[117] Delegates of the garrison informed Polkovnikov that they would obey only those orders which were countersigned by the revolutionary military committee.

At that moment, perhaps, an energetic action on the part of the government might still have saved the situation.

There was little doubt about what was going on. The decision of the bolsheviks to launch an uprising had leaked out, and the well-known writer Vladimir L. Burtsev sounded daily warnings in his paper, pointing out that the insurrectionists were "deriving their main strength from the weakness of the government."[118] However, counsels of prudence prevailed, and the government decided to negotiate. There was a strong disinclination to use force even against armed rebellion. Polkovnikov had no other choice but to order his soldiers and officers to stay in the barracks. He instructed them, quite ineffectually, that they were not to obey any orders which did not emanate from military authorities.

In the meantime, the revolutionary situation was maturing. The internal conflict within the government broke into the open with a speech by the minister of war calling for early peace. He was given an immediate leave of absence, but the ensuing crisis rendered the government incapable of devoting proper attention to subduing the insurrectional threat.

Meanwhile, the revolutionary military committee was drawing up plans for the uprising. November 4, proclaimed "day of the Petrograd soviet," saw large mass demonstrations which not only heightened the fever of the masses but enabled the insurgents to carry out "invisible maneuvers."[119] Individuals assigned the mission of seizing specific buildings or installations were ordered to familiarize themselves with the layout, see with their own eyes the spots most vulnerable to attack, determine the most suitable methods of capture, observe the local defense arrangements, enter target buildings and silently practice capture. The demonstrations provided cover for these rehearsals.[120]

[117] Bunyan and Fisher, pp. 81 f.

[118] Mavor, *op. cit.,* p. 147.

[119] Curzio Malaparte, *Tecnica del Colpo di Stato* (Milan, Bompiani, 1948), pp. 117 f.

[120] Mavor, *op. cit.,* pp. 147 f.; see also, Malaparte, *loc. cit.*

On November 5, the executive committee of the Petrograd soviet, in an official announcement, reasserted the authority of the revolutionary military committee. It confirmed that the commissars appointed by the committee were representatives of the Petrograd soviet with command authority. Yet the commandant of the St. Peter and St. Paul fortress refused to recognize the commissars, and was upheld by his troops. As a counter, it was proposed that the fortress garrison be called into a meeting and be won over by "persuasion and argument." Trotsky and Lashchevich (a member of the revolutionary military committee) successfully addressed the garrison, which promptly joined the bolsheviks. Another government stronghold had crumbled.

The government no longer could delay counteraction. On November 6, Polkovnikov issued an order removing all commissars appointed by the Petrograd soviet and initiating legal investigations into unlawful acts perpetrated by them. Bridges across the Neva were occupied by loyal cadets, who also took over the protection of the Winter palace, the seat of the government. Military units were placed throughout the city. The revolutionary papers were closed.

In reply, the revolutionary military committee proclaimed the Petrograd soviet to be in danger and ordered every regiment to be in readiness and to await further orders. "Any delay or failure to obey this order will be considered a betrayal of the revolution."[121]

Within a few hours the various military organizations under the control of the committee were directed to their battle stations. A commissar was appointed to the cruiser *Aurora,* then under repair in the Petrograd yards. Disregarding the objections of the commanding officer, the commissar took the ship through the shallow channel of the Neva river into the city of Petrograd.

Contending that the revolution was forced to adopt measures of self-defense, the revolutionary military committee, in the name of the Petrograd soviet, issued the call for the uprising.

The timing of the attack came as a surprise to the government, which had expected it one day later. Whether or not this was deliberate deception, or whether the date of the uprising was advanced by twenty-four hours to avoid the consequences of a security leak (as asserted by Stalin),[122] is not known.

[121] Bunyan and Fisher, *op. cit.,* pp. 85 f.
[122] *History of the Communist Party, op. cit.,* p. 207.

The actual uprising involved the occupation of key spots within the city. There were no barricades, no old-fashioned street fighting. The insurrection was carried out by military units under the command of the commissars, by Red guard companies, and by revolutionaries working inside the target installations. The bolsheviks, helped by left social revolutionaries, acted primarily as cadres. There were few, if any, special units.

Attack plans were based on extensive intelligence, procured partly by the prior rehearsals described above. Target seizure was accomplished by simple penetration into the building, by a sudden *coup de main*, by penetration from the sewer system, or by "political conquest," that is, capture from the inside.

Each assault team comprised specialists with particular knowledge of the target. For example, detachments taking power stations included electrical engineers and electrical workers; telephone workers participated in the seizure of telephone installations, and so forth.

Only a very few targets, such as the Winter palace, the military headquarters, and some military schools, had to be taken by assault; but nowhere did really serious fighting occur.

The attack began with the seizure of the main telegraph station and the government news agencies. Within a few hours the power plants, munition and food stores, the water works, several bridges, the telephone exchange, the state bank, the big printing plant, the remaining telegraph stations, the central post office, and the railroad stations were seized.

The bolsheviks saw to it that the early morning papers announced the overthrow of the government as an accomplished fact. They alleged that state power already had passed into the hands of the revolutionary military committee. This, of course, was a ruse of war. Trotsky apologized. "The leaders of an insurrection are not historians; in order to prepare events for the historians they have to anticipate them."[123]

It is not true, as has been asserted, that the attack was directed chiefly against the government apparatus of physical power, such as the public utilities. Such targets were included on the target list. But the primary targets of the insurrection were the telecommunication centers and the means of public information. These were of the greatest strategic importance, since the spreading of the revolution

[123] *Ibid.,* p. 233.

throughout Russia depended on their control by the bolsheviks. If the government had retained possession of its communication channels (it preserved merely a secret line to the high command at Mogilev), it would not have been isolated, its demise could not have been announced before the event, the opportunities for counterattack might have been far better.

As soon as the news of the Petrograd uprising and the end of the Kerensky government was flashed all over the country, revolutionary military committees—which had been formed in the major cities and in many of the large military units—constituted themselves as the chief authority, launching uprisings which followed the general tactics of the Petrograd model.

Only the Moscow uprising followed a different course. Stronghold of the bourgeoisie, Moscow was in a less revolutionary mood than was Petrograd, the citadel of the proletariat. To create the prerequisite revolutionary fever, the Moscow insurrection was combined with a general strike. At the beginning of the coup, the bolsheviks held the Kremlin, but later, after the bolsheviks had lost heavily in street fighting, they were forced to evacuate it and accept an armistice. During this truce the bolsheviks redeployed their forces, particularly their artillery, and moved reinforcements into the city. As soon as sufficient strength was concentrated, they resumed fighting and subjected the Kremlin to heavy bombardment. The council of the Russian church enjoined the combatants to end the bloodshed and save the Kremlin from destruction. The antibolsheviks, as usual, were victims of the illusion that a compromise could be arranged, and declared their willingness to conclude an armistice. When, as a result, the garrison (with the exception of the Cossacks) gradually went over to the bolshevik side, Moscow was surrendered to bolshevik control. By November 14, the fighting was over.

GOVERNMENT PARALYSIS

ALTHOUGH even a cancer when diagnosed early enough can be arrested, a minor infection left unattended may cause death. Similarly in politics; for, once a revolutionary situation reaches a certain level, and the authority of the state begins to break down, little can be done to keep the malady under control.

By early November 1917, the situation in Russia had deteriorated to such a point that a catastrophe was inevitable. Yet even this late in the day the course of history might have been changed. If the anti-bolsheviks had put up a strong resistance to the Petrograd uprising, the bolsheviks might have been weakened fatally and the revolution might not have spread to the rest of Russia. If the government had retained the support of but one or two regiments, the rising might have been aborted. Even after the start of the uprising, the government and its component parties underrated the danger and hesitated to use force. Encouraged by this attitude, the bolsheviks, throughout the insurrection, negotiated over possible compromises and coalition governments and promised to halt the uprising which, they intimated, had arisen quite spontaneously, like a catastrophe of nature. Since the moderate socialist parties consumed their energies in argument, Kerensky, during the last hours of his regime, was forced to rely most heavily on the support of liberal and bourgeois groups with whom previously he had co-operated but little. These latter organizations, especially the cadet party, had been the target of incessant government propaganda labeling them as archreactionary and counterrevolutionary. The desperate last-minute reorientation of Kerensky's politics, of course, lent credence to the bolshevist claim that the provisional government was organizing a counterrevolution.

During the night of November 7, when the revolutionary units were mounting their attack, Kerensky at last decided to call upon the Cossack units stationed in Petrograd. Serviced with only poor intelligence, he was certain the Cossacks would obey his orders without delay. But to Kerensky's surprise, the Cossack regiments suddenly posed conditions. Not content with the order of their military superiors, they wanted, first, a direct order from the generalissimo. Kerensky signed the order. Then, they wanted assurances that, this time, their sacrifices would not be in vain as in July when the bolsheviks were captured, then released without punishment. Kerensky gave this assurance. Moreover, the Cossacks asked for infantry support. Kerensky made another promise. Still the Cossacks did not appear. The government made one frantic telephone call after the other, only to be told each time that the Cossacks were still debating the issue but were about ready to saddle their horses; occasionally the Winter palace was told that the Cossacks actually were saddling their horses. This went on throughout the night, but the troops never moved. When the chief of staff, General Dukhonin, was informed that the Petrograd garrison was siding with the bolsheviks and that the Cossacks were evading the government's directives, his contribution was the suggestion: "With God's help everything will be straightened out."[124]

Realizing that it was impossible to organize resistance within the capital, Kerensky, in the early morning hours of November 7, ordered the commander of the northern front at Pskov to dispatch Cossack units by rail. However, the revolutionary military committee had anticipated such a move and had instructed its subordinate committees not to permit the movement of military units to Petrograd. "Use persuasion and, if that fails, do not hesitate to use force. This order should be read to all soldiers. Any attempt to conceal it from the soldier masses will be regarded as a revolutionary crime and punished with all the severity of the revolutionary law."[125] Officers withholding active support from the new revolution were to be arrested.

Nothing could be done at Petrograd. Kerensky left the city to organize resistance from without. Units from all over the military zones had been entrained en route to Petrograd. Some units, under the influence of the commissars, refused to move; others held meetings and delayed compliance. A few units under the command of the energetic General P. N. Krasnov did reach the outskirts of Petrograd when they were suddenly stopped by General Cheremisov, commander of the northern front, whose area they were crossing. If Krasnov's forces had reached Petrograd on November 8, as planned, the uprising might well have been subdued.

On the testimony of Lenin himself, Cheremisov contributed more to the triumph of the uprising than did anyone else.[126] There is little doubt that Cheremisov was on good terms with the revolutionary committee of his command.[127] He explained his decision by pointing out that the provisional government was no longer in existence and that the appointment of a member of the cadet party as acting prime

[124] Oldenbourg, op. cit., pp. 154–56.

[125] Bunyan and Fisher, op. cit., p. 104.

[126] Oldenbourg, op. cit., p. 9. Cheremisov had been appointed to his position despite the objections of General Kornilov.

[127] Ibid., p. 195; Bunyan and Fisher, op. cit., p. 106.

minister in Kerensky's absence, and of another cadet as governor of Petrograd, "created a sharp break [in the attitude] of the army organization at the front, not in favor of the provisional government."[128] His main job, Cheremisov contended, was to maintain his positions against the Germans. Although he would have sent troops to Petrograd if the majority of the troops had demanded it, the dispatch of troops without majority consent would have provoked opposition, and probably fighting, among his soldiers. In this case, the Germans would have been able to break through the Russian front. Also, Cheremisov affirmed that the revolutionary military committee would maintain order. The bolsheviks, a small minority, would be unable to run the country alone and in the end would be compelled to agree to a satisfactory compromise.[129]

However, Cheremisov's explanations do not seem entirely honest. When called upon by General Dukhonin to explain his actions, he stated that he had secured Kerensky's prior approval and testified further that Kerensky had intended to resign his post as generalissimo and appoint Cheremisov supreme commander in chief. This, quite probably, was a barefaced lie. When Dukhonin attempted to check Cheremisov's alibi with Kerensky personally (the latter at that time was at Pskov), Cheremisov refused to call the prime minister to the telephone.[130] Under normal circumstances, Cheremisov would have been arrested, but neither Kerensky nor the high command was willing or able to act in a decisive manner.

Some desultory fighting took place near Gachina, on the approaches to Petrograd, but it was fairly obvious that the loyal troops and the Cossacks were entirely lacking in fighting spirit. Revolutionary military committees had, in many cases, seized control of telecommunications. Moreover, the railroad workers announced on November 11 that they would call a strike if the civil war were not stopped forthwith, which meant that Kerensky had to give up his attempt to recapture Petrograd.[131]

The bolsheviks began negotiating with the various military com-

---

[128] Bunyan and Fisher, *op. cit.*, p. 141.

[129] Oldenbourg, *op. cit.*, p. 298.

[130] Bunyan and Fisher, *op. cit.*, p. 144.

[131] This great power of railroad unions was entirely of the provisional government's making.

manders, and even General Krasnov found himself compelled to sign an armistice. Kerensky vacillated, and issued a declaration saying that the provisional government was ready to stop its forceful repression of the revolt and was willing to "liquidate" the insurrection through negotiation for a reconstitution of a legal government.[132]

In the negotiations between Cossacks and bolsheviks, the latter declared themselves ready to compromise if Kerensky were handed over to them. The main bolshevik negotiator, Pavel E. Dybenko, offered to exchange Lenin for Kerensky and promised that Lenin and Trotsky would be excluded "from the government pending proof of their innocence of treason."[133] The Cossacks agreed to these conditions, but Kerensky escaped, losing all influence over events (November 14).

In the meantime, various antibolshevik organizations had opposed the new regime in Petrograd by force of arms, but without success. Antibolshevik politicians formed a "committee to save the country and the revolution." They informed General Dukhonin that a peaceful settlement was possible with the chairman of the preparliament as prime minister and Dukhonin as commander-in-chief. However, the general was told that the chances of such a settlement were dependent on the removal of Cheremisov and the dispatch of considerable reinforcements into the Petrograd area.[134] Dukhonin took only part of this advice; he appointed himself commander-in-chief *per interim* but halted troop movements toward Petrograd and left Cheremisov in command.

Still, antibolshevik resistance was not over. Boris Savinkov, a well-known revolutionary and assistant war minister in the Kerensky cabinet, began organizing a new march on Petrograd from Luga. Savinkov believed, perhaps with some justification, that his forces could be trusted to fight the bolsheviks, and he wrote Dukhonin suggesting a resumption of the advance. As usual, Dukhonin hesitated, but the revolutionary military committee took no chances—they sabotaged telephone equipment and, together with the railroad workers, cut the rail lines. On November 17, Dukhonin confirmed his previous order and stopped the movement of troops in Savinkov's area. This order reached the Luga units on November 18, and the troops

[132] Oldenbourg, *op. cit.*, p. 340.
[133] Bunyan and Fisher, *op. cit.*, p. 171.
[134] *Ibid.*, pp. 172 f.

returned to their former positions.[135] Thus the last military threat against the bolsheviks disappeared.

On November 22, Dukhonin, who refused to enter into armistice negotiations with the Germans, was dismissed as generalissimo, but declined to relinquish his post and attempted to stop the newly appointed commander-in-chief, the bolshevik Nikolai V. Krylenko, from taking over the command. On December 3, however, Krylenko, with a contingent of revolutionary soldiers and sailors, occupied the Stavka at Mogilev. General Dukhonin was lynched under the very eyes of his more vigorous replacement, Krylenko.

CONSOLIDATION OF POWER

THE RUSSIAN civil war, which lasted from 1918 to 1921, may be considered the last step in the bolshevik seizure of power.

By the end of 1917 the bolsheviks had established authority, recognized by many foreign nations, over large parts of central Russia. Whatever the legalities of the situation, the bolsheviks controlled the state in the most populous areas of Russia, although with an apparatus shot through with weaknesses and with many inoperative parts. Despite the shaky structure of the bolshevik state, its control of the administrative bureaucracy, as well as of the soviets, won it the spontaneous allegiance of many Russians and the relatively willing compliance of those who were not inclined to participate actively in revolutionary undertakings.

The "White" competitors of the bolsheviks, *de facto* rulers of peripheral provinces largely inhabited by ethnic minority groups, were in worse shape. Not only faced with the normal difficulties of rebels against established authority, they also suffered from the bad morale inevitably accompanying recent defeat. Their cause lacked appeal; they fought for a system which all knew and no one liked.

The antibolshevik leftist parties within Russia proper spent their time arguing against every single one of the courses open to them. They were not inclined to take risks or to seek help from abroad. They were paralyzed by the fear that forceful counteraction would

[135] Oldenbourg, *op. cit.,* pp. 409–15.

lead to the crushing of their February revolution, long since deceased.[136]

The direction of antibolshevik operations, therefore, fell to the military Whites, who had not prepared themselves for the task, had failed to set up chains of command or salvage forces and materials. Compelled to rely on hasty improvisation and haphazard recruiting, their effort was confused and unco-ordinated. It completely failed to enlist the latent support available to them in the ranks of the middle peasants and the urban non-communist left.

By decree of November 15, 1917, the bolsheviks proclaimed the right of self-determination for the many peoples encompassed in tsarist Russia, to the point of separating from Russia and forming independent states.[137] On December 7 they went one step further and appealed to the Russian Moslems to defend the revolution, which alone could give them a free national and religious life. By contrast, the Whites upheld the motto of "Russia one and indivisible," favoring the continuation of the traditional Great Russian policy, thereby alienating the inhabitants of the very areas which the Whites had to use as bases for their operations.

Compromise with the social revolutionaries, the only serious competitors of the bolsheviks, or concurrence in policy envisaging the breakup of Russia, was impossible for the Whites. There was only one chance to crush the bolshevik dictatorship: an alliance between the Whites and foreign powers. Since the World War was still going on, the Whites, theoretically, could choose between the allies and the central powers. While the Germans were occupying large parts of Russia and were supporting the bolshevik regime, the allies were far away, and totally lacked the capability of intervening effectively. Hence the Whites were compelled to attempt to arrange something with Germany if only to deprive their opponents of their foreign support.

This unpalatable fact was recognized only halfheartedly. Milyukov, formerly foreign minister in the first provisional government, entered into unofficial negotiations with the German foreign office.

---

[136] James Bunyan, *Intervention, Civil War, and Communism in Russia, April–December, 1918, Documents and Materials* (Baltimore, Johns Hopkins Press, 1936), pp. 188 ff.

[137] Bunyan and Fisher, *op. cit.*, pp. 282 f. Needless to add, this decree was later forgotten.

He did not fail to discern that "the Germans . . . will doubtless try to come to an agreement with those Russian groups that are willing to make the greatest concessions."[138]

But the Whites were unwilling to compromise, insisting during the negotiations on the integrity of the Russian empire, except for Finland and Poland. The bolsheviks were, of course, ready to yield far broader concessions. Moreover, the bolsheviks delivered the goods— the Brest-Litovsk treaty, which took Russia out of the war and ceded large territories to Germany. The Germans, realizing that any other government of Russia would be compelled to cancel the treaty, held to their alliance with the bolshevik regime. The communists were thus freed to throw their forces against the Whites. When the final defeat of Germany in November 1918 compelled the Germans to withdraw their forces from Russia, they abandoned large amounts of military matériel to the bolsheviks, who through this transaction gained in battlefield strength.

The bolsheviks fully understood the value of the German alliance and stuck to it at great sacrifice. They vigorously opposed the demand of the left social revolutionary party that revolutionary war be waged against Germany. In order to provoke war, the social revolutionaries had gone so far as to assassinate Count Mirbach, German ambassador to Moscow. But neither the Germans nor the bolsheviks could be provoked.

To oppose this firm German support of the bolsheviks, the Whites had only a paper alliance with the allies. The Whites undertook futile operations to prepare and support allied landings, but these landings either did not materialize, came too late, or were carried out with insignificant forces. Allied forces which actually were landed were withdrawn when trouble arose. Material aid was given, but according to the too-little-too-late practice. Moral support, the indispensable prerequisite for the unification of the Whites, was entirely lacking—in the summer of 1918 there were more than twenty "governments" in the areas not controlled by the bolsheviks.[139]

Throughout the entire civil war, bolsheviks disposed of a superior war potential, controlling a larger population, the bulk of the country's industrial resources, and the best parts of its transport system. Moreover, the bolsheviks enjoyed the great advantage of fight-

[138] Bunyan, *op. cit.*, p. 178.
[139] *Ibid.*, p. 277.

ing along interior lines. Possessing also a superior transport system, they were able to cope with their opponents one by one. The Whites, by contrast, never managed to establish communications among themselves, let alone co-ordinate their strategy or carry out concentric operations.

The White generals fought the war in a conventional military fashion, paying little attention to morale or indoctrination. Nor did the Whites wage propaganda warfare. Their lack of a political program and the unpopularity of some of their objectives handicapped them considerably. Still, they could have waged a negative propaganda campaign against the bolsheviks who, after all, were none too popular. Their failure to enlist sympathy for their cause prevented them from using the weapon of partisan warfare against the bolsheviks and, at the same time, rendered them highly vulnerable to this form of attack.

Notable, also, was White inability to exploit the unrest within the bolshevik area. In May 1918, there was a Red army revolt at Saratov. In July, the right social revolutionaries started revolts in many cities surrounding Moscow, and, almost concurrently, the left social revolutionaries started revolts in Petrograd and in Moscow itself. During the same month, the bolshevik commander-in-chief of the Volga front, Muravyev, turned against the regime. In August, the leadership of the regime was crippled: Lenin was wounded severely in an attempt on his life. Many other cases of unrest, from the very start of the bolshevik regime until the Kronshtadt rebellion of the erstwhile Red sailors in March 1921, offered opportunities to the Whites. Yet none of these events was followed up or exploited. Even in the field of conventional strategy, White leadership showed complete lack of imagination and resourcefulness.

There were numerous reasons which accounted for the failure of the White armies. The most fundamental cause, perhaps, was that, after years of war, revolution, civil war, and terror, and in the absence of strong moral and material support from abroad, the Whites were mentally and physically exhausted. It is remarkable that so many fought so long against such obstacles. The remnants of the White armies which, by the end of 1920, were evacuated from the Crimea to Constantinople could point to the fact that without their sacrifice and resistance communist Russia might have embarked on a revolutionary offensive war which would have engulfed eastern and central Europe. If they could have foreseen history, they might well have claimed to have saved eastern Europe from 25 years of bolshevik terror.

THE REVOLT IN THE BLACK SEA

AFTER the defeat of imperial Germany, the western democracies apparently possessed the military strength, and occasionally even the will, to eject the bolshevik regime just come to power in Russia.[140] While many economic and political factors prevented France and England from continuing World War I in Russia, a chief cause of the failure of western intervention was the inability of the western powers to cope with the communist techniques of warfare used against them and, more specifically, to prevent the disintegration by the bolsheviks of the French forces in the Black Sea area.

The communists regard their action against French military and naval forces during 1919 as an important model of streamlined strategy and tactics. They study this model on the basis of a detailed history written by André Marty, prominent French communist and erstwhile naval officer participant in the Black Sea mutiny.[141]

Early in 1919, the French sent eight regiments of troops and eighteen warships, including six battleships, into the Black Sea. The mission of these units was ambiguous, but by and large the French aimed at strengthening the anticommunist forces in southern Russia and the Ukraine. Scattered operations took place in the Crimea and Bessarabia, as well as in the areas of Sebastopol and Odessa.

The French soldiers and sailors just had finished four years of fighting against Germany. Understandably enough, they were disappointed when it turned out that victory did not mean, for them at least, the end of hostilities. Also, some of the units which the French

[140] "If the fate of intervention had been dependent on the mathematical and technical relationship of strength, the allies would have won, without the shadow of a doubt." L. Alfred, J. Dupont, and Kurt Fischer, *Revolutionaerer Anti-Militarismus, aus der Geschichte der antimilitaristischen Arbeit* (Metz, Imprimerie Populaire de Lorraine, no date), p. 110. This book will be discussed at length in Chapter 4.

[141] André Marty, *La Révolte de la Mer Noire* (Paris, Éditions Sociales, 1949). Marty's history has had at least four editions and was even issued during the German occupation of France. At present, the book is enjoying wide distribution.

high command had sent to Russia without, at the same time, insti-
tuting an equitable policy of rotation had previously been involved
in breaches of discipline and in rebellions. Every one of these battle-
weary units comprised a large number of socialists and communists
as well as other elements who, for one reason or other, were opposed
to the resumption of war. The spirit of rebellion was stimulated by
the revolutions and mutinies which were taking place in Russia,
Germany, Austria and Turkey. To make things worse, the supply
situation of the French Black Sea forces was very poor; the improvised expedition was launched before the logistics had been straightened out, and local supplies were all but unobtainable. Little concern
was paid to the morale of the French enlisted men.

Since the bolsheviks did not have the strength to oppose the French
in military battle, they decided to wage an all-out propaganda war
while co-operating closely with the mutinous elements within the
French forces. It did not take them long to decipher the psychology
of the battle-weary *poilu,* model 1919.

The main propaganda arguments were as follows. The resumption
of war is a great evil for France and every single French soldier. The
bolsheviks cannot be defeated by small means and small wars. Hence,
the expedition is simply the start of a full-fledged war against Russia.
This war, obviously, will last indefinitely and cannot be won by the
French, not only because Russia is too big, but because the revolution has made Russia invincible. The Russia of Nicholas II is not the
Russia of Lenin. The war is being fought against a people which has
freed itself from slavery. French soldiers are supposed to fight in the
interest of French capitalists who mean to seize the wealth of Russia
and are willing to pay for it with the blood of French workers and
peasants. "You must continue to suffer and die so that you conquer
for the millionaires, while your family must wait for you in misery."[142] Did the French worker-soldiers want to become the "executioners" of the proletarian revolution?

The crushing of the revolution, the bolsheviks said, would be
against the interests of the French soldiers. These soldiers were nothing but workers and peasants in uniform and, therefore, the brothers
of the Russian workers. Hence, the French troops should fraternize
with the Russian revolutionaries. The rebellious ardor of the French

[142] *Ibid.,* p. 168.

soldiers was being stimulated by fake news about revolutionary events in France.

This propaganda was designed, in Lenin's words, to "tear away the soldiers from the imperialists." It was carried out through agitation, the distribution of leaflets, meetings, demonstrations, revolutionary songs, and the use of communist visual symbols. In order to reach the crews of the French warships, radio was employed on a large scale. This early use of radio warfare achieved full tactical surprise and proved highly effective.

Another method utilized was the deliberate return of prisoners to their units. Before being set free, these prisoners were exposed to thorough communist indoctrination. Upon return, they told of the atrocities committed by the antibolsheviks, of the good behavior and the "progressive" ideas of the bolsheviks, and of the unjust character of the intervention. Unsuspecting, the French command reintegrated these returners into their units, with the result that communist cells crystallized in large numbers. The infiltrators, helped by propagandists from the outside, induced the singing of the *International* and the hoisting of red flags by French units and on warships. Whenever this happened, the particular unit became a source of mass desertion.

As a fortuitous circumstance, the French forces came into close contact with German soldiers who were being repatriated. After almost two years of fraternization with communists, and impressed by the revolution in Germany, these Germans were badly infected by the bolshevik virus. The French and Germans fraternized, and the virus spread into the French units. Many French soldiers were questioning the sudden change of national policy: after France had been fighting the Germans in alliance with the Russians, the French now were supposed to help the Germans go home and continue Germany's "war of plunder" against Russia. In Marty's words, the French and German imperialists were eager to establish a united front between their respective general staffs, but the fraternization of German and French soldiers with the Russian proletariat assured the success of the revolution.[143]

As a result of propaganda and fraternization, discipline among the French broke down rapidly. In the beginning, military courtesies

[143] *Ibid.*, p. 142.

were disregarded. Then, units failed to carry out routine assignments such as guard duty, foraging, and the loading of coal. In the end, they refused to go into combat or, if already on the battlefield, disobeyed orders to fight, abandoned positions, and withdrew without permission. Occasionally, such refusals to fight were preceded by assurances to the bolsheviks that the French soldiers would not shoot.

When it turned out that the French command was unable to enforce discipline but actually resorted to the repatriation of some of the rebellious units, open mutinies occurred. This was particularly true of the crews on warships, which, in several instances, disarmed their officers and took command. After the mutiny had reached fever pitch and the military hierarchy had proved its impotence, the mutineers simply sailed the ships back to French home bases. The remaining ships were withdrawn, by order from Paris.

According to Marty, the mutinous sailor is a phenomenon of great historical importance who has been found in the vanguard of most modern revolutions. On the basis of a sociopsychological analysis of class differences on board ship, Marty predicted that naval mutinies would always play a crucial role in revolutions. He intimated that, in future, the air force would become a second hearth of revolutionary activity.[144] Marty stressed that to subvert a military unit, an infiltration by relatively small numbers is sufficient. The mutiny of one French regiment was led by only thirty soldiers.

The 1919 strategy of the bolsheviks was summarized by Marty as follows: propaganda to gain support among the majority of the Russian people; operations by the Red army co-ordinated, on the one hand, with guerrilla activities and, on the other, with insurrections in cities close to the front; neutralization of hostile Russian and foreign troops and, if possible, their enlistment on the side of the revolution.[145]

The disintegration attack against the French troops in Russia was paralleled by intensive communist activities in France itself. Quite naturally, the developments in the Black Sea had their repercussions in the various French naval bases where they led to demonstrations and unrest of all types. The communists made great efforts to prevent the loading of ships ordered to the Black Sea and to stimulate the mutinous behavior of their crews. Whenever possible, they attempted

[144] *Ibid.*, pp. 392–97.
[145] *Ibid.*, pp. 184, 185.

to co-ordinate unrest among the military forces with unrest among the civilian population and to combine, on a local scale, mutiny with insurrection.[146] Through these tactics they prevented the French naval command from dispatching some of the reinforcements destined for Russia.

Political agitation campaigns on a national scale challenged the policy underlying the French intervention in Russia. One of the chief arguments was that the "war" had not been declared in a constitutional manner. Prolonged debates in the *Chambre des députés* publicized the mutiny and led to a *de facto* alliance between the communists and the non-communist opposition against the government. Liberals and communists clamored for an end to the intervention and for leniency against the mutineers; communists and some conservatives demanded the immediate demobilization of the fleet, the latter on the theory that this was the only method to stop the spreading of the revolutionary movement. And indeed, the French government "mastered" the mutiny by demobilizing the naval reservists, that is, by disarming the fleet.

As a sequel to this acrimonious debate, prominent liberal politicians worked for the amnesty of the Black Sea rebels. Among these politicians were men who subsequently achieved great influence on French policies, including the prime ministers Édouard Herriot, Henri Queuille, Édouard Daladier, and Paul Ramadier.

Among the mutineers (amnestied after a few years) was Charles Tillon, who set up communist partisan units during World War II; later he became secretary of the air force, minister of armaments, and minister of reconstruction—all positions for which his background provided him with singular qualifications. André Marty himself became secretary of the central committee of the French communist party; in 1927 he fomented mutinies among French troops in Morocco and later participated prominently in the Spanish civil war. He never lost touch with antimilitary disintegrative work.

Insofar as the future was concerned, Marty drew five lessons from the Black Sea experience. First, communists should guard against the error of thinking that mutinies would occur spontaneously: they must be prepared thoroughly and systematically. Second, preparation must begin long before a new "anti-soviet war" will occur. Third,

[146] *Ibid.*, p. 586.

once this war starts, slogans of immediate applicability, largely designed to interfere with mobilization, must be circulated. These slogans should concentrate on the theme: "Stop the war before it gets out of control." Fourth, the most important propaganda task is to describe the war as unjust. According to Marty, the belief that a war is unjust is "the fundamental motive of all mutinies." Fifth, the soldiers must be told that they do not fight in the pursuit of their own interest. "This is not our war, it is the war of our exploiters and murderers."[147]

Marcel Cachin, the senior European communist, wrote a preface to Marty's book. He, too, invited the comrades to study the Black Sea revolt because, he said, after thirty years the same enemies of bolshevism are attempting to strike the blow which they could not strike in 1919. Russia is being encircled, and, still according to Cachin, the "imperialists" are building "more than 200 bases of aggression."

Hence, the question is asked of the workers of France and the entire world: Do they understand that it depends on them, on their actions and unity, whether a new anti-soviet war will be prevented? In 1919 the sailors and soldiers of France knew how to stay the arm of the murderer. At that time they were only a small band of hardened and courageous men. Today, millions of proletarians in France and everywhere on the earth should know the example of 1919 and be ready to follow it. . . . This book must be on the night-table of all communists. It was not written for dusty archivists, it is a weapon for militant men who want to learn, always to learn more, in order to prepare themselves for the action necessary to win peace.[148]

Peace, the communists teach, cannot be achieved by incantations. It can only be the result of a stubborn fight—a fight to disintegrate the armed forces of the opponent.[149] A useful lesson.

AN EVALUATION IN RETROSPECT

WHAT does the October revolution demonstrate of bolshevik operational techniques?

[147] *Ibid.*, pp. 571–76.
[148] *Ibid.*, pp. 11 f.
[149] *Ibid.*, p. 577.

Stalin stated that the bolshevik uprising in Russia succeeded with "comparative ease" due to a set of external and internal circumstances.[150] The most important factor was that the "two principal imperialist groups" were "engaged in mortal struggle between themselves," and "had neither the time nor the means to devote serious attention to the struggle against the October revolution." The second facilitating factor (still according to Stalin) was that the uprising began during an imperialist war at a time when the masses were suffering from exhaustion and fatigue and were thirsting for peace. The war armed the proletariat with "the mighty weapon of peace, furnished the opportunity of connecting the soviet revolution with the ending of the hated war, and thus created mass sympathy for it both in the West among the workers and in the East among the oppressed peoples." The third external circumstance was that revolutionary crises were maturing in the West and in the East. The working-class movement in Europe acted as an ally of the bolsheviks.

Among the unfavorable external circumstances, Stalin mentioned the "isolation" of the bolshevik movement and "the absence near it, or bordering it, of a soviet country on which it could rely for support." Future revolutions, obviously, would not be handicapped in this respect. Internally, Stalin stated, the uprising was made possible by three factors: novel insurrection technique; a highly revolutionary situation accentuated by an exceptionally weak and irresolute government; and the emergence of dual power.

This interpretation is accurate as far as it goes, but it does not provide a complete picture. The most important external circumstance was not the war between two imperialist groups, but the military defeat of Russia. Furthermore, the revolutionaries allied themselves with one of the warring powers, acting in support of the military operations of this enemy. Third, the antirevolutionary forces did not find effective outside support. On the contrary, they were forced by their allies into further military defeats and irresponsible adventures, only to be left in the lurch.

The bolsheviks did develop an entirely new insurrectional tech-

---

[150] "The October Revolution and the Tactics of the Russian Communists," in Stalin, *Problems of Leninism* (Moscow, Foreign Languages Publishing House, 1940), p. 86. Grotewohl's book is an official Stalinist handbook on how to avoid mistakes in revolutionary strategy, on how *not* to make a revolution.

nique. Yet the essence of this technique does not lie in the replacement of street fighting by the seizure of key control points. The real
novelty lay in the creation of the revolutionary military committee,
the appointment of revolutionary commissars to military units, and
the assumption of control over the armed forces *prior* to the uprising.

The importance assigned by both Stalin and Lenin to the development of dual power is justified. The transfer of the army's allegiance
from the government to the bolsheviks (camouflaged as soviets) related directly to the existence of dual power. Yet, actually, there were
not dual but multiple power structures rivaling the government.
Without the existence of numerous competing political and semi-
legislative bodies, and without the existence of quadruple control
channels into the armed forces, the bolshevik uprising could not have
developed as it did.

While the dispersion of authority weakened the government to the
point of almost complete impotence, and while the extreme "democratic" character of the political parties condemned them to inac-
tion, the strict discipline which ruled in the communist party gave the
latter an influence entirely out of proportion to its numbers. This discipline and, during the critical hours, Lenin's one-man rule provided
the communist party with its exceptional ability to adjust tactics to
changing conditions and permitted it the flexibility necessary to out-
maneuver its opponents.

Stalin emphasized that the "fundamental strategic rule of Leninism" consisted in isolating the "compromising parties, as the most
dangerous groups in the period of the climax of the revolution."[151]
This cryptic sentence points out that if the moderate and liberal parties had correctly understood the bolshevik threat, they would have
unified their forces. To prevent this development, the bolsheviks arranged for the insurrection not to take place under the banner of
communism. *Communism never became the issue in 1917,* nor did
the auxiliaries of the bolshevik insurrection, in their overwhelming
majority, have the slightest inclination to install a communist system.
The insurrection was supported because it seemed to be the only
method to obtain peace.

Contending that stabilization of the provisional government, and
the promulgation of an agrarian law by the constituent assembly,

[151] *Ibid.*, p. 104.

would deprive the peasants of their newly acquired land holdings, the bolsheviks pulled in peasant support as well. Lenin left no doubt about the nature of bolshevik tactics: "We achieved victory because we adopted *not our own agrarian program,* but that of the social revolutionaries."[152]

Nothing would be more erroneous than to assume that the course of events was the result of foresighted bolshevik planning. There was no great design which led inexorably to the October uprising. Despite the often repeated bolshevik argument against the spontaneity of revolutionary movements, Stalin himself admitted that the party "invariably relied in its struggle upon the spontaneous upsurge of the mass revolutionary movements," particularly among the peasants.[153] He insisted, however, that while relying on this spontaneous upsurge, the bolsheviks maintained "undivided leadership of the movement" and thereby formed the "mass political army for the October insurrection."[154]

The most important steps which led to the bolshevik seizure of Russia would seem to have been not of bolshevik making. The establishment of the soviet and of numerous other bodies was the work of the socialists. The destruction of the armed forces was accomplished mainly by the provisional government supported by socialist reformers. The failure to suppress the bolshevik conspiracy was due to the vacillation of the government. The break between army and government was due to personality conflicts and to illusionary government policies, and the peasant riots were generated mainly by socialists. Lastly, the lack of military resistance and the inefficiency of the resistance which did occur were the result of the irresolution and irresponsibility of some high-ranking officers. The provisional government, the socialists, and the military leaders created, themselves, the revolutionary situation; the bolsheviks simply collected the dividends and eventually captured the entire corporation.

[152] *Selected Works,* X, 286. (Italics added.) Yet thirteen years later the bolsheviks were to revert to their own program and collectivize agriculture.

[153] "The October Revolution," *op. cit.,* p. 103.

[154] *Ibid.,* p. 104.

3. Doctrinal Ferment · 1918–1928

> *"The French revolutionary people . . . remoulded the whole system of strategy, they broke all the old laws and customs of war; and in place of the old army they created a new revolutionary people's army and introduced new methods of warfare."*
>
>

LENIN, MAY 27, 1917
War and the Workers, London, Lawrence and Wishart, 1940, page 7

LENIN ON THE THEORY OF REVOLUTIONARY WAR

WHILE Lenin recognized that the differences between military and non-military (peace) means are neither basic nor always distinguishable, he did feel that success through war is more likely and more permanent than success through the utilization of non-violent and quasi-violent weapons. The thing that counts is policy; whether the policy is implemented by forcible or non-forcible techniques is entirely a matter of expediency and opportunity. At one time Lenin put down this strong sentence: "Civil war decides *all* serious questions of politics when history places the dictatorship of the proletariat on the order of the day."[1]

Lenin admitted that war is a great disaster. To the revolutionary, however, the question of disaster or welfare is regarded as not usually germane to the problem at hand. The revolutionary must analyze any historical phenomena, including war, from the point of view of proletarian, that is, party, interests.

He must evaluate war not by the number of casualties, but by its political consequences. Above the interests of the individuals perishing and suffering from war must stand the interests of the class. And if the war serves the interests of liberation from the yoke . . . such a war is progress, irrespective of the victims and the suffering it entails.[2]

[1] Lenin, *Selected Works* (New York, International Publishers, 1943), X, 5.

[2] Lenin, *Sobraniye Sochinenii* (Moscow), VI, 457, quoted from Timothy Taracouzio, *War and Peace in Soviet Diplomacy* (New York, Macmillan. 1940), p. 53.

In 1915, Lenin stated that Marxists "have always stood for revolutionary wars against counter-revolutionary peoples."[3] And at another place: "War is not only a continuation of politics but also a summation of politics."[4]

According to Lenin, socialists cannot be pacifists. They cannot oppose war per se without ceasing to be socialists. They must struggle against capitalism, which is the root of war. "But inasmuch as capitalism has not been exterminated, we [the communists] are struggling not against wars in general but against reactionary wars and for revolutionary wars." The class struggle within a single nation "may come into collision with a war between different nations. . . . Therefore, we cannot deny the possibility of revolutionary wars, i. e., of wars resulting from class struggle, which are waged by the revolutionary classes and have a direct bearing upon revolutions."[5]

Lenin realized that socialism cannot be victorious simultaneously all over the globe, but would win first in one or a limited number of countries. This is the so-called "law of the uneven development of capitalism" which has played a great role in Stalin's thinking. It outlined, in official bolshevik view, "a new and complete theory of the socialist revolution, a theory affirming the possibility of the victory of socialism in separate countries, and indicating the conditions of this victory and its present prospects."[6]

In turn, victory of socialism in one or more countries would create friction and, according to Lenin, a desire on the part of the bourgeoisie to overthrow the proletarian states. A war would result, but, from the standpoint of the socialist states, it would be a "legitimate and just war." It would be fought for socialism and "for the liberation of other peoples from the yoke of the bourgeoisie."[7] Clearly, this "law" is merely an ambiguous phrasing of the idea that a proletarian state must oppose other states by war.

[3] *Ibid.*, XVIII, 250, quoted from *ibid.*, p. 30.

[4] *Selected Works, op. cit.*, VIII, 68.

[5] *Sobraniye Sochinenii*, XIII, 453, and XXX, 332 f., quoted from Taracouzio, *op. cit.*, p. 26.

[6] *History of the Communist Party of the Soviet Union (Bolsheviks), Short Course* (New York, International Publishers, 1939), p. 169.

[7] Lenin, *Collected Works, 1916–1917* (New York, International Publishers, 1942), p. 325. This statement was reasserted by Stalin, *History of the Communist Party, loc. cit.*

No revolutionary class can denounce revolutionary war, for it would mean condemnation to a ridiculous pacifism. . . . It is possible to denounce such a war. This would mean Tolstoiism and the pitifulness of the bourgeoisie; it would mean forgetting all the science of marxism, all the experience of European revolutions.[8]

A clear exposition of Lenin's doctrine was given in an article written in the fall of 1916 entitled "The Military Program of the Proletarian Revolution."[9] In that article Lenin opposed disarmament because wars will remain inevitable as long as there are capitalists. Re-emphasizing that socialists never have been "nor can they be, opposed to revolutionary wars," he called on the socialists to intervene on the side of the "oppressed" in national and colonial wars of liberation. Lenin went on to state that "civil wars are also wars"—a statement which was repeated in the *Theses and Statutes of the Communist International,* 1920. Anyone who accepts the necessity of class struggle must recognize that civil wars are a natural, and sometimes inevitable, consequence.

The victory of socialism in one country must lead to wars fought by that country for socialism and for the liberation of other nations from the bourgeoisie. Quoting Engels, Lenin denied the possibility of peaceful development. The very thing that distinguishes opportunists from revolutionaries is that the former refuse to "think about and reflect on the fierce class struggle and class *wars* that are necessary for the achievement of world socialism."[10]

Summing up his doctrine, he stated: "Every war is the exercise of violence against nations, but that does not prevent socialists from being in favor of revolutionary war."[11] Lenin wrote in 1915 and repeated in 1918: "We must prepare to wage war, it is inevitable, it is coming, it will come."[12] And Sinovyev aped the master in March

[8] *Sobraniye Sochinenii,* XIV/1, 300, quoted from Taracouzio, *op. cit.,* p. 47.

[9] *Collected Works, op. cit.,* XIX, 362 f.

[10] *Ibid.,* p. 364. (Lenin's italics.) Class struggle is a translation of the German word *Klassenkampf.* There is a frequently overlooked but clear distinction between class struggle and class war. While the older socialist writers wrote mostly about class struggle, the expression *voina klassov* (class war) predominates in the terminology of the bolsheviks and especially in that of Stalin. The expression *borba klassov* (struggle) or variations of this term are rarer.

[11] *Selected Works, op. cit.,* V, 175.

[12] *Ibid.,* VII, 308.

1918: "Revolutionary war . . . is inevitable, is coming and will come."[13]

LENIN AND THE PRACTICE OF REVOLUTIONARY WAR

UPON SEIZURE of power in November 1917, the Lenin government was confronted with three military tasks: to defend itself against counterrevolutionary action by the Whites; to unite the areas dominated by the communists throughout Russia; and to defend Russia against the German army.

Upon seizure of power in November 1917, the Lenin government was confronted with three military tasks: to defend itself against counterrevolutionary action by the Whites; to unite the areas dominated by the communists throughout Russia; and to defend Russia against the German army.

Peace negotiations at Brest-Litovsk in early 1918 revealed Germany as a predatory power whose demands were aimed at depriving Russia of a large portion of its most valuable territory. The majority of the communist leaders favored revolutionary war against Germany. Lenin, however, took the position that the armistice had to be accepted at whatever price. Although he had no objection against revolutionary war as such, he insisted that in spring 1918, Russia was unable to wage revolutionary war successfully. "We cannot joke with war."

But even under the condition of Russian demobilization—"if we meant war, we had no right to demobilize"—Lenin did not rule out war entirely: "Had the Germans said that they demanded the overthrow of the bolsheviks [as a condition of peace], then we should have to fight." Yet the Germans were satisfied with the bolshevik government. They did not intend to take Petrograd or Moscow, nor did they attempt to install a more conservative government. They were willing to help the bolsheviks consolidate themselves in power. This consolidation was the first requirement of world revolution; all the rest was "phrase mongering."

On February 23, 1918, Lenin said: "It is time to put an end to

[13] Lenin and G. Sinovyev, *Gegen den Strom, Aufsaetze aus den Jahren 1914–1916* (Hamburg, Verlag der Kommunistischen Internationale, 1921), p. xiii.

revolutionary phrases and get down to real work . . . to carry on a revolutionary war, an army, which we do not now have, is necessary." And, at another place:

> To tie one's hand beforehand, openly to tell the enemy who is at present better armed than we, whether and when we shall fight him, is stupidity and not revolutionariness. To accept battle at a time when it is obviously advantageous to the enemy and not to us is a crime.[14]

A matter of expediency pure and simple.

Revolutionary war requires two conditions: the nation embarking on the war must believe in its purpose, and the attacked nation must be in the throes of a revolutionary crisis.[15] Lenin denied that these conditions existed during the spring of 1918. While he believed that a revolutionary situation was ripening in Europe, he was careful to distinguish between the second and the ninth month of political pregnancy.

Lenin's decision was entirely realistic: "History causes the military problem to become the essence of the political problem." Hence, the first conclusion was that the communists "should have but one slogan—seriously learn the art of war."[16] Learn it from whom? "The bourgeoisie teaches the proletariat how to use its arms."[17]

The second conclusion was to create the Red army. This decision was made consciously in line with Marx's dictum that "the revolution will have to fight modern instruments and arts of war with modern instruments and arts of war."

Thus, in the spring of 1918, Lenin rejected the ridiculous suggestion to wage revolutionary war without an army. But he did so specifically to prepare for successful war at a later date: "Clench your teeth, don't brag, but prepare your forces. *The revolutionary*

---

14 *Selected Works, op. cit.,* X, 119.

15 Criteria for the maturity of the revolutionary situation are given in *ibid.,* X, 137.

16 *Ibid.,* VII, 304; E. Wollenberg, *The Red Army* (London, Secker and Warburg, 1938), p. 1. The proletariat should master "all means of warfare," even though circumstances may not always permit them "to use weapons that are most dangerous for the enemy, weapons that are most quickly death-dealing." *Selected Works, op. cit.,* X, 139.) Obviously, if the communists have weapons that are "most quickly death-dealing," they should use them. "If . . . we are able to master all means of warfare we shall certainly be victorious because we represent the interests of the really advanced . . . class." This is a hint on the communist attitude about the atomic bomb.

17 Wollenberg, *op. cit.,* p. 15.

war will come, there is no disagreement among us about that."[18]

Trotsky had his own thoughts on the advisability of revolutionary war in 1918. Referring to the French revolutionary wars, he commented:

France was the richest, and most civilized country on the European continent, whereas twentieth century Russia was the poorest and most backward European land. The revolutionary task of the French army was more superficial in character than the revolutionary tasks before us now. In those days the main objective was the overthrow of the "tyrants" and the abolition or modification of feudal serfdom. Our mission . . . is the complete destruction of exploitation and class oppression.[19]

The general line of Lenin's strategy at that time was described by the Russian term *peredyshka,* meaning "breathing spell." After an exhausting race the runner must catch his breath; only after full recovery should he compete again. Peredyshka is not a defensive concept, as is often believed. A global offensive must be carried out step by step. After each advance a consolidation period is necessary. Lenin invited his opponents to check Clausewitz on the importance of force relationships and on the strategic potentialities of retreat into the interior of Russia.[20] Peredyshka tactics have become a standard soviet method: armistices and negotiations are used for regrouping and strengthening communist forces and for outmaneuvering, propagandizing, and demoralizing enemy forces.

Lenin was not in favor of abdication vis-à-vis Germany. Nor was he willing to live up to the provisions of the "peace." He anticipated that the Brest-Litovsk agreement would prove a "Tilsit peace," that is, a very provisional arrangement with a temporarily stronger power about to be defeated by its other enemies.

Lenin signed the treaty of Brest-Litovsk without bothering to read it. "I don't mean to fulfill it, except insofar as I am forced," he allegedly said. Lenin's intention was to exploit, for bolshevik purposes, the "contradictions" in the capitalist camp: the West would save the communist regime from the Germans.

On their part, the Germans miscalculated badly. They exhausted

[18] *Selected Works, op. cit.,* VII, 311, speech of March 8, 1918. (Italics added.)

[19] Quoted from Wollenberg, *op. cit.,* pp. 78 f.

[20] *Selected Works, op. cit.,* XII, 358. This reference may be to Clausewitz, *Der Feldzug 1812 in Russland und die Befreiungskriege von 1813–15* (3rd ed., Berlin, 1906).

themselves in futile attacks against the West and banked on the Brest-Litovsk arrangement to supply them with food and raw materials. To keep them quiet, the communists abandoned the Ukraine from which, Lenin said, "you can get as much grain and coal as you like, that is, of course, if you are able to get them." Lenin doubted that the Germans had the capability of getting much out of the Ukraine, and, by obstructing German efforts, he proved himself right. In the end, Germany did get a little grain, but the treaty "brought bolshevik disintegration into Germany."[21] The Germans could be maneuvered so easily because they "hated England with all their heart and soul." Lenin thus rediscovered the old truth that emotions can be manipulated to further the self-destruction of the emotional group.

In more than one way the German high command played directly into bolshevik hands, particularly in refusing to help the antibolshevik Russians. In a memorandum probably originated by the *Oberste Heeresleitung* (Supreme Headquarters) and sent to General Wilhelm Groener, military administrator of the Ukraine in Kiev, we read:

Germany is to play the fool. The bolsheviks are to be chased out of Russia and the reactionaries put in their place. The latter then will follow exactly the same course with respect to Germany which the tsarist government followed in the last few decades. . . . We ourselves therefore would be guilty of putting our enemies back in power. We should have at present only one purpose in Greater Russia: to further the disintegrating forces and to keep the country weak. . . . It is therefore to our interest that the bolsheviks stay in power. . . . The Russian system of transportation, industry and commerce must be controlled by us. We must succeed in exploiting the Eastern territories.[22]

Accordingly, the Germans were willing to make common military cause with the bolsheviks against the counterrevolutionary elements. Groener realized that it would be "catastrophic" if the Germans were "to fight together with the bolsheviks against the decent elements of the country." But his "worst fears" were confirmed. The soviets on their part, through Foreign Commissar Chicherin, proposed joint

[21] Bolshevik propaganda in Germany was very extensive. It was most effective on the eastern front where leaflets were air-dropped and smuggled into the trenches and where fraternization was rampant. Five hundred thousand copies of a German newspaper *Die Fackel* were printed by the bolsheviks daily.

[22] *Groener Papers*, National Archives, unsigned memorandum, no date, Box 27, Index 254, II.

action to the Germans, while the German foreign office, as well as the army, contemplated "complete marriage with the bolsheviks."[23]

Brest-Litovsk taught the bolsheviks how to exploit hostility between two enemy camps "in such a way that in the long run both lost." Stalin maintained: "We are at present between two foes. If we are unable to defeat them both we must know how to dispose of our forces in such a way that they fall out among themselves."

The "imperialists" were unable to destroy the bolsheviks only because they were fighting each other. Locked in conflict, they could not, in 1918, prevent the communists from marching "in this brilliant, triumphal procession" through European Russia, from spreading into Finland, and from beginning "the conquest of the Caucasus and Rumania." (Sic!) Conflict among the enemies of communism was thus an essential precondition of revolutionary war.[24] If there was no such conflict, it was to be incited. "If we are obliged to tolerate such scoundrels as the capitalist thieves each of whom is preparing to plunge a knife into us it is our direct duty to make them turn their knives against each other."[25]

This approach was patterned after that of Richelieu, who almost until the end of the Thirty Years' war contrived through neutrality tactics to improve the relative and absolute power position of France vis-à-vis the other countries of Europe. This strategy of the *tertius gaudens* aims at having somebody pull one's own chestnuts out of the fire. Since Stalin often used this simile, the technique can be described as "chestnut strategy."[26]

As long as the bolsheviks have not "conquered the whole world" and are weaker than their opponents, they must adhere to this basic rule: contrive that your opponents weaken each other, and prevent them from uniting against you. "Had we not adhered to this rule, everyone of us would have long ago been hanging on an Aspen tree, to the satisfaction of the capitalists."[27]

[23] *Groener Papers, Tagesbuchnotizen,* National Archives.

[24] *Selected Works, op. cit.,* VII, 289.

[25] *Ibid.,* VIII, 279, 282, 288.

[26] The general idea of "chestnut strategy" was expressed by Stalin as early as 1901. See Stalin, *Sochineniya* (Moscow, Orgis, 1946), I, 23.

[27] In accord with Lenin's idea that the "communists must use one country against another," it is noteworthy that he mentioned—on November 26, 1920—the following exploitable international antagonisms: Japan versus United States; Japan versus China; Germany versus the Entente. This showed some foresight, although he was entirely wrong when he also anticipated an Anglo-American conflict. *Selected Works, op. cit.,* VIII, 288.

The bolsheviks, of course, did not overlook the possibility of weakening the Germans through revolutionary antimilitarism and subversion. Agitation continued on the front, but, even better, the soviet ambassador to Germany, Adolf A. Joffe, took a hand in fomenting revolution. The Germans expelled Joffe shortly before the Kaiser's overthrow and later, in a radiogram to the Russian government, officially accused him of having acted in bad faith. The Germans complained that Joffe had engaged in propaganda and had purchased arms and ammunition for German revolutionaries, spending for this purpose 105,000 marks.

The cocksureness of the bolsheviks may be gleaned from the answer Joffe sent on December 4, 1918:

With reference to the radiogram of December 3 . . ., which accuses the former embassy of the soviet government in Berlin not only of spreading bolshevik propaganda but also of purchasing arms, I wish to state that the said propaganda was carried on with the help of the independent social-democratic party. As regards the purchase of arms . . ., the amount mentioned in the radiogram is not correct. Minister Barth received not 105,000 marks but several hundred thousand marks for the purpose of acquiring arms. I desire to make known the real facts in the case and consider it as to my credit that by means of my above-mentioned activities, which were in full accord with the independent (socialists) . . ., I contributed to the full extent of my power to the triumph of the German revolution.[28]

As the collapse of imperial Germany was approaching, the idea of revolutionary warfare again came to the fore. On October 3, 1918, Lenin wrote a letter to the central executive committee in which we read:

The result of the crisis in Germany . . . will surely be the capture of the government by the German proletariat. The Russian proletariat is watching the course of events with close attention and great enthusiasm. . . . The Russian proletariat must realize that it will soon be necessary to make great sacrifices in the cause of internationalism. The time is approaching when circumstances will demand that we help the German people . . . against Anglo-French imperialism. Let us begin to prepare at once. Let us show that the Russian worker can work much more energetically, make greater sacrifices, and die more bravely when fighting for

28 James Bunyan, *Intervention, Civil War, and Communism in Russia, April–December, 1918, Documents and Materials* (Baltimore, Johns Hopkins Press, 1936), p. 156.

the cause of the international proletarian revolution. . . . Let us . . . increase our efforts to organize the Red Army . . . of workers and peasants, ready to make every sacrifice for the cause of socialism. This army is growing stronger and more experienced. . . . It was our intention to have an army of a million men by spring, but now we need an army of three millions. We can and will have it. The history of the world during the last few days has quickened the pace of the proletarian world revolution. The most rapid changes are now possible. It may be that German and Anglo-French imperialism will join forces against the Soviet Government.[29]

On the following day, the central executive committee accepted Lenin's proposal, and declared:

. . . to the whole world that Soviet Russia will offer all its forces and resources to aid the German revolutionary government. The All-Russian central executive committee has no doubt that the French, English, American, and Japanese proletariat will be in the same camp as Soviet Russia and revolutionary Germany.[30]

In implementation of this new concept, three measures were adopted: (1) An extensive program to reorganize and strengthen the Red army was launched; (2) An order was given (but not carried out) "to create at once a supply of food for the toiling masses of Germany and Austria-Hungary to aid them in their fight against internal and external aggressors;" and (3) A lump-sum tax of ten billion rubles was levied on the "propertied classes in cities and villages."[31]

There are indications that the bolsheviks went one step further.

According to Milyukov, the soviets concluded, late in 1918, a secret "treaty" with the German communist Karl Liebknecht. Allegedly this treaty stipulated that a Russian army would take the offensive to support a Spartacist uprising in Berlin. Liebknecht promised, once the revolution was victorious, that he would raise a German Red army of 500,000 men.

In March 1919, the soviets possibly concluded a similar treaty with the Hungarian communist Béla Kun and initiated the preparations for offensive revolutionary war against "the Entente, and particularly against Poland and Rumania."[32] The Red army actually

[29] *Ibid.*, pp. 149 f.
[30] *Ibid.*, p. 151.
[31] *Ibid.*, pp. 152 f.
[32] P. Milyukov, *La politique extérieure des Soviets* (Paris, Giard, 1937), p. 34.

had started marching through the Ukraine to Ruthenia when Béla Kun's collapse rendered further operations impractical.[33]

A second plan for offensive revolutionary war against Germany was developed in 1919 by Karl Radek. The plan envisaged the offensive use of Russian prisoners of war still kept in Germany.[34]

All these grandiose plans failed. Yet, on the authority of the *Great Soviet Encyclopedia* (first edition), the soviets fought at least two revolutionary wars under Lenin, the wars against Poland and Georgia. That the "liberation" of Georgia, then ruled by what Stalin called "menshevik nationalists," was the result of Russian military intervention was admitted by Lenin himself.[35]

By contrast, Trotsky was a little squeamish about this point, and in a long talmudistic dissertation replete with finely split dialectical hairs tried to explain away soviet intervention. However, even Trotsky admitted the following facts: the insurgents availed themselves of Red army support and chose to stage their insurrection at the border rather than at Tiflis, the capital of Georgia. The Russian army, in Trotsky's fiction, was needed to prevent English and French intervention and to forestall a possible attack by General Wrangel from Constantinople. The fate of menshevik Georgia had been decided, anyway, by communist victory in the Crimea, that is, by military action outside of the country! In any event, the Russian army came, and has remained there ever since.[36]

Trotsky admitted that the communist uprising in Azerbaijan "co-

[33] Béla Kun had participated, quite prominently, in uprising and civil-war activities in Russia. It is unlikely that he returned to Hungary without previous conversations and contingent agreements with his highly placed bolshevik friends.

[34] Milyukov, *op. cit.,* p. 35. There is some doubt as to whether the soviets actually concluded these agreements with German communists, and in what form. While it is possible that Milyukov fell for a plant, it seems more probable that his information was accurate and that at least informal agreements were reached. Radek advocated a program of national bolshevism for Germany and favored an alliance between Russian bolsheviks and the German general staff. In 1921 he was sent to Berlin, and negotiated with the Reichswehr the basis for a subsequent secret Russo-German military collaboration. See Ruth Fischer, *Stalin and German Communism* (Cambridge, Mass., Harvard University Press, 1948), p. 528.

[35] "The soviet republic in Russia obtained no political or military assistance from anywhere. . . . The soviet republics of the Caucasus obtained political and . . . military assistance from the R.S.F.R. This is a fundamental difference." *Selected Works, op. cit.,* IX, 203.

[36] Leon Trotsky, *Die Grundfragen der Revolution* (Hamburg, Verlag der Kommunistischen Internationale, 1923), pp. 313–15.

incided" with the approach of the Russian army. It may be added that Asiatic Russia almost in its entirety was sovietized through the Red army rather than through communist insurrections.

The case of the Polish war of 1920 is more complex. Poland started the attack—about this there is no doubt. The Polish Marshal Pilsudsky allegedly was convinced that a soviet attack on Poland was impending. It is possible that either Pilsudsky misread soviet intentions or that he simply made use of an old propaganda trick to justify his own aggression.

However, his information may not have been entirely inaccurate. It is a fact that the Russians rallied for a strong counteroffensive in a suspiciously short time. It is a second fact that the soviets repulsed the Poles and then decided to transform their allegedly defensive fight into an offensive fight and into an offensive revolutionary war:[37] not only was Poland to be bolshevized but also Germany and even France. Russian units raced to the borders of East Prussia, but when they reached Germany the battle of Warsaw had been lost by the Red army and the Russians were compelled to withdraw.

Soviet Russia's overbold strategy in penetrating too deeply into Poland was based on the assumption that there would be revolutionary fraternization with Polish workers and revolutionary uprisings in Germany. Both hopes were disappointed, although there was considerable unrest in Germany, and the nucleus of a Polish Red army and a committee for national liberation were formed in Bialystok.[38] A few more days of victorious advance, Lenin said, and the communists would "not have merely captured Warsaw; we should also have shaken the Versailles peace treaty to its foundations. That is the international significance of our war with Poland."[39]

[37] See Wollenberg, op. cit., p. 142.

[38] Soviet hopes and disappointments were described by Tukhachevsky in his lectures on "The March beyond the Vistula," February 1923. These lectures were reprinted in Marshal Joseph Pilsudski, L'Année 1920 (Paris, La Renaissance du Livre, 1929). See particularly Tukhachevsky's discussion on pages 230–32 on the "exported revolution." The later Marshal Boris Shaposhnikov also analyzed the Polish war and concluded that if communist subversion had disorganized the Polish rear more effectively, the soviet offensive might have been more successful.

[39] Wollenberg, op. cit., p. 148. In connection with soviet plans for Germany, it is now known from the unpublished notes of the German social democrat, Arthur Crispien, that German socialists attended a meeting in Moscow where Lenin outlined his idea to start a war against Poland, secure the support of the German workers, and then proceed against France and England. The German socialists refused to play the game. This incident indirectly supports

The bolshevik leaders realized that there is a

fundamental difference in the proletariat's position before and after the seizure of power. Before the seizure, the proletariat cannot but organize its armed strength in the form of partisan units. Afterwards, however, the proletariat has its proletarian state and therefore the capability of setting up a regular Red army to throw back the regular troops of the bestial bourgeoisie.[40]

Henceforth, then, bolshevik strategy and tactics were geared toward war between capitalist and communist states. In Trotsky's words: "Revolutionary violence is the means of attaining the freedom of the toilers. From the moment of assuming power, revolutionary violence assumes the form of an organized army."[41]

According to Lenin's final opinion, the correct communist program was "to arm the proletariat in order to conquer and expropriate the bourgeoisie." "Boycott war—is a stupid phrase. Communists must take part even in the most reactionary war."[42] "They must prepare for the defeat of the imperialist powers at the hands of Soviet Russia."[43] "As soon as we are strong enough to defeat capitalism as a whole we shall immediately take it by the scruff . . . of the neck." The disarming of the bourgeoisie is the historical mission of the proletariat.

TROTSKY MISSES THE POINT

WHEN the bolsheviks took power in Russia, their ideas about military matters were very confused. Many old-time communists had

---

Milyukov's information about the agreement with Liebknecht. *The New Leader*, New York, February 12, 1951; see also Samuel Gompers, *Out of Their Own Mouths* (New York, Dutton, 1921), p. 158.

[40] S. I. Gussev, *Die Lehren des Buergerkrieges* (Hamburg, Hoym, 1921), p. 22.

[41] *Makers of Modern Strategy, Military Thought from Machiavelli to Hitler*, ed. by E. M. Earle (Princeton, N. J., Princeton University Press, 1943), p. 339. See also, H. Bergmann, J. Smilga, L. Trotsky, *Die russische sozialistische rote Armee* (Zurich, Internationaler Verlag, 1920), p. 52: "Each step which the socialist army advances equals [a] thousand steps in the advance of world revolution. Every breakthrough of an enemy front is a new hole in the wall of capitalism. The Red army is conscious of the fact that it is not only a Russian but an international army . . . the army of world revolution."

[42] *Selected Works, op. cit.*, X, 317.

[43] *Ibid.*, VIII, 87.

fixed ideas about revolutionary procedures and showed themselves unwilling to adjust techniques to meet new conditions. The bolshevik right wing persisted in recognizing only old forms of combat, uprisings, and partisan warfare, and were unable to accommodate themselves to new and more effective methods. The left wing was correspondingly oversold on the idea of revolutionary warfare, leaning toward the unconditional repudiation of old forms.

The leftists failed to understand that, according to Lenin, it is the duty of communists "to master all forms," to learn how to switch with great rapidity from one form of combat to another, to substitute one weapon for another, and to adapt "tactics to every change that is called forth by something other than our class, or our efforts."[44]

The bolsheviks had trained themselves in demoralizing and disrupting armed forces. Yet, from 1917 onward they were masters of a state and were compelled to build armed forces rather than destroy them. According to Stalin,

> either we create a real worker and peasant—primarily a peasant—army, strictly disciplined army, and defend the republic, or we perish.[45]

It took some time before Stalin himself arrived at this conclusion. During the early months of the bolshevik regime most communist leaders hoped that the Red guard would become "the shield of the Russian proletariat against the enemy operations of foreign and native counterrevolutionaries."[46] Red guard officers were elected, not appointed; discipline was based on communist "spirit"; orders were often arrived at by discussion. No wonder the fighting value of the Red guard was very poor. Early in 1918, German advances demonstrated the uselessness of the Red guard.

In the countryside, communist guerrillas sprang into existence. The peasants defended their newly gained land against the counterrevolutionaries who, according to communist propaganda, desired to undo the real or presumed benefits of land distribution. Many bolsheviks who were still "liberal" enough to be antimilitaristic hoped that guerrillas would prove adequate for the defense of Russia; they strongly favored this "democratic" form of military organization. Guerrilla operations offered many advantages, especially in

[44] *Ibid.*, X, 147.
[45] *History of the Communist Party, op. cit.*, p. 235.
[46] Wollenberg, *op. cit.*, p. 28.

impenetrable swamps and forests; but whenever the guerrillas were forced to accept open battle, they were destroyed. Obviously, since battle must be waged sometime if the enemy is to be defeated and the war to be won, the guerrilla idea, too, had to be abandoned. There was no possibility of an unorthodox, "progressive" reform army.

Reluctantly, but firmly, the soviets decided to establish regular armed forces. They also determined that the Red army was to be built along modern lines as a reliable instrument of combat powerful enough to brave any enemy. Since it was impossible to organize the army without professional help, former officers of the tsarist army had to be utilized.

On January 15, 1918, the council of people's commissars defined the task of the new army as follows:

The defense of the soviet authority, the creation of a basis for the transformation of the standing army into a force deriving its strength from a nation in arms, and, furthermore, the creation of a basis for the support of the coming socialist revolution in Europe.[47]

The military oath was, in its first version, straight out of the textbook on revolutionary enthusiasm. The Red soldier took it upon himself to give aid "in the hard and holy wars of the oppressed peoples" and to fight "worthily and without fear" for the "triumph of socialism." Trotsky redesigned the oath and eliminated the reference to the "holy war." But the Red army man still pledged himself to "spare neither strength nor life in battle for the Union of Socialist Soviet Republics and for the cause of socialism and the fraternization of all races."[48]

The Red army having been established, the question arose: what should its doctrine be? Should the Red army become just another army? Should it be built according to ideas of ultramodern strategy? Or should it be developed as an instrument of specifically proletarian methods of war?

Many of the professional officers reintegrated into the army became acquainted with Marxism and inevitably hit on the idea that Marxism and military science ought to be married. They saw the possibility of making strategy more effective through coupling with

[47] *Ibid.*, p. 249.
[48] *Ibid.*, pp. 178 f.

it the revolutionary art and through making Marxism more powerful by the addition of the military art. They suggested that there was a need for a "special military doctrine of the revolutionary proletariat."[49]

Quite unexpectedly, these excursions by the officer-communists into the field of theory were ridiculed by Trotsky, then commissar of war. As a chief theoretician of the party, he tolerated little competition, least of all from recent converts. He contended that the officers had not yet assimilated Marxism. In any event, the officer's job was not to think but to provide his soldiers with rations, teach rookies to clean weapons, grease boots, and learn how to shoot. It must have been a spectacle to see Trotsky in the role of a Colonel Blimp.

Trotsky stated that the idea of a Marxist military doctrine "would be similar to the evolving on Marxian lines of a theory of architecture or a veterinary textbook." Trotsky warned the officers of the budding Red army against abandoning old military doctrines. According to him, war was neither science nor art.[50] The trouble with Trotsky was that he never outgrew being a littérateur.[51]

The young military Marxists believed that mobility, maneuver, and the offensive spirit were the essential characteristics of revolutionary strategy. Trotsky insisted that the development of the technological and economic basis of the army was more important and, in any event, more urgent. He denied the great merits of the offensive principle; strategy should be "elastic." Trotsky was opposed to the idea of using the Red army as an instrument of revolution. To him, the revolutionary uprising remained the master weapon. An early *Official History of the Communist Party of the Soviet Union,* written by Popov, summed up the situation by saying that Trotsky had "social democratic prejudices," meaning that he misunderstood the power problem.

[49] *Ibid.,* p. 151.

[50] Part of this historic debate may be found in *Osnobnaya voyennaya sadacha momenta, diskussiya na temu o yedinoi voyennoi doktrinye,* stenograficheskii otchet 2-vo dnya sovyechshaniya voyennykh delegatov XI-vo s'yezda P.K.P. 1-bo aprela 1922 g (Moscow, 1922). Participants in this discussion included Trotsky, Frunze, Tukhachevsky, Budyonny, Voroshilov, *et al.*

[51] In later years in Mexico, Trotsky stated that power was a burden. While he was in the government, he said, he had his best time on vacations writing books. This throws much light on why he lost influence and political power.

Other communists took a more realistic attitude. Bukharin, for example, suggested that the dictatorship of the proletariat may have to give "armed assistance" to the proletariat of those lands where "the struggle with the bourgeoisie has not yet been carried to a successful issue." Bukharin criticized the socialists "nurtured in the peaceful atmosphere of petty-bourgeois villaindom" who pay no attention to "the possibility of, or the need for, organizing a proletarian army in the period of the fight for socialism." The armed struggle would be protracted. Europe "would have to pass through a phase, not only of socialist revolutions, but also of socialist wars." Hence the importance of the military question which tended to be overlooked by most socialists.[52] "The day when the Red army can be permanently disbanded will be the day on which will be signalized the final victory of the communist system."[53]

This debate continued till 1927 when D. B. Ryazanov again proclaimed that Marxism could not construct a theory of war different from bourgeois war doctrine. It was an illusion to think that something new and better could be worked out. Ryazanov was in favor of a defensive soviet strategy and considered the theory of the "revolution from the outside" as very dangerous. Armed intervention and soviet occupation would engender resentment and drive communist sympathizers into the camp of the opposition. The reserve of foreign workers and sympathizers would be the stronger, the less they required open military assistance. Ryazanov, who also was given to liberal illusions, thought that the pretended successes of the proletarian revolution would prove so impressive by themselves that they would revolutionize the West. If civil wars in other countries were to continue the class struggle and the revolution with other means, the most advantageous situation would be created. Ryazanov admitted that war might become inevitable; if so, only one way would be left: revolution combined with war. In this case, *war of the proletarian states would be the "continuation of the revolution by other means."*[54] A neat formula.

---

[52] See N. Bukharin and E. Preobrazhensky, *The ABC of Communism* (Communist Party of Great Britain, 1924), pp. 214 f.

[53] *Ibid.*, p. 225.

[54] D. B. Ryazanov, "Voyennoye delo i marksizm," in *Voina i voyennoye iskusstvo v svete istoricheskoye materializma,* ed. by M. N. Gorev, Sbornik statei (Moscow-Leningrad, 1927), p. 23.

It may be observed that both Trotsky and Ryazanov missed the point entirely. It is undoubtedly true, and was undisputed by their opponents, that Marxists could not do without the experience, science, and military art developed by bourgeois soldiers. Yet, unlike bourgeois armies, the soviet forces aim at remaking society on a global scale. If for no other reason, the soviets needed a specific military doctrine to clarify what role their army should play in the process of world revolution. They also needed a theoretical guide to indicate the particular capabilities possessed by a military force working in co-operation with organized revolutionary groups.

THE LESSONS OF THE CIVIL WAR

THE PROBLEM of civil war, which heretofore was only of peripheral interest to theoreticians of national armies, frequently confronts the communist strategist. Reasoning from the experience of their own civil war, the young Turks of the Red army acquired the firm conviction that entirely new strategical and tactical vistas had been thrown open. Far more than World War I itself, the internal struggle should serve as a model for future communist operations. Revolutionary warfare would take the form of "international civil war."

The lessons to be drawn were cogently summarized by S. I. Gussev.[55] Civil war, according to him, is a class war in which essentially three classes participate: the bourgeoisie, the revolutionary proletariat, and the petty bourgeoisie. The latter is opposed to the war, tries to end it, and frequently switches sides.

In a civil war, the front is ubiquitous. There are no unbroken lines; the front is ahead, in the rear, and on both flanks, sometimes along an arc of 360 degrees. Hence, both parties must often employ "strategic *carré*" formations.

Gussev noted that while the civil war lasted, the bourgeois armies were compelled to recruit unreliable elements, thus diluting the purity of their "class structure." Desertion was frequent on both sides. As the hostile armies advanced, they entered into populated areas

[55] Gussev, *op. cit.* See also the official military history of the civil war, *Grazhadanskaya Voina 1918–1921,* ed. by A. S. Bubnov, S. S. Kamenyev, M. N. Tukhachevsky, and R. R. Eideman (3 vols., Moscow-Leningrad, 1930).

and gained control over "human reserves." Whenever the proletarian army entered industrial and densely populated areas, it likewise was able to mobilize large numbers and to increase its strength. *Therefore, territorial conquest is of special importance in a civil war.*

Since the front is everywhere, forces were relatively small (relative to the size of the territory held). The war must become a war of movement, rendering mobile forces of great importance. "In the age of the socialist revolution, war came out from the wet trenches, liberated itself from the complicated net of wire obstructions and entered into the free air of the battlefield."[56] Gussev held no brief for the old-fashioned horseman with lance and saber, but he stressed the role of armored cavalry equipped with mounted machine guns, combat vehicles, mobile artillery, and airplanes. (Use was made during the civil war of armored railroad trains which showed great effectiveness in the roadless steppes of Russia.) Infantry also must be mobile, although, with Russian roads in mind, Gussev was less convinced of the usefulness of tanks.

Gussev insisted that the revolutionary officers' corps ought to utilize military experts—officer deserters from the bourgeois armies. Proletarian commanders must be trained very thoroughly and in large numbers. He emphasized the key importance of an effective intelligence service, the need for unity between rear and front, and the need for political commissars. Since, according to him, *the socialist revolution will take place under conditions created by a preceding imperialist war,* and therefore under conditions of a disintegrating industry and a disorganized transport system, civil-war operations must be conducted strictly according to the principle of economy of force.[57] Military operations can be rendered relatively cheap if they are co-ordinated with guerrilla operations and urban uprisings in the opponent's hinterland.

Gussev warned the European proletariat that it should not repeat the mistakes of the Russian revolution. He underscored the need for discipline and insisted that compulsory discipline *(Zwangsdisziplin)* remained necessary, despite liberal illusions to the contrary. Evidently not anticipating the "Bonapartism" of Stalin, Gussev maintained, nevertheless, that revolutionary discipline is different from the discipline in a bourgeois army. It is not based on the need to keep

[56] *Ibid.,* p. 19.
[57] *Ibid.,* p. 64.

together members of hostile classes but on comradeship and class solidarity, or so he believed.

Gussev went to great lengths to explain that, after the seizure of power, the proletariat must organize its armed strength in a proper fashion. The leftist error—that military power ought to be organized in the form of partisans—is one of those "inevitable errors which each revolution experiences."[58]

In the Ukraine, for example, guerrilla warfare "developed into a mass manifestation and assumed dimensions unparalleled in history." But guerrillas often became bandits, incessantly changing sides and more often than not fighting for loot. Frequently they interfered with regular operations. While the partisans of the Ukraine developed more power and strength than any earlier guerrilla organization in history, they were incapable of winning decisive victories. "Such victories were won only by the regular Red army."[59] Gussev concluded that the first and only task of the victorious proletariat is to organize a Red army immediately upon seizure of power.[60]

On this point, other soviet theoreticians were not basically at issue with Gussev. According to Trotsky, the guerrilla movement "was a necessary and adequate weapon in the first period of the civil war."[61] But as the war grew in scope the guerrilla movement became, as Gussev concluded, a hindrance to the Red army.

According to Wollenberg,

the fundamental error of the adherents of guerrilla warfare was that they carried their theory of revolutionary warfare to the pitch of trying to apply their organizational form and fighting tactics to situations entirely different from those which had rendered them necessary, or at any rate inevitable, for armed proletarian units at a certain stage in the development of the class war.[62]

In accordance with the best thought being developed, soviet leaders decided to incorporate the guerrillas into the regular forces. Many bands refused, and were liquidated. Other bands, including one led by the later Marshal Budyonny, were taken over, and for a time served as "regular guerrillas" side by side with the army.

[58] *Ibid.,* p. 21.
[59] *Ibid.,* p. 11.
[60] *Ibid.*
[61] Wollenberg, *op. cit.,* p. 38.
[62] *Ibid.,* p. 40.

The leftist overemphasis on guerrilla combat made the creation of the Red army unnecessarily difficult. However, Gussev added, it would be a rightist error to abolish partisans entirely.

The correct interpretation of the inter-relationship between the regular army and the partisans is that while the regular army is decisive and the most important form of strength, the partisans are an auxiliary force supporting the operations missions of the regular army.[63]

This is as good a place as any to let the record refute the often held opinion that guerrilla warfare is the soviet master weapon; for example, "the men in the Kremlin confidently rely on communist guerrilla warfare to over-balance the industrial and atomic superiority of the West, whether in time of war or in time of so-called peace."[64]

The men in the Kremlin, of course, are not guilty of this antique "leftist deviation," although they cannot object if some in the West misunderstand them. Guerrillas are just one of the communist weapons. They are used if and when expedient and opportune. In a given instance, they might comprise the "master weapon"; in other cases, they would play their normal role of auxiliary force.

The usefulness of guerrillas is beyond doubt. They may fight in occupied areas to deny the enemy the fruits of territorial conquest. In ground battle they may enhance regular military strength; force enemy dispersal; support flank attack; foul up enemy logistics and rear communications; attack enemy command posts; facilitate survival and withdrawal of encircled units; and make possible desertion from the enemy army. Granted these important functions, they are neither the shock troops nor the showdown forces of revolutionary war. According to official Leninist doctrine, they constitute a combat organization fighting chiefly during the interval between major battles. Guerrilla tactics are inevitable when the masses have reached the phase of uprising, but prolonged guerrilla warfare lowers the consciousness of the proletariat to the level of "drunken bums." Hence, it never can be the principal form of struggle.[65]

[63] Gussev, *op. cit.*, p. 20. See also below, p. 257.

[64] Stewart Alsop and Samuel B. Griffith, "We Can Be Guerrillas, Too," *The Saturday Evening Post,* December 2, 1950.

[65] "Lenin o voine v svyazi s zadachami revolyutsii," *Voina i voyennoye iskusstvo, op. cit.,* pp. 183–85.

It is useful to distinguish between guerrilla and partisan warfare. Guerrillas are revolutionary *civilians,* more or less organized, emerging more or less spontaneously, and fighting, in most cases, in the vicinity of their homes. Partisans are *soldiers* or professional revolutionaries cut off from their units, left behind, or sent into the enemy rear for the accomplishment of assigned missions. They are tightly organized (in some cases they are nothing but specialized military units), highly mobile, and in general fulfill the tactical missions of the old-fashioned cavalry.

The function of guerrillas and partisans is similar: to disorganize the enemy's rear. Partisans are often assigned to the setting-up of guerrilla units. Guerrillas who have been operating a long time and who have acquired organizational stability gradually become partisans, that is, "irregular regular soldiers." Thus, the distinction between partisans and guerrillas tends to be artificial.

The point is, however, that partisan warfare can be waged in areas where the population is non-co-operative and unwilling to start guerrilla warfare; and that guerrilla warfare can be undertaken without the close support of a near-by army and without the help of military technicians sent into the area for the purpose of organizing the peasants. The second point is that partisan warfare may pay off if waged merely on a hit-and-run basis, while guerrilla warfare may prove useful even if waged in remote areas, provided the guerrillas can endure for a long while and tie down hostile forces.

Mao Tse-tung, reportedly the strongest communist advocate of irregular warfare, has taken pains to point out that partisans are only an auxiliary weapon, especially useful in periods of "positional warfare." In periods of mobile warfare, which are decisive for the outcome of war, guerrillas and partisans have merely limited usefulness, although they should be employed whenever possible. Mobile and positional warfare may be different phases of war, but they also may occur simultaneously. Some areas may be the scene of mobile warfare fought by regular forces, but in other areas, guerrilla operations may predominate.[66]

Mao has an offensive and transitional concept of guerrilla and partisan warfare. To him, partisans are not primarily useful as attack forces against the enemy's logistics. The chief mission of partisans

[66] Mao Tse-tung, *On a Prolonged War,* 1938, quoted from Robert Payne, *Mao Tse-tung, Ruler of Red China* (New York, Schuman, 1950), p. 175.

is the "capture of spoils": guerrilla and partisan warfare is a primary method of recruiting a revolutionary army in hostile territory.[67]

TUKHACHEVSKY

MIKHAIL N. TUKHACHEVSKY was perhaps the most original military thinker of communism. Despite his premature end during the purges, Tukhachevsky's teaching greatly influenced the nascent Red army, and probably continues to be influential, though without proper footnoting or credit.

Tukhachevsky's main contribution is contained in a book entitled *The War of the Classes.*[68] To him, the terms "class war" and "civil war" have not only national but also international connotations. Revolutionary seizure of power, he said, can be carried out by two methods: by revolutionary uprisings within one country, or by armed intervention of a proletarian state.[69] The first method is a conventional revolution; the second is a "revolution from outside" *(revolyutsiya isvnye).*

Both methods have exactly the same purpose: proletarian dictatorship. If there is only a weak internal revolutionary spirit, the revolutionary movement cannot strike effectively. If the indigenous revolutionary movement has strong morale but cannot find arms, or if the government has superior military strength and is willing to use it, a conventional revolution is not feasible.[70] In such cases the revolution must come from the outside, or it cannot succeed.

Even if a revolutionary uprising is successful, the foreign enemies of the revolution may support the defeated government. In this case, the civil war is transformed into an "international class war,"[71] requiring the intervention of the proletarian army.

The dictatorship of the proletariat must commit its armies to the overthrow of world bourgeoisie—if only for "defensive purposes." Therefore, revolutionary war will become both inevitable and necessary. Before revolutionary war is waged, however, one must evaluate

[67] Mao Tse-tung, *The Strategic Problems of China's Revolutionary Wars,* 1941, quoted from Payne, *op. cit.,* p. 191.

[68] M. N. Tukhachevsky, *Voina klassov, stat'i 1919–1921* (Moscow, 1921).

[69] *Ibid.,* p. 51.

[70] *Ibid.,* p. 53.

[71] *Ibid.,* p. 51.

the attitude of the workers and peasants toward the Red "liberators." If this attitude is favorable, there is no reason to wait.[72] If the attitude is unfavorable, one should be very careful: the bourgeoisie must be prevented by propaganda from exploiting "armed assistance" for purposes of "chauvinism." If the proletariat remains reluctant to support the proffered "armed assistance," intervention must be camouflaged and drawn out. Protracted hostilities will lead almost automatically to the revolutionary disintegration of the bourgeoisie and to a more favorable attitude of the proletariat.

Whether or not the technique of revolution from the outside is utilized is a matter of expediency.[73] Tukhachevsky was inclined to

[72] *Ibid.*, pp. 56 f.

[73] Trotsky was the main opponent of the revolution from the outside. He summarized his position during the hearings in Mexico: If a revolution occurred, and if the new government called for help, he would not, if he still were in the soviet government, refuse assistance. (*The Case of Leon Trotsky: Report of Hearings on the Charges Made Against Him in the Moscow Trials* [New York, Harper, 1937], p. 305). He admitted that war can accelerate revolution but this acceleration may be unfavorable to the proletariat "if it is not prepared for the revolution" (p. 364). He thought it impossible to make an artificial revolution. "Revolution is a historical event which must be produced by the development of society." Asked whether he considered war as desirable in the interests of socialism, he answered: "It is almost the same as if the question were asked: What is your opinion of cholera and epidemics for human civilization? . . . When there was cholera—there was in Russia, and is now from time to time—we revolutionists thought by illegal leaflets to help the peasants. We denounced the regime of the tsar. You know it is an interesting parallel. The Black Hundreds, our specific Russian reactionaries, accused us of spreading the germs of cholera. There were pogroms against the doctors, the students, the radical intelligentsia, and Jews, as a vengeance for spreading cholera. It was the measure of the reaction to reject the responsibility about sanitary conditions and to replace it on the radical elements. I thank you very much for your questions because I find the analogy very important. I assure you, under tsarism we had twenty-five years of revolutionary activity, and I never asked for cholera. . . . The same with war. If war comes in spite of us, we will use all the means to place the responsibility on the ruling classes and to accelerate the revolution. But to wish a war—it is absurd from every point of view. What do we need with artificial means for revolution? We have a revolution in Spain without war, but we are not capable of being victorious yet. We had in Germany two and three revolutions. There was in 1918, and in 1923 during the Ruhr occupation, a totally revolutionary situation. Before the victory of Hitler we had a totally revolutionary situation. The lack was not objective revolutionary situations, but revolutionary parties which had the necessary confidence of the masses and adequate leadership. Now, we need the creation of such parties and such leadership. For that we need time, and not to provoke artificial revolutionary situations with the purpose of losing them and so to allow millions of workers, hundreds of thou-

think that revolution from the outside will usually prove to be more effective than the conventional revolution from the inside. This means that war is a more effective revolutionary technique than insurrection. War, Tukhachevsky explained, is the most forceful as well as the most risky action which policy can use.[74] It is the ultimate means of politics.

War is used under two conditions: when, in order to improve one's own position, it becomes an absolute prerequisite, unattainable by non-military means, to weaken or destroy the powers of the opponents; or when circumstances make war particularly expedient— when the chances of victory are good.

It cannot be forecast, reasoned Tukhachevsky, whether the final overthrow of the bourgeoisie will come through internal uprisings or through external attack, or by a combination of both methods. It is in the nature of things that the proletarian state will try to expand to the neighboring territories and ultimately to the entire world; hence, the communist armed forces[75] must play a key role in world revolution.

The Red army of Russia is the cadre of the Red army of the world.

No Red army will ever fight alone. It will get the help of the working classes of the country with whose bourgeoisie it is at war.[76] This help will come not only in revolutionary explosions in the enemy's rear but also through the recruitment of revolutionary manpower and prisoners of war directly into the ranks of the Red army and its auxiliary units.[77] Such a parasitic build-up will take place at the expense of the bourgeois army and reserves. Thus, through the dis-

---

sands, to perish in the defeat. . . . The more a party, a workers' party, is revolutionary, the less is the danger of war, because the only handicap for the imperialists in beginning a new war is the fear of a new revolution. If the danger is real, if the working class is penetrated with a revolutionary spirit, we can postpone the war and the revolution can proceed and not only make war impossible, but the revolution can replace war." (Pp. 308 f.) Trotsky evidently based his theory on an overly optimistic estimate of insurrectional capabilities: Not one of the revolutions mentioned by him was successful; not one of these revolutionary situations was really "total." Stalin and his group of realists never could have believed that the communist parties in Europe and America would be able to execute the program outlined by Trotsky.

[74] "K voprosu o sovremennoi strategii," in *Voina i voyennoye iskusstvo, op. cit.,* p. 119.

[75] Tukhachevsky, *op. cit.,* p. 61.

[76] *Ibid.,* p. 75.

[77] *Ibid.,* p. 14.

integration of the bourgeois army and society will the Red army gain strength.

In Tukhachevsky's opinion, the Third International ought to assume leadership over the world revolutionary movement of which the socialist war is only a part.[78] The International should set up revolutionary movements within the various nations and co-ordinate them with the support activities based on the proletarian states. It must be at the helm of the socialist effort of the world proletariat against world capitalism.

If coordination and leadership of all military operations with the labor class on the broadest world scale are flawless, the means of the world revolution will be multiplied tenfold.[79]

Accordingly, Tukhachevsky invited the communists to consider the question of war "seriously."[80]

The Communist International must prepare the proletariat for the forthcoming [international] civil war from the military point of view. It must make the proletariat ready for the moment when the world offensive by all armed proletarian forces will take place against armed world capitalism.

The world civil war should not come as an unexpected surprise. The Communist International must be recreated as a general staff and must deliberately work out the military problems of socialist war.[81] Under this general staff, the labor classes must become able to form regular Red armies and Red army support units.

By contrast, Trotsky thought that such a general staff could be formed only on the basis of national general staffs existing in several proletarian states. As long as such proletarian states did not exist, an international general staff would remain "a caricature."[82]

At various points in his doctrine, Tukhachevsky was carried away by bolshevik illusions.[83] For example, he believed that capitalist

[78] *Ibid.*, p. 59.
[79] *Ibid.*, p. 59.
[80] *Ibid.*, p. 139.
[81] *Ibid.*, p. 140.
[82] Wollenberg, *op. cit.*, p. 201.
[83] It is hardly necessary to point out that his reliance on the "labor classes" was entirely misplaced. Under conditions of growing "capitalism," the workers tend to become highly conservative. Poor peasants, déclassé intellectuals, and impoverished members of the middle class are more likely to become radicals than workers.

states can never use their industry as fully as socialist states. In a socialist nation, general mobilization can be carried out without disorganizing the industry, but in a capitalist society the act of mobilization allegedly operates as a dislocating factor.

Tukhachevsky fell into similar errors concerning manpower and morale. The raising of a multimillion-man army, he thought, might prove suicidal for a politically unstable state. Hence, not every state, even if possessed of a large population, can wage war effectively.[84] This, he claimed, is particularly true of capitalist states in a prerevolutionary condition.

Man-power requirements of modern war are enormous. Therefore, countries unable to replace their losses from within their own borders must rely on allies and principally on colonies. This, he alleged, is a reason why "imperialism" cannot survive without colonies.

If a war should last a long time, Tukhachevsky asserted, disintegrating tendencies would operate even in the stable capitalist countries and would affect their armies regardless of training and equipment. The greater the successes of the Red army, the faster would disintegration progress,[85] especially if such armies are fighting against communist forces rather than against other imperialist units.[86]

Tukhachevsky acknowledged that in case of Red army failure and capitalist victories the disintegration of bourgeois armies and states would be retarded or not take place at all. That a proletarian dictatorship, too, may be subject to disintegration did not seem to occur to him.

Tukhachevsky opposed the blitzkrieg doctrine and asserted that no major war can be decided by a single strike.[87] However, the attacker should score significant victories during the early phases of operations: early successes will weigh decisively on the ultimate outcome of the conflict. How can initial victories be secured? Industrial mobilization takes a long time. The first phases of war must be fought with the reserves and stockpiles accumulated during peace. Hence, the belligerent entering the war at a relatively higher level of logistical readiness will gain considerable immediate advantages.

[84] "K voprosu," *loc. cit.*, p. 125.

[85] *Ibid.*, p. 135.

[86] Article "Voina" in *Sbornik Voyennoi Akademii RKKA imeni M. V. Frunze* (Moscow, 1926), I, xxiv.

[87] "K voprosu," *loc. cit.*

The advent of the atomic bomb scarcely invalidated the realism of these statements.

Tukhachevsky had practical command experience, and, as commander-in-chief during the war against Poland (1920), was responsible for the rapid advance to Warsaw. During the course of this campaign he devised the strategy of encircling Warsaw from the North so that the Red army would reach the borders of friendly Lithuania and Germany and stimulate revolutionary movements in central Europe.

Stalin critized this plan; at least, he did so after the event: attack from the North required an offensive through agricultural areas where the soviet army could not pick up local support. Poland's industrial districts were situated to the South and Southwest of Warsaw, particularly around Lvov. According to Stalin, the main communist advance should have been directed through the industrial South where the Polish workers would rally to the Red flag. Unfortunately for Stalin's sociological theory, proletarian Lvov actually put up a stiff resistance, thus exposing the Russian southern army to dangerous flank attacks. Both communist strategists were wrong: the Polish workers neither rallied to the Russian army, nor did the German workers make a revolution.[88]

In a later critique of his own campaign, Tukhachevsky maintained that he had good reason to believe that local revolutionary movements would help his operations. "From East-Prussia came hundreds and thousands of volunteers who formed a German rifle brigade under the banner of the Red army."[89] In defense of Tukhachevsky, it must be granted that a revolution from the outside was a distinct possibility, in which case the Polish war would have served as the connecting link between the October revolution and the proletarian revolution in western Europe. The fundamental failure was that the soviets did not succeed "in depriving the Polish bourgeoisie of its bourgeois army." Tukhachevsky had overrated the ripeness of the revolutionary situation.

Marshal Pilsudsky, Tukhachevsky's opponent, thought that the calculations of the communist leader were "based on the idea that the bayonets need only give the word, and then there would be a

[88] Wollenberg, *op. cit.*, p. 139.

[89] Tukhachevsky, "The March beyond the Vistula," *op. cit.*, p. 231.

chance for the soviet revolution to develop its power in the land it had invaded."

Trotsky believed that the overestimation of the revolutionary character of the Polish internal situation led to a careless driving forward and to a reckless offensive. He summed up the theory of the revolution from the outside in these words:

In the great class war now taking place, military intervention from without can play but a concomitant, co-operative, secondary part. Military intervention may hasten the denouement and make the victory easier, but only when both the political consciousness and the social conditions are ripe for revolution. Military intervention has the same effect as a doctor's forceps; if used at the right moment, it can shorten the pangs of birth, but if employed prematurely, it will merely cause an abortion.[90]

According to Stalin, the advance into Poland was unorganized. The troops were not allowed to consolidate their positions; advance detachments were led too far ahead; reserves and ammunition were left too far in the rear. The front was stretched out endlessly and underequipped with ammunition, thus enabling weak enemy forces to break through. If we are to believe Stalin,[91] world revolution was slowed down largely for military reasons.

Trotsky concluded from the failure of the revolutionary war against Poland that the revolutionary movement abroad must be strengthened. Stalin concluded that the Soviet Union must be strengthened. The *vozhd* (leader) found no fault with the doctrine of revolution from without.

Tukhachevsky himself was taught a hard lesson. He learned that overemphasis on offensive action, a bolshevik version of the discredited *"offensive à outrance,"* is perilous, especially for a technologically backward army. Henceforth, he paid great attention to technology and particularly to mechanization. Since the defensive is feasible with means of "technical simplicity," he became more inclined to think in defensive terms and shed early illusions about the "special maneuverability" of the Red army.

Of great significance for the future were Tukhachevsky's ideas on air-borne warfare. Undoubtedly, General William Mitchell can lay claim to the paternity of the idea, but Tukhachevsky must be given

90 Wollenberg, *op. cit.*, pp. 145 f.
91 *History of the Communist Party, op. cit.*, p. 242.

credit for having been the first commanding general to take the concept of air-borne operations seriously, both tactically and strategically. He tried to combine tanks and planes by proposing an armored car which could be transformed into an airplane, and back again. As an intermediary solution he suggested large aircraft capable of transporting tanks.

Tukhachevsky envisaged the use of air-borne forces as support for revolutionary and partisan movements. Air-borne units landed directly in areas inhabited by people openly in sympathy with the invader would strengthen the revolutionaries, open "fronts" in the enemy rear, and reduce the logistical requirements of the air-borne forces. Tukhachevsky studied the possibility of landing air-borne infantry in the Ruhr, in East Prussia, and in the territory between Berlin and Saxony, so that they might

hasten to the assistance of the German proletariat in the event of revolution. . . . The conception of a parachute corps is therefore closely connected with the idea of an international socialist revolution.[92]

Toward the end of his life Tukhachevsky became more and more conservative in his thinking and criticized the military theories of J. F. C. Fuller, B. H. Liddell Hart, and Charles de Gaulle. He ended up leaning strongly in the direction of conservative French military doctrine. Actually, during the first year of the Russo-German war, the tactics of the Red army followed closely the spirit of French field instructions, except that the Russians applied these tactics in larger spaces, with greater skill, more equipment, and enormous manpower reserves.

Mikhail Frunze

WHEN Trotsky got hopelessly entangled in his struggle with Stalin, he was replaced as commissar of war by Mikhail V. Frunze (1924), a confidant of the dictator[93] and a partisan of the new school

[92] Wollenberg, op. cit., p. 195. Wollenberg was one of the soviet military delegates to the German communist party and may have assisted the Russian marshal in this planning.

[93] Frunze died of an operation ordered by the Politburo. There is speculation that he, too, got himself involved in a conflict with Stalin.

of military thinking. Frunze recognized the need for, and took steps to develop, an inclusive Marxian doctrine of war.

A short while after his appointment to the commissariat of war, a complex system of advanced colleges in which foreign communists were trained as professional revolutionaries was established. The universities in this system were the Lenin Institute for the training of western communists, and the University of the Peoples of the East, created three years earlier, which trained communists from Asia and the colonial areas, and also American Negroes, who were considered to be colonials, and the Sun Yat-sen University for the education of Chinese party members.[94]

The faculty staffs included the highest-ranking Russian officers and politicians, including such figures as Tukhachevsky, Bukharin, and occasionally Stalin himself. The students were recruited mainly among reliable foreign communists, but included Russian nationals selected for liaison duty. All were trained in the traditional arts and techniques of the communist agitator and propagandist. All learned the tricks of sabotage and espionage, of infiltrating and running labor organizations, and of directing industrial strikes.

The students were also taught the art and science of creating and conducting armed uprisings. They were instructed that uprisings can take place either in isolation or in conjunction with the Red army, with the second type considered the more important. In accordance with this concept, specially selected students were given military training. Frequently, the training schedule included classes and discussions at the Frunze Academy, the staff school of the Red army. The foreign military students became full-fledged experts in subversive, partisan, revolutionary, and military support operations. The more outstanding among them were appointed officers in the Red army.

The formal establishment of this training system indicated that the communists had firmed their ideas concerning their military requirements. They no longer were content to leave the business of revolution in the hands of amateurs. To them, world revolution was a careful art and science to be grasped more thoroughly than the art and science of the physician. No technique was meant to be over-

---

[94] The first bolshevik party schools were established after the revolution of 1905 on the island of Capri and at Longjumeau near Paris. Maxim Gorki taught at Capri, and Lenin instructed at Longjumeau.

looked, and no scruples were permitted. The "leaders of the proletariat" were given a type of instruction that surpassed anything ever taught at military schools anywhere. Thorough on-the-job training and much experience were prerequisites to admission to the universities. The courses of study required student revolutionaries to remain in residence for extensive periods, sometimes for more than three years. Afterwards, they again would get plenty of on-the-job experience.

Thus, the world communist movement was put into the hands of practitioners fully conversant with the theory and practice of war and revolution. The keynote of the theoretical instruction was Lenin's statement that Marxism is distinguished from other forms of socialism in that *it does not tie down the struggle to any specific form of struggle*. It does not hesitate to adopt any form of combat. It recognizes that "new forms of struggle . . . must *inevitably* arise as the given social situation changes." It demands that the struggle be developed within its historical setting.[95]

The appointment of Frunze signified the adoption of a realistic military program. Frunze believed that the waging of war is dependent upon the internal politics and conditions of a country. Domestic politics determine foreign policy and influence the conduct of military operations. Military doctrine must therefore be adapted to the policy of the ruling class. It must be tied in with national objectives and resources and cannot be improvised or invented freely.

The components of a doctrine are given by circumstances. A true military doctrine should be responsive to circumstances and to the military needs and purposes of a nation. In developing its doctrine, the Red army ought to determine the social forces by which it is surrounded. It must analyze the military problem as given to it by the character of the proletarian dictatorship. The peculiarities of the Red army, its specific battle methods and capabilities, must be taken into account. The rules of military science and art must be in-

---

[95] *Voina i voyennoye iskusstvo, op. cit.,* p. 178. This book, published in 1927, probably served as the original textbook on theory within the revolutionary universities. Lenin's statement appears in *Sobraniye Sochinenii, op. cit.,* X, 80, and is also contained in an American-published communist textbook, *Strategy and Tactics of the Proletarian Revolution* (New York, International Publishers, 1936), p. 29. A prefatory note states that the quotations of which the latter book is made up were compiled by V. Bystryansky and M. Mishin.

tegrated with the requirements of the revolutionary era.[96] The proper execution of doctrine must be insured both in the material and in the moral fields.

According to Frunze, the Soviet Union will never conduct a national war against foreign peoples. It will wage a revolutionary class war against the enemies of the working classes. "The struggle for the liberation of our oppressed brothers . . . would be a most popular slogan for the Red army and for the whole country."[97]

Between the proletarian government and the rest of the bourgeois world there can be nothing but a state of long, persistent, and desperate war, not for life "but unto death." The external form of this relationship may change. The conduct of this struggle may be modified. Open war may cede its place to other, non-military forms of the struggle, for example, to diplomatic treaties. There even may be peaceful coexistence—to a certain degree—but such coexistence is impossible for a prolonged period.[98]

The general policies of an aggressive class, a class aiming at victory over the bourgeois world, must be aggressive to the highest degree. But, since an aggressive communist policy is determined by the resources of the U.S.S.R., there are temporary limits to soviet offensive capabilities. Hence, there may be delays before the class can strive for ultimate victory, though resources alone are not always the limiting factor.

The difference between Frunze and the earlier Tukhachevsky lay in the former's distinction between the offensive and mere dash and drive. Frunze recognized that offensive warfare must be based on effective strength; that it must be carried out systematically and by steps; that each new offensive requires previous consolidation of conquered territory; and that prior to mounting an offensive, large reserves must be accumulated. Frunze was strongly in favor of offensive strategy, agreeing with Stalin, who once asked: "Who wants a military leader incapable of understanding that the opponent is not going to surrender—that he must be crushed?"[99]

[96] M. V. Frunze, *Yedinaya voyennaya doktrina i krasnaya armiya* (reprint from 1921, Moscow, 1941), pp. 10–13.

[97] A. Golubev, *M. V. Frunze o kharaktere budushchei voiny* (Moscow, Voyennaya Akadmiya RKKA imeni M. V. Frunze, 1931), p. 20.

[98] Frunze, *op. cit.,* p. 14.

[99] Michel Berchin and Eliah Ben-Horin, *The Red Army* (New York, Norton, 1942), pp. 130 ff.

The first principle of soviet high strategy, according to Frunze, is that victory will belong to him who will find the moral strength to attack. The side that limits itself to defense is doomed to failure. The very nature of the revolutionary process shows that the "labor class" will be forced to attack "capital" as soon as circumstances are favorable. "On this point the requirements of the military art are in full agreement with general politics."[100]

The base of the proletarian attack will not be Russia alone. If proper preparations are made, the Russian proletariat will receive support from the world proletariat.

The victory of Sadowa (1866) was attributed to the Prussian schoolteacher. The victory of the world revolution must be prepared by the communist schoolteacher and propagandist. Hence, *the economic difficulties of the Soviet Union are not necessarily of first importance and should not weigh too heavily on communist freedom of action.*

In his *Doktrina,* Frunze discussed various other methods by which technical inferiority can be neutralized, but a 1937 editor of this paper held them no longer useful. Although this comment may have been based on the editor's observation of Russia's industrial progress, it is more probable that Frunze's proposed methods of compensating for technological inferiority have been superseded by more streamlined means. By implication, the editor suggested that the rest of Frunze's writings still was considered valid.

Frunze took issue with the doctrine of the revolution from the outside. A revolution is a lengthy process of social and economic change developing within the classes of a state. The revolution can mature only if many objective and subjective conditions exist in addition to the military capabilities of the revolutionaries or their foreign supporters. The inevitable simile of pregnancy was used. Revolution is like the birth of a baby: the doctor can assist and speed up the act of birth but cannot create the process from the outside (unless, of course, he was with the mother nine months earlier).

Socialist states can and must assist revolution abroad. But they cannot artificially force the birth of a revolution before the internal conditions in the target countries have ripened. Frunze clearly overlooked the possibility of prior "revolutionary insemination."

Frunze opposed the concept that military intervention is the only

[100] Frunze, *op. cit.,* p. 16.

method of revolutionary expansion. The relationship between the victorious proletariat in Russia and the proletariat in other countries is very complex and takes many forms, in addition to wars. Hence, he believed that the victorious proletariat must assist the still oppressed proletariat in many different ways, depending on time and situation. In years of peace, help should be economic, organizational, and cultural. In periods of civil war and foreign clashes, assistance may be both quasi-military and military in nature.[101]

However, Frunze did not take issue with the idea that revolution should be helped by military intervention from the outside. His point was that intervention by socialist armies is not enough for the creation of revolution and that social, economic, and political processes are also required. He was thinking of revolution as a process of social restructurization, but not about the mechanics of power seizure.

Frunze believed that armed intervention should coincide with significant social changes and revolutionary situations in the target countries. Military strategy is part of political strategy[102] and must take into account mass movements, class struggles, and the relative strength of organized social groups.

The fundamental strategic plan of the soviets is to transform the isolated Russian revolution into a world-wide revolution. This will be brought about by three forces: the proletariat in the capitalist countries; the revolutionary movement in the colonial and dependent areas; and by the U.S.S.R. itself. First, the internal power of the Soviet Union must be strengthened. Then, the soviets should wait for the moment when the "rising of the revolutionary movement will weaken the capitalist camp and will create conditions favorable for the beginning of a decisive attack by the proletarian army."[103]

The resulting war would be vastly different from past wars. The capitalist world would be shaken up violently. Its social and political disintegration would be exploited by the tactics of the soviet forces. "Strategy is the highest military art which must consider not only the purely military elements such as the numbers of armies, etc., but also the elements of the political situation."[104] Even battle tactics must be conceived on the basis of numerical strength,

[101] Golubev, *op. cit.*, p. 33.
[102] *Ibid.*, p. 30.
[103] *Ibid.*, p. 31.
[104] *Ibid.*, p. 46.

technical means, and the social composition of the hostile forces.[105]

Since the imperialist armies will be composed largely of workers, Frunze felt that mobilization would necessarily transfer the class contradictions and struggles from the bourgeois society into the armed forces, making them highly vulnerable. However, the Soviet Union should not expect imperialist defeat to come from any resultant disintegration. *Disintegration would come from defeat.* The first and foremost job is to destroy the armed forces of the capitalist enemy *in a physical sense,* and then to enlarge the defeat *into political disintegration by revolutionary means. Revolution is the consummation of military victory.*

To put it into different terms: the revolution as a social act never can go fast and deep enough unless it is preceded, accompanied, or stimulated, by military defeat. The destruction of the capitalist state apparatus requires military means and the effective use of violence. The greater the devastation wrought by war, the better the revolutionary cause is served.

Accordingly, Frunze advocated a political-economic-military strategy of attrition rather than a strictly military strategy of annihilation. By contrast, he expected that the bourgeoisie would resort to blitzkrieg tactics because these were safer politically and socially: capitalist armies may go under in a drawn-out conflict but are unlikely to disintegrate during a fast and victorious war.[106]

Frunze believed that the idea of a blitzkrieg against Russia was based on a misunderstanding. The internal contradictions within the imperialist camp would prevent the opponents of the Soviet Union from uniting against the bolsheviks. Many capitalist states would try to remain neutral, although ultimately they, too, would be drawn into the war. (Frunze did not foresee that the most powerful capitalist states would actually ally themselves with the Soviet Union.) World capitalism has been unhinged to such a point that never again will it possess crushing superiority of strength. Since communist power is concurrently growing rapidly, the Soviet Union cannot be defeated with one big blow whatever the composition of the anti-soviet alliance.[107]

[105] *Ibid.,* p. 19.

[106] *Ibid.,* p. 50. Frunze preceded German military scientists in using the term "lightning blow" (*molniyenosnyi udar*) as early as 1925.

[107] *Ibid.,* p. 22.

The capitalists are losing the masses, Frunze thought. Hence, they put overemphasis on technology. However, technology, manpower, and morale are not entirely interchangeable. The country which can put into the field a politically reliable and well-equipped mass army possessing superior numbers should be victorious. Frunze believed that only in the Soviet Union were the conditions favorable for the simultaneous development of numerical strength, political reliability, and technological superiority.

At the time of Frunze's writing, "peace" was objectively the form of struggle most advantageous to the Soviet Union. But Frunze considered it naïve to assume that these conditions would last forever. The life-and-death problems arising from the conflict of social systems and state organizations cannot be solved by peaceful means. In language reminiscent of Bismarck, Frunze stated that "they must be solved by iron and blood."

Frunze anticipated a thought expressed in 1937 by Mao Tse-tung. According to Mao, a communist revolution must pass through a compromising, a contending, and an offensive phase. During the first phase after the seizure of power, the communists must concentrate on staying in power. During the second, they must develop their offensive strength and whittle down the strength of their opponents. When the third phase arrives, the communists must strike "death-blows" at capitalism.

Thus, the Soviet Union must strengthen itself industrially; communist movements abroad must be organized, and the Red army must be brought to the highest pitch of combat efficiency and attain a maximum of strength. Once these conditions exist, offensive revolutionary war should be waged by the Red army allied with the foreign proletariat. "The proletariat can and will attack. *With it, as its main weapon, will march the Red army.*"[108]

THE INTEGRATION OF RUSSIAN TRADITION

SINCE Ivan the Terrible, the Russians have been masters in what Hitler called "extended strategy." The bolsheviks were naturally unwilling to abandon techniques which had proved their worth

[108] Italics added. Frunze, *op. cit.*, p. 17. The Russian expression for main weapon is *glavnoye oruzhiye.*

in the past. A former tsarist officer, Alexander Svechin, was one of those given the job of marrying the strategical heritage of old Russia with the new bolshevik doctrine.[109]

Svechin pointed out that the Russians were honor students of the Mongols and experts in Oriental practices of war. They adopted from the East "a deep respect for accurate shooting, for the leading of an army in battle from the rear, for division of a big army into right and left wings, into vanguards and reserves, for organizing light cavalry to fight like infantry, and we have learned to attach great importance to espionage and security service." Asian strategy, Svechin continued, necessitated cunning and foresight.

All means were considered good, provided they would lead to military success. . . The Mongols did not scruple to break promises, and all the means to oppose one group of dynastic interest to another were taken advantage of. . . . Most probably, a military expedition on a larger scale was undertaken only when assurance could be obtained that in the state organism of the neighbor, there appeared deep dissensions.[110]

The Russians learned from an unknown Chinese military writer the methods by which such dissensions could be created. This writer outlined the following strategic formula:

Disorganize everything that is good in the enemy's country, try to entangle representatives of the highest spheres in criminal undertakings, compromising their position and afterwards, according to opportunity, give publicity to their transgressions. Enter into contact with the lowest and most objectionable individuals in your enemy's country. Hamper the activities of the government of the country. Propagate disagreement and dissatisfaction among the citizens. Instigate the young against the old. Try to make your enemy's army suffer continually from deficiency in supplies and equipment. Introduce sensuous music; loosen the old customs. Send licentious women to complete the work of degradation. Be generous in your offers, in your gifts, whenever it becomes necessary to obtain information on what is going on in the enemy's country. Do not spare money, the more money you spend, the more profit you will get therefrom. Money spent thus brings huge returns. You should keep spies everywhere. Only a man who has such tools at his disposal in his activities, who knows how to use such methods and how to disseminate disso-

---

[109] Since Svechin's history of the military art was not available to the author, he was compelled to rely on a summary given by Włodzimierz Bączkowski, *Towards an Understanding of Russia, A Study in Policy and Strategy* (Jerusalem, Liphshitz Press, 1947), pp. 20–34.

[110] *Ibid.*, pp. 20, 22.

lution and dispute everywhere, only such a man is entitled to govern. He is a treasure for his master and the pillar of the state.[111]

Russian history is indeed replete with pertinent examples. Tsarevitch Alexis, the son of Peter the Great, was kidnapped on his father's order and murdered. In 1703, the Russian ambassador in Constantinople [Istanbul] succeeded "not only in depriving the Grand Vizier hostile to Russia of his post but also in causing him to be beheaded."[112] In 1709, an attempt was made to murder Charles XII of Sweden. These practices of kidnapping, provocation, and murder were continued under Catherine the Great, Nicolas I, and, of course, under Stalin (kidnapping of Generals Müller and Kutyepov, the assassination of Ignace Reiss and Leon Trotsky, and so forth).

In numerous past instances, the Russians interfered in Polish and Turkish affairs by means of bribery, espionage, and subterfuge. For example, in 1794 the Polish insurgents captured the files of the Russian ambassador, which revealed that 110 prominent Poles, including the king, had been receiving money from Russia in addition to a larger list of lower Polish police functionaries and officials also on the payroll. During the Napoleonic period, no less a person than Talleyrand was the recipient of Russian bounties. So was the Prussian police minister of 1810.

The military successes of Russia in 1812 were due partly to the fact that the Russian government had concluded a secret treaty with Austria's Metternich. This treaty enabled the Russians to attack the French army at the most inopportune moment when it was recrossing the Berezina river. The Russians also persuaded large parts of the Prussian army to desert their French allies on the battlefield and to join the Russian ranks. By contrast, Svechin observed, the French showed little skill in the craft of extended strategy. Napoleon failed to proclaim the liberation of the serfs and use the peasants as a rebellious force against the tsar. Hence, he was unable to provoke insurrections in the Ukraine, which might have proved decisive. This very theme was taken up later by the prominent soviet historian Eugene Tarlé.[113]

Time and again the Russians showed their mastery of sociological warfare. The Caucasus was conquered partly by means of "disinte-

---

[111] *Ibid.*, p. 19.

[112] *Ibid.*, p. 27.

[113] *Ibid.*, p. 29. Eugene Tarlé, *Napoleon's Invasion of Russia, 1812* (New York, Oxford University Press, 1942).

grative propaganda," bribery of influential persons, and the inciting of Caucasian tribes against each other.[114] The Russians also organized numerous Greek and Armenian revolts against Turkey. During the Crimean war they employed feigned truces, fraternizations, and propaganda, with the purpose of making the British believe that the French were negotiating a separate peace.

Other notable examples from the perennial arsenal of Russia may be found in the activities of the Russian secret police in France, which between 1891 and 1914 aimed at producing and cementing the Russo-French alliance. For this purpose the Russian covert operations arm resorted to the systematic bribing of newspapers, the production of fraudulent documents (including the notorious *Protocols of the Elder Men of Zion*), and, most probably, to terrorism by means of bomb attacks, including bomb throwing in the French parliament.[115]

Needless to add that the bolsheviks themselves have had great experience with provocation. The cases of Asev and Malinovsky are only the most sensational.[116]

The communists were not reluctant to learn from the history of Russia as well as from that of their own party. Hence, they decided to develop, on a large scale, the "secret elements" of armed force. They did not content themselves with establishing these weapons as mere auxiliaries, but ascribed fundamental importance to the paramilitary organizations and methods. *"The whole army was to become the factor of subversion against hostile countries."*[117]

JOSEF STALIN

STALIN'S writings are applicable both to revolution and to war. Political and military strategy are twin brothers and are subject to the same rules of behavior. Military experience clarifies political

---

[114] Bączkowski, *op. cit.*, p. 30. This strategy was proposed as early as 1834 by Platon Zubov, in his *Caucasian Essays*. Zubov was prominent in court circles.

[115] Henry Rollin, *L'apocalypse de notre temps* (Paris, Gallimard, 1939), particularly Chaps. 10, 11, 15, 16, 17.

[116] Boris Nikolajewsky, *Aseff, the Spy, Russian Terrorist and Police Stool* (New York, Doubleday, 1934). On Malinovsky, see David Shub, *Lenin* (New York, Doubleday, 1948), pp. 118–126.

[117] Bączkowski, *op. cit.*, p. 38. The author is indebted to Professor Bączkowski for the quotes from his outstanding book.

problems, and vice versa. Both military and political strategy must master all forms of fighting.[118]

The most startling aspect of Stalin's operational thinking is its systematic and comprehensive character. Everything must be considered. Everything must be planned. A strict sequence of strategic methods must be observed. There is great emphasis on extreme tactical flexibility, but strategy is conceived by him in a rather rigid pattern. "Tactics must be adapted to the aims and possibilities of strategy."[119] Hence, strategy controls tactics. The difference between the two is defined after Clausewitz: "The aim of strategy is to win the war . . . the aim of tactics . . . is to win engagements and battles and . . . conduct campaigns and operations."

Over-all soviet strategy is conceived within the framework of Lenin's theory of the uneven development of capitalism, which holds that communism can expand only by steps, leaps, and bounds. The simultaneous victory of socialism in all countries is impossible. Socialism must be victorious first in one or a limited number of countries, as the rest temporarily remains bourgeois. The victorious proletariat of the country in which socialism has been established, "having expropriated the capitalists and organized its own socialist production, would stand up *against* the rest of the world, the capitalist world, attracting to its course the oppressed classes of other countries."[120]

Stalin commented that this theory differs from previous illusionary Marxist interpretations which assumed that socialism would be introduced simultaneously in all civilized countries. The original theory has become obsolete. The law of uneven development opened up new revolutionary perspectives. It taught the foreign proletariat to take advantage of war situations to organize the attack against their own national bourgeoisie.[121]

Stalin developed another aspect of this uneven development. One capitalist country forges ahead of the others; therefore, it must try to increase its share in the world market and, by military means, strive for the redivision of an already divided world. This course

[118] *Strategy and Tactics, op. cit.,* pp. 23, 31.

[119] *Ibid.,* pp. 27 f.

[120] Lenin in 1915, quoted by Stalin in *History of the Communist Party, op. cit.,* p. 169.

[121] *Ibid.,* p. 170.

sharpens the conflicts in the capitalist camp, weakens world capitalism, and creates favorable conditions for new break-throughs of capitalist fronts by the world proletariat.[122] Communist strategy is concerned with exploiting this development of capitalism for the expansion of revolution.

Stalin's strategy is embedded in the geopolitical concept that the October revolution threw "a bridge between the socialist West and the enslaved East and formed a new revolutionary front from the proletariat of the West via the Russian revolution to the suppressed peoples of the East." This entire front of world revolution is directed against world imperialism. The task of the communists, then, is to break the centuries-old enslavement of the eastern peoples, infect the colonial workers and peasants with the spirit of revolution, educate them for the struggle, and deprive "world imperialism" of its "bottomless manpower reserves." Without depriving the imperialist countries of the human resources of Asia and enlisting the eastern masses on the side of the Soviet Union, there can be neither a complete victory over imperialism nor a final success of socialism. *"Don't forget the East,"* Stalin exclaimed as early as 1918.[123]

What are the basic operative ideas of Stalinist strategy? First, by breaking the capitalist chain at several points, the proletariat must aim at replacing the "capitalist encirclement" of the Soviet Union by a "socialist encirclement" of the main capitalist powers. This is the main prerequisite for ultimate communist victory. Secondly, there is the requirement for the "coordination of the economic with the military struggle and the coordination of the attack from without with the attack from within."[124]

On the basis of the two master ideas of socialist encirclement and the fusing together of the military and non-military tools, the determination of the direction of the "main blow" devolves upon strategy.[125] This direction must be selected with great care because

to define the direction of the main blow means to determine the character of the operation throughout the duration of the war and consequently to determine to the extent of nine-tenths the fate of the war itself. That is the aim of strategy.[126]

[122] *Sochineniya, op. cit.,* IX, 106.
[123] *Ibid.,* IV, 166–72.
[124] *Ibid.,* V, 120.
[125] *Ibid.,* p. 163.
[126] *Ibid.,* p. 164; *Strategy and Tactics, op. cit.,* p. 27.

The problem is to choose the location of the battlefield, of the area from which the enemy is to be attacked, and of the "moral battlefield" where the maximum of demoralization can be achieved. The purpose is not only to maximize the immediate results but to prepare further strikes, which, if the original effort succeeds, should be developed forthwith.

Against what target should the blow be directed? The blow should fall against "that single link in the chain of events which, if seized upon, will enable us to keep hold of the whole chain and prepare the ground for the achievement of strategic success."[127] Such success will be facilitated greatly if the key link is also the enemy's most vulnerable spot.

Where is the most vulnerable spot? Stalin criticized Bukharin's idea that "the imperialist chain will break where the *economic* system is weakest." He substituted for it Lenin's statement that "the capitalist chain will break where *it is weakest*"—very clearly a substitution of a strategy of power for purely economic strategy. If the key links are invulnerable to attack, the main blow should be directed against the weakest links in the chain.

The choice of the targets for attack should be influenced by sociological analyses of the "class structures"[128] of the belligerents. Attack has a "class nature."

> They talk loudly about attack. But an attack on *which* class and in alliance with *which* class? . . . Is it *any kind* of attack we want, or not an attack against a definite class, in alliance with a definite class?[129]

For example, during the Russian civil war, the anticommunist General Denikin selected the Donets basin as his battlefield, thus committing the serious error of advancing into a region whose population was hostile to him. By contrast, Stalin once planned an attack on Rostov by leading his troops by a tortuous route but through areas friendly to the soviet army.[130]

Stalin derided the customary overemphasis on flank security which often prevents deep penetration movements.

[127] *Strategy and Tactics, op. cit.,* pp. 34, 45.
[128] *Sochineniya, op. cit.,* IV, 325.
[129] *Strategy and Tactics, op. cit.,* pp. 40 f.
[130] Klim Voroshilov, *Stalin and the Red Army* (Moscow, 1942), p. 23.

The troops must be taught to rid themselves of the fear of open spaces at their flanks. It is not necessary to seek elbow liaison but to operate through the utmost possible concentration of forces in the most important operative direction.[131]

This is a strategy of tactical boldness which seeks security in movement and sociology.

Once the direction of the attack has been determined, the blow must be timed correctly. The attack should be initiated at the moment "when the crisis has attained its highest pitch." An objectively favorable situation is found when revolutionary emotions are boiling over; when slogans fall behind the movements of the mass; when the enemy camp shows signs of disintegration; and when the apparatuses of administration and repression collapse or fall paralyzed.

In order to become "ripe," the situation must be sparked by a "revolutionary incident." Yet even the ripest situation can be exploited only if the revolutionary military forces have been organized, disciplined, trained, equipped, and have accumulated adequate striking power. Once the situation is "right," Stalin explained, this strength should be demonstrated openly in order to incite clashes and increase the moral and material power of the revolutionary forces. Then a test of strength[132] should be undertaken and, if successful, the main attack launched.

The attack having been launched, "it must be pursued no matter what difficulties and complications may be encountered on the road." The "grievous error well known to sailors as 'losing the course'" must be avoided.[133]

If the attack fails, the revolutionary forces must retreat in an orderly fashion "to gain time, to disintegrate the enemy and to accumulate forces in order to assume the offensive later."

One of the most important problems of revolutionary strategy and leadership is the proper use of the "reserves of the revolution." According to Voroshilov, Stalin is

a military leader and a strategist of the proletarian revolution which disposes not only of the armed forces under its immediate command, but

[131] *Ibid.*, p. 38.
[132] *Sochineniya, op. cit.,* V, 75.
[133] *Strategy and Tactics, op. cit.,* p. 36.

also of vast potential reserves of manpower along the main strategic direction. It is these reserves, the vast potentialities of the developing proletarian revolution . . . that Stalin, with his genius for strategy, fully and unerringly, took into consideration in his remarkable plan [against Rostov].[134]

In communist terminology, the term "reserve" means any force that can be exploited for soviet interests. The term often is used as just another word for "force." Stalin distinguished between the direct and indirect reserves. The direct reserves listed by him are: the peasantry and intermediate strata of a nation's population; the proletariat and the international movement; the revolutionary movement in the colonies and dependent countries;[135] and the achievements of the proletarian dictatorship.

The indirect reserves include: contradictions and conflicts among nonproletarian classes; and contradictions, conflicts, and wars among bourgeois states which "can be utilized by the proletariat in its offensive or in maneuvering in the event of a forced retreat." This is the theoretical basis of chestnut strategy.[136]

With respect to tactics, Stalin made three main points. First, those procedures and combinations of procedures should be used which are "best suited to the conditions prevailing during the ebb and flow of the movement at a given moment." There are no restrictions on means, provided they are effective. Second, tactical attacks should be concentrated against the decisive link within the situation. And third, "changes in the forms of struggle" must be "accompanied by corresponding changes in the form of organization."[137]

The struggle must be vitalized by slogans, changed according to the situation. Party slogans (tactical directives) must be transformed into slogans for the masses (for propaganda and agitation). But mass support for the struggle cannot be achieved by propaganda and agitation alone. Support must be obtained through action and political experience. *"The broad masses should learn from own personal suf-*

---

[134] Voroshilov, *op. cit.,* p. 38.

[135] *Sochineniya, op. cit.,* VIII, 26.

[136] Stalin, *Problems of Leninism* (Moscow, Foreign Languages Publishing House, 1940), p. 62.

[137] *Ibid.,* pp. 61, 66, 68.

ferings that the overthrow of the given system . . . is inevitable and that the establishment of a new political and social system is inevitable."[138]

The strategic plan must arrange for an effective deployment of all forces. "The task of strategic leadership is to make proper use of all these reserves for the achievement of the main object of the revolution at the given stage of its development."

Stalin paid a great deal of attention to defensive problems. His main defensive preoccupation was the security of the rear (*tyl*), which, to his mind, did not simply mean security of rear communications but sociological and political safety. As early as 1919 he insisted on a triple command structure dealing with supply, military operations, and political security.[139] This preoccupation with internal security in case of war partly, though not wholly, explains Stalin's infatuation with the political police.

With reference to Poland's attack in 1920, Stalin stated that the advance of the Polish army into Russia deprived it of its effective moral support and exposed it to attack from hostile national groups, including the Russian peasantry. The soviets fell into a similar error when they carried out what Stalin euphemistically called the "forward movement" to Warsaw; during that campaign, the Russian "reserves fell behind" and the solidity of the Russian rear gave way. The soviets had to retreat to strengthen their rear through such means as the New Economic Policy: concessions to the old way of life.

Stalin is best known for his theory that Russia has become the base of world revolution. The October uprising

has ushered in a new era, the era of proletarian revolutions in the countries of imperialism . . . of colonial revolutions which are being conducted in the oppressed countries of the world in alliance with the proletariat and under the leadership of the proletariat.[140]

[138] Italics added. *Strategy and Tactics, op. cit.,* p. 48. This statement by Stalin is at variance with Trotsky's discourse about cholera, quoted above. Yet, its meaning is clear enough: Without mass suffering, there will be no support for the revolutionary movement, and no revolution.

[139] *Sochineniya, op. cit.,* IV, 216.

[140] "The International Character of the October Revolution," *Problems of Leninism, op. cit.,* pp. 198, 200. This paper was published in November 1927. It has been republished regularly since. See *Sochineniya, op. cit.,* (1949) X, 241, 243.

The bolshevik seizure of power "jeopardized the very existence of world capitalism *as a whole*."[141] Read again: *world capitalism is threatened in its entirety.*

And why? Conflicts and armed clashes are inevitable; so is "unprecedented slaughter." Attrition is "washing away, bit by bit, the very foundations of world imperialism." The October revolution inflicted a "mortal wound" on world capitalism from which it "will never recover."[142]

But more than that. The October uprising also has created

a powerful and open base for the world revolutionary movement. . . . It has created a powerful and open center of the world revolutionary movement . . . around which it now can rally and organize a united revolutionary front of the proletarian and oppressed nations of all countries against imperialism.[143]

The dictatorship of the proletariat in Russia is "a base for the overthrow of imperialism in all countries. The revolution is spreading beyond the confines of one country; the period of world revolution has commenced."[144]

In another typical formulation, Stalin stated that the erstwhile task of overthrowing the national bourgeoisie of Russia has been replaced by the new task of overthrowing the international bourgeoisie.[145] Obviously, he is here blowing the trumpets of world revolutionary war.

As a corollary, the Russian proletariat, the vanguard of the international proletariat,[146] must prepare to receive the main blows of international capitalism. The establishment of socialism in one or several countries must create friction with the bourgeoisie, which must try to overthrow the victorious proletarians.

In such cases a war on our part would be a legitimate and just war. It would be a war of socialism, for the liberation of other nations from the bourgeoisie.[147]

141 *Problems of Leninism, op. cit.*, pp. 20 f.; *Sochineniya, op. cit.*, X, 245.
142 *Sochineniya, op. cit.*, p. 246.
143 *Ibid.*, p. 246.
144 *Problems of Leninism, op. cit.*, p. 60.
145 *Sochineniya, op. cit.*, V, 82.
146 The term "vanguard" is a communist circumlocution for the term "elite." The Russian communist party is the elite of the elites. There is not only Marx, but also a great deal of Pareto, in Stalin.
147 Lenin in 1916 quoted by Stalin in *History of the Communist Party, op. cit.*, p. 169.

The weakness of Russia's war potential originally imposed on the communists a policy of temporary agreement, a policy of gaining time and peaceful coexistence. This policy was facilitated by the circumstance that capitalism, too, needed time to catch its breath. The soviets must make use of the pauses in world revolution to develop their capital and technical resources to the maximum—and at the same time continue the disintegration of their enemies. Peaceful coexistence, like peredyshka, is a tactic (not a strategy) designed to further the cause of communism. It does not signify acquiescence in any given *status quo.*

Although, for a long time, Stalin preoccupied himself with the internal economic development of Russia, the Soviet Union was, and still remains, the base of the world revolutionary movement, the leader of revolutionary movements in all countries, and the fatherland of the world proletariat.[148] The industrialization of Russia was undertaken to strengthen the military power of the soviets, to enhance the position of the world proletariat, and to increase the chances for world proletarian victory.[149] It was not undertaken to improve the standard of living of the Russian people. Industrialization, let it be repeated, aims predominantly at increasing the soviet war potential. In fact, the organization of the soviet economy served as model for German *Wehrwirtschaft*;[150] even the term is nothing but a translation of Stalin's expression *oborono sposobnosti.*

During the early phases of the Russian revolution many soviet theorists placed great hopes in the capabilities of foreign revolutionary movements. They expected these movements to come to the rescue of the Soviet Union. Hence, the bolsheviks, particularly those associated with the Communist International (for example, Sinovyev, Radek, and Bukharin), showed eagerness to organize revolutionary uprisings wherever and whenever possible. However, Lenin did not overrate the communist insurrectional capability. Stalin, too, had many misgivings about the practicability of uprisings in Europe[151] and, by 1925, realized that the early strategy of fomenting these revolutionary uprisings was amateurish. One of the reasons for Stalin's

[148] *Sochineniya, op. cit.,* XI, 151.
[149] *Ibid.,* IX, 27.
[150] Organization of the economy in time of peace, in view of maximum output of military goods and minimum loss of time for industrial mobilization, or the permanent militarization of the economy.
[151] *Sochineniya, op. cit.,* III, 42.

re-evaluation of strategy was his understanding that the revolutionary movement in the West was incapable of effective action and, in case of war, would not lighten the burden on the Soviet Union.[152]

Hence Stalin modified the early theory in a fundamental fashion: while formerly the Soviet Union was supposed to support revolutionary movements abroad, if necessary by means of revolutionary war, *he now proclaimed that the foremost function of revolutionary movements outside of Russia was to support the Soviet Union.*

In order to stimulate world revolution, "the defense of the Soviet Union must be considered paramount."[153] An internationalist is he who unhesitatingly supports the U.S.S.R. Whoever thinks of helping the world revolutionary movement apart from or against the U.S.S.R. goes against the revolution and helps the revolutionists' enemies.[154] "Communists will call upon all toilers to work, with all the means at their disposal and at any price, for the victory of the Red army over the armies of the imperialists."[155]

Thus, revolutionary movements are no longer the key weapon of revolution that must be supported by the U.S.S.R., as Tukhachevsky had imagined. *The Soviet Union has become the key instrument of revolution that must be supported by the revolutionary forces abroad.* This great theoretical change led to the program of the Communist International of 1928.

This modification, of course, did not mean that the soviets would withhold help from foreign revolutions. After all, valid revolution abroad must strengthen the communists in Russia, but communist revolutions like that in Hungary (1919), which was crushed because of its isolation, do not advance the cause. Nevertheless, Stalin vowed that the dictatorship of the proletariat would never again look on quietly while the interventionists (the capitalist countries) were defeating a revolutionary movement. Stalin did not commit himself clearly as to the methods by which, in such a case, the Soviet Union might react.

---

[152] *Sochineniya, op. cit.,* VII, 26.

[153] *Strategy and Tactics, op. cit.,* p. 96.

[154] *Sochineniya, op. cit.,* X, 51.

[155] "Seventh World Congress of the Communist International, Resolutions on the Report of Ercoli," quoted from *Strategy and Tactics, op. cit.,* p. 96. "Ercoli" is the Italian communist Palmiro Togliatti.

It is not absolutely necessary to make territorial contact with the revolutionary country. It is enough to bite the interventionists in those places on their own territory where they are most vulnerable in order that they would feel the danger and understand the reality of proletarian solidarity.[156]

Stalin clearly grasped the advantages of a strategy of indirect approach.

War is inevitable, Stalin severely criticized Sinovyev, who considered it merely "possible."[157] Yet emphasis on military methods does not mean that the Soviet Union must rush into aggressive war. In line with the traditional strategy of exploiting antagonisms arising between foreign countries, Stalin's prescription, model 1925, was as follows:

If war begins we shall not be able to remain sitting on our hands. We shall be forced to enter into it. *But we must enter it last.* We shall enter the war in order to throw a decisive weight on the scales and thus change the balance of power. Hence, the conclusion: we must be ready for everything.[158]

To leave no doubt about his basic intention, Stalin took time to raise weighty objections to pacifist literature. We need, he explained, a literature describing the horrors of imperialist wars but not of other wars. This literature ought to explain the need to overthrow imperialistic governments. But it should not state or imply that bolsheviks are against all wars. Bolsheviks are against imperialist and counterrevolutionary wars. *They are for wars of liberation and anti-imperialistic, revolutionary wars,* and this despite the fact that even "progressive" wars are not free of bloodshed but actually are very bloody.[159]

Stalin never became untrue to his fundamental principle which he formulated first in 1905 at Tiflis:

What revolution can be victorious without arms and what revolutionary would say down with arms? . . . What do we need in order to win? We need three things: first—arms, second—arms, third—arms and arms again.

[156] *Sochineniya, op. cit.,* II, 147. Stalin's strategy during the Korean war was in line with the above quotation.

[157] *Ibid.,* X, 47.

[158] *Ibid.,* VII, 13. (Italics added.)

[159] *Sochineniya, op. cit., XI,* 176, written in 1930.

4. Doctrinal Consolidation · 1928–1939

> *"Capitalism will not collapse automatically; it will not collapse if it is not given a push. No class, said Lenin, no regime falls unless it is pushed."*
>
> D. Z. MANUILSKI,
> *International Press Correspondence,*
> *Sept. 15, 1933, page 892.*

THE SIXTH WORLD CONGRESS

I. The Program

IN 1928, the Communist International was called into congress. It convened at a time when the usurpation of power by Stalin was virtually complete. The purpose of the congress was to prepare the proletariat for the war which the bolsheviks thought the impending economic crisis soon must generate.

The congress issued three different documents: the *Program* of the Communist International, the *Resolutions* on communist activities in colonial and dependent areas, and *The Struggle against Imperialist War and the Tasks of the Communists*.

These three documents bear the imprint of Stalin's thinking. They form the most comprehensive statement ever issued by the communists, and still must be considered as *the* basic communist program. The documents were never withdrawn or criticized. There are changes in detail and emphasis, and there are later additions, but communist international strategy and tactics have never been defined more authoritatively and thoroughly. And, most significantly, they have stood the test of time.

Despite the great importance of the Sixth World Congress, these documents are little known. The *Program* and the *Theses* on communism in the dependent areas are quoted occasionally, but the *Resolutions* on the tasks of the communists in case of war are rarely considered. Yet together they form the *Mein Kampf* of the bolshevik movement.

The *Program* of the Communist International was based on the premise that imperialism "inevitably" will give rise to wars which will shake the system of international relationships and, therefore, "inexorably" lead to the world proletarian revolution.[1]

A second assumption was that the struggle between the imperialist bourgeoisie and the proletariat more and more was assuming an "international character." In full agreement with Tukhachevsky's criticism,[2] this superseded the old Marxian idea that the struggle between bourgeoisie and proletariat takes place largely on the national scene.

The Comintern *Program* described itself as the "supreme critical generalization of the whole body of historical experience of the international revolutionary proletarian movement" and as the "program of struggle" for world communism.[3]

The *Program's* analysis demonstrated that local crises and wars were giving way to world crises and world wars. Struggles between isolated and single groups were becoming nationwide conflicts which ultimately must lead to international struggles of the world proletariat against the world bourgeoisie. The workers and oppressed peoples were teaming up against the capitalists.[4] This development had been enhanced by the proletariat's seizure of state power and its newly won capability of conducting the struggle on an "enormous and really world scale." "The working class of the world has now its own state—the one and only fatherland of the international proletariat."[5]

As a result "of the first round of imperialist wars," a fundamental antagonism arose between the Soviet Union and the capitalist world.[6] Together with the conflicts between imperialist states, the rising of the masses in the colonial countries, and the action of the revolutionary proletariat in the imperialist states, this antagonism is corroding the power of world capitalism. The international revolution is developing under the "hegemony exercised over the whole world revolu-

---

[1] *Blueprint for World Conquest as Outlined by the Communist International,* with an introduction by William Henry Chamberlin (Washington-Chicago, Human Events, 1946), p. 149.

[2] M. N. Tukhachevsky, *Voina klassov, stat'i 1919–1920* (Moscow, 1921), p. 50.

[3] *Blueprint for World Conquest, op. cit.,* pp. 151 f.

[4] *Ibid.,* p. 161.

[5] *Ibid.,* p. 174.

[6] *Ibid.,* p. 175.

tionary movement by the proletarian dictatorship in the USSR."[7]

Before the revolution can succeed, there must be a long period of transition, replete with general crises, proletarian civil wars, national wars, and colonial rebellions. There will be both peaceful and belligerent periods of coexistence between the capitalist and socialist systems. New soviet republics will emerge and unite. *Ultimately there will be a period of wars fought by the imperialist states against the soviet states.*[8]

Wars are recognized as *"constituent parts of the world proletarian revolution."* The final showdown between capitalism and socialism will assume the form of war.

The dictatorship of the proletariat is defined as the "continuation of the class struggle under new conditions." It is also defined as a "stubborn fight . . . against *external* capitalist enemies,"[9] as well as against the traditions of the old society, and against a new bourgeoisie that may spring up despite the victory of communism.[10] This stubborn fight will be bloody, violent, and military, but it also will make use of non-violent, economic, pedagogical, and administrative means.[11] (Psychological, political, and sociological means are not mentioned specifically, but there seems to be no doubt that these means would also be used.)

The dictatorship of the proletariat must bring about a "cultural revolution." Socialism calls for a "mass change of human nature."[12] The working class can transform itself during the transition period, but only by means of a violent revolution.

Hence, revolution is not only necessary because there is no other way of overthrowing the ruling class, but also because only in the process of revolution is the overthrowing class able to purge itself of the dross of the old society and become capable of creating a new society.

This is the exact counterpart of the German nationalistic doctrine of the *Stahlbad.* The nazis also hoped to regenerate mankind through war. *Les extrêmes se touchent.* Or, two horses from the same stable?

[7] *Ibid.,* p. 178.
[8] *Ibid.,* p. 184.
[9] Italics added.
[10] One of the contentions of Tito is that a new bourgeoisie has emerged in Russia in the form of soviet bureaucracy.
[11] *Blueprint for World Conquest, op. cit.,* p. 200.
[12] *Ibid.,* p. 206.

The Comintern *Program* presented a classification of the types of revolution. Revolutions can take place in highly developed capitalist countries, such as the United States, Germany, or Great Britain; in countries with a medium development of capitalism, such as Spain, Poland, or Hungary; in colonial or semicolonial countries, such as China or India; in dependent countries; or in truly backward countries as found in some parts of Africa. The *Program* also catalogued four roughly corresponding types of revolution: purely proletarian revolutions; revolutions of the bourgeois-democratic types which grow into proletarian revolutions; colonial revolutions; and wars of national liberation.

All these types of revolution will be used in the world revolutionary process. It is historically "inevitable" that the proletariat will come to power by a variety of means and at different rates of speed in various areas. The world dictatorship of the proletariat "comes only as the final result of the revolutionary process."[13] This constitutes a restatement, within a different context, of the idea that wars are a part of the world revolution and that peace will not come to the world until the communists have established a world dictatorship.

In countries with less than full development of capitalism, socialism may well be introduced by stages. The need for gradual progress is even more pronounced in colonial and backward areas. Struggles for national liberation and bourgeois-democratic revolutions may be a detour to socialism "provided they receive the assistance and support of the proletarian dictatorship and of the international proletarian movement generally." Once the intermediate stage is reached, for example, a bourgeois-democratic revolution accomplished, it must be driven forward into a communist seizure of power.[14]

In highly developed capitalist countries, no intermediary stages need be introduced. There should be a direct transition to the dictatorship of the proletariat. The *Program* was silent as to the means by which this rapid transition can be effected, nor did it state explicitly that the Soviet Union would provide help and assistance to the revolutionary movements in the advanced capitalist countries. *It is probable that the idea of the one-stage revolution in the advanced capitalist countries has since been modified as the magnitude of the task and*

---

[13] *Ibid.,* p. 208.
[14] This is a generalization from the Russian experience of 1917.

the revolutionary unreliability of the western proletariat has become apparent.[15]

The world revolutionary duties of the Soviet Union are recognized:[16] "The USSR inevitably becomes the base of the world movement of all oppressed classes, the center of international revolution, the greatest factor in world history." It is "the international driving force of the proletarian revolution that impels the proletariat of all countries to seize power." If the imperialist states should declare war on the U.S.S.R., the "international proletariat must retaliate . . . and struggle for the overthrow of the imperialist government."[17]

Thus, the interrelationship between war and revolution is emphasized. Yet it is partially concealed behind the contention that the imperialist states will attack the U.S.S.R. and that both proletarian revolution and revolutionary war would be merely measures of defense. There is no doubt that, at least till the advent of the atomic bomb, the soviets would have preferred war to come about through imperialist, rather than through communist, "aggression." Nor is there any doubt that the soviets will always camouflage aggression as a defense measure, or set up provocation disguising their opponents as the ostensible aggressors.

Imperialist war upon the Soviet Union must inevitably lead to mighty revolutionary outbreaks which will overwhelm capitalism "in a number of the so-called civilized countries," unleash victorious revolutions in colonies, broaden the bases of the proletarian dictatorship, and "with tremendous strides, bring nearer the final world victory of socialism."[18]

War is the road to communist revolution and to the world dictatorship of the communist party.

[15] Mao Tse-tung is one of those who does not believe that revolution can be successful "in a single throw." See his *New Democracy*, 1940, quoted from Robert Payne, *Mao Tse-tung, Ruler of Red China* (New York, Schuman, 1950), p. 183. Also, the familiar strategy of first popular and united front, then coalition government, and, finally, a people's democracy is based on the idea of bringing about revolution through a series of steps, alternating between violence and infiltration. Revolution by steps is also implicit in some of William Z. Foster's writings. A recent statement on the bourgeois-democratic phase of the communist revolution may be found in Otto Grotewohl, *La Rivoluzione del 1918 in Germania, Insegnamenti della Storia del Movimento Operaio Tedesco* (Rome, Rinascita, 1952), p. 147.

[16] *Blueprint for World Conquest, op. cit.,* p. 220.

[17] *Ibid.,* p. 223.

[18] *Ibid.,* p. 223.

II. Military Tasks of Foreign Communists

THE *Resolutions* of the Sixth World Congress dealing with *The Struggle against Imperialist War and the Tasks of the Communists* are based on the Comintern *Program*. They outline the strategy and tactics which communist parties in non-communist states should adopt during war. Since the *Resolutions* are addressed exclusively to communists outside the soviet orbit, and are designed to tell foreign communists how to support the Soviet Union, neither the role of the Russian communist party nor the tactics of the soviet state and armed forces are defined. The theme of revolutionary offensive war is alluded to, but never developed.

The *Resolutions* were concerned with defining the tasks of a foreign communist party when its particular nation was engaged in war. Three types of war were defined: wars between imperialist states; wars of imperialist counterrevolution against the proletarian revolution or against countries in which socialism is being built; and national revolutionary wars, especially of colonial countries against imperialism.[19]

Somewhat unobtrusively, the *Resolutions*[20] alluded to a fourth type of war as well, the "war staged by the proletariat itself, or by the proletarian state against imperialism." This, of course, is the offensive revolutionary war.

In the discussion of these various kinds of war, the *Resolutions* held that during World War I both sides were waging an imperialist war. During the subsequent war of intervention against the Soviet Union, only the imperialists waged a reactionary war, while the proletarian dictatorship was waging a revolutionary war. In an imperialist war against the Chinese revolution, should one occur, the capitalist powers would be engaging in an imperialist war, but the Chinese would be waging a just and revolutionary war. The war of an op-

[19] *The Struggle against Imperialist War and the Tasks of the Communists,* Resolution of the Sixth World Congress of the Communist International, July–August 1928 (New York, Workers Library Publishers, 1932), p. 10.

[20] *Ibid.,* p. 11. The communists decided early that any analysis indicating the importance of war in their theory and practice would hurt their cause. Therefore, they called for a systematic propaganda campaign to cover their tracks. (*Ibid.,* p. 7.) Seen from the vantage point of a later generation, it is clear that this propaganda campaign was successful. Many people are as yet unaware of the true communist doctrine on war.

pressed nation against imperialism must be considered "a part of the proletarian world revolution."

In the treatment of national liberation wars, the *Resolutions* specifically do not state that they will occur only in Asia and Africa. Such wars also may occur in Europe, where many national minorities are being oppressed. "Poland and Rumania cruelly oppress with a bloody hand the White Russian, Ukrainian, and Bessarabian populations—who look longingly towards their soviet fatherland."[21] Also forecast were "national wars of the Latin American countries against United States imperialism." There is a tendency, we are told, for these wars and rebellions to transform themselves into "proletarian wars and rebellions."[22]

As these various wars arise, the tasks of the communists of the nations concerned are clearly described. The proletariat must fight against imperialist wars "with a program of defeatism and the transformation of the war into a civil war against the bourgeoisie." If imperialists fight other imperialists, the proletariat in both camps has an identical program of bringing defeat and civil war to both countries. In an imperialist war waged against a socialist or national revolutionary state, the proletariat must support the nonimperialist side and organize "for the defense of national revolutions and of the countries of the proletarian dictatorship." In an offensive revolutionary war, the duty of the proletariat is to defend the socialist country.

If the character of war changes, the strategy of the proletariat must change accordingly. An excellent example is found in the behavior of the U.S. communist party which, on June 22, 1941, reversed its attitude toward World War II, stopped its pacifist campaign, and became vociferously interventionist, all in accordance with doctrine laid down thirteen years before.

The conventional differentiation between offensive (that is, aggressive) and defensive wars is meaningless. It does not matter who fires the first shot. The nature of a war should not be analyzed in a military, but in a historical and political, sense: "The question primarily is not, who is the aggressor, who is waging an unjust war, but, who represents reaction, the counter-revolution and exploitation; who is on the imperialist side, and against the national pro-

21 *Ibid.*, p. 33.
22 *Ibid.*

letarian revolution?"[23] By definition, the aggressor is he who "represents reaction, the counter-revolution and exploitation." The others are angels—always and everywhere.

How should the communists go about their various tasks? First and foremost, they must infiltrate, even before the war, into the armed forces and the civilian defense organizations. Military disintegration work should never be considered from an "abstract, purely propagandist and agitational point of view."[24] The communists in the armed forces must fight for the right of the soldiers to organize in trade unions and to attend political meetings. Such demands must be properly timed—army morale and the political situation must be taken into account: "For example, the demand for the election of officers, as a rule, can be advanced only when the army has reached an advanced stage of disintegration."[25]

Under certain conditions the communists should skip such intermediate steps and strike directly for a complete disintegration of the armed forces.[26] In this connection, great emphasis was laid on the fraternization between "hostile" soldiers at the front. This technique is based on the premise that "in their imperialist war, the bourgeoisie must place weapons in the hands of the workers"; and that "in critical military situations, defeats, etc., they [lose] command over the mass armies."[27] According to the *Resolutions,* experience "has shown that mass fraternization inevitably leads to class differentiation in the armies and to armed conflicts between soldiers and officers."[28] Fraternization is a most powerful method of disintegrating military organizations.

Proposals for all-out reorganization are considered another means of attaining such an ambitious objective. For example, if there is a professional army, it should be reorganized as a national army, using "national militia" or "armed nation" slogans. When the situation is ripe, disintegration work must be superseded by the establishment of a revolutionary army.[29]

In addition to disintegrating the armed forces per se, the commu-

[23] *Ibid.,* p. 11.
[24] *Ibid.,* p. 36.
[25] *Ibid.,* p. 43.
[26] *Ibid.,* p. 42.
[27] *Ibid.,* p. 26.
[28] *Ibid.,* p. 24.
[29] *Ibid.,* pp. 47–49.

nists must work toward disarming and dissolving the gendarmerie, police, special security forces, and "fascist leagues."[30]

In short, the *Resolutions* follow Engels's idea that *mass militarization must result in the disintegration of all armies from within.* Hence, communists must not boycott bourgeois armies, but join them, learn the trade of arms, stimulate and seize revolutionary control of the process of internal disintegration. "At the proper moment [they must] turn their weapons against the bourgeoisie."[31]

Simultaneously, the communists must work politically against the government, that is, accelerate deterioration of home morale through lavish use of the peace slogan and prepare for insurrection.[32] The revolutionary situation will probably occur "as the result of military defeat."[33] If a revolutionary situation exists, if "the broad masses of the working class" are in favor of rebellion, and if there is a communist "capacity for mass action,"[34] then the uprising must be carried out offensively.

In the case of war against the Soviet Union, the same general rules hold, although additional action is demanded. In countries where the local communist party disposes of strong revolutionary organizations, guerrilla units should be formed immediately.[35] The party should employ at the earliest possible moment, even "prior to the outbreak of the war and during mobilization, . . . the weapon of mass strikes and the general strike."[36] The communists should see to it that "the conditions favorable for transforming a war against the Soviet Union into civil war against the bourgeoisie will be much

---

[30] *Ibid.*, p. 40. These concepts are developed more fully below in the subchapter entitled "Antimilitarism."

[31] *Ibid.*, p. 23. On the interesting subject of mass armies, see Hoffman Nickerson, *The Armed Horde 1793–1939, A Study of the Rise, Survival and Decline of the Mass Army* (2nd ed., New York, Putnam, 1942).

[32] The peace slogan—the call for *immediate peace*—must not be used always. It applies only to communists living in states which are fighting an imperialist and counterrevolutionary war. The *Resolutions* repeated Lenin's saying that the revolutionary proletariat "cannot be against every war," since war "is a continuation of the politics of certain classes by other means." (P. 10.) The proletariat must make a careful study of the historical and political class meaning of each war, analyze the war from the "viewpoint of the international revolution." The only criterion is to help the revolution and the Soviet Union.

[33] Nickerson, *op. cit.*, p. 26.

[34] *Ibid.*, pp. 20 f.

[35] *Ibid.*, p. 24.

[36] *Ibid.*, p. 29.

more speedily created than in an ordinary imperialistic war."[37]

In a conventional war, actual rebellion should be undertaken only if the chance of success is good. However, in the case of a war against the Soviet Union, the interests of the "class struggle at home in each country" must be subordinated to "considerations for the outcome of the war at the front."[38] In this event, workers in capitalist countries must not allow themselves to be scared away from supporting the Red army and from expressing this support by fighting against their own bourgeoisie.[39]

En clair: uprisings may have to be launched even if there is no chance of success, provided the insurrection facilitates the operations of the Russian armed forces. Thus, as already pointed out, the fully developed soviet doctrine demands that revolutionary forces abroad be used as auxiliaries of the Red army.[40]

The *Resolutions* pose a strange riddle: it is stated specifically that "the overthrow of capitalism is impossible without force, without armed uprising and proletarian wars against the bourgeoisie."[41] But we are also told that the communists "in the interests of the masses of the workers and of all the toilers who bear the brunt of the sacrifice entailed by war, wage a persistent fight against imperialist war and strive to prevent imperialist war by proletarian revolution."[42] The overthrow of the bourgeoisie, therefore, requires war, and yet the communists committed to that overthrow are opposing war.

Actually, the solution to the puzzle is not difficult to find. According to the communists, war is inevitable. War will come regardless of any pacifist propaganda which the communists make or fail to make. Imperialist wars can be prevented only through the elimination of the bourgeoisie in the most important countries,[43] but such

---

[37] *Ibid.,* p. 28.

[38] *Ibid.,* p. 29.

[39] *Ibid.,* p. 29.

[40] The oath of membership in the U. S. communist party contained this vow: "I pledge myself to rally the masses to defend the Soviet Union, the land of victorious Socialism." See J. Peters, *A Manual on Organization* (New York, Workers Library Publishers, July 1935), p. 105. This important manual was reproduced by the Bi-Partisan League of Ohio under the title *Secrets of the Communist Party Exposed* (Columbus, Ohio, State Publishing Company, 1947).

[41] *The Struggle against Imperialist War, op. cit.,* p. 9.

[42] *Ibid.,* p. 12.

[43] *Ibid.,* p. 8.

an event is most improbable before the outbreak of hostilities. Hence, the soviets devised a strategy of eating their cake and having it, too. A resolute opposition to war would provide the communists with gradually increasing popular support and give them a chance to stimulate pacifist sentiments, that is, lay the foundations for tactics of "defeatism." By posing as champions of peace, the communists would derive strength from those elements who, in the course of the war, lose their patriotic fervor and become inclined to terminate the war at whatever price. Thus, the fight against war is seen as the best cover and lever to build up a revolutionary organization. By fighting for defeat and immediate "peace" or surrender, the communists exploit war to create revolutionary situations and to launch revolutionary attacks.

War and revolution are two sides of one coin. On the one hand, wars against the Soviet Union will arise necessarily and inevitably.[44] On the other, the revolutionary war of the proletarian dictatorship is but "a continuation of revolutionary *peace* policy 'by other means.' "[45] It is all in line with Marx's dictum that the last word of the social sciences will be war and the bloody struggle for annihilation.[46]

III. The Oriental Flank

THE COMMUNISTS must learn how to utilize each and every conflict, to develop such conflicts and to broaden their significance, to connect them with the agitation for revolutionary slogans, to spread the news of these conflicts among the wide masses, to arouse these masses to independent, open manifestations in support of their own demands.[47]

[44] *Ibid.*, p. 31.

[45] *Ibid.*, p. 31. (Italics added.)

[46] Timothy Taracouzio, *War and Peace in Soviet Diplomacy* (New York, Macmillan, 1940), p. 25.

[47] "Theses and Resolutions of the Sixth World Congress of the Communist International, Theses on the Revolutionary Movement in the Colonies and Semi-Colonies," *International Press Correspondence* (Vienna, December 12, 1928), VIII, No. 88, p. 1668. The terms "colonies" and "semi-colonies" refer less to dependent areas in Africa than to countries like China, Egypt, Mexico, and so forth. It should not be forgotten that the Soviet Union also possesses a vast colonial empire in Asia.

As we have seen, the Sixth World Congress taught the communists how to exploit war in the interest of revolution. It also taught them to combine class war with race war. This unexpected combination climaxed a long history of revision of traditional socialist concepts.

The origins of the eastern orientation. What is the geopolitics of bolshevism? By what route do the bolsheviks plan to conquer the world? It is frequently asserted that Europe is the primary goal of soviet expansion and, even, that the bolsheviks are committed to start the world revolution in Europe. They are assumed to believe that with Europe under their control, the whole globe would be theirs.

It was axiomatic during the early period of the communist movement that the revolution would be carried out by the proletariat. Hence, it had to take place in countries possessing an industrial proletariat. The failure of the revolution of 1905 forced Lenin to reevaluate this traditional reliance on the proletarian class. Never embarrassed by dogmatic ballast, Lenin began to argue that there must be an alliance between proletariat and peasantry, or there would be no revolution. Lenin's new sociological strategy was borne out by events: the October revolution of 1917 was made, essentially, by the peasant-soldier. It never would have happened but for the alliance between proletariat and peasantry.[48]

Once the ideological hurdles were cleared and the peasant was recognized as a revolutionary force, it was inevitable that the bolsheviks should become interested in the Orient. By August 1908, Lenin took notice of the "sharpening of the revolutionary democratic struggle in Asia." Born strategist that he was, he comprehended the world revolutionary significance of the Oriental crisis: "The Russian revolution possesses a great international ally both in Europe and in Asia."[49]

In 1911, under the impact of the Chinese revolution, Lenin spoke about a "progressive Asia" which he contrasted with a "backward Europe," intimating that, perhaps, the revolution in the Orient was

---

[48] Lenin, "The Two Tactics of Social Democracy in the Democratic Revolution," *Selected Works* (New York, International Publishers, 1943), III, 72, 82, 109. By contrast, this alliance was not accomplished in the German revolution. See Grotewohl, *op. cit.,* p. 83.

[49] *Selected Works, op. cit.,* IV, 303.

closer at hand than a communist triumph in the Occident. Within a few months he latched on to a very significant fact: "In very many and very essential respects Russia is undoubtedly an Asiatic country and, moreover, one of the wildest, most medieval and shamefully backward of Asiatic countries."[50]

It seems that, even at that early juncture, Lenin's interest in the Orient was not entirely platonic. During 1911, one of his trusted assistants, Veltman-Pavlovich, established, on Lenin's orders, close contacts with Oriental liberation movements, especially with Turkish, Persian, and Hindu groups.[51] These contacts primarily served the exchange of tactical information. But they also laid the foundations for subsequent strategic co-operation.

Between 1912 and 1917, Lenin's attention quite naturally centered almost exclusively on European affairs. However, in various papers discussing the "national question," he called attention to developments in China, Persia, and in the colonial dependencies. He also pointed out the connection between the revolutionary struggles in the West and the national liberation movements in the East.[52]

It is amusing to note that Stalin, allegedly the originator of the eastern orientation of bolshevism, in his book on *Marxism and the National Question* (1913), discussed nationality problems in Austria and Russia, the Jewish question, and racial tensions in the Caucasus, but made only cursory remarks about Asia. He merely stated that Russia was situated between Europe and Asia and, more specifically, between Austria and China. He also held that the growth of the liberation movement in Asia was inevitable. But that was all.

Immediately after the bolshevik seizure of power in Russia, Lenin and Stalin, in one of their first major governmental acts on December 7, 1917, issued a proclamation to the *Moslem workmen of Russia and the East*. This proclamation called on the Moslems to rise up against their oppressors and put an end to foreign domination. It was dictated by the needs of the incipient civil war and by the bolshevik desire to extend its power over Asiatic Russia. Eager to obtain peace from Turkey, the proclamation promised that Constantinople would remain in the hands of the Mohammedans. The bolsheviks

[50] *Ibid.*, IV, 306.

[51] *La Vague rouge,* Paris, December 1929, p. 15. This information was derived from speeches made at Veltman's burial.

[52] For example: *Selected Works, op. cit.*, V, 275 f., written in March 1916.

also aimed at reducing British freedom of action against the Islamic parts of Russia.

One year later, on the occasion of the first anniversary of the bolshevik coup, Stalin wrote an article entitled *The October Revolution and the National Question*. According to him, the international significance of the revolution lay in the fact that it was erecting "a bridge between the socialist West and the enslaved East, having created a new line of revolutions against world imperialism, extending from the proletarians of the West, through the Russian revolution, to the oppressed nations of the East." For the first time, the "fight against imperialism" was linked explicitly with "the question of the emancipation of the colonies."[53]

Outlining the tasks of the Third International in July 1919, Lenin took to task the socialist parties in the capitalist countries which "fail to wage a revolutionary struggle within 'their own' colonies for the overthrow of 'their own' bourgeoisie, which do not systematically assist the revolutionary work which has already commenced everywhere in the colonies, which do not send arms and literature to the revolutionary parties in the colonies." In other words, the Third International was called upon to organize the revolutionary struggle in the colonies and to send arms and literature to the various revolutionary movements in the Orient.[54]

To defend themselves against the British invasion of the Caucasus and to stave off contemplated British forays into Turkestan, the bolsheviks did their share in stimulating the independence movements that were springing up in Egypt, Afghanistan, and India. Offensively, to be sure, the bolsheviks were concentrating on a revolution in Germany. But when it was clear that this revolution had failed, and that the European revolutionary tide was "ebbing," Lenin thought that the Orient held out the greatest promise for revolutionary expansion.

In a speech delivered to the second congress of the Communist International (July 19, 1920), Lenin treated his listeners to a few basic statistics. According to him, 1,250,000,000 colonial and semicolonial people were living "in oppression." Another quarter of a

---

[53] Stalin, *Marxism and the National and Colonial Question* (New York, Marxist Library, International Publishers, no year, probably around 1935), pp. 75 f.

[54] *Selected Works, op. cit.,* X, 46. (Italics in original.)

billion people were living in countries defeated during the war, and had fallen "into economic dependence upon America." Only one quarter of a billion people were living in the advanced capitalist countries and were benefiting from the partition of the world. Thus, Lenin divided the world into 14 per cent "haves" (disregarding the class cleavages within the victorious capitalist countries) and 86 per cent "have-nots." "I would like you to memorize this picture of the world, for all the fundamental contradictions of capitalism, of imperialism, which are leading to revolution . . . are all connected with this division of the population of the world."[55]

Lenin called upon the second world congress to amalgamate the proletariat in the advanced capitalist countries with the oppressed masses of the eastern countries.

World Imperialism must fall when the revolutionary onslaught of the exploited and oppressed workers in each country, overcoming the resistance of the petty-bourgeois elements and the influence of the small upper stratum of the labor aristocracy, will unite with the revolutionary onslaught of hundreds of millions of people who up to now have stood outside of history and have been regarded merely as the object of history.[56]

A few days later, on July 26, 1920, Lenin changed his statistics somewhat and concentrated merely on the 70 per cent of the world population which, in the Orient, were suffering from imperialist oppression. "This distinction, the idea of dividing the nations into oppressing and oppressed nations,"[57] became the cornerstone of bolshevik strategy. It supplemented, and occasionally superseded, the old division between oppressing and oppressed classes.

Lenin went one step further and suggested that it might no longer be necessary in backward countries to initiate the establishment of the proletarian dictatorship by a bourgeois-democratic revolution. Thus, he scrapped one of the oldest tenets of Marxism, that the socialist revolution could occur only after a capitalist "mode of production" has been organized.

The communist international must lay down, and give the theoretical grounds for, the proposition that, with the aid of the proletariat of the most advanced countries, the backward countries may pass to the soviet

[55] *Ibid.*, X, 183.
[56] *Ibid.*, p. 197.
[57] *Ibid.*, p. 240.

system and, after passing through a definite stage of development, to communism, without passing through the capitalist stage of development.[58]

The second congress adopted the notorious "conditions of admission to the Communist International." These conditions included Point 8, drafted by Lenin, which called for support of colonial liberation movements, for the expulsion of the imperialists from the colonies, and for agitation "among the armed forces . . . against all oppression of colonial peoples."[59] In short, the second world congress of the Communist International (1920) was the true starting point of the bolshevik "eastern orientation."

As a follow-up, there met at Baku a *Congress of the Peoples of the East* (September 1920).[60] Actually, this was predominantly a congress of Near and Middle East peoples. The main effort was directed at the Moslems, whom Sinovyev summoned to a "holy war" against British imperialism. A short while later, when the bolsheviks extended their rule to the areas east of Lake Baikal and got into trouble with Japan, they convened at Moscow a new congress which preoccupied itself, almost exclusively, with the Far East (January 1922).[61] This congress symbolized an ever more radical departure from the erstwhile European orientation and initiated the specifically far-eastern strategy of the bolsheviks.

In the meantime, Stalin, the party's expert on the national question, had elaborated on the theory of the Oriental revolution. Reporting to the tenth congress of the Russian communist party on the *Immediate Tasks of the Party in Connection with the National Problem* (March 10, 1921), Stalin pointed out that, as a result of colonial expansion, the old national states of the West "ceased to be national states" and hence had become more vulnerable to revolutionary at-

[58] *Ibid.*, p. 243.

[59] *Ibid.*, p. 203. The *Program* discussed above did not accept this particular view of Lenin's.

[60] The creation of the University of the Peoples of the East in 1921 was another follow-up. It preceded by several years the founding of the Lenin Institute devoted to the education of western communists. Both the Baku congress and this university, as well as a simultaneously created Scientific Group for the Study of the Orient which was placed under the central committee, were organized by Veltman-Pavlovich.

[61] *Der Ferne Osten, Erster Kongress der Revolutionären Organisationen der Ostvölker* (Hamburg, Hoym, 1922).

tack. He asserted that part of the power of the imperialist states was based on the colonies. Colonial competition between the imperialist powers produces contradictions which "give rise to war." "These contradictions do exist," he repeated, "and it is on them that the activities of the people's commissariat of foreign affairs are based."[62] And Stalin went one step further: "The abolition of national oppression in Europe is inconceivable without the emancipation of the colonial peoples of Asia and Africa from the oppression of imperialism. . . . The former is organically bound up with the latter."[63]

In January 1923, Sun Yat-sen, China's most prominent political leader, met the soviet emissary Adolf A. Joffe in Shanghai and worked out with him a basis of co-operation between the Kuomintang and the bolsheviks. The choice of Joffe as chief bolshevik negotiator is self-revealing. During 1918, Joffe had been ambassador to Germany where he served as main contact man between the bolsheviks and the German revolutionary movement. His transfer to China signified a fundamental change in strategy: China replaced Germany as the primary target of communist expansion.

Inasmuch as Joffe negotiated the admission of the Chinese communists into the Kuomintang, the agreement with Sun Yat-sen also signified a considerable change in tactics: for the first time, the Trojan-horse technique was applied on a truly strategic scale. Infiltration and policy perversion were to be used as the chief weapons of the communist revolutionaries in China at that time.

While Joffe was traveling to China, Lenin's health broke down. On March 2, 1923, the bolshevik leader dictated what was probably his last coherent statement; only one later communication from Lenin has become known, a brief note of March 5, 1925, announcing the severance of "all personal and comradely relations with Stalin."

Lenin's last article is entitled: *Better Fewer, But Better*. It revealed many doubts in the dictator's mind. He had become greatly worried about the survival chances of the bolshevik regime. But there was one great hope:

In the last analysis, the outcome of the struggle will be determined by the fact that Russia, India, China, etc., constitute the overwhelming majority of the population of the globe. And it is precisely this majority of the

---

[62] *Marxism and the National and Colonial Question, op. cit.*, pp. 100–5.
[63] *Ibid.*, p. 112.

population that, during the past few years, has been drawn into the struggle of its emancipation with extraordinary rapidity, so that in this respect there cannot be the slightest shadow of doubt what the final outcome of the world struggle will be. In this sense, the final victory of socialism is fully and absolutely assured.[64]

Rephrased, Lenin told us that the final victory of socialism is dependent upon revolution in India and China. *Revolution in the Orient is the indispensable condition for the attainment of bolshevik world rule. This theorem is Lenin's true political testament.* It far overshadows in importance his much more famous and somewhat earlier "testament" bequeathing to posterity his opinions about the comrades in the Politburo.[65]

In August 1923, Chiang Kai-shek went to Moscow and negotiated an outright alliance between the Kuomintang and soviet Russia. This alliance led to the appointment of the notorious Mikhail M. Borodin as political adviser to the Chinese government. In November 1923 a new communist uprising failed in Germany. In the face of this new disaster in Europe, the fifth congress of the Communist International (1924) decided to shift the revolutionary offensive against the East. The "marching route" of the communist forces was changed. The new road to world victory led through Asia.[66]

In a subsequent speech of March 1925, Sinovyev gave three reasons for this change of route. First, the East contains "the great reserves of the revolution," which, translated from bolshevik lingo, means that outside of Russia the Oriental revolutionary movements constitute the main force of the world revolution. Furthermore, the revolutionary situation was maturing much more rapidly in the East than in the West. And third, as a result of the Oriental turmoil, the class struggles in the western countries would become intensified.[67]

With the fifth world congress and this speech of Sinovyev, the Leninist phase of bolshevik world strategy came to a close.

Lenin was barely dead when Stalin delivered his lectures on the

[64] *Selected Works, op. cit.,* IX, 400.

[65] Dated December 25, 1922, with a postscript of January 4, 1923.

[66] G. Sinovyev, *Die Weltpartei des Leninismus* (Hamburg, Hoym, 1924), pp. 227 f. According to Sinovyev, Lenin "during the last years of his life" often asserted "that what is happening in the West is very important, but what is happening in the East is even more important because it gives world significance to the revolution." *Ibid.,* p. 193.

[67] Sinovyev, *Ueber die Bolschevisierung der Parteien* (Hamburg, Hoym, 1925), pp. 20, 28.

Foundations of Leninism at the University of Sverdlov and thus established his claim to the theoretical and ideological leadership of world communism. With respect to our present problem, Stalin laid down the following points: (1) Germany is no longer the center of the revolutionary movement;[68] (2) "A coalition between the proletarian revolution in Europe and the colonial revolution in the East in a united world front of revolution against the world front of imperialism is inevitable"; (3) This coalition between the western proletariat and the eastern masses derives its special importance from the fact that "under imperialism wars cannot be averted";[69] (4) "The chain of the imperialist front must, as a rule, give way where the links are weaker and, at all events, not necessarily where capitalism is more developed." Stalin implied that while this chain still may break in Germany, it was more likely that it would break in India or in other Oriental countries.[70] Particular hopes were placed by Stalin on the concept that the combination of proletarian revolution with peasant wars and wars of national liberation "could not fail to jeopardize the most deep-seated reserves of capital."[71]

For the next three years, the theory of Oriental revolution did not change. During the summer of 1927, however, the failure of the communist maneuvers in China forced Stalin to re-evaluate his tactics. He came up with the following additional points:

(1) At certain periods the national bourgeoisie in colonial countries may support the revolutionary movement against foreign imperialism. Hence, the revolutionaries should enter into temporary alliances with such a national bourgeoisie.

(2) Colonial revolutions take place in three stages rather than in

[68] Stalin, *Problems of Leninism* (Moscow, Foreign Languages Publishing House, 1940), pp. 7 f.

[69] *Ibid.,* p. 19.

[70] *Ibid.,* pp. 21, 54 f.

[71] First expressed on the fifth anniversary of the revolution, November 7, 1923, *Marxism and the National and Colonial Question, op. cit.,* p. 187: "The October revolution undoubtedly represented that happy combination of a peasant war and a proletarian revolution. . . . The proletariat can seize power and retain it, provided it is able to sever the middle strata, especially the peasantry, from the capitalist class and provided it is able to convert these strata from reserves of capital into reserves of the proletariat. . . . The October revolution went further and . . . managed to achieve a combination of the proletarian revolution" not only with "a peasant war" but also with a national war. Stalin pointed out that "oppressed nationalities are usually oppressed not only as peasants and as urban working tradesfolk, but also as nationalities." See also, Stalin, *Sochineniya* (Moscow, Orgis, 1946), V, 334 f.

two, as is usual in capitalist countries. In Russia, the bourgeois-democratic revolution, "with the agrarian movement as its main axis," was followed by the proletarian seizure of power. In China, the first stage of the revolution was characterized by the attack of the national united front against foreign imperialism. The second stage was the bourgeois-democratic revolution which developed to a point where "the bourgeoisie deserted the revolution and the agrarian movement grew into a mighty revolution." The third stage will be the soviet revolution.[72]

(3) The proletariat participating in an Oriental revolution must "put forward a radical agrarian program." Otherwise, "it will be unable to draw the peasantry into the revolutionary struggle and will forfeit its hegemony in the national liberation movement." "We are decidedly in favor of the land actually being seized by the masses from below."[73] Once in power, revolutionary governments must be identified with the agrarian revolution.

(4) The role and weight of the proletariat in Oriental societies, however, should not be underrated. Industrial strikes must be organized to give the growing proletariat "class-consciousness."

(5) The work of communist cells in the army must be intensified[74] to disintegrate hostile divisions, disorganize the rear, and give assistance to peasant uprisings.

(6) The communists must arm the workers and peasants and establish their "own reliable army." "Otherwise there can be no guarantee against failures."[75]

(7) The communists within the Kuomintang must exploit their positions of infiltration "to secure the resignation or expulsion of the Rights from the Kuomintang." Reliable (that is, communist) elements must be placed in the central committee of the Kuomintang to change "the present structure" of that organization. Infiltration must be enlarged to effect capture[76] and bring the Kuomintang under communist control. The erstwhile alliance was to be replaced by domination.

[72] *Marxism and the National and Colonial Question, op. cit.,* p. 235. According to Stalin, the Chinese revolution in 1927 was passing through the second phase of its development.

[73] *Ibid.,* p. 249.

[74] *Ibid.,* pp. 239, 249. This was directed against the Kuomintang armies at the very time when the communists still held membership in that party.

[75] *Ibid.,* pp. 240, 249.

[76] *Ibid.,* pp. 240, 249.

(8) Peasants committees must be transformed into "actual organs of power, accompanied by armed self-defense." The revolutionary forces must take and hold territory.[77]

Perhaps the most significant statement on communist Oriental strategy was made by Stalin as early as 1921:

If Europe and America may be called the *front,* the scene of the main engagements between socialism and imperialism, the non-sovereign nations and the colonies, with their raw materials, fuel, food and vast store of human material, should be regarded as the *rear,* the reserve of imperialism. In order to win a war one must not only triumph at the front but also revolutionize the enemy's rear, his reserves. Hence the victory of the world proletarian revolution may be regarded as assured *only* if the proletariat is able to combine its own revolutionary struggle with the movement for emancipation of the toiling masses of the non-sovereign nations and the colonies against the power of the imperialists and for a dictatorship of the proletariat.[78]

The Codification, 1928. The true significance of the "eastern orientation" lies as much in the change of the "marching route" as in the change of sociological strategy: the peasant became the most important soldier of the revolution. As already pointed out, the old concept that the communist revolution must needs be accomplished by the proletariat had been modified, quite openly, before and during 1917. During the Sixth World Congress it was abandoned, except in wording. The proletariat had proved disappointing as a revolutionary vehicle. Of course, the proletariat was not written off as a revolutionary force, but the stringent need for additional revolutionary energies was recognized.

The Sixth World Congress told the comrades all over the world that they must mobilize these additional energies among the Oriental peoples and, more specifically, among the peasants of Asia. And, in fact, the thesis of the Orient's probable revolutionary development proved more valid than the idea of the proletarian world revolution. More than thirty years of history show that, far from being the liquidator of capitalism, communism as a home-grown movement usually flourishes in countries with precapitalist economies.[79] In the

[77] *Ibid.,* p. 240.
[78] *Ibid.,* p. 115. (Italics added.)
[79] G. F. Achminow, *Die Macht im Hintergrund, Totengraeber des Kommunismus* (Ulm, Spaten Verlag, 1950), pp. 33 f. Achminow is a young Russian emigré whose book presents an excellent sociological analysis of soviet

truly capitalist countries, the working classes buy real estate and common stock but do not invest in expropriation and revolution.

The general idea of communist colonial strategy, as codified by the Sixth World Congress, was that "the colonies have become a perpetual source of conflicts and wars between the imperialists"; that they were a most vulnerable sector of the "imperialist front"; and that, at the same time, "the vast colonial and semi-colonial world has become an unquenchable blazing hearth of the revolutionary mass movement."

The revolutionary movement in the colonies and semicolonies, the communists were told, has

an immediate connection with the great epoch-making struggle between the capitalist and socialist systems—a struggle which at present is being conducted on a world scale by imperialism against the USSR and inside each separate capitalist country between bourgeois class rule and the communist movement.[80]

Communists should use the colonies and dependent areas as a lever to induce and stimulate international conflict. They should incite disputes over, and troubles within, the colonies. Revolutionary movements in the colonies are auxiliary forces of the Soviet Union and the communist movement. "Cooperation of the revolutionary proletariat of the whole world and of the toiling masses of the colonies represents the surest guarantee of victory over imperialism."

The strategy for the utilization of colonial revolutionary movements was conceived dialectically. The communists in the colonies were to organize revolutionary activity either openly or secretly within a national liberation movement. Simultaneously, they were to co-ordinate their efforts with the communist parties in the parent countries. The western parties, in the parent countries themselves, were instructed to agitate for colonial "emancipation," to develop the colonial question as a cleavage in domestic politics, and to weaken or prevent repressive military action against colonial unrest.

The communists expected that international conflicts and political disturbances in the colony-holding countries would facilitate colonial

society. He emphasizes that the communist movements in capitalist countries are not based on the proletariat but on the impoverished intelligentsia and on would-be industrial managers and technicians (p. 89).

[80] "Theses and Resolutions," *International Press Correspondence, op. cit.,* p. 1661.

revolution. Intervention against one colonial rebellion would contribute to risings in other colonies.

Armies of the imperialist powers fighting in the colonies were considered vulnerable to attack through antimilitarist action and propaganda. Western soldiers and colonial troops were to be induced to fraternize with the colonial revolutionaries and thus to help the revolution in the East and West.

Thus, the scheme is as follows:

Thesis: Colonial rebellions and revolutions lead to crises in capitalist countries, to military intervention, and to international conflict.

Double Antithesis: Intervention and conflict enable the western communists to increase the scope of their activities. Part of these activities are designed to aid colonial rebellions.

Intervention and conflict disperse the military and economic strength of the imperialist powers. Antimilitarist attack reduces the reliability of capitalist armies.

Synthesis: The Soviet Union will be strengthened.

The capitalist states will be weakened economically, politically, and militarily.

Revolutionary movements in the East and in the West will be strengthened.

Possible additional results: Revolutions, both of a communist or a national democratic type, may be successful either in the East or in the West, or in both. If so, the capitalist states would be deprived of bases, manpower, and resources—which may be added to the side of the revolution.

The communists recognized that revolutionary programs in the colonies involve methods different from those utilized in industrial countries. A proper proletariat is not found in a colonial country, nor is there a "revolutionary mass consciousness." Hence, the communists were instructed to further the tendencies of local bourgeois movements, to demand emancipation, and to associate themselves with nationalism and self-determination.[81] They also were to advocate the industrialization of the colonies, stimulate the growth of a proletariat, help build up trade unions, and thus create the social basis of a true communist revolution.

While furthering nationalism, the communists were to show to the colonial peoples that ultimately their problems could be solved only through communism. The "emancipatory movements" must be convinced "that there is no salvation for them except through alliance with the revolutionary proletariat, and through the victory of the world proletarian revolution over world imperialism."[82]

If the opportunity arose, and if the social and economic bases for a true proletarian movement had come into existence, communists were to push beyond the bourgeois-democratic rebellion into a truly communist revolution. While it was anticipated that most colonial revolutions would be accomplished by stages, the possibility was not excluded that a revolutionary attempt "may be able in one single mighty wave to achieve the conquest of power by the proletariat and peasantry."[83]

In addition to nationalism, the agrarian question was described as the second "axis" of approach. Slogans must accord with local agricultural conditions. "Class contradictions" in the villages must be enhanced. Agitation and propaganda should create revolutionary attitudes among the poorer peasants, who were to be told that communism would free them of "pre-capitalist and colonial conditions of exploitation and bondage." The communists, of course, did not contemplate a simple agrarian reform. They aimed at the "nationalization of the land."[84]

[81] *Ibid.*, p. 1670. Nationalism was to be embraced not only against the imperialist powers but also regionally, against the subjugation of one colonial people by another.

[82] *Ibid.*, p. 1661.

[83] *Ibid.*, p. 1669.

[84] *Ibid.*, p. 1665.

Furthermore, the communists were instructed to organize the urban poor, coolies, land tenants, students, women; to agitate against race, caste, and sex inequalities; and, above all, to win over the youth.

The Sixth Congress of the Communist International makes it obligatory for all communist parties in the colonies to render all possible assistance in the creation and development of the communist youth movement.[85]

The organizational approach of the communists in the colonies was to follow along three distinct lines: infiltration, the establishment of communist parties and organizations, and the setting up of "Red armies."

Infiltration was to be practiced on a maximum scale, particularly in those countries where open communist appeals showed little strength. Prescribed especially for use against peasant unions,[86] it was also to be employed against factories, trade unions, and political organizations. However, infiltration was never to be carried to the point where the communists would abandon the advocacy of a distinct political line: while working in non-communist organizations, communists never should cease working for communism. The communists were instructed not to trail other movements but to dominate and lead them. On the other hand, they were cautioned not to indulge in a radicalism which would isolate them from the masses.

The existence of a strong communist party "with a big mass influence" was described as the most important prerequisite for the "transition of the revolution to the socialist phase." The communists realized that there was an "excessively marked disproportion between the revolutionary situation and the weakness of the subjective factor." Hence, the creation of revolutionary organization and striking power represented "one of the most important and primary tasks of the Communist International." The party was told to work in the economic and ideological fields and to combine legal with illegal methods. As a colonial specialty it was acknowledged that "intellectuals" were to form the main cadres and propagandists of communist organizations.[87]

The tasks of the communist parties in the parent countries were

[85] *Ibid.,* p. 1672.
[86] *Ibid.,* p. 1671.
[87] *Ibid.,* pp. 1670 f.; see also pp. 1665, 1675.

to co-ordinate the revolutionary movements in the colonies and in the capitalist countries; to organize opposition and unrest against imperialism; to weaken, through propaganda, transport strikes, infiltration, and fraternization, the armies used in the colonial areas; and to oppose the colonial policies of the Second International.[88]

The establishment of Red armies was advocated, but the revolution was still seen in terms of "armed insurrection as the sole path to the completion of the bourgeois-democratic revolution and to the overthrow of the power of the imperialists, landlords and national bourgeoisie."[89] Since the problems of guerrilla and peasant war, as well as the importance of territorial conquest in civil war, were not discussed, these aspects of the *Theses* must be considered as out of date.

In 1928, the Comintern stated that "not a single section of the Communist International in the capitalist countries has succeeded to an adequate degree in mobilizing the masses for active support of the Chinese revolution." Since the Chinese revolution is now an accomplished fact, and since, at the second try, the Chinese communists were supported very effectively by their comrades in the capitalist countries, it will be interesting to see what other colonial revolutions the communists have in mind.

In addition to China, the Sixth World Congress concerned itself with the revolutionary movements in the following colonies and semi-colonies: Korea, India, Indonesia, Egypt, French North Africa, and Latin America. It may be deduced that these countries are among the primary objectives of revolutionary expansionism—a deduction borne out by the case of Korea as well as by subsequent events in Africa and the Middle East.

The *Theses* also discussed the "black belt" in the United States and the world position of the Negroes. What is the significance of this?

Would a revolutionary attack against the United States (as distinguished from a military attack) be planned to follow the pattern of a proletarian uprising? Perhaps, but the communists would hardly rely on a purely proletarian approach. Among other methods, they doubtless also would apply a "colonial" strategy against the United

---

[88] *Ibid.*, p. 1675.

[89] *Ibid.*, p. 1672; see also p. 1667. It should not be overlooked that insurrections would take place in conjunction with international war.

States. This kind of attack would be conducted through Latin America and to the extent possible, through the U.S. Negro population.[90]

The Sixth World Congress described Latin America as "one of the most important junction points of the antagonisms of the whole imperialist colonial system"[91] and called for its development as an area of intense revolutionary activity. The revolutionary fight in Latin America was to be directed against the landowners and the church and against American and British imperialism. Communists were instructed to co-ordinate their activities in Latin America and to work through "corresponding international organizations and also with the revolutionary proletariat in the United States."[92]

Revolutionary action in Latin America was to take the form of mass demonstrations, industrial strikes, general strikes, peasant and agricultural laborer risings, mutinies, partisan war, and military revolutions.

The *Theses* stressed the revolutionary usefulness of the following slogans: eight-hour working day, improvement of working conditions, expropriation of big land properties, confiscation of foreign and big enterprises, repudiation of state debts, liquidation of foreign controls, and the establishment of worker and peasant governments. The communists also called for the organization in Latin America of worker and peasant armies and for the conversion of standing armies into worker and peasant militias.[93]

It is well to bear in mind that while the *Theses* mentioned twelve Latin American countries, most of the specific discussion was devoted to Mexico.[94] Nor are the soviets oblivious to the world importance of the Latin American oil industry.

Insofar as the Negroes are concerned, the *Theses* divided them into four broad groups: the Negroes living in Central Africa; the colonial or semicolonial Negro states (for example, Haiti); the Union

[90] Since the exhumation of panslavism during World War II, the soviets have been devoting some attention to the possibility of attack through slavic minorities. The Chinese minority in the United States should not be forgotten in this connection.

[91] "Theses and Resolutions," *International Press Correspondence, op. cit.,* p. 1675.

[92] *Ibid.*

[93] *Ibid.*

[94] *Ibid.,* p. 1661.

of South Africa "where the negroes are the majority in relation to the white colonists"; and the U.S. and some Latin American countries where the Negroes constitute a significant minority.

The status of the American Negro was described in a way which the reader can imagine without difficulty. "The growth of a negro proletariat" in the United States was considered "the most important phenomenon of recent years."[95] The Comintern gave instructions to stimulate the "struggle for a complete and real equality of the negroes." It also ordered the setting-up of revolutionary Negro organizations.

Yet communist strategy went far beyond these standard measures; it envisaged that the predominantly Negro areas in the United States were to be given the "right of self-determination." The southern regions "in which compact negro masses are living" should be established as independent states. No more and no less.[96]

The white proletariat of these southern areas must be convinced that, together with the Negroes, it should fight against the "barbarous exploitation" by the American bourgeoisie.

Only the victorious proletarian revolution will completely and permanently solve the agrarian and national question of the southern United States in the interests of the overwhelming majority of the negro population of the country.[97]

In short, the communists aim at *the partition of the United States.* Fantastic? Let us not forget another pertinent quote from the *Theses:*

The proletariat of the USSR and the workers movement in the capitalist countries, headed by the Communist International, . . . are supporting and will more and more effectively support *in deeds* the emancipatory struggle of all colonial and *other dependent* peoples.[98]

[95] *Ibid.,* p. 1674.

[96] On the failure of this policy and on communist twists in the Negro question, see these thorough books: William A. Nolan, *Communism versus the Negro* (Chicago, Henry Regnery Co., 1951); Wilson Record, *The Negro and the Communist Party* (Chapel Hill, N. C., University of North Carolina Press, 1951).

[97] "Theses and Resolutions," *International Press Correspondence, op. cit.,* p. 1674. The same concept, of course, could equally apply to the Mexican minority in the continental southwestern states. It is unnecessary to remind the American reader that the hopes which the communists placed on our colored citizens were quite in vain.

[98] *Ibid.,* p. 1661. [Italics added.]

It cannot be said that the communists have failed to give solemn and early warning.

ANTIMILITARISM

EARLY in 1928 the bolsheviks decided to go all out for anti-militarist work. This decision was probably one of the most important in soviet history.

Demoralization of hostile armies had long been a communist objective. In 1908, Lenin wrote an article on the subject and praised the antimilitarist work done in Belgium and France.[99] The purpose of the article was to criticize both the right-wing socialist position that antimilitarist propaganda was unnecessary and the opposite thesis, propounded by Gustave Hervé, that all wars could be prevented by organized large-scale desertions and military strikes on the day of the declaration of war. Lenin argued that the proletariat cannot obligate itself to oppose every war. He cited Marx and Engels, who had called for wars by Germany and England against Russia[100] and reasoned that opposition to every war would deprive the proletariat "of the choice of the moment for the decisive battle and [leave] that choice to its enemies." Moreover, the specific device of the military strike might not be practical in the face of repressive measures.

The proletariat, Lenin said, may reply to war by military strike "if it finds it expedient and appropriate." But "it is not in the interests of the proletariat to bind itself down to this 'tactical recipe.' "[101]

[99] "Militant militarism and the anti-militarist tactics of social democracy," *Selected Works, op. cit.,* IV, 324–33. He called attention to the device of the "soldier's sou" practiced in France: Every week a worker paid one sou to the union. The sums were sent to the soldiers to remind them "that even while in soldier's uniform they belong to the exploited class and that they must not forget this under any circumstances." (P. 331.)

[100] *Ibid.,* pp. 331 f. The notes appended by the party publisher in 1943 give quite a few details on Marx's and Engels's attitude on war, already discussed in the first chapter. Marx wrote in 1853: "Let Russia get possession of Turkey and her strength is increased nearly half, she becomes superior to all the rest of Europe put together. Such an event would be an unspeakable calamity to the revolutionary cause." Hence, Marx and Engels "tried to influence public opinion in England in order to induce the latter to go to war against Russia" (Crimean war, and again in 1877). See *ibid.,* p. 444.

[101] *Ibid.,* p. 329.

Yet in 1928 the bolsheviks decided that antimilitarism should be adopted, if not as a tactical recipe, then as a standard auxiliary procedure. For this purpose, communists from all over the world, including the United States, went to Moscow to work out the details of demoralization tactics.[102] The Sixth World Congress ordered the communist parties outside of Russia to engage in antimilitarist activities. The parties were instructed to study the military question. It was made clear that *antimilitarism is fundamentally different from pacifism*. It is an integral part of the general struggle against the capitalist system and is closely tied to the defense of the socialist state.[103]

A few months after the closing of the Sixth World Congress, the Comintern prepared a handbook on fission techniques against military organizations. Naturally, this book was not for public sale. It was distributed to the higher echelons of the various communist parties, including the communist party of the United States.[104] This guide to action ought to be studied, together with a more theoretical discussion of antimilitarism by a veteran bolshevik Emilyan Yaroslavsky [Jaroslavski].[105]

Every bourgeois army, the communists tell us, is subject to contradictions. The army is the most powerful instrument of class oppression. It is officered by members of the ruling class. Yet the soldiers who are to defend the interests of capitalism must be recruited from among the workers and peasants whose interests are irreconcilable with those of the capitalists. Hence, according to soviet

[102] *Hearings before the Committee on Un-American Activities, Testimony of Paul Crouch* [U. S. Congress, 81st, 1st sess., House. (Washington, D. C., Govt. Print. Off., 1949), pp. 185–88].

[103] *Bolshaya Sovyetskaya Entsiklopediya* (2nd ed., Moscow, 1950), II, 506–8. Is there any other encyclopedia which contains an article on antimilitarism?

[104] L. Alfred, J. Dupont, and Kurt Fischer, *Revolutionärer Anti-Militarismus, aus der Geschichte der anti-militaristischen Arbeit* (Metz, Imprimerie Populaire de Lorraine, 1929). The date of publication was reconstructed from the text. It is noteworthy that the book was published in France but in the German language. The authors' names, of course, are pseudonyms. It is possible that L. Alfred stands for Alfred Lange, as mentioned below.

[105] It was impossible to determine the date of Jaroslavski's book. Despite its importance, the text seems to be unavailable except in a Spanish translation, apparently published during the Spanish civil war. See *El Trabajo de los Bolcheviques en el Ejército antes de la Revolución de Octubre* (Barcelona, Edeya, no date).

dogma, there is a class struggle between officers and enlisted men.

To succeed with insurrection, it is necessary to neutralize the army as an organization and draw individual soldiers and military units to the side of the revolutionaries. To neutralize the army, while winning over elements of it, antimilitarist work must be directed at the soldiers but not at the officers (as was attempted by the old Russian revolutionary organization *narodnaya volya*). Officers sympathizing with the revolution should be enlisted merely for information and help in training.[106]

To win the soldiers, most of whom are workers, it is necessary to influence them before they enter the army. The stronger the workers' movement, the easier the work of antimilitarism. The communist task within the army is largely one of co-ordinating the chaotic, natural, antimilitarist tendencies of conscripted soldiers. At the next echelon of control, the revolutionary movement within the army must be co-ordinated with the revolutionary movement of the workers and peasants.[107]

The handbook *Revolutionärer Anti-Militarismus* was written around the theme that revolution cannot become a mass movement without penetration of the army. The 1920 *Conditions of Admission to the Communist International,* and particularly Point 4 of that schedule of requirements, were recalled:

Persistent and systematic propaganda and agitation must be carried on in the army, where communist groups should be formed in every military organization. Wherever owing to repressive legislation agitation becomes impossible, it is necessary to carry on such agitation illegally. But refusal to carry on or to participate in such work should be considered equal to treason to the revolutionary cause, and incompatible with affiliation to the Third International.[108]

The Comintern textbook pointed with pride to communist successes in demoralization work.[109] Examples which are quoted again

---

[106] It is doubtful whether the communists still stick to this axiom.

[107] Jaroslavski, *op. cit.,* pp. 6–9, 29, 32.

[108] *Blueprint for World Conquest, op. cit.,* p. 67.

[109] The German term *Zersetzung* is far stronger than the English word "demoralization." It means organizational break-up or decomposition. The communists aim at more than mere demoralization. During the late twenties, the German communist party had a specific *Z-Apparat* for *Zersetzung* and a *T-Apparat* for terror. *T* and *Z* work a powerful combination.

and again were: the 1917 mutiny of the French army;[110] the French naval mutiny in the Black Sea, 1919; the military strike of French reservists, summer 1927; and the successful communist infiltration into each annual contingent of French conscripts. To this date, communist work within the French armed forces serves as model of revolutionary antimilitarism.

Modern militarism is extremely vulnerable—this was the central thesis of the book. This vulnerability of modern armed forces is due to the merging of front and rear; the dependence of the military establishment on industry, transportation, and labor; the mass character of modern armies which have to take in millions of men who, in communist opinion, are politically unreliable. The organization and structure, per se, of the armed forces also were considered vulnerable to fission attack. Particular importance was ascribed to transportation as a target for antimilitarist work. Railroads are a key to military power as well as to industrial production and civilian life.

Programs of disintegration must be maintained not just during war but constantly. Wartime successes must be prepared during peace.

There are specific "peace missions" for communist fractions in the army. The use of the armed forces against demonstrations, strikes, and revolutionary uprisings must be prevented; and fraternization between soldiers and workers must be facilitated.

Communists in the armed forces must live up to the general principle that revolutionary work is a full-time job. It is the revolutionary's duty to carry on "termiting" everywhere and always.[111] There must be no unemployment among the workers for the dictatorship of paradise.

Who are the targets of the antimilitarist effort? In addition to the soldiers themselves, agitation must be directed at the broad masses whose attitudes condition the views of the military rank and file: workers, peasants, women, young people, men about to be drafted, soldiers about to leave the army, reservists, and soldiers belonging to national or religious minorities.

Soldiers on foreign occupation duty are easily demoralized and can be induced to fraternize with the local population, including

[110] Alfred, *et al., op. cit.,* p. 109.
[111] *Ibid.,* pp. 22, 24, 91.

members of communist organizations. During the occupation of the Ruhr, for example, French soldiers often refused to shoot at German "workers": "The German communist youth and the young communists in uniform competed in courage and skill in distributing antimilitaristic leaflets. The sympathy of the French soldiers was visibly on the side of the revolution."[112]

Much of the antimilitarist work, of course, must be undertaken in the barracks, but an attempt should be made to reach soldiers outside. Locations where contacts can be made include: railroad stations, canteens, transit camps, port cities, embarkation points, restaurants, and places of amusement.

In addition to communists within the armed forces, many other categories can be used as bearers of propaganda: railroad workers, seamen, longshoremen, taxi drivers, civilian supply personnel, waitresses, and other females—all those whose daily business brings them into normal contact with military personnel.

In its early phases, antimilitarist work must be, first and foremost, a negative propaganda based on existing grievances. For example, Rumanian soldiers allegedly were compelled to stay on duty for fifteen to sixteen hours a day. They were permitted to leave the barracks only occasionally for two or three hours. They were forbidden to ride street cars sitting down. Nor were they allowed to go to movies or theaters or read anything except patriotic and religious literature. The barracks were dirty and uncomfortable. Soldiers slept on narrow straw mattresses, and the food was deplorable.

This example served to describe the character of exploitable grievances. It was emphasized that living conditions for soldiers everywhere, if properly exploited, are sufficiently bad to lead to opposition and mutinies.[113]

Great attention was devoted to the various possible themes of antimilitarist propaganda. Barracks-room discussions should cover the material and legal situation of the soldier, officers privileges, the danger of war (or the next battle), the nature of the external enemy ("why shoot at your fellow workers?"), the role of elite units, military organization, revolutionary work, disarmament and demobilization, and the role of the army in revolution.[114] Great emphasis was to be laid on the slogan: "Never fight for the enemies of the people."

[112] *Ibid.*, pp. 78, 79.
[113] *Ibid.*, p. 26.
[114] Jaroslavski, *op. cit.*, p. 21.

According to Yaroslavsky, "Tolstoyan pacifism" proved effective in sapping the fighting spirit of the Russian soldiers.[115]

The fundamental basis of antimilitarist propaganda is to describe any war waged by a "capitalist" against a "socialist" nation or a war waged between "capitalist" states as unjust.

The Comintern book listed about one hundred slogans which, in April 1929, had been worked out by the antimilitarist section of the French communist party. These slogans were considered applicable all over the world.

* The "central antimilitarist slogans" are: Fight the preparations for imperialist war by opposing the bourgeoisie more strongly; Support the U.S.S.R. with all means; Support the Red army and the Red fleet; Assist the fight of the colonial peoples against imperialism; Fight the social democrats who participate in the armaments of the bourgeoisie—but who oppose the arming of the proletariat; Oppose conscription; Dissolve the imperialist army; Arm the proletariat; Resist training for imperialist war; Demand training for revolutionary war; Ally the workers, peasants, reservists, soldiers, and sailors in the fight against imperialism; Join the organizations of conscripts; Organize soldiers and sailors committees, and so forth.

Other slogans oppose the calling up of conscripts and reservists; call for the broadening of soldiers' rights such as the right to organize and demonstrate; demand the amnesty of soldiers arrested for revolutionary activities. Nor are various special demands overlooked: free travel on street cars and railroads; better barracks; improvement of military justice; elimination of security surveillance; right to wear civilian clothes, and so forth.

Additional slogans deal with food, military pay, leave, service regulations, hygienic matters, and the status of reservists.

Soldiers belonging to linguistic minorities are urged to request that instruction be given in their own language and that they be used only in their home areas.

Soldiers under medical care should ask for the right, while on active duty, to obey instructions given by their private physician.[116] Another comparable gem is found in the demand that soldiers should be given the right to request a new assignment every three months. Such a rule would make any army unmanageable.

Few western armies have taken precautions against this type of

[115] *Ibid.,* p. 25.
[116] Alfred, *et al., op. cit.,* pp. 33–38.

attack, although agitation along these lines could tie up even a good army, especially at times of crisis. Military reforms aimed at under-cutting such propaganda attack must avoid the double danger of overlooking some real grievances and of demonstrating communist propaganda to be effective.

According to communist teaching, the media of antimilitarist work include: the communist and fellow-traveling press in general; a spe-cifically antimilitaristic press; and papers designed for soldiers and preferably written by soldiers. Within the soldiers' press there must be specialization: papers and magazines directed to new recruits, to veterans, and to reservists; garrison papers; unit papers; and papers for special arms. Newspapers must be supplemented by posters, leaf-lets, and booklets.[117]

Concurrently with such agitation, which can be carried out in part from outside the armed forces by politicians and activists spread-ing the slogans of disintegration and military reform, the communists must also establish fractions, or nuclei, within the military unit. Cells should be organized particularly in the capital city, in garrisons of key importance, and in the most significant services. As the infiltra-tion proceeds, communist cells must strive for the establishment of soldiers' committees patterned after the military soviets of 1917. (Demands for the reorganization of the entire military establishment were discussed in the section *The Tasks of the Communists*.)

There must be co-ordination between the work within the armed forces and the revolutionary work in the factories. Such co-ordina-tion can be achieved, for example, by organizing meetings between the workers of a given factory and the communists in a near-by mili-tary unit. The workers should undertake "collections" for the sol-diers. They should "adopt" a military unit and give it "moral" sup-port in case of conflict or mutiny. The soldiers should support the workers if these should go on strike.

Contacts must not, however, depend upon mere geographical con-tiguity but also should be established by weapons' categories. For example, the labor force of a tank factory should be in contact with the enlisted men of an armored unit; the labor force of an aircraft factory should co-operate with air force mechanics, and so forth.

---

[117] According to Jaroslavski, the lessons of the 1905 revolution pointed to the need of an antimilitaristic subversive literature. First communist efforts in this field began in November 1905.

Obviously, vertical co-operation of this kind would faciliate sabotage.

The standard immediate mission of the antimilitaristic effort is to turn the army into an unreliable instrument for the bourgeoisie and to use it for the military training of the communists.

The ultimate and most important goal of antimilitarist work is to support Red army operations. Communist soldiers are never loyal to the bourgeois army in which they serve. Wherever physically located, they must be loyal to the army of the international proletariat, the Red army.[118] They aim to destroy the army of their country from within by agitation, infiltration, espionage, desertion, and mutiny. But when the time comes, they must strengthen the forces of the revolution, join revolutionary uprisings, and support revolutions from the outside, that is, the invasion of the Red army.

There is evidence that the soviets have paid great attention to antimilitarist work in the United States. The Young Communist League was in charge of these activities, following the precept of Karl Liebknecht: "Those who have the youth, have the army."

In 1934, a training manual was issued for the benefit of young American communists.[119] This manual couched its instructions in the form of historical analysis. Some historical examples were taken over from the *Revolutionärer Anti-Militarismus;* others were added. The manual stressed examples of antimilitarist work accomplished in neutral countries during World War I—an obvious allusion to American preoccupation with neutrality. It stressed American experiences and explained that the "hundreds" of members of the Young Peoples Socialist League of America who refused to take up arms instead should have joined the army to fight against the war.[120] It told how young Italian socialists "tried to master the methods of illegality." "The mass movement in the Italian army had undoubtedly weakened its militancy."[121]

There were instructions on how to write letters and send presents to the front and how to work among recruits and soldiers on leave. The importance of soldiers' newspapers was stressed.

[118] Alfred, *et al., op. cit.,* p. 120.
[119] I. V. Motyleva, *Youth in the World War* (New York, Youth Publishers, 1934). Acknowledgments to James B. Greene for the reference.
[120] *Ibid.,* p. 31.
[121] *Ibid.,* p. 36.

An effort was made, also in 1934, to infiltrate the National Guard. For this purpose a secret manual[122] was prepared which gave precise instructions on how to get into the National Guard; how to select the place to join; what to do upon joining; what information to procure; how to make friends; how to work with special contacts; what issues to raise; how to exploit grievances; legal and illegal methods of agitation; how to gain the confidence of enlisted men; how to organize committees and clubs; how to operate in camp; how to relate the work in the Guard with that of the Young Communist League; how to recruit for communist mass organizations; and how to form fractions in the National Guard.

It seems likely that there existed similar manuals on work in the regular American forces and in the ROTC.

Communist cells operated in various army camps and on some naval ships, especially the battleship *Oklahoma*. There was sabotage on the *Colorado* and also in the Akron base for dirigibles.

Characteristic of these American manuals is their great emphasis on fraternization, not only between soldiers at the front, but between workers and soldiers and between campus and camp.

During World War II some worker-soldier fraternization was generated, for example by systematic letter writing between home and front through the medium of special "fraternalist" magazines issued by front organizations.

Revolutionary antimilitarism is not a thing of the past. It is a chief weapon in the struggle which is raging at present. The *Great Soviet Encyclopedia* asserted that the United States has become the leader of the militaristic, imperialistic, and antidemocratic camp, that it openly prepares for new wars, and that its policy is being opposed by a tremendous antimilitarist movement throughout the whole world. For the first time in history, we are told, there is an organized peace front which bases itself on the socialist states, the peoples' republics in Europe and Asia, the communist parties, the fighters for national liberation and the labor movement. There is also a permanent peace commission which was organized in 1949 at Paris and

---

122 *House Committee on Military Affairs, To Make Better Provision for the Government of the Military and Naval Forces of the United States by the Suppression of Attempts to Incite the Members thereof to Disobedience* [U. S. Congress, 74th, 1st sess., House (Washington, D. C., Gov. Print. Off., 1935), p. 137].

Prague. The Partisans for Peace, the World Federation of Trade Unions, and international and women youth organizations all play important roles.[123]

On February 16, 1951, in a statement to *Pravda*, Stalin reaffirmed the antimilitarist doctrine. He directed communists to describe the United Nations war with North Korea and China as "unjust." American and British soldiers were invited to "perform their duties on the front in a formal way without faith in the righteousness of their mission and without enthusiasm." If they would do so, even "the most experienced generals and officers can suffer defeat."

Stalin set the propaganda stage for World War III by explaining that the capitalists need "super-profits" and plunder and "regard war as an item of income." He voiced the belief that peace could be preserved only "if the peoples will take the cause of preserving peace into their own hands and will defend it to the end"—a restatement of Engels's position of 1891. Demoralization and revolutionary antimilitarism will be among the chief weapons which the communists will apply against the United States. "The wide campaign for the maintenance of peace . . . is now of first-rate importance."

But is antimilitarism enough? Following Lenin, Yaroslavsky emphasized that agitation and infiltration are only "passive approaches" and are inadequate to break up an army. *The infiltrated army must be engaged, weapons in hand;* otherwise the vacillating elements never can be won for the cause of communism. The communists must fight for the support of the army.[124]

Thus, we have the following doctrine:

Capitalism must be broken by force. "In modern battle the only organization of force is military organization" (Lenin). Hence, in order to make a revolution, the military organization of the bourgeoisie must be weakened while at the same time a revolutionary military force must be built. Battle must be joined and the hostile army neutralized as an effective organization, with elements of it swung over to the revolution.

The revolutionary army, according to Lenin, consists of the organized workers and peasants; the organized cadres or vanguards of these classes; and of military units deserting to the revolution. This revolutionary army must be created in the course of battle. As it

---

[123] *Bolshaya Sovyetskaya Entsiklopediya, op. cit.,* p. 507.
[124] Jaroslavski, *op. cit.,* p. 13.

comes into existence, the capitalist army will be fatally weakened and defeated.

This doctrine applies both to insurrection and war. The disintegration of bourgeois armies makes uprising possible and victory in war certain.

To put the doctrine, as it applies to insurrection, in a dialectic sequence:

Thesis: The government army is the key to revolutionary success.

Double Antithesis: The government army must be disintegrated.

The revolutionaries must build a military organization.

Synthesis: Through battle, parts of the government army are meshed into the revolutionary organization. A revolutionary army emerges.

New Thesis: The revolutionary army is the key to revolutionary success.

Applied to war, the dialectic sequence is as follows:

Thesis: The bourgeois army is the key to soviet victory.

Double Antithesis: The bourgeois army must be weakened from the inside and heavily infiltrated.

The soviet army must be strengthened to the maximum.

Synthesis: Through battle, the bourgeois army will be disintegrated. Parts of it will desert to the soviet army, other parts will revolt.

New Thesis: The victorious soviet army holds the key to world communism.

This is a type of dialectics which will probably amaze the college professors teaching Hegel and Marx. Yet this is how abstract philosophy can be applied in practice. The true meaning of communist dialectics is that the communists draw up their operational plans according to the dialectic scheme: Each problem is attacked simultaneously by a positive and a negative solution. These solutions are combined through the process of time to produce the "negation of the negation," that is, recreate the original problem in a different fashion. Dialectics is less an interpretation of the world than a guide to dynamic action.

COMINTERN TEXTBOOKS ON UPRISINGS

THE *Resolutions* of the Sixth World Congress developed the concept of combining war with revolutionary uprisings. Communists all over the world prided themselves on their insurrectional propensities, but since October 1917 no communist uprising in the classical style had been successful. To make the combination of revolutionary war and armed insurrection work with a reasonable degree of assurance, uprising techniques had to be perfected. Foreign communists and Russian soldiers busied themselves with inventing combined military insurrectionist tactics.

Tactical innovations and training procedures were laid down in numerous secret documents and manuals. Foreign communists studying at Moscow familiarized themselves with soviet writings on the strategy and tactics of uprisings and irregular warfare. Large libraries at the central building of the Comintern in Moscow and at the Frunze Academy collected materials on the military aspects of communist expansion.

It was strictly forbidden to take documents and books from these libraries. However, since not all professional communists could be trained in Russia, some training had to be done abroad. Due to this circumstance, two of the secret communist manuals have become available. These manuals dealt with uprisings only, that is, with only one of the several communist techniques. While it is fortunate that they found their way into non-communist hands, it is important to remember that these texts did not tell the whole story.

The first of these manuals, originally written in German, was entitled *Der Weg zum Sieg* or *The Road to Victory, a theoretical dis-*

cussion of Marxism and revolution. The author's name was given as "Alfred Lange."[125]

The second manual was entitled *Der bewaffnete Aufstand* or *The Armed Uprising.*[126] A. Neuberg signed as author. We have it on the testimony of Dimitrov himself that "this book is in the library of every revolutionist. It is the duty of every revolutionist to educate himself further."[127] It is generally believed that Neuberg was a pseudonym of the German communist Heinz Neumann, participant in many European and Chinese insurrections and ultimately a purge victim;[128] however, his authorship has not been established beyond doubt.

Lange's book was published early in 1928. The precise date of publication of Neuberg's book is not known; it was, however, published after the Sixth World Congress of the Comintern, probably in 1929.[129]

---

[125] "Lange" was a pseudonym either of Hans Kiepenberger, former chief of the German communist party's military apparatus, or of the Finnish communist, Tuure Valdemar Lehen (or Leino), erstwhile husband of Hertta Kuusinen. Lehen is still an active communist in Finland. Kiepenberger was probably purged. According to experts working for the House of Representatives Foreign Affairs Committee, "Lange" probably stands for Lehen, but the author is inclined to think that circumstantial evidence points to Kiepenberger as the author of *The Road to Victory*. The booklet was published by Ernst Schneller, a leading German communist and onetime editor of the secret monthly *Oktober*, a magazine devoted to the problems of military insurrection and irregular warfare.

[126] For purposes of educating anticommunists, *The Armed Uprising* was published in abbreviated version in France. The editor did not change the original text but cut out a few case studies. See Léon de Poncins, *Le Plan communiste d'insurrection armée; documents originaux resumés et commentés* (Paris, Les Libertés Françaises, 1939).

[127] *International Press Correspondence, op. cit.,* October 13, 1933, p. 993.

[128] See *International Press Correspondence, op. cit.,* 1933, p. 1174. Heinz Neumann's widow spent several years in Russian slave labor camps, and was subsequently turned over to Germany where she spent an additional five years in a nazi concentration camp. She was liberated by the American army. Her case pointed up the intimacy between the soviets and nazis in 1940. See the very valuable memoirs by Margarethe Buber-Neumann, *Under Two Dictators* (New York, Dodd, Mead, 1951).

[129] The author also had the opportunity to consult *Bolshevist Civil War Regulations,* an English mimeographed translation of a Russian text. Internal evidence of the text as well as the source from which the *Regulations* were procured leave little doubt about their authenticity. The *Regulations* were written during or before 1926 and presumably were one of the early manuals which students at the Lenin Institute must have found useful.

Neuberg discussed military tactics in greater detail than did Lange, who devoted his attention more to public opinion and broad strategy.[130] Both authors used many identical quotes from Marx and Lenin, but neither mentioned Stalin once—perhaps a clue to their untimely, though not necessarily unfortunate, demise.

Lange's book dealt with the art of the uprising; the choice of the moment of attack; the concentration of force; the offensive; and the prevention of enemy tactical concentrations. Neuberg's book was broken down into three parts: the preparation of uprisings; the tactics of insurrection; and case studies.

Both authors agreed that the uprising is the first phase of civil war.[131] Neuberg underscored the need of using violence. He pointed out, in orthodox Marxian fashion, that violence has a "creative" role and that only force can solve the great problems of history.[132]

Both authors quoted Marx's oft-repeated statement of 1852 that "uprising is an art, just like the art of war." Neuberg added Lenin's comment that, therefore, the uprising should be prepared both politically and militarily. Without systematic military preparation, the uprising must fail like the communists' insurrection in Germany (1923).[133]

On the other hand, uprising is a special military art and, in some respects, differs from conventional warfare. Lange summarized the differences as follows: The front of the armed uprising is everywhere; the revolutionary army consists of untrained and largely improvised troop units; its size cannot be predetermined; the rebels must organize their army in the course of fighting and do not enter battle in a combat-ready condition; the participation or nonparticipation of great masses decides the fate of the uprising.

If popular opinion is favorable to the uprising, this will not only guarantee the support of the masses, but also affect the morale of the insurgents. It will bring courage and self-confidence to the revolutionaries and uncertainty and dissolution to the counter-revolutionaries.[134]

[130] The *Regulations* deal mostly with organization.

[131] According to the *Regulations,* uprising must be preceded by a period of political preparation and a period of organization and technical training.

[132] Neuberg, in Poncins, *op. cit.,* pp. 12, 20.

[133] *Ibid.,* p. 31.

[134] Lange, Chap. 1. This book was available only in mimeographed form and cannot be quoted by pages.

Neuberg added that it is necessary to procure arms, to demoralize the government, army, and police, and to utilize the nuclei which the communists have previously emplaced within the military and political organizations of the ruling class. On the other hand, the revolutionaries must be careful not to fall under the influence of capitalist agents placed in proletarian organizations.[135]

An insurrection must be timed correctly. It must not be launched before the masses of the people are sympathetic toward the revolutionaries. A revolutionary situation is a *conditio sine qua non* of a fight to the bitter end. If a revolutionary situation emerges, but the revolutionary forces are not ready, revolt is premature.

Lange stated that revolutions cannot be plotted beforehand with a calendar. Correct timing is essentially a problem of leadership which must organize the insurgents as the revolutionary situation moves toward its peak. According to Neuberg, one danger is that the "degree of the revolutionary situation" will be overrated; the other danger is that the revolutionaries may underestimate their own strength.

These timing problems occur mainly in long-range planning. In the short run, the date and hour of the insurrection must be fixed accurately by those who "have influence on the masses" and therefore exert limited control over the situation. The uprising should begin at night or during early morning hours when most of the defenders of the government are fast asleep and can be surprised in their beds.[136] Operations should be run with extreme punctuality and with strict adherence to timetables. A delay of two minutes proved fatal to the insurrection at Reval (Tallin).

Very often the timing of attacks was made dependent on the changing situation itself; in line with this or that contingency, signals such as light shells, lamps, or sounds were to start new moves. Experience showed that signals are unreliable. Hence, operations must be conducted as far as possible according to a preplanned timetable.

Both Lange and Neuberg attempted to define the term "revolutionary situation." There must be a revolutionary upsurge of the people and vacillation, cowardice, and defeatism within the government. The revolutionary classes must be organized and be willing

---

[135] Neuberg, in Poncins, *op. cit.,* pp. 59 f.

[136] The *Regulations* point out that insurrectionists should find it easier, given adequate training, to fight at night.

to take up arms. The vital interests of a large segment of the population must be involved. The masses must favor a change of government.

Enlarging on Lenin and Sinovyev, Neuberg listed four factors which, if they occur simultaneously, denote a revolutionary situation: First, a crisis within the ruling class which no longer can maintain its domination and cannot continue on as in the past; second, an abnormal deterioration in the economic circumstances of the oppressed classes; third, eagerness of the masses to resort to action; and fourth, moral and material disintegration of army and police. In Neuberg's opinion, the infection of army and police with the revolutionary spirit is the best portent of a revolutionary situation.

A revolutionary situation may occur as a result of an economic or political crisis. It is "inevitable," said Neuberg, after war and defeat.

Revolutionary acts may enhance the revolutionary situation. A revolutionary incident, such as a specific military defeat or an act of terror, also may sharpen the crisis.

However, the revolutionary situation by itself does not produce revolution. There must also be an organized force capable and willing to exploit the opportunity. If the bolsheviks had not exploited the situation of October 1917, the crisis would have passed as did, one year later, the crisis in Germany.

Of course, even a strong revolutionary force cannot launch a successful insurrection at any time it pleases. To attack without considering the revolutionary temperature is called "putschism."[137] Neu-

[137] In communist parlance, "putschism" often is called "blanquism," after the French revolutionary Auguste Blanqui, 1805–81. Communist opposition to blanquism sometimes is misinterpreted to mean that the communists are opposed to military uprisings. Lange criticized Blanqui on the ground that in all his uprisings he fought with inferior forces. "This mistake can be accredited to the fact that Blanqui did not grasp the necessity of numerical superiority in an uprising because he did not understand the role of the broad masses as an active participant in the armed revolt." (Chap. 3.) Neuberg, however, called Blanqui the predecessor of modern Marxism. Blanqui was a communist and a materialist but not a dialectician. He wanted to take power by means of a well-organized, armed, secret, and centralized force. He did not understand that the revolutionary situation is a precondition of victorious insurrection. The need to organize the military uprising and his insistence on the fatality of an armed clash with the ruling class—this is Blanqui's legacy to Marx and Lenin. Yet, according to the Marxists, Blanqui did not understand the economic and social causes of revolution nor the need for a powerful revolutionary upsurge of the proletariat. Trotsky thought that Blanqui was right in believing that tactical weakness condemns insurrection to defeat but was wrong

berg critized the theory of "constant offensive pressure" by quoting Lenin's opinion that even in the period of decline, capitalism remains capable of strong counterattacks. The remaining strength of capitalism should not be underestimated.

Both Lange and Neuberg commented at length on Marx's rules of uprising.

First, one should never toy with an uprising unless determined to endure all consequences. Uprising is a calculation with many unknowns. Government forces have the advantage of organization, discipline, and equipment. The revolutionaries must throw overwhelming numerical strength against the forces of order, or they will be defeated.

Second, once the uprising has started, the revolutionaries must act with the utmost resolution and fight offensively. The defensive is the death of every armed insurrection.

Third,

surprise the opponent when his troops are scattered, be sure to win daily small victories,[138] maintain moral superiority which your first successful rising will bring, draw each vacillating element, which always goes over to the strongest and the one who is most apt to win, over to your side, force your enemies to retreat before they can gather their forces, in short, follow the word of Danton, the greatest master of revolution up to now: "de l'audace, de l'audace, encore de l'audace."[139]

These are the orthodox rules of the art. Obviously, they are applicable both to insurrection and to war. It would be a mistake to assume that the bolsheviks did not make some progress since Marx.

---

in assuming that technically correct insurrectionary tactics must guarantee victory. "The insurrectionary tactic of blanquism corresponded to the character of the old Paris, the semi-handicraft proletariat, the narrow streets and the military system of Louis Philippe. Blanqui's principal mistake was to identify revolution with insurrection. His technical mistake was to identify insurrection with the barricades. The Marxian criticism had been directed against both mistakes." *The Triumph of the Soviet* ("The History of the Russian Revolution," Vol. III [New York, Simon and Schuster, 1932]), 170.

[138] The *Regulations* speak of the "principle of partial victory."

[139] Marx's statement was originally made in *Revolution und Konterrevolution in Deutschland*. It entered communist folklore when it was taken up by Stalin in 1906 in an article discussing the unsuccessful rising of 1905. Lenin discussed it in 1917 in an article entitled "Can the bolsheviks retain state power?" *Selected Works, op. cit.,* VI, 292. See Lange, Chap. 1, and Neuberg, in Poncins, *op. cit.,* pp. 35, 77.

Any insurrection must be planned with great care. There should be an over-all strategic plan covering the entire country and subsidiary tactical plans for the various cities and regions. The strategic plan must determine, for example, which cities or areas are vital to the uprising. It must also state whether or not the insurrection should be co-ordinated with a general strike.[140]

The tactical plan must estimate the force relationships within target areas, determine the geographic base of the uprising,[141] define command and liaison structures, select the primary and secondary targets to be seized by the insurgents, allocate forces to targets, lay out missions after seizure of the initial targets, anticipate courses of action in the case of failure, prescribe measures to prevent the arrival of troops and enemy reinforcements, spread propaganda to lure new forces into the fight, and prepare for the distribution of arms, the suppression of enemy leaders, the establishment of Red army units, and the enactment of laws.[142]

For example, the plan of the Hamburg insurrection of 1923 envisaged the following sequence of events: surprise action against weapons depots: the disarming of the police and of antirevolutionary organizations in the suburbs; concentration of the now armed revolutionary units in the center of Hamburg; attack toward the River Elbe, seizure of the bridges and initiation of a two-front pitched battle—all this while concurrently blocking the main highways leading into the city, and seizing, by internal *coups de main,* the post and telegraph offices, the railroad stations, the airfields, and the public utilities.[143]

In order to execute a plan of this type, tactical intelligence is required. Static targets should be put under "observation." Movements of government forces must be watched by "reconnaissance." Since the insurgents are native to the target city, they should have no trouble determining the best observation points, procuring suitable security covers, and gaining access to points of importance.

Revolutionary intelligence must obtain complete layout plans of

[140] Neuberg, in Poncins, *op. cit.,* p. 82.

[141] The *Regulations* state that the insurgents should avoid fighting in the open country but rather stick to fighting in cities where the army cannot use its full power and is reluctant to operate effectively for fear of hurting the population.

[142] Neuberg, in Poncins, *op. cit.,* p. 82.

[143] *Ibid.,* p. 96.

installations, determine guard arrangements, hours of shift, communications setups, street and house addresses, and personal habits of target individuals. Most important is the locating of armories, automobile garages, and truck depots.

In addition, "social city maps" indicating the geographic distribution of friendly and unfriendly "classes" and groups must be prepared. These social maps can be developed into military situation maps showing the deployment, armament, and morale of revolutionary and antirevolutionary forces in the various sectors of the town. Other maps must show the city's transportation, communications, and sewer systems. Other types of intelligence the professional planner of city uprisings must have are: a tactical evaluation of the city's key buildings, street intersections, squares, bridges; a listing of the house blocks suitable for defensive or offensive action; and data on surface and subsurface lines of retreat.

Both authors stressed the need for offensive action. Even an unsuccessful local offensive may help the insurrection, while the defensive, although tactically successful, must contribute to strategic defeat. According to Lange:

There is only one theoretically possible situation in which stalling could be beneficial to the revolutionists and change the power relationship to their advantage, namely: the possibility of military support from a foreign country, in which the revolutionary class has already seized power.[144]

This is the revolution from without, as seen by the revolutionary on the inside.

The main purpose of incessantly offensive action and of partial victories is to prevent the tactical concentration of antirevolutionary forces and to break down cohesion and liaison between hostile units. Attacks must be launched against the "strongholds of reaction"; fighting in so-called "Vendée" districts tends to disorientate and discourage the antirevolutionaries. Thwarting enemy concentrations and scattering already massed formations are "the best tactics for the revolutionists."

The strongest offensive effort must be directed against the "key" or "life force" of the counterrevolution. The life force is that element of strength which, if destroyed, must eliminate a group's power.

[144] Lange, Chap. 4.

To put it differently, it is the life force which binds together a political entity. (In this case it is the sociological equivalent to the geographic "key to the country" discussed by Clausewitz.) Or, it is the element which can do most damage to the group's opponents.

The life-force concept, which is related to Stalin's concept of the "decisive link," is a simple one. For example, subduing a person by tying his arms and legs is difficult and requires full use of one's entire strength. However, once an individual is paralyzed by a night stick on the head, the tying of his arms and feet is routine. Accordingly, the life force is the primary target of revolutionary attack. Its survival or fall determines the outcome of the operation.

But in terms of specific targets, what is the life force? Lange and Neuberg asserted that this depends on the situation. The life force may be political or military in nature. It may be the enemy's weakest or his strongest point. Very often it may be the arsenals and weapons depots, especially for the reason that in order to succeed, the revolutionaries must arm themselves in addition to disarming the opponent. The capital of a country, the administrative centers of the provinces, the government army, the physical bodies of the members of government, the technical government apparatus, telecommunications, public utilities, selected industries—all these, depending on the situation, could qualify as life-force targets.

Whatever the life force may be, it must be attacked with vastly superior strength and with crippling effect. *The center of gravity of the attack must be directed against the life force. This fundamental rule must be applied to all military and non-military operations.*

What happens if this rule is disregarded? In the Canton insurrection of 1927 the key objective was to neutralize a certain cadet regiment. However, a second life-force objective, the city's weapons depot, was overlooked. The rising failed. Similarly, at Reval, the life force was not included among the targets: the insurgents attacked many different types of objectives and were crushed by the very force which their first blow ought to have destroyed.[145]

Initial successes usually decide the final outcome of an uprising. In turn, initial success depends greatly on surprise. The communists do not expect that the enemy can be kept entirely ignorant of the impending blow. They do not believe that preparations for an uprising can or should be kept entirely secret: exaggerated secrecy

[145] Neuberg, in Poncins, *op. cit.,* pp. 66 f.

would preclude the very mobilization of the revolutionary forces. Lenin taught that "the masses must know that an armed, bloody, and desperate conflict will be begun."

According to communist doctrine, surprise will be achieved if the attack comes at a moment when enemy strength is dispersed; if the timing and tempo of the blow, as well as the strength and morale of the attacking forces, can be kept secret; and if the exact operational tactics are not anticipated by the opponent.[146] The initial blow must be accompanied by terror, that is, by arrest, incapacitation, or liquidation of hostile political leaders and military commanders.[147]

As the uprising progresses, the insurgents should mobilize ever increasing numbers. They should arm themselves rapidly by seizing arsenals and stores, disarming enemy forces, and manufacturing weapons of opportunity. If there is a weapons shortage, the revolutionaries should not hesitate to disarm soldiers with their "bare hands."[148]

The offensive proceeds through the systematic occupation of all major targets, governmental building, barracks, business offices, industrial installations, military command stations, communication centers, newspapers, and so on. Attacks from without must be combined with attacks from within.[149] Through the disintegration and disorganization of the enemy the revolutionary units must be strengthened.

The best way to put down an uprising, Lange observed, is to prevent the disintegration of the government forces and to keep strong reserves beyond the reach of revolutionary attack. If the revolutionaries do not succeed in dispersing these reserves (that is, if the government has had sufficient foresight to maintain an invulnerable protection force), the insurrection will fail.

Once it is clear that the insurrection is unsuccessful, the communist party must lead the retreat. The insurgents should counterattack whenever possible, especially against the enemy's flank and rear, and

[146] Lange, Chap. 5; Neuberg, in Poncins, *op. cit.*, pp. 71 f.

[147] Lange, Chap. 4; Neuberg, in Poncins, *op. cit.*, p. 68.

[148] Lange, Chap. 1; Neuberg, in Poncins, *op. cit.*, p. 55.

[149] The *Regulations* define the purposes of decomposition work: (1) to enlist elements of the army on the side of the revolution, and to neutralize the rest; (2) to destroy the functioning of the government's military and police arm; (3) to destroy equipment and thus to weaken the government strength.

try to wear out the government forces. They may still outlast the counterrevolution. If this is not possible, a complete retreat must be undertaken. The revolutionaries should console themselves with Engels's dictum that defeat is an excellent school: this retreat is just a prelude to future offensives.

Neuberg placed great emphasis on the strictly military aspects of the insurrection. The revolutionaries must have a combat organization capable of fighting against the army. Such an organization cannot be improvised. It must be organized, trained, and armed systematically.[150] The training of the cadres and combat leaders must include the theoretical study of revolutions and war, as well as drill, experimental tactics, maneuvers, and participation in uprisings and war.

The armed forces remain the key factor deciding the outcome of the insurrection. The army will disintegrate only if there is a revolutionary situation; if it has been infiltrated on a massive scale; and if it is engaged successfully by the combat forces of the revolutionaries or, it may be added, if it is being defeated in war.

Neuberg warned against the idea that war is the only road to revolution. Naturally, there are always countries where military morale can be disintegrated by means short of war. Some important countries possess no strong military organization, perhaps as a result of disarmament imposed by defeat in a previous war. Experience has shown that the establishment of a communist combat organization may be tolerated. However, in countries with strong administrative and military morale, adequate armed forces, and semimilitary anticommunist units, and where subversive combat organizations are not tolerated, revolution is possible only through the midwifery of war and defeat.

[150] The *Regulations* prescribe a variety of organizational devices. The party leadership on the national and provincial levels must create military revolutionary committees to co-ordinate political and military work. Similar committees must be created in all organizations participating in the uprising. Operations and operational headquarters must be under a single command, but the commander must have two principal assistants: one directing the decomposition work in the hostile forces, the other directing the military activities of the insurgents. This triple-command structure must be maintained on all levels. The insurgent forces should have an organization paralleling as much as possible the organization of the government forces. Fighting units should be small, not more than ten men, and should be commanded by one trained chief; if possible, they should comprise a few specialists in technical weapons such as artillery and gas.

Lange ended his treatise by pointing out that the fight for the destruction of the armed forces must be waged both from the outside and from the inside. He believed that *pacifist propaganda is the best preparation for the armed conflict. Si vis bellum, garri pacem.*

THE AFTERMATH OF THE SIXTH WORLD CONGRESS

SHORTLY after the Sixth World Congress in December 1928, the industrialization of the Soviet Union was put into high gear. The Russian army was to be the main weapon of world revolution. The Russian people were called upon to forge that weapon. First, the forge had to be built. "Industrialization also means the development of our war industries."[151]

The first Five Year Plan, adopted in April 1929, was not entirely a military measure,[152] but industries "which will play the main role in consolidating the defensive powers of our country" were to be developed before industries needed to improve the standard of living. The bolshevik doctrine that technology is one of the keys to victory was put into practice.

The theoretical justification for the plan was given by Stalin. He quoted Lenin to the effect that the proletariat which had been victorious in one country must organize its own socialist production and, "in the event of necessity," come out "even with armed force against the exploiting classes and their states."[153]

The organization of socialist production, that is, the equipping of Russia with a modern war potential, was regarded "as a guarantee against intervention and restoration." In 1935, Stalin commented that without this planned creation of Russian industry the soviets would have had no tractors, automobiles, planes, and tanks. "We

---

[151] Sergei N. Kournakoff, *Russia's Fighting Forces* (New York, Duell, Sloan and Pearce, 1942), p. 66.

[152] In Stalin's *History of the Communist Party of the Soviet Union (Bolsheviks), Short Course* (New York, International Publishers, 1939), p. 296, the plan was juxtaposed with the conflict about the Chinese Eastern Railroad. "The imperialists provoked a conflict between China and the Soviet Union." However, the fighting followed the adoption of the plan.

[153] *Problems of Leninism, op. cit.*, pp. 160, 162. Lenin's statement dates from 1915 (*Selected Works, op. cit.*, V, 141). It was taken up by Stalin in 1926 and since then reoccurs in each reprinting of the *Problems;* for example, see *Sochineniya, op. cit.*, VIII, 68.

would have found ourselves unarmed in face of foreign foes . . . we would have fallen captive to the bourgeoisie, home and foreign."[154]

A second significant step taken in the wake of the Sixth World Congress was the streamlining of the Red army school system. The Frunze Academy was split into two major departments: one to train senior staff officers, and one to graduate specialists for military service in Asia.[155]

In 1929 a system of study groups to analyze military problems for the Communist Academy was founded. The academy as a whole was under the central committee of the communist party and specialized in the study of applied Marxism. It held, in this field, the same supreme position which the Academy of Sciences still holds with respect to science in general.

The announced purpose of the academy's military studies was to apply dialectics to war and to formulate Marxian concepts of strategy and tactics.[156] The lessons of the civil war, Lenin's theory of rebellion, and the military experience of the communist party were emphasized. These studies resulted in a communist "science of victory." (This term was borrowed from the title of Marshal Alexander V. Suvorov's eighteenth-century treatise.) The details of this new science were not revealed.

Clues, however, to the course of development of soviet military doctrine may be found in the provisional field service regulations written in 1936, probably by Tukhachevsky. In summary, the regulations hold that the battle conduct of the Red army ought to aim at the enemy's complete annihilation. The main objective of the soviet army is to win a decisive victory and to destroy the enemy. The only means to reach this goal is battle.

But the military destruction of the enemy's armed forces does not necessarily imply victory, because even defeated troops can still derive strength from a morally and economically strong rear. *The destruction of the military power in its totality alone can assure final and definitive success.* Hence, communist strategy should not aim only at winning military encounters but must comprise all of the following elements:

[154] *Problems of Leninism, op. cit.,* p. 541.

[155] Nikolaus Basseches, *The Unknown Army; the Nature and History of the Russian Military Forces* (New York, Viking, 1943), p. 139.

[156] Fedotoff White, "Soviet Philosophy of War," *Political Science Quarterly,* LI (1936), 347.

(1) The moral defeat of the enemy forces, their political disintegration, and the diminution of their resistance and maneuverability.

(2) Seizure and destruction of enemy matériel, attrition of the opponent's weapons supply, and reduction of his fire power.

(3) Weakening of the enemy's initiative through exhaustion and immobilization of his reserves.

(4) Seizure of the enemy's territory.[157]

A decisive battle must be forced upon the enemy and must be waged by all available weapons. In the listing of these weapons, that of air power was included as early as 1921: the field service regulations at that time assigned to the air forces the mission to support ground forces and to attack, independently, the enemy's rear and reserves. Air mastery was considered highly important and was defined as the ability of the air forces to carry out their assigned missions.[158] According to the 1921 version, air mastery should be won by surprising the enemy before he has deployed his aerial forces and by attacking air bases and the aeronautical industry. The potentialities of air-borne operations were emphasized. A few Russian authors contended that air mastery is not required for air-borne attacks which, they felt, could be executed under the protection of surprise.[159] It would be surprising if the Russian air staff still holds this belief.

EXCURSUS ON CADRES

IN 1935, Stalin applied a new interpretation to his theory that man power was the most decisive factor in the historical process. When Russia was still a vast country with enormous man power but without technology, the communists issued the slogan "technology decides everything." This slogan helped to reduce Russia's technical and industrial handicaps. But it turned out that technology per se was

157 Théodore M. Makhine, L'Armée rouge, La puissance militaire de l'URSS (Paris, Payot, 1938), pp. 79 f.

158 Ibid., p. 105.

159 Ibid., pp. 107 f.

not enough. In a speech to the graduates of the Red Army Academy, Stalin stated:

In order to get technology going and to utilize it to the full, we need people who have mastered technology. We need cadres capable of mastering and utilizing this technology according to all the rules of the art. Without people who have mastered technology, technology is dead. In the charge of people who have mastered technology, technology can and should perform miracles. . . . That is why emphasis must now be laid on people, on cadres, on workers who have mastered technology; that is why the old slogan "technology decides everything" which is a reflection of a period already passed, a period which suffered from a dearth of technology, must now be replaced by a new slogan, the slogan "cadres decide everything."[160]

This was a rephrasing of an idea which Stalin expressed as early as 1918. When told that the reverses of the Red army were due to the technical superiority of the enemy, and specifically to his superiority in artillery, Stalin is said to have replied:

But are not our reverses due to inadequate political training? Behind the gun there is a man. No matter how many guns an army commander may have at his disposal, if his men are not properly trained by propaganda,

[160] *History of the Communist Party, op. cit.,* p. 337. The author took the liberty of using the word "technology" instead of "technique" employed in the official translation. In connection with this emphasis on cadres, Stalin opposed the traditional Russian indifference to loss of human lives: "I recall an incident in Siberia where I lived at one time in exile. It was in spring floods. About thirty men went to the river to pull out timber which had been carried away by the vast, swollen river. Towards evening they returned to the village, but with one comrade missing. When asked where the thirtieth man was, they replied indifferently that the thirtieth man had 'remained there.' To my question, 'How do you mean, remained there?' they replied with the same indifference, 'Why ask—drowned, of course.' And thereupon one of them began to hurry away, saying, 'I've got to go and water the mare.' When I reproached them with having more concern for animals than for men, one of them said, amid the general approval of the rest: 'Why should we be concerned about men? We can always make men. But a mare . . . just try and make a mare.' (Animation.) Here you have a case, not very significant perhaps, but very characteristic. It seems to me that the indifference of certain of our leaders to people, to cadres, their inability to value people, is a survival of that strange attitude of man to man displayed in the episode in far off Siberia that I have just related." *Problems of Leninism, op. cit.,* p. 544. This is good thinking, but unfortunately Stalin did not always remember it. As a result of his actions, many millions of people "remained there," and the bolsheviks, indeed, were not too successful in making mares.

he will be powerless against men who are inspired by revolution even if they are less supplied with artillery.[161]

Analyzing the civil war from the vantage point of hindsight, Stalin explained the communist victory by the policy of the soviet government. This policy allegedly corresponded to the "interests" of the people; it secured the loyalty of the Red army and the support by the people; and it proved itself in the ability of the soviets to control the rear and serve the needs of the front: "An army without a strong rear to support the front in every way is doomed to defeat."[162]

Stalin gave additional reasons for the communist victory in the civil war: high morale of the Red army induced by their understanding of the war aims; bolshevik control over the army and the rear; maintenance of "bolshevik discipline"; the production by the Red army of first class soldiers, political educators, organizers, agitators, and commissars; the support which the Red army got from revolutionary forces operating in the enemy's rear; and finally the support of the world proletariat which allegedly forced "the imperialists to call off the intervention."[163] The point is not whether these factors explain communist victory in 1921. The point is that Stalin considered these factors as elements of soviet strategy and as constituent parts of a future communist victory.

The Midwives of the Nazi Reich

The famous proposition that communist tactics are an enigma wrapped in a mystery inside a puzzle is not generally valid. However, communist policies in Germany at the time of the nazi conquest of power have remained enigmatic. What was the communist plan? Did they wish the nazis to come to power? Were the nazi successes an incidental result of communist policies aiming at other objectives? Or did the communists do their best to defeat Hitler's hordes?

The basic facts are clear enough. On many occasions the German

---

[161] I. Minz, *The Red Army* (New York, International Publishers, 1943), p. 109.

[162] *History of the Communist Party, op. cit.*, p. 254.

[163] *Ibid.*, pp. 245 f.

communist party voted with the nazis against the Weimar government. Time and again the communists refused to vote with the social democrats and the democratic parties. They were even unwilling to limit their opposition to simple abstention from voting. At two critical junctures, during the fall of 1932 and during January 1933, the communists offered motions of no confidence, forced the dissolution of the Reichstag, and thus brought about new elections. These tactics contributed to the rapid growth of the nazi movement and culminated in the appointment of Hitler as chancellor of Germany. Without the constant elections and the parliamentary instability of the government partly induced by the communists, the German political and economic crisis never need have led to the nazi coup.

Phrased differently, due to the parliamentary balance of power in Germany during 1932, it was in the hands of the communists to preserve the Weimar republic and to break the tidal wave of national socialism. Yet, instead of applying their loudly proclaimed policy of the "united front" against reaction, the communists performed yeoman service for the nazis and actually paved for them their road to power while, at the same time, engaging in numerous skirmishes and street battles against the brown-shirt troops. The question is: Was the help which the communists afforded the nazis intentional or was it "coincidental midwifery"—an undesired by-product of another program?

What would have been a logical line for the communists? Early in 1932 the communists tried to organize a conflict of class against class. This struggle would have cut across party lines and was supposed to lead to a revolutionary united front of the poor and impoverished classes, that is, of the majority of the population. Since a nazi dictatorship was sure to mean a fundamental change of system, the suppression of all freedoms and the destruction of the communist party, as well as a long postponement of revolution in Germany, it would have seemed imperative for the communists to adopt either of two tactics: (1) an all-out assault against the national socialists, aiming at their incapacitation or, (2) in the absence of a capability to carry out such a plan successfully, "peaceful" united-front tactics designed to prevent nazi electoral and parliamentary victories. Such tactics would have required a temporary truce with the parties supporting the Weimar regime and especially with the social democrats. Moreover, an alliance with the social democrats would have been the main condition of effective assault tactics against the nazis; that is, it was basic to both tactics.

This alternative was clear to many German communists at that time. The assault method was proposed by the left wing of the German communist party under the leadership of Heinz Neumann but was ruled out some time in summer of 1932 and officially condemned by the central committee of the German communist party.[164] The united-front method was preached by the right wing but was never applied except in the form of provocative negotiations designed to put the socialists "on the spot." The obvious idea that the communists should band together with the socialists against the avowed enemy of labor was neutralized by the slogan that the popular front should be organized "from below," meaning that it should be a practical co-operation among workers but not a co-operation among organized political parties.[164A]

There might have been a third policy which, though risky, would have made sense, at least in retrospect. The Russian Politburo (as distinguished from the Comintern and the German communist party) might have estimated (1) that German communism had no chance to seize power or to accomplish anything worth while for communism or Russia; (2) that nazism was a native and truly revolutionary movement, a modified but authentic German version of Russian bolshevism, while historical Marxian communism could find no indigenous roots in Germany; and (3) that the establishment of nazism would produce wars as well as revolutions all over Europe. On the basis of such an estimate, it would have been logical for the Russians to leave German communism to its fate and help Hitler carrying out his "national revolution."

But what precisely was the communist policy?

There is no doubt that, immediately after Hitler's first successes,

[164] International Press Correspondence (Berlin, October 27, 1932), XII, 1015.

[164A] In 1935, Wilhelm Pieck, Russian-installed president of East Germany, stated that the communists should have directed their main attack against the nazis instead of against the social democrats. He asserted that the strength of the nazi movement had been underrated and that the policy aimed at enlisting the support of individual socialists was caused by the "sectarian" spirit of the German communists. Quite so; only he forgot to add that this policy had been decided upon at Moscow. See Wilhelm Pieck, Der neue Weg zum gemeinsamen Kampf fuer den Sturz der Hitlerdiktatur (Berlin, Neuer Weg, 1947), pp. 24–30.

the communists got ready to take a strong line. But as time went on, they became ever more cautious in their tactics, violent and otherwise, against the nazis. What is more surprising, they reduced their propaganda output against the nazi movement and omitted altogether to prepare agitprop materials on some of the topics most vitally needed in the anti-nazi struggle. By the end of 1932 the self-styled "fighters against fascism" fought a very desultory battle indeed. Why?

There is available testimony by two witnesses which may throw some light on the matter. The first witness, Erich Wollenberg, met Stalin in January 1933 at Moscow and discussed with him the German situation.[165] According to Wollenberg, Stalin did not believe that Hitler would come to power, partly because the *Reichswehr* was against a Hitler government and partly because the western powers would intervene. Stalin also expressed the belief that the Weimar republic was in no position "to break the chains of Versailles." The German problem was to be considered not only from the point of view of internal German politics but from that of the international interests of the communist movement. Pressed a little further, Stalin admitted that Hitler might come to power after all. To Wollenberg's remark that this would mean a military attack upon the Soviet Union, Stalin reputedly answered: "This war is unavoidable." Wollenberg objected that a socialist revolution in Germany would prevent such a war. In reply, Stalin broke off the discussion.

To stop the argument at just this point signified that, in Stalin's opinion, Wollenberg was hopelessly confused. Stalin must have considered that a German revolution was no protection against war and that the problem was not to avoid war but to postpone it. On the basis of his intimate knowledge of the Kremlin's political thinking, Wollenberg explained that, according to Stalin, a socialist revolution in Germany would lead to immediate armed intervention by the West and would therefore accelerate the coming of world conflict. However, at that time the Soviet Union was in the midst of agricultural collectivization and also in the throes of a catastrophic famine. It was in no position to risk a large-scale military conflagration, as clearly evidenced by the unprofitable sale of the Chinese Eastern Railroad to Japan in 1932. Wollenberg's interpretation becomes even more plausible if it is remembered that Japanese opera-

[165] *Plain Talk,* May 1950, pp. 59–64.

tions in Manchuria posed a threat to the then almost undefended eastern parts of Russia and that, true to his dislike of a two-front war, Stalin was disinclined to add western complications to his problems in the East. It is only logical, therefore, if, according to Wollenberg's testimony, "the central committee of the K.P.D. [German communist party] had received from Moscow the strictest orders to refrain from anything which could have led to a socialist way-out of the German crisis."[166]

An explanation which, at first glance, is contradictory was supplied by a second witness, Dr. Karl August Wittfogel:

> The Comintern engineered the fight between the German communists and the social democrats . . . to bring Hitler to power, not because they were political perverts but because they wanted a big war in the West. . . . They would have preferred a military conservative government. They took Hitler. He was the lesser evil.[167]

Wittfogel had an extensive range of personal acquaintances among communist leaders. During the summer months of 1932 he lived in Moscow and engaged in many discussions about the German situation. According to his testimony, he was told by prominent second-echelon leaders of the Comintern that Hitler must and should come to power even if "20,000 of the best labor leaders in Germany will have to be killed." "This was the great line of the Comintern, to bring Hitler to power, not because they loved him; they did not. They thought that through him they would get the big thing going." And Wittfogel commented:

> I myself thought at first the Russian communists were just dumb. Gradually, I realized myself that this was a very big strategy to get one of the great wars of modern times going. This took some time, but it succeeded in 1939.

The two testimonies are not in conflict: To avoid immediate war, but to provoke war at a later time, it was "reasonable" to sacrifice

[166] *Loc. cit.*, p. 63.

[167] *Hearings before the Subcommittee to Investigate the Administration of the Internal Security Act and other Internal Security Laws of the Committee on the Judiciary, The Institute of Pacific Relations, Part I* [U. S. Congress, 82nd, 1st sess., Senate. (Washington, D. C., Govt. Print. Off., 1951), pp. 323 f.].

the German communist party and transform Germany into an aggressively revisionist power. A closer study of the documented party line does not contradict this interpretation. However, it indicates that the situation was more complex and, also, more confused. There may have been less "grand strategy" and more day-by-day expediency, and even more a misreading of the nazi threat, than these testimonies indicate.

Ample documentation can be culled from the pages of *International Press Correspondence* (*Inprecorr* for short) which, at that time, was the main informational organ of the communist world movement. Inprecorr disseminated authoritative statements, interpretations, and Comintern instructions to communist organizations in all countries. Since the soviet archives have not been opened, the *International Press Correspondence* must be considered as one of our main, and most reliable, sources of information on questions of this type.

Several points can be established with clarity. There was no question in communist minds that another imperialist world war was not only inevitable but impending. For example, the issue of March 10, 1932, carried the headline: "The world is drifting into an imperialist world war." The same issue also affirmed that the redistribution of the world stood "immediately on the order of the day."[168] On September 1, 1932, Inprecorr reprinted an article from *Pravda*, originally dated August 27, which reads:

We are in the transition to a new epoch of war and revolution. . . . Capitalism has reached a catastrophic stage, a phase of violent class struggles, of attempts to re-divide the world by means of war.[169]

On October 20, 1932, celebrating the fifteenth anniversary of the October revolution, the Comintern house organ asserted: "Never has there been so great a danger of military attacks on the U.S.S.R. as there is now."

What nations were causing this danger of war? Again, the communists were perfectly outspoken. In March 1932, Japan, England, France, Poland, and Rumania were mentioned as the chief aggres-

[168] P. 213.

[169] P. 815. It should be remembered that this was the period when the depression was at its bleakest.

sors. In September, Japan and France were considered the main warmongers. And in October,[170] Japan, France, and Britain were appointed the leading culprits. This last enumeration is particularly important since it was published in an *official* statement by the twelfth plenum of the executive committee of the Comintern. The twelfth plenum also issued a resolution[171] in which we read:

The imperialist powers, and first of all, the imperialists of France and Japan, are exerting every effort to extend and strengthen the anti-soviet block in order to deliver a decisive military blow at the basis of the world proletarian revolution, the U.S.S.R. . . . At the same time, direct preparations for intervention against the U.S.S.R. are being carried on under the guidance of France, Poland, Rumania and the Baltic countries.

This estimate, which implied that Germany was not considered a danger to the Soviet Union, may be posed as a first premise. If, as a second premise, it is assumed that a strongly nationalist Germany would not come to terms with France or Britain but would abrogate the Versailles treaty and therefore join in mortal conflict with the West, the conclusion would be inevitable that heavy German rearmament—which could be obtained only as a result of the seizure of power by the nazis or other right extremists—would improve the security position of the U.S.S.R. A nazi victory, or a victory by militant nationalists, would deflect the attention of the western powers from the Soviet Union to Germany.

There is, of course, an obvious argument against this reasoning: Must not the nazis or a strongly rearmed Germany be expected to turn against the Soviet Union? The reply probably would have been that national socialism simply is another form of bourgeois rule, and, therefore, it really made no difference. Moreover, the national socialist government would be dominated, behind the scenes, by a Reichswehr which for more than ten years had been co-operating closely with the soviets. The military leaders of Germany were on record as favoring an alliance with Russia. In any event, they were opposed to war against Russia and could be relied upon both to prevent a Russo-German war and to plump for a war with France.

It is not without interest to remember that during 1931 and 1932 the German market was flooded with books pleading for German-

[170] October 6, 1932, p. 939.
[171] October 20, 1932, p. 1055.

Russian collaboration and extolling the similarities between the bolshevik and the nazi revolutions. Nazism was indeed described as the German form of bolshevism, and an elusive phenomenon called "national bolshevism" was hailed as the nemesis of senile, tottering capitalism. Some of these books were written by authors known for their allegedly conservative leanings and their romantic opposition to "business economics"; the identity of other authors was more dubious: in fact, there was a strong incidence of pen names.

The German communist party cultivated some programs (under the direction of dissident Reichswehr officers) aiming at an understanding with the nazis. There was one widely read magazine which at one and the same time was strongly anticapitalist, pro-Russian, pro-German nationalism, pro-German expansion in the direction of the Danube valley, and pro the romantic idealization of the "toilers." It is now known that this magazine was infiltrated by cryptocommunists. Two medium-sized publishing houses specialized in hybrid literature of a pronazi and, simultaneously, pro-Russian and even probolshevik character. Thus, indications are fairly strong that the communists engaged in a peculiar type of ideological warfare designed to orient the minds of German nationalists.

To return to Inprecorr. The next point that can be established clearly is that the communists had elected the social democrats rather than the nazis to be their main enemy. For example, in the issue of January 28, 1932, it is stated that "the chief attack of revolutionary policy must be directed against the main social fortress of the bourgeoisie, the social democracy."[172] The central strategic task of the communists was described as the "winning of the majority of the proletariat for communism." This task allegedly could be accomplished only as a result of the destruction of the social democratic party.[173]

Time and again the socialists were described as the "main social support of the bourgeoisie." The communists professed to see no difference between Carl Severing, the socialist minister of the interior in Prussia, or Hindenburg, and Hitler.[174] W. Knorin, the Russian representative in the Comintern, acknowledged that there were differences between the democratic socialists and the national so-

[172] P. 73.
[173] This was repeated, for example, on March 3, 1932, p. 176.
[174] For example, January 14, p. 23; also, March 24, 1932, p. 276.

cialists but "these differences of opinion are between two fractions which are striving to maintain capitalism and fighting against the proletarian revolution."[175] Knorin continued:

The communists have declared a thousand times that there is only one enemy which must be overthrown, namely the bourgeoisie. In order to overthrow the bourgeoisie it is necessary that the majority of the working class exert all their efforts. The social democracy holds the workers back from the struggle. . . . It [the social democracy] helps the bourgeoisie and is therefore the chief enemy within the working class and unless it is shattered, the bourgeoisie cannot be overthrown.

Even after Hitler had gained power the chief significance of this event was seen to lie in the "second historical downfall of social democracy" and in the resultant "exit" of the "broad working class masses" from the socialist party.[176]

Hence, according to this communist theory, the nazis, objectively speaking, *accomplished the primary revolutionary task: the destruction of social democracy.*

The question naturally arises: Was this antisocialist line a bona fide policy? If so, communist assistance to the nazis could be interpreted as unintentional. It just so happened that the nazis profited from the attack on the socialists and that the communists did not see any good reason to abandon their antisocialist line simply because the nazis derived advantages from the situation. Such an interpretation, of course, would assume great naïveté on the part of the communists. Hence, the other question arises: Was the antisocialist policy a cover operation designed to conceal the true communist policy, which was to support the nazis? Unfortunately, this question cannot as yet be answered.

A fourth point that can be established is that the communists, to the bitter end, underrated the power and effectiveness of the nazi movement. In fact, they knew very little about it.[177] For example,

[175] April 21, 1932, p. 348.
[176] March 17, 1933, p. 304.
[177] Ignorance and underestimation of the nazi movement was typical of the time. From the vantage point of posterity, it is hard to see how anyone could have underrated the nazis. In order to understand the decisions of the time, however, we must remember that Hitler was generally considered a clown who would be pushed aside easily. The nazi party was considered an agglomeration of contradictory interests which could not weather a serious storm. A nazi government was believed possible by many, but it was assumed that it would last only a short time or that its control would pass into the hands of the army, the bureaucracy, and big business.

it was only in June 1932 that Inprecorr began a series of articles on the nazi party, admittedly to improve the knowledge of the communists which was "still very unclear and in part undecided." Actually, this series of articles was smuggled into Inprecorr by "deviationist" elements within the German communist party.[178]

But apparently this attempt at enlightenment did not help very much. The official communist theory was that the nazi dictatorship would not mean a fundamental change of system and that the bourgeoisie would not be strengthened by a nazi conquest of power. It appears that at least some prominent communists considered the nazi dictatorship as inevitable and as a "necessary intermediary stage" to the proletarian revolution in Germany.[179]

In point of fact, the nazi ascension to power was seen as the beginning of a true revolutionary crisis. There were allegedly strong anticapitalist tendencies among the nazi masses. These basically anticapitalist nazis were expected to turn against Hitler if he exposed his true role as the savior of the capitalist system. The exposure of subservience to capitalism both of the socialists and of the national socialists would drive the workers into the arms of communism.

Even if there were no widespread disillusionment, the nazification of Germany would lead to the destruction of the workers' organizations and the abolition of the "revolutionary achievements of the working class." Paradoxically, such an event would accelerate "the process of mobilizing the forces of the proletariat."[180] On October 11, 1932, *Pravda* stated that the setting up of a fascist dictatorship in Germany would not mean the strengthening but the weakening of the German bourgeoisie. The Russian communists confessed to believe that in a country where the proletariat constitutes the absolute majority of the population, where it possessed "great Marxist traditions," and where, moreover, the communist party has become a mass organization, "in such a country it is impossible for a government of terror to last any length of time."[181] All of this may seem

---

[178] Personal statement to the author by K. A. Wittfogel.

[179] June 2, 1933, p. 526. This phrasing is contained in a resolution of the central committee of the German communist party and is directed against the policies allegedly advocated by Heinz Neumann. It is a favorite trick of Stalinist organizations to accuse opponents of the very mistakes they committed themselves.

[180] July 28, 1932, pp. 673 ff.

[181] Knorin, July 28, 1932, pp. 673 ff.

slightly contradictory, but the meaning is quite clear: nazism is not really dangerous. Or, as Manuilsky expressed it: "If it required many years for the shattering of social democracy, . . . a much shorter period will, of course, be necessary for the collapse of fascism."[182]

The communists supported their estimate by pointing out that leading German industrialists, too, were of the opinion that "Hitler means civil war and then everything would be lost" for the capitalist system.[183]

For whatever reasons, the communists would not, for one moment, support the "bankrupt Weimar regime." That is the fundamental fact: the *consistency* with which communist tactics furthered the purposes of the nazis. The only point at issue is the hidden purpose of these tactics.

After Hitler had come to power, the Russian communists expected that, as a result of the events in Germany, a revolutionary crisis would mature not only in Germany but "in the whole of Europe."[184] The general theory was propounded by the irrepressible Manuilsky, who proclaimed: "The appearance and growth of fascism are due to the over-ripeness of capitalism and the belatedness of the proletarian revolution."[185]

Overripeness and belatedness or not, there is at least indirect confirmation of the theory that Stalin did not then desire a communist revolution in Germany. In January 1932 the German communists issued bloodthirsty slogans to stimulate the domestic class struggle. They came out loudly for a socialist soviet Germany and its alliance with the Soviet Union and the world proletariat. In June, the communists still described themselves as the "only party" which could organize the "revolutionary way out of the crisis." The central committee of the German communist party stated:

Hitler fascism must never take over government power in Germany. The terrorist bands of the nazis must never set up their bloody regime of the German proletariat.[186]

[182] September 15, 1933, p. 892.

[183] March 10, 1932, p. 215.

[184] Knorin, March 9, 1933, p. 263, reprint from an article originally published in Russian on February 10, 1933. As of these dates, Germany was said to be "on the threshold of a revolutionary crisis." In reality, the communists got kicked in the shins.

[185] October 29, 1932, p. 983.

[186] June 6, 1932, p. 528.

It called for political mass strikes and for "extra-parliamentary mass fights" against fascism, hunger, and imperialist war, as well as for a powerful "red mass self-defense."

Later, however, this revolutionary phraseology was dropped. The communists contented themselves with ideological struggle, united-front tactics, and propaganda work among the unemployed, youth, women, emigrants, peasants, and national liberation movements. There were also calls to engage in antimilitarist work.[187] By clear implication, the strong effort against nazism was called off. The extraparliamentary mass fight had become a tame struggle with words.

It goes without saying that this policy of playing intentional or accidental midwife to the nazi revolution was not accepted without a great deal of opposition. There were violent clashes within the ranks of the German communist party, which is quite understandable, since it was the leaders of this very party who were risking their own necks. There was, furthermore, dissension between the Russian and the German communists. For example, in Inprecorr of June 9, 1932, an editorial from *Pravda,* in which the advent of a "fascist dictatorship" was calmly accepted as inevitable, was reprinted together with an appeal by the German central committee calling for a strong fight against the "bloody" nazi threat.

There are many indications that the discussions about the German policy caused a serious dispute within the Comintern itself. For example, on July 28, 1932, an article by Knorin on the German situation was reproduced with the non-customary warning that this article which had appeared in *Pravda,* the central organ of the C.P.S.U., was published "as expressing the views of an important press organ." For the communists, *Pravda* represented a great deal more than an "important press organ." Needless to say, the opposition did not get very far, and, even more needless to add, the opponents of 1932 did not survive the purges of 1936.

Hence, the communist German policy of 1932 may be summarized as follows: (1) There is a great danger of war, which could be lessened if Germany would rearm immediately and on a massive

[187] October 20, 1932, p. 1006. Incidentally, revolutionary antimilitarism was to be organized for the active defense of the Soviet Union, as would be expected. It is rather unexpected that this work was also to be done for the active defense of China and the Chinese soviets. There were no longer any appeals to do something about the sorry plight of the German communist party.

scale. Such rearmament could be brought about only by a nazi government or by a government controlled by seminazis and the Reichswehr. (2) The social democrats are the main enemy and must be destroyed. Once in power, the nazis would destroy them. (3) The nazis are not really dangerous to Russia and the world communist movement. However, they would temporarily incapacitate the communist party of Germany. This loss must be accepted. (4) A communist revolutionary solution to the German crisis is impossible and, in any event, premature. It would endanger the safety and security of the Soviet Union.[188] (5) The seizure of power by the nazis would usher in a profound revolutionary crisis not only threatening Germany but also weakening Europe as a whole. Failing this, the nazis would be unable to consolidate themselves and would be destroyed through war which also might undermine the western powers.

Insofar as the soviet government was concerned, it eagerly renewed, during May 1933, the Berlin treaty of 1926 on neutrality and nonaggression. In the words of *International Press Correspondence,* the prolongation of this Russo-German treaty was the "correct continuation of [the] struggle for peace in the interest of the toilers of the whole world."[189]

If everything is said and done, communist policy of 1932 may not have been so "rational" as these various acrobatic arguments would seem to suggest. It is impossible today to state categorically what the communist concept really was. There is throughout a strong suggestion of confusion and compromise. It is possible that events moved much faster than the communists expected. For instance, the overthrow of the Schleicher government after only two months in

[188] In this connection it is worth recording that, according to a most knowledgeable German source, "during the depression years, German industry was kept afloat largely because it received substantial orders from the Russians," especially gold and raw materials. Without these Russian orders, the economic crisis in Germany would have been intensified to the breaking point, and almost inevitably a revolutionary crisis would have arisen. The Russian orders kept German capitalism alive, although this may have been a matter of economic compulsion—the first Five-Year Plan had just been put into operation—rather than political choice. Certainly, this Russian trade policy was not in contradiction with the concept that a communist revolution in Germany was as yet to be avoided. For some of the documentation, see Robert Strausz-Hupé and Stefan T. Possony, *International Relations in the Age of the Conflict between Democracy and Dictatorship* (New York, McGraw-Hill, 1950), p. 745.

[189] June 2, 1933, page 535.

power came as a complete surprise to everybody. It had been widely anticipated that General Schleicher would run Germany for a very long time. It is quite conceivable that communist policies were based on an estimate that the two prenazi governments were relatively stable.

On the other hand, there is a clear-cut pattern of almost unceasing collaboration between German nationalists and Russian bolsheviks. This collaboration started in 1914, or even earlier, reached a climax during 1917 and 1918, after a short break was resumed in 1920, led to Rapallo and the Berlin treaty,[190] and, via 1932, culminated in the pact of 1939 and the negotiations of 1940. During the war this collaboration was resumed in the form of the free German committee and continued into the period of Russian occupation of eastern Germany.[191] Could it be that, in 1932, the bolsheviks simply adhered to this pattern, wishing, quite primitively, to stick to the one non-communist group with which they had been able to maintain a semipermanent semialliance—the German conservatives and the military?

However that may be, an official interpretation of the Comintern nazi policy was revealed in December 1933.[192] Appropriately, it was couched in Aesopian language and classical quotations.[193] A

[190] The text of the Rapallo and Berlin treaties is reprinted in Strausz-Hupé and Possony, *op. cit.,* pp. 752–56.

[191] For these events, see Chap. 5, p. 278.

[192] *International Press Correspondence,* December 15, 1933, p. 1241.

[193] Some people believe that the term "Aesopian language" was invented *ad hoc* to confuse American politics. In 1917, Lenin wrote in the Preface to the Russian edition of his *Imperialism, the Highest Stage of Capitalism:* "This pamphlet was written with an eye to the tsarist censorship. Hence, I was not only forced to confine myself strictly to an exclusively theoretical, mainly economic analysis of facts, but to formulate the few necessary observations on politics with extreme caution, by hints, in that Aesopian language—in that cursed Aesopian language—to which tsarism compelled all revolutionaries to have recourse, whenever they took up their pens to write a 'legal' work." To which the editor added: " 'Aesopian,' after the Greek fable-writer Aesop, was the term applied to the allusive and roundabout style adopted in 'legal' publications by revolutionaries in order to evade the censorship." See *Selected Works, op. cit.,* V, 5. In his Preface to the French and German editions, written in 1920, Lenin explained the continuing need for the employment of such language: "To a certain extent it will be useful to many communists in advanced capitalist countries to convince themselves by the example of this pamphlet, legal, from the standpoint of the tsarist censor, of the possibility—and necessity—of making use of even the slight remnants of legality which still remain at the disposal of the communists, say, in contemporary America or France." *Ibid.,* p. 7.

French socialist had confessed to his inability to understand "the reasons which induced Stalin's representatives to seek connections with the leaders of Italian, German, and Austrian fascism. The threat of a Russo-Japanese conflict does not justify it."

The communist answer was given in the words of Friedrich Engels:

Marx and I do not find the matter itself [that Wilhelm Liebknecht, as member of the Saxon Diet, took the prescribed loyalty oath] in any way so dangerous. . . . *You* must know whether *"Paris vaut bien une messe,"* as Henry IV said when he became a catholic.[194]

And, indeed, why should a communist not become a nazi?

THE SEVENTH WORLD CONGRESS: TROJAN HORSE TACTICS

THE Seventh World Congress of the Communist International met in 1935. Predictions made during the Sixth Congress that a new war was impending had not yet been realized, but "fascism" had become the major political factor in Europe, and "fascism is war."[195] The Soviet Union felt itself directly menaced by both Germany and Japan and was disturbed by the possibility of Chiang Kai-shek crushing the Chinese communists and retaking the soviet-ized lands of Northwest China.

In 1935 the Soviet Union was just recovering from the ravages of collectivization and industrialization. The second Five Year Plan had not been completed. The soviets were too weak for war, especially for a war in which they would be isolated, without outside sources of supply and without allies who could attack their enemies from the rear. Accordingly, the Soviet Union improved its relations with France, called off, temporarily, the French communist party from its antimilitaristic demoralization work,[196] attempted to forestall the conflict through the League of Nations, and accommodated

[194] Engels to Bebel, November 24, 1879.

[195] Georgi Dimitrov, *The United Front, The Struggle against Fascism and War* (New York, International Publishers, 1938), p. 262.

[196] Stalin's reported promise to this effect to Pierre Laval when the latter signed the Franco-Russian alliance in 1935 was confirmed by D. C. Manuilsky, *The Work of the Seventh Congress of the Communist International* (New York, Workers Library Publishers, 1936), p. 26.

itself with the United States, in line with Stalin's alleged opinion that:

Victory will be won by the side which is allied to the United States.[197]

At the same time, of course, revolutionary work was not abandoned. While predicting war and subsequent revolution, Stalin came out strongly against what Kuusinen called "opportunist reliance on spontaneity." The revolution would not result automatically from the oncoming war but had to be prepared by "the greatest intensification of . . . bolshevik activity."[198]

The problem was, on the one hand, to gain allies among nations whose government and social structure the communists were determined to destroy and to gain some measure of control over these allies; and, on the other hand, to continue preparations for revolution both against the coveted allies and the fascist countries, where police-state controls copied from the soviet system made subversive work very difficult.

To solve this difficult problem, the communists came up with one of their inimitable dialectical schemes. They wanted their allies strong, but they also wanted them procommunist, or, in any event, not actively anticommunist. The solution was, first, to reassure the proletariat of these allied countries that they were fighting a "national liberation war" against "fascism," on the side of the Soviet Union. They were, therefore, engaged in a "just" war. Secondly, the communists were told that they should strive to transform the war for national independence into a genuine "people's war," on the model of the Chinese communists.[199] They must secure the arming of the whole people in order that "the war may be waged in a Jacobin, in a revolutionary manner."[200]

[197] Yves Delbars, *Le Vrai Stalin* (Paris, Editions "Je sers," 1950), p. 432.

[198] *Abridged Stenographic Report of Proceedings, Seventh Congress of the Communist International* (Moscow, Foreign Languages Publishing House, 1939), p. 470.

[199] Manuilsky took great pains in pointing out the importance of the Chinese movement for the whole world. He emphasized that the Chinese communists had a number of military tricks which should be imitated in other peoples' wars: guerrilla warfare in the rear of the enemy, utilization of antagonisms in the opposing camp, preservation of initiative, counteroffensive, and political demoralization. *Ibid.*, pp. 52 f.

[200] Manuilsky, *op. cit.*, p. 25.

The purpose was to link the military struggle of the U.S.S.R. with communist-controlled mass movements abroad. The soviets wanted to enlist maximum support for the war by entering into agreements with any and every group. They worked to extend "the democratic rights and liberties of the masses of the people," meaning the position and influence of the local communist party.[201]

Dimitrov, then secretary general of the Comintern and subsequently prime minister of Bulgaria, explained that the movement toward the people's war, among other things, should aim at the disarming and disbanding of anticommunist organizations and at the purging of anticommunists from state bureaucracy, army, and police.[202]

There were to be alliances between the capitalist countries and Russia. The capitalist nations were to be reorganized in order to be capable of fighting a people's war;[203] and the organization of the people's war was to lead to communist participation in the government and, ultimately, to communist seizure of power.

The general objective was to shift most of the burden for the dirty work both for war and revolution to the shoulders of the capitalists. Due to their foolish disarmament policies, the western powers needed the assistance of Russia in their defense against Germany and Italy. Hence, the western powers were to be held in their dependence on Russian help, partly by preventing reconciliation between the hostile camps and especially by preventing a Franco-Italian *rapprochement;* partly by insisting on a domestic policy which would not arouse Russia's "suspicions." The capitalist nations were to do most of the fighting, they were to admit more and more communists to the helms of command—to keep faith with Russia and to organize the people's war—and they were to tolerate the emergence of an ever more powerful and revolutionary domestic communist movement. As the fascist armies would sap the strength of the capitalists, the communists inevitably would fill the vacua of political power. Thus, capitalism would call in communism as its savior and, indeed, would be saved in truly communist fashion. While this scheme was unsuccessful at the time, it served after June

---

[201] *Ibid.*, p. 52.
[202] Dimitrov, *op. cit.*, p. 47.
[203] Manuilsky, *op. cit.*, p. 63.

1941, in a slightly modified version, as the theoretical basis for communist participation in the resistance movement.

This new concept of world revolution could not work so long as communists' motives and intentions were being "mistrusted." From a propaganda standpoint, communism had not made much headway among the western nations. The soviets realized that their publicity campaign had lacked appeal, since it was couched in language completely incomprehensible to those not steeped in Marxian terminology ("sectarianism").

In order to gain more followers, stereotyped forms of political activity had to be abandoned. Only if the communists could find a "common language" with the people would it be possible to end "the isolation of the revolutionary vanguard from the masses of the proletariat and all other toilers, as well as overcoming the fatal isolation of the working class itself from its natural allies in the struggle against the bourgeoisie, against fascism."[204]

The fear of fascism was selected by the Seventh Congress as the bait by which the "united front" of all "anti-fascists" could be formed under communist leadership.[205] The partial abandonment of the Marxian vocabulary in favor of "liberal" and "democratic" language and the concentration on concrete issues rather than abstractions became the means by which the communists hoped to gain the support of non-communists.

United-front tactics required the western European communists to advocate the strengthening of national defense systems. Dimitrov quoted an article written by Lenin in 1914 entitled "On the National Pride of the Great Russians," in which it was stated that Russian revolutionaries might very well have "national pride." After all, Russia had created a revolutionary class and had given to humanity "great examples of the struggle for freedom and socialism." While a revolutionary should hate the "slavish past" of his country, he

---

[204] Dimitrov, *op. cit.,* p. 92.

[205] Talking about China, Stalin said in 1927: "A united front can have revolutionary significance only if it does not hinder the communist party from conducting its independent political and organizational work, only if it does not prevent it from organizing the proletariat into an independent political force, rousing the peasantry against the landlords, openly organizing a revolution of workers and peasants and thus preparing the conditions necessary for the hegemony of the proletariat." *Marxism and the National and Colonial Question, op. cit.,* p. 208.

should be proud of his fatherland's national and cultural achievements.[206] Naturally, everything can be argued both ways.

United-front tactics not only posed ideological problems but also required the creating of suitable organizational devices. Dimitrov called for the strengthening of "transmission belts" between party and people, particularly trade unions, women's organizations, antifascist and antiimperialist "fronts." He also suggested penetration of mass organizations not yet under communist control. In short, the communists were to make use of any appeal and any organization provided they could do so effectively.

Special attention was devoted to the United States, where the communist party enjoyed only a small local following. Dimitrov pointed out that fascism in the United States would be disastrous for the fate of world communism. He intimated that, in its sectarian form, the communist party could do nothing to prevent such a threat. Hence, parties should be established which would be acceptable to the American people, perhaps a "workers and farmers party." The communists should accept the fact that such a party would be neither socialist nor communist, although it might oppose such institutions as the trusts and banks. There were only two requirements: The party must be "anti-fascist" and *must not be anti-communist."*[207] Dimitrov warned the comrades that the initiative for an American "third party" should not pass into the hands of elements who would create an anticommunist and antirevolutionary organization.

The new tactics would achieve their greatest success if the communists were admitted into "united front governments." A united-front government was not designed to be what the liberals believed it should be, namely an honest leftist and progressive coalition, within the framework of democracy, uniting all antireactionary and antifascist forces.

Dimitrov quoted Lenin to the effect that great attention should be devoted to "searching out forms of transition for the proletarian revolution." He added that the united-front government would prove to be one of the most important transitional forms from bourgeois democracy to communist dictatorship. According to Dimitrov, the left doctrinaires always avoided and misunderstood this

[206] Dimitrov, *op. cit.,* p. 79.
[207] *Ibid.,* p. 42. (Italics in original.)

useful idea of Lenin's. The point is to get into the government by hook or by crook, carry out "fundamental revolutionary demands," and arm the proletariat.[208] To make his meaning clear, Dimitrov quoted the horrid examples of united-front governments in Saxony and Thuringia where the communist cabinet members did not exploit their positions for revolutionary purposes but simply acted as conventional ministers of state.

Dimitrov left no doubt that a united-front government cannot bring "final salvation." It cannot overthrow "the class rule of an exploiter" nor remove the danger of counterrevolution. As a transition device, it can go only so far. Therefore, in addition to setting up and participating in coalition governments, it is necessary to "prepare for the socialist revolution." Dimitrov added ominously: "Soviet power and *only* Soviet power can bring salvation."[209] Clearly, Frunze's thesis that the Red army was the main weapon of the communist movement was not abandoned by the Seventh World Congress.

The most authoritative version of united-front and coalition government tactics was given later, in 1940, by Mao Tse-tung in his book *China's New Democracy*.

Mao's interpretation of the significance of coalition tactics can be summarized as follows: *Lenin insisted on the usefulness of communist participation in parliaments. There is an even greater revolutionary usefulness in communist participation in governments.*

United fronts and coalition cabinets constitute an effective device to split the opposition, isolate the anticommunists, gain non-communist support, and make full use of all "progressive" movements. Coalition tactics are a real addition to the art of seizing power. They remove the difficulties inherent in the 1917 tactics of dual power; it may be very difficult to recreate such a situation which requires overt competition with the entrenched authority. Transfer of power from the government to another "sovereign" group like the soviet no longer needs to be engineered.

On the contrary, communist participation in government prepares for the usurpation of power in such a fashion that seizure can take place through the regular institutions. This is so because communist cabinet ministers will sabotage policy, weaken and destroy

[208] Dimitrov, *op. cit.*, pp. 74 f.
[209] Italics in original.

state power, infiltrate their agents into key control positions, manipulate and even neutralize the armed forces. Mao's *New Democracy* "enveloped the communist pill in the sweetest sugar coating ever given it, and redoubled the effectiveness of the dose at the same time."[210]

So much for communist strategy with respect to the prospective allies of the Soviet Union.

The Seventh World Congress also studied the possibility of revolutionary work in hostile countries where "the fascists are in power."[211] This was described as perhaps the most important problem facing the communists.

The Achilles's heel of the fascist dictatorship was considered to be its social basis which, Dimitrov thought, was "extremely heterogeneous." Since fascism is a dictatorship exercised by the "big bourgeoisie" over various classes and strata of society, it "must inevitably come into conflict with its mass social basis."[212] This faulty sociological analysis may have been one of the reasons why communist work proved ineffective in nazi Germany and fascist Italy.

Dimitrov and his associates hoped that a revolutionary movement could be built on the exploitation of local and temporary grievances without the emergence of an over-all political "consciousness." Day-to-day problems would give the communists opportuni-

---

[210] *House Committee on Foreign Affairs, The Strategy and Tactics of World Communism, Supplement III, Communism in China* [U. S. Congress, 81st, 1st sess., House. (Washington, D. C., Govt. Print. Off., 1949), pp. 31–35]. It should be remembered that ideas of "evolutionary revolution" were discussed in 1917. Stalin was in favor of this approach until turned around by Lenin, while Kamenyev and Sinovyev continued to favor this tactic to the very end. Kamenyev hoped that Kerensky would pass from the scene if and when the bolsheviks became the majority party in the central executive committee of the All-Russian soviet. Stalin allegedly said: "No, we must prepare for battle. If Kerensky falls by himself as a result of our propaganda, like the walls of Jericho fell from the sound of Joshua's trumpets, so much the better. But we must be ready for the worst." Workers and coalition government tactics were discussed even prior to World War I. They were reconsidered during the Fifth World Congress in 1924, particularly by Radek who saw much promise in the device. Sinovyev admitted the possibility of seizing power through workers' governments and thought that the coalition idea was useful propagandistically. But he believed that seizure of power in a strong and advanced country would require civil war and that conclusive success through coalition tactics was improbable. *Die Weltpartei des Leninismus, op. cit.,* p. 108. The development of the soviet doctrine is toward ever greater tactical flexibility.

[211] Dimitrov, *op. cit.,* p. 47.

[212] *Ibid.,* p. 49.

ties for agitation. Such a hope was in contrast to the basic tenets of Leninism and Stalinism. It was hardly taken seriously and was probably expressed only to bolster the morale of German communists.

The soviets, of course, realized that internal agitation and propaganda were impossible in a country run by a secret police like the Gestapo. *Except war, infiltration is the most effective method of fighting a dictatorship.* The communists were told that they must obtain posts in organizations like the nazi labor front, the Hitler youth, sports clubs, *Kraft durch Freude,* and so forth. Surprisingly, Dimitrov did not mention the German army and the Gestapo. Was this oversight intentional?

Infiltration tactics were to be patterned after the

... ancient tale of the capture of Troy. Troy was inaccessible to the army attacking her, thanks to her impregnable walls. And the attacking army, after suffering many sacrifices, was unable to achieve victory until with the aid of the famous Trojan horse it managed to penetrate to the very heart of the enemy's camp. We revolutionary workers, it appears to me, should not be shy about using the same tactics with regard to our fascist foe, who is defending himself against the people with the help of a living wall of his cutthroats.[213]

A revolutionary who fails to understand the necessity of using such tactics may be an excellent man, Dimitrov said, but he is also a windbag and not a true revolutionary! The communist movement must grow outside and inside the fascist organizations and thus become the "battering ram" to shatter the fortress which seemed "impregnable to many."

Manuilsky admitted that the new tactic would encounter great difficulties, such as early discovery or the "acclimatization" of the infiltrators to their new surroundings and consequent loss of their usefulness. "We have not much experience to go by at this work yet, and it is a difficult matter to sum it up publicly."

The need for new organizational forms to be devised for rank and filers engaged in "open mass work" was recognized as well as the need for cadres of "legal" (secret) communists who "must penetrate into the fascist mass organizations." Public discussion being impossible, Manuilsky invited the communists to "decipher" the Trojan horse tactics.[214]

[213] *Ibid.*, p. 52.
[214] Manuilsky, *op. cit.*, pp. 69, 70.

The Seventh World Congress did not invalidate the resolutions of the Sixth Congress. These resolutions were maintained in their entirety, though somewhat altered to fit a changed world situation and improved in respect to "termiting" tactics. The Seventh Congress simply enriched the tactical arsenal of communism.[215]

However, the communists were unable to infiltrate the nazi state apparatus effectively. While they achieved some influence over their "capitalist allies," the measure of control gained by them in the late 1930's was inadequate to insure success of this strategy. Hence, it must have seemed to the soviets that they would be compelled to abandon revolutionary strategy and concentrate on old-fashioned defense. The bolsheviks were relieved when they discovered that the main premise of their concept—that the fascist states were preparing war against the Soviet Union *only*—was not entirely valid and that it was possible to conclude an alliance with fascism. The fiasco of the Seventh World Congress strategy against the fascist states led to the reversal of soviet policy in 1939.

FOOTNOTE ON THE SPANISH CIVIL WAR

ACCORDING to a statement by Ercoli-Togliatti, the Spanish civil war was "after the October socialist revolution of 1917 . . .

---

[215] The basic strategic concept developed by the Seventh Congress may be summed up dialectically as follows:

Thesis: The fascist states are preparing for war against the Soviet Union. The fascist states must be weakened by infiltration. Their advance must be stopped by war.

Antithesis: The main burden of the war should be carried by the capitalist states. The Soviet Union must ally itself with some capitalist states. The Soviet Union must establish partial or full control over its capitalist allies; this control can be obtained by infiltration, by organizing a people's war, and by participation in a coalition government.

Synthesis: The war must be used to press forward to gradual seizure of power in the allied capitalist states. The fascist states, weakened by infiltration, must be defeated in battle; defeat will lead to revolution.

This was a very ambitious strategy of killing three birds with one stone, but it was a trifle oversophisticated.

the biggest event in the emancipation struggle of the masses of the people in capitalist countries."[216] One would expect, therefore, that the Spanish civil war contributed greatly to the development of communist conflict techniques. But this is not the case. On the contrary, the Spanish civil war bears out the contention that the political structure of the soviet dictatorship and its internal conflicts may react unfavorably on communist capabilities abroad. The purge of the bolshevik "old believers" coincided with the Spanish incident. It undercut the support to, and the leadership of, the revolutionary forces in Spain and, in the last analysis, made a very substantial contribution to the victory of General Francisco Franco.

The overthrow of Primo de Rivera's benign dictatorship and the subsequent fall of the Spanish monarchy (1931) initiated a series of events which, in communist terminology, could be described as the first phase of a "bourgeois-democratic revolution." The years after the fall of the monarchy were a "time of trouble." There were frequent and large-scale industrial strikes which hampered the progress of the economically backward country. Strong separatist movements sprang up in Catalonia and in the Basques Provinces. Communists, anarchists, and syndicalists organized numerous local uprisings, especially in the mining districts of Asturias. At that time, the Stalinist communists had a small and rather uninfluential party: Spanish revolutionaries flocked to the more unruly Trotskyite and anarchist organizations.

Following the decisions of the Seventh World Congress, the Spanish Stalinists joined the other leftist parties in a "popular front" which achieved an electoral victory early in 1936. A leftist coalition government was formed, and the communists got ready to enlarge their positions, with a view toward achieving, first, influence and, later, control over the Spanish popular front.

As soon as the popular front was in power, there developed a revolutionary crisis. In many ways Spain began to resemble the Russia of early 1917. One need only read the *International Press Correspondence* of the time to realize that the communists confidently expected uprisings and a leftist revolution to occur within the near future. Undoubtedly, they also made preparations for such contingencies. However, they still were weak, and their influence

[216] Ercoli, "Specific Features of the Spanish Revolution," *International Press Correspondence* (October 24, 1936), p. 1292.

on events was far less significant than that exercised by other leftist groups. In any event, it was not the leftists who seized the initiative, but the Spanish army which had decided to act (July 1936) and prevent Spain from going down the road of Russia. Where Kornilov had failed, Franco succeeded, not only because the Spanish military forces had not yet entirely succumbed to leftist disintegration, but also because the Spanish generals had secured military and political support abroad, especially in Germany and Italy, at that time the only nations following a clear-cut antisoviet and anticommunist course of action.

Franco's coup was not a full success. Part of the army and navy sided with the government, and the army's seizure of power was incomplete. The military rebels secured a great deal of territory, but the government retained control over vital parts of the country, including the capital city. As a result, a civil war followed in which both sides controlled territory and, with regular armies, waged a campaign for the capture of more territory. Aside from the fact that the war was fought within one nation, it was an orthodox war of the traditional type.

The outcome of the civil war was by no means a foregone conclusion. The government had retained control over most of Spain's industrial war potential, its banking system, and its gold reserves, and it possessed land communications with France, then also ruled by a popular-front government. The workers and the lower middle classes, as well as the anticlerical liberal elements, sided with the government. Franco was able to compensate for his original weakness by better military leadership and organization and by gaining strong support among the mass of the Spanish people, the peasants, the catholics, the traditional parties, and the upper classes. He was able to secure weapons and military advisers from Germany and Italy while the loyalists, due to the so-called nonintervention agreement, proved unable to procure supplies in adequate quantities from France and Britain.

Russian intervention into the Spanish civil war was slow in coming. While there was a counterrevolution against socialism and an excellent chance to bring about a communist victory on a truly international scale, the soviets limited themselves for many months after the outbreak of hostilities (when Italy and Germany already were rushing help to Franco) to the sending of "observers" and to the making of propaganda on a minor key. It was only late in September or early in October 1936—if the *International Press Correspondence* may serve as a clue—that a more massive intervention was decided upon at Moscow. And even then, while a fair amount of war matériel was being dispatched to Spain, Russian policy and diplomacy remained extremely cautious. Soviet help was to be secret and furtive. The soviets hinted broadly that they would not take serious risks for the sake of the Spanish republic, nor would they take steps to assure the delivery of their supplies to the loyalists. Thus, while German and Italian munitions flooded unimpeded into Spain, occasionally under the very protection of the axis navies, Russian supplies time and again were intercepted and sunk. Yet, the soviet leaders were apparently resolved not to be provoked. They definitely wanted to avoid being drawn into a premature international conflict.

The communist military advisers included some very high-ranking soviet officers, yet their advice seems to have run along traditional lines. The loyalists barely made an attempt to work out truly modern tactics. There was not even an up-to-date technique of combining front with rear warfare, although civil wars offer the most favorable opportunities for rear operations. From the point of view of communist conflict management, then, the Spanish civil war offers but few points of interest.

However, there is one feature which deserves attention. According to Stalin, "the liberation of Spain from the yoke of the fascist reactionaries is not the private affair of the Spaniards, but the common cause of all advanced and progressive mankind."[217] On this basis the communists made a major recruiting effort all over the world and organized the dispatch of specialists, technicians, and volunteer soldiers and officers into Spain. Most of the recruits came from western and central Europe and from the United States. In this fashion the Comintern mobilized the "war potential" which the revolutionary movement possessed in the various countries of the world outside of Russia; to phrase it differently, part of the military strength of the western nations was put to work for the communist cause. The fighting of a war with foreign volunteers, of course, is a neat device to carry out military operations and yet reduce to a minimum the risk of international conflict.

[217] *International Press Conference* (November 14, 1936).

Once in Spain, the volunteers were organized into international brigades which, on the whole, gave a good account of themselves. These volunteers received thorough training in military and secret operations and, upon return to their mother country, contributed their newly acquired skills to the local revolutionary movement. While in Spain, many of the volunteers had been incorporated into various Russian organizations, including intelligence and control agencies. In turn, the Russian apparatus obtained valuable contacts and facilities, for example, the passports of killed volunteers. Last, but not least, the agitation about the Spanish civil war made possible the recruitment of sympathizers into the communist movement or into front organizations.

In most other respects, however, the communists played a very clumsy game. Gratuitous religious persecution—undertaken in violation of the principles of the Seventh World Congress—alienated a large part of the Spanish population. More particularly, it made it impossible for the communists to gain support among the peasants, thus precluding the setting up of guerrilla operations behind the lines of the Franco army. The encroachments and stupidities of the Russian secret police, which gradually took over the control of the republican rear, caused dissensions among, and defections from, the loyalist ranks and repelled even those leftist groups which wanted to collaborate with, but did not desire to be submerged by, the Stalinists. These tactics, too, violated all the precepts of the united front.

The communists took advantage of the deteriorating military situation and, largely through Russian intervention, put men of their confidence into the key governmental positions (May 1937). But this cryptocommunist seizure of power proved a hollow success. It did not lead to the organization of a true "people's war," although the GPU made desperate attempts to mobilize for such a war by methods quite incompatible with the psychology of the Spanish people. Heavy repression and terror became instruments to avoid early collapse. To make things worse, the Russian purges carried over into Spain, and the Russian advisers, technicians, and even police agents were liquidated one by one. The temporary survivors among the Russian missions had other worries than the civil war and concentrated on efforts to save their own hides, quite to the detriment of military operations. These cleavages and confusions led to various uprisings and civil wars within the civil war. Communist tactics lost all sense and meaning, except as a reflection of the domestic struggles in Russia.

By the end of 1937 it was becoming clear that the loyalist cause was lost. Simultaneously, the purge craze in Russia reached unprecedented heights, and Hitler was getting ready to start the *Drang nach Osten*. Under the circumstances, the soviet government deemed it wise to disengage itself from the Spanish entanglement. Supply programs were gradually eliminated and soviet support operations of all kinds reduced and, in many cases, terminated. One interest remained: to prolong the war as long as possible in order to restrict the freedom of action of the European powers. Otherwise, the Spanish adventure was written off.

Communist policies in Spain cost many innocent lives and proved a dismal and contemptible failure. Yet the Spanish civil war yielded to the Soviet Union four important assets: the rejuvenation of the western communist parties through the international brigades; a considerable increase in the capabilities of the communist espionage apparatus; the testing of Russian weapons in competition with foreign munitions, as well as the training of Russian officers and staffs in actual combat; and the gold treasure of Spain which the Soviet Union took into custody but forgot to return to its rightful owner.

VYSHINSKY'S DOCTRINE OF REVOLUTION IN A DICTATORSHIP

DURING the Seventh World Congress, Manuilsky's reluctance to reveal soviet methods of attacking a dictatorship from the inside became apparent. Yet, circumstances demanded that at least a portion of the soviet doctrine be made public.

Between 1936 and 1938, Stalin carried out the notorious purge trials which eliminated all prominent bolsheviks actually or potentially critical of his leadership. Hitler had demonstrated the benefits accruing to the dictator who eliminates competition by simply shooting his opponents: The nazi purge of 1934 revealed a mind preoccupied with brute force. Stalin's method of preceding executions by public admissions of guilt reflected a preoccupation with demoralization techniques. The Soviet dictator was not content with the mere physical destruction of his enemies. He also

wanted the moral submission of his opponents and the political per-
dition of their cause.

The purge trials showed another of Stalin's character traits. It
must have been apparent to the dictator's mind that, for political
and personal reasons, the bolshevik old guard had to be liquidated.
But, for many years he proceeded cautiously, gradually increasing
the pressure, emasculating and dividing the opposition step by step;
yet, he shunned drastic action.

Suddenly, an incident occurred which made radical action politically feasible and psychologically almost inevitable: the assassination of Kirov, the Leningrad party secretary. This assassination
might have been unexpected,[218] but in any event, once the incident
had set the stage, Stalin struck with utmost resolution and cruelty.
This was no longer the cautious Stalin of the legend but a ruthless
aggressor willing to take substantial risks. When the one-sided battle was over and the enemy destroyed, Stalin liquidated the bloodthirsty and hated executioners of his policy, including Yezhov and
Yagoda, the chiefs of the political police. Thereupon, Stalin reap-
peared on the scene posing as the great "pacifier."

That the trial proceedings conducted by Andrei Y. Vyshinsky as
state procurator were a sham need not be proved in detail.[219] Although Stalin's enemies, and even some of his friends, were accused
of major crimes, their guilt was not established in legal and orderly
fashion. The accusations were unsupported and contradictory, yet
the defense was entirely ineffective. Convictions were based almost
entirely on the "confessions" of the defendants, although many of
the latter could not possibly have committed the crimes of which
they accused themselves; some of them had been in prison when
they allegedly "prepared" their acts. Individual defendants, particularly Bukharin, were able to disprove some of Vyshinsky's statements. From abroad, Trotsky refuted most of the allegations.[220] To

[218] There are indications that it was possibly a GPU provocation.

[219] F. Beck and W. Godin, *Russian Purge and the Extraction of Confession*
(New York, Viking, 1951).

[220] The "evidence" presented at the purge trials was analyzed and demol-
ished by an international commission meeting in Mexico during 1937. See:
*Not Guilty; Report of the Commission of Inquiry into the Charges Made
Against Leon Trotsky in the Moscow Trials* (New York, Harper, 1938); also,
*The Case of Leon Trotsky: Report of Hearings on the Charges Made against
Him in the Moscow Trials* (New York, Harper, 1937).

remove any lingering doubt, the seizure of the German archives in the closing days of World War II failed to reveal corroborative evidence for Vyshinsky's contentions.

It is known, however, that the nazis sent deception materials through doubled intelligence channels to the soviets in the form of fraudulent "evidence" against high-ranking Russian military officers. By transmitting fabricated evidence of treason, Hitler hoped to decapitate soviet *military* leadership. But no such operation was directed by the nazis against the old-guard bolsheviks.[221]

While the specific criminal charges were fabricated by the regime, most of the defendants were political opponents of Stalin who, as experienced revolutionaries, undoubtedly had considered ways and means of removing Stalin and returning themselves to power. Perhaps one or the other defendant had gone beyond purely "verbal conspiracy" and was preparing revolutionary acts, if only in the form of administrative inefficiency and policy sabotage. If so, no convincing evidence has been adduced.

The trials took place in a country which is very well informed on revolutionary methods and techniques. In order to make even a formal case against the defendants, Vyshinsky was forced to hypothecate a line of action, a *modus operandi,* by which the accused actually could have overthrown the Stalin dictatorship. To appear plausible in the eyes of his audience, Vyshinsky had to present an argument which made good revolutionary sense. Whether or not he delved into the professional knowledge of the communist leadership, whether he obtained his ideas from the Lenin Institute, or whether, as the trials went on, he himself had made up a doctrine of antidictatorship revolution is purely conjectural.

The fact remains that Vyshinsky did develop a doctrine on revolu-

---

[221] According to Walter Hagen, *Die Geheime Front* (Zurich, Europa 1950), pp. 54–68, this fabrication operation was originated by Reinhardt Heydrich who, with Hitler's and Himmler's approval, produced a voluminous correspondence between key Russian generals and the German Reichswehr. The material was delivered to the Russian embassy in Berlin. According to Winston Churchill, some of the incriminating information may have been directed to Moscow via Prague. Hagen stated that Heydrich sold the documents for three million rubles. It turned out later that the communists paid him in counterfeit money. One of Heydrich's assistants, SS General Hermann Behrens (executed in 1946 by Tito), believed that the soviet secret police had suggested, and participated in, the provocation. The truth of this aspect of the affair has not been ascertained.

tion against modern dictatorships. This doctrine was and is consistent with bolshevik theory and practice.

In 1934 the defendant L. B. Kamenyev, one of the highest-ranking bolsheviks, brother-in-law of Trotsky and once the oldest and
closest friend of Stalin, wrote a preface to a Russian edition of
Machiavelli. Machiavelli, wrote Kamenyev,

... made his treatise into an astonishingly sharp and expressive catalogue
of the rules by which the ruler of his time was to be guided in order to
win power, to hold it and victoriously to withstand any attacks upon it.

Vyshinsky commented: "You had a good teacher, Kamenyev, but
you, and you must be given credit for it, have excelled your teacher.
[You] adopted the rules of Machiavelli, you developed them to the
utmost point of unscrupulousness and immorality, you modernized
them, you perfected them." What was the "perfection"?

To Machiavellism was added the tactic of infiltration, or "Aze-
vism."[222] Vyshinsky described the alleged program of the conspira-
tors:

Their program of home policy was confined to murder; their program of
foreign policy was confined to the defeat of the U.S.S.R. in war; their
method was perfidy, cunning and treason.[223]

The doctrine expounded by Vyshinsky during the trials can be
summarized in this fashion:

To ensure the success of a revolution, it must be directed from
at least two centers; the reserve center must act if the first has been
destroyed. (This rule is standard communist practice.)

Once the double command post of revolution has been established, agents must be placed in high government and control positions. Exactly what and where these positions are is not overly important, since damage can be caused from almost any point in the
hierarchy. For example, physicians who count high-placed persons
among their clientele are always handy. However, to infiltrate agents

---

[222] Asev was an Okhrana *agent provocateur* who operated before World
War I against the bolsheviks and who might have been a double agent work-
ing for them. He was one of the most effective infiltrators of history. See,
Boris Nikolajewsky, *Aseff, the Spy, Russian Terrorist and Police Stool* (New
York, Doubleday, 1934).

[223] *The Case of the Trotskyite-Zinovievite Terrorist Centre,* People's Commissariat of Justice of the U.S.S.R. (Moscow, 1936), pp. 138–40.

into the decision-making levels of government, into the armed forces, the diplomatic service, and leading economic circles is, of course, far preferable. The agents' tasks are to sabotage policy, to undermine the economic strength of the nation, to weaken the nation's defenses, and to stultify any attempt to repress revolutionary or subversive activities.

Infiltration and military defeat are the practical revolutionary weapons against dictatorship. The revolutionaries must conclude an alliance with a foreign nation and suck it into an attack on their own nation by promising territorial concessions, for example, or by direct provocation, such as assassination of its diplomats. The foreign attack must be co-ordinated with internal efforts aimed at undermining the target nation's military and moral power. Cells in the armed forces should be on the "combat-ready." Espionage bases must have been established. Upon the launching of the foreign military attack, the nation's top leadership should be assassinated.

As hostilities continue, defeatist work proceeds on a large scale. Insurrections should be attempted in the rear of the army and at the periphery of the country. (Vyshinsky alleged that insurrections had been planned in Uzbekistan, in the North Caucasus, and in the Far East). All over the territory there should be sabotage, especially against railroads, chemical factories, and coal mines. Under certain circumstances, bacterial warfare should be used, or whatever will but cripple the defense industries and "strike palpable blows at the most sensitive places."[224]

If possible, the front should be opened to the enemy: Revolutionaries in the armed forces, especially in the higher-command echelons, should work toward defeat and never prevent the "caving-in" of military units. The revolutionaries should wait until the enemy approaches the capital city, then stage an armed uprising and overthrow the government. This, Vyshinsky contended, was called the "Clemenceau thesis."[225]

---

[224] *The Case of the Anti-Soviet Trotskyite Centre,* People's Commissariat of Justice of the U.S.S.R. (Moscow, 1937), p. 11.

[225] *The Case of the Trotskyite-Zinovievite Terrorist Centre, op. cit.,* p. 131. The reference to Clemenceau arose from a distortion of a remark by Trotsky. Actually, Vyshinsky betrayed ignorance of the facts: Clemenceau was the exact opposite of a defeatist; his policy aimed at victory. He came to power through a legal change of government when France needed him most to stop the Germans. The identification of "Clemenceau-ism" with defeatism is an example of the misinformation stuffed away in the heads of soviet leaders.

Economic support operations include weakening the financial powers of the nation, creating discontent with taxes, holding up wage payments (and military pay, one may presume), destroying savings accounts, and producing inflation. Agents located at industrial control centers must see to it that output lags and is technologically inferior.

According to Vyshinsky, the revolutionaries developed an entire plan of sociological warfare. They had determined that "capitalist psychology" was not yet dead in Russia. The peasants were dissatisfied with collectivization. Wide strata of the Russian people objected to forced industrialization. Therefore, the revolutionaries allegedly decided on a capitalist restoration in the U.S.S.R. Their program proposed revival of small farms, liquidation of the collectives, and the leasing of industrial concessions to foreign capitalists —in short, the controlled reestablishment of private property. This was designed to enlist the support both of the native population and of foreign nations.

It is readily apparent that sociological warfare can be applied not only against socialist states but, through the inversion of this program, also against capitalist nations. The soviets never fail to resort to sociological attack, for example, by proposing land reform, nationalization of banks and armament factories, expropriation of foreign holdings, and so forth.

In the absence of broad popular support, unobtainable in a dictatorship which does not tolerate subversive propaganda and agitation, revolutionary seizure of power requires terrorist methods and a "palace coup d'état."[226] In Vyshinsky's analysis, terrorism is a tool of the *coup d'état;* the main terrorist effort is directed against the leaders of state. The liquidation of leadership is the oldest method of revolution, already discussed by Machiavelli. "The whole matter is in the top, therefore the top must be removed. . . . Heads are peculiar in that they do not grow on again."[227]

While under the influence of the failure of the *narodnaya volya,* the early Marxists rejected individual terrorism as the main form of revolutionary attack. However, Vyshinsky expounded a new method

[226] *The Case of the Anti-Soviet Bloc of Rights and Trotskyites,* People's Commissariat of Justice of the U.S.S.R. (Moscow, 1938), p. 21.

[227] *The Case of the Trotskyite-Zinovievite Centre, op. cit.,* p. 16.

and an improved variant: *terrorism coupled with infiltration, socio-economic warfare, and defeatism.*

Sometimes it is advisable to remove key figures by "imperceptible means." Physicians are the indicated tool for this operation; terrorism has been dubbed "surgical intervention." Assassination through the physician is simple: If a sick person is deliberately given "contra-indicated" therapy, he has little chance of recovery. Most target personalities of terror campaigns are beyond the prime of life; hence, they are already suffering from some ill or are under a doctor's care, and disease can be induced easily.

Imperceptible murder is a method of infiltration. Frequently an agent cannot be placed in a strategic position until the incumbent is removed. If the latter be qualified, trusted, and invulnerable to character assassination, only death can quickly create the vacancy. Vyshinsky put it to the defendant Yagoda that, by medical and bacterial means, he had removed W. R. Menzhinsky, his predecessor at the helm of the GPU.

Yet, the head of state must not be removed quietly or secretly. He must be killed publicly, before an international forum. If the leader of the state were removed through an arranged automobile accident, for example, his head would not grow again, it is true. But, if he were removed in a dramatic fashion, the incident would give rise to maximum confusion in the established leadership.[228] If the assassination should coincide "with some big political event of international importance," such as a military defeat, it could throw the country into chaos and would facilitate seizure of power.

---

[228] Trotsky's position on assassination is worth noting: Whether or not terrorism is successful depends on political circumstances. Confusion may be caused by murder of key personnel, but the state does not rest on the ministers and cannot be destroyed with them. The state will always find new men: "The mechanism remains intact and continues to function." "If it is enough to arm oneself with a revolver to reach the goal, then to what end are the endeavors of the class struggle? If a pinch of powder and a slug of lead are ample to shoot the enemy through the neck, where is the need of a class organization? . . . What need is there for a party? What is the need of meetings, mass agitation, elections, when it is so easy to take aim at the ministerial bench?" And, in another version: "The bureaucracy can replace Stalin and Molotov. That is why individual terrorism is stupid." *The Case of Leon Trotsky, op. cit.,* pp. 259, 374. Of course, if the target personalities cannot be replaced easily and fast—and this possibility certainly exists—Trotsky's theory does not hold. Besides, terrorism need not be an isolated act but could be combined with "class organization."

All in all, Vyshinsky's hypothecation envisaged a combination of internal and external attack. His antidictatorship tactics took their inspiration from the termite, the parasite, and the gangster. But the provocation of war and the causing of defeat were considered the keys to the overthrow of a strongly organized state.

PERFECTING STRIKE STRATEGY

IN A DEMOCRACY, Trojan horse tactics can be applied more easily than in a dictatorship, particularly within the labor movement. Success as a labor leader requires knowledge and leadership ability, especially in the conduct of industrial strikes. Hence, the communists strive to become strike experts—a skill useful in military, political, and economic warfare.

An industrial strike may be undertaken to remedy grievances, increase wages, or improve working conditions. The right to strike is acknowledged by all democratic nations. Since workers often have real and serious grievances, the industrial strike may be, and frequently is, a weapon of legitimate self-defense.

But the interests of the labor movement and world communism cannot be equated. A strike organized by communists and sympathizers is not meant primarily to serve the economic interests of workers but the political interests of the communist party. It is a step on the road to power. If the strikers are predominantly noncommunists, the communists will employ Trojan horse tactics to obtain control over the movement and to exploit it as a transmission belt. Such a capture of a trade union directly increases communist strength.

A strike undertaken by a captured union may deteriorate the economic conditions of the strikers. This is not always unwelcome to the communists. Although it may reduce their influence temporarily, it acts to intensify the class struggle.

Strikes are an integral part of revolution. They can be used for the mobilization of revolutionary forces. They are a training school for revolutionary organizations. They can be exploited for the preparation and support of revolutionary uprisings and civil war. In discussing the revolution of 1905, Lenin indicated that there was a relationship between an ever growing wave of strikes and the emergence of a revolutionary situation. A revolutionary strike parallels mutiny in the armed forces. It is an instrument of active defeatism and contributes to the creation of a revolutionary army.

Industrial strikes may serve as a weapon wielded by a foreign power to reduce a nation's war production, interfere with logistics and military operations, and bring about a change in policy.

The general strike is a revolutionary act which, in theory, could by itself lead to the overthrow of government. In case of revolution, it would facilitate insurrectional seizure of power. In case of war, a sustained general strike would make military defeat inevitable.

"General strikes" in the literal meaning of the term—strikes in *all* enterprises everywhere throughout a country—have been exceedingly rare in history, if they ever happened at all. General strikes in cities have occurred. But there is no need for a general strike. Political, economic, and military effectiveness can be achieved by a paralyzing strike: the stoppage of production in basic or key industries or public utilities sooner or later must entail general effects all over the nation. Such strikes in key industries or transportation have occurred time and again but, in most cases, did not last long enough to affect the entire economy. The chief revolutionary problem in organizing paralyzing strikes is to make them long lasting.

In case of civil or international war, the effect of strikes may be enhanced by mass sabotage campaigns or by aerial bombing. A strike in the oil industry, for example, combined with mass sabotage of railroads and air attacks on chemicals or, to take another example, a strike in telecommunications supported by mass sabotage in power stations and air attacks on the steel industry would constitute devastating combinations. If successful, the strikers and *saboteurs* would gain in organizational strength and ultimately might be in a position to reach out for territorial control and even seizure of power.

Obviously, then, industrial strikes are key weapons in the communist arsenal.

The setting up of efficient strike machinery and the calling and winning of strikes have always been considered as vital tasks of communist parties everywhere.

The communists consider that the strike, like rebellion and war, is an art. The rules of warfare must be applied to them. Four principles of Lenin's spiritual grandfather, Clausewitz, are regarded as particularly applicable: "To bend all strength to the very utmost"; "to concentrate all possible forces there where it is necessary to deliver a decisive blow"; "not to lose time" but to strangle rapidly enemy undertakings and gain public support; and "to utilize all . . . victories with the greatest of energy."[229]

However, the differences between a regular army and an army of strikers must be understood. Strikers join voluntarily and are not subject to disciplinary compulsion; they lack mobility, since they must fight close to their place of work; strike leaders are less well trained and selected than are military leaders; and also, they rarely have studied strategy or tactics and are usually unfamiliar with the experience of other strike undertakings. The staffs of strike organizations are easily penetrated and corrupted and seldom dispose of an effective propaganda machine.

According to William Z. Foster, a chief theoretician of American communism, "fundamental to the carrying out of a good strike strategy is a thorough preliminary organization for the struggle." Foster emphasized that there must be an equivalent to the recruiting and training services in an army because "drilled troops are better fighters than new recruits." "Good preparations give the workers incomparably greater striking power."

The strike staff should be organized functionally to handle picketing, publicity, propaganda, relief, morale, intelligence, and, though this is sometimes glossed over, strong-arm squads. Picket captains must be selected and briefed. All the necessary paraphernalia must be procured—signs, cards, identification papers, strike headquarters, meeting halls, communications, cars, motorcycles, messengers, bodyguards, flying squads, canteens, first-aid stations, and so forth.

Since the build-up of organization will never be complete before the strike, the organization must be perfected as the strike is proceeding.[230] This parallels the idea that the demoralization of an army cannot climax before that army is engaged in battle and that a revolutionary army must be created through the revolutionary act. While one should aim at maximum efficiency and plan at long range, organization should always allow for initiative, improvisation, and rapid adaptation—an important organizational principle.

Every strike must be prepared propagandistically. The probable

---

[229] John Steuben, *Strike Strategy* (New York, Gaer, 1950), p. 64.
[230] *Ibid.*, p. 108.

immediate gains are to be stressed. The workers must be convinced that strike is the only means by which they can attain their objective. The families of the strikers must be influenced so that they do not oppose the strike but willingly accept the sacrifices involved. Efforts must be made to win public support through newspapers, advertisements, radio, leaflets, meetings, parades, and organizations.

There should be propaganda transmission belts such as citizens, women, or veterans committees. Participation of veterans is especially important because of their prior training, discipline, and tactical knowledge.

The blow should be struck only when preparations have been completed. The walkout should affect as much of the labor force as possible and should come by surprise. Although full surprise is unlikely, tactical and timing surprise must be achieved.

The picket line is the life force of the strike. The general rule is: "The longer the line the shorter the strike." The stronger the line and the higher its morale, the greater is its influence on the workers, its effect on public opinion, and its value in restraining strike breakers. "Mass picketing is the surest road to victory."[231]

Staff work is needed to run picket lines effectively. How many pickets are needed? At what time and what places? What points of the factory must be covered by what numbers? Where is it easy for strike breakers to get into the factory? How can pickets be reinforced rapidly? How can communications be maintained? How can the morale of the pickets be improved? How can pickets be fed and protected against bad weather?

Unity among the striking workers must be maintained. Differences, for example race conflicts, should be composed beforehand. Workers who at first did not join the strike should not be criticized but should be convinced.

In addition to pickets, there must be reserves, who include the non-picketing strikers and workers in similar and related industries, in near-by factories, in the same community, particularly if connected with transportation and public utilities, in near-by cities, as well as the unemployed, women, and even children.

The strike should be run offensively. According to William Z. Foster, "workers like soldiers (and they are the same human beings and subject to the same psychological laws) fight best on the offen-

[231] *Ibid.,* p. 130.

sive. They are then fired with a sense of power and victory; defensive fighting demoralizes them and fills them with defeatism." An offensive strike is a strike which is spreading. Additional forces of reserves should gradually be thrown into the battle. Increasingly large numbers of units should participate. The ultimate ideal would be to call a general strike.

If the strike cannot spread, *the offensive may be maintained by preventing the employers from developing an offensive of their own.*

Since it is postulated that the employers' offensive usually takes the form of terror, the task is to "nip the planned terror in the bud."[232] This is best done by counterterror. Obviously, terror is one method to give a strike revolutionary meaning.

The strikers should agitate against law enforcement and advocate prohibitions against industrial police units. Municipal and other authorities should be put under political pressure not to authorize the use of force. *Agents provocateurs* must be eliminated from the ranks of the strikers. Top management should be held responsible for all acts of violence: intimidation.

In addition, the strikers must be able to fight it out on even terms. Violence, it is said, usually comes against picket lines. It must be defeated by "solidarity" and "technical equipment." This technical equipment should include cameras to take pictures acceptable in court testimony. It is left to the imagination of the reader to determine what other types of equipment would be helpful in such situations.

The general rule is to prevent the opponent from taking violent action by propagandizing against such measures and, at the same time, by describing violence by the strikers as self-defense, advocating the deputizing of strikers and the forming of a mass defense organization capable of protecting strikers, pickets, labor leaders, installations, and families. "The younger strikers, particularly veterans, can give substance to such a strikers' defense organization."[233]

It is clear that such defense organizations could be used offensively as well as for purposes of unrest and sabotage. They could be transformed into a modern version of the Russian Red guard

[232] *Ibid.,* p. 154
[233] *Ibid.,* p. 261.

and employed for insurrectional tasks. They could also become the nucleus of an irregular force fighting in the rear of a nation engaged in war against the Soviet Union. Through militant organizations, violence arising from strikes could spread, in crescendo fashion, across a nation and reach a fortissimo of insurrection and civil war.

Once the strike has induced a conciliatory attitude on the part of the employers, or has lasted so long that it cannot be prolonged, it must be wound up by negotiation. In dealing with the employers, the strikers must be firm and flexible. They should be ready to sacrifice nonessentials while insisting on their main demands. It is imperative that proper precautions be taken. For example, it should be agreed before the negotiations that the settlement will constitute an improvement over the status before the strike.

If the strike is a defeat, rout and demoralization must be prevented and an organized retreat undertaken. The purpose is to preserve solidarity and loyalty of the strikers. One way to minimize reverses is not to think in terms of all-out retreat but to develop a counteroffensive.[234]

A victory, on the other hand, must be consolidated; the strike organization must be strengthened and expanded. "A victory is not an end but a beginning, a springboard to even greater organization, which means ever greater victory."[235]

According to Lange's *The Road to Victory* a revolutionary party preparing for armed conflict should base its organization on the factories. The forces of the proletariat can be reached most easily at their places of work. In the "battles with their employer," the proletarians gain combat training and experience. These battles serve to select revolutionary leaders. They immunize revolutionary organizations against infiltration. Hence, solid organization in the factories is "extraordinarily important from the point of view of the armed uprising." Strike and uprising are complementary forms of attack which may be employed independently, successively, and simultaneously. An effective industrial strike organization is a powerful weapon of communist strategy. It is a weapon of revolutionary defeatism, insurrection, irregular warfare, and revolutionary war.

[234] *Ibid.*, p. 110.
[235] *Ibid.*, p. 299.

MAO TSE-TUNG'S CONTRIBUTIONS TO THE COMMUNIST SCIENCE OF CONQUEST

THE TACTICS of the Trojan horse were reinvented in China during the early 1920's when the communists concluded an agreement with Sun Yat-sen and entered the Kuomintang as political organizers and military advisers. These united-front tactics suffered their first defeat when Chiang Kai-shek expelled the communists from the Kuomintang, put down several communist uprisings, and chased the representatives of the Third International from China.

According to their party critics (of the Monday morning quarterback variety) the early Chinese communists suffered from "revolutionary adventurism." They undertook uprisings, especially in Canton and Shanghai, before a truly revolutionary situation had emerged. The original strategy of the Chinese communists called for local uprisings in small cities. After a large number of small cities had been seized, it was hoped that capture of the big cities would be possible. Once the big cities were in communist hands, China would fall in its entirety. The predilection for city uprisings was purely doctrinaire: The Marxian book said that revolution would be carried out by the proletariat. Since the proletariat lived in cities, uprisings had to be organized there, and there alone. The chief exponent of this doctrine was Li Li-san.

The strategy of city uprisings, combined with infiltration of the Kuomintang high command, failed. Violent discussions ensued at Moscow. Stalin himself took great interest in the Chinese revolution. He recognized the agrarian character of China and realized that the Chinese revolution had to be predominantly agrarian in character.[236] It followed that the conventional technique of uprisings was inapplicable. The military factor and the creation of a revolutionary army, rather than the organization of the urban proletariat, were to be the most important elements in the struggle for China.[237] The revolutionary army, in addition to its military activities, would act as a transmission belt by propagating the idea of the communist revolution. The Red army was to be organized as soviets were established in "liberated" provinces.

[236] *Sochineniya, op. cit.,* IX, 284.
[237] *Ibid.,* VIII, 362–64.

More clearly than other communists, Mao Tse-tung understood the limitations of the orthodox proletarian strategy in China. He liberated himself radically from the shackles of dogmatism and proceeded to organize the revolutionary movement, not in the cities and not with a few miners and railroad workers, but in the country with the peasant masses. "To reject the poor peasants is to reject the revolution." Mao did not deny the importance of the proletariat but concluded that "if the whole revolution was represented by the figure 10, then its success in the cities might be accounted as 3, and among the peasants as 7."[238]

These heretical views were not accepted easily by the bolshevik leadership. Mao simply went ahead, organized a revolutionary army, captured territory, and proved his thesis through successful practice.

Mao Tse-tung is both a practical strategist and tactician, and a military theoretician. His main victory was the conquest of China, perhaps one of the most significant events of modern times. His main military writings are: *On a Prolonged War,* 1938; *The Chinese Revolution and the Communist Party of China,* 1939; and the *Strategic Problems of China's Revolutionary Wars,* 1941. These texts were summarized very conveniently by Robert Payne.[239]

The enormous contribution of Mao lies in the fact that he taught the communists how *to fight war successfully with a minimum of matériel.*

Having no weapons, Mao started out in the late twenties by enlisting the good will of the villagers and by setting up extensive intelligence warning nets among the civilians. At first, his forces did not possess one single machine gun, or so it is said, but gradually they acquired arms by luring nationalist forces into ambush and capturing weapons in combat. The weapons of morale and intelligence served to procure firearms.

Basing his practice on the teachings of the world's oldest military classic written by the Chinese Sun Tsu (about 500 B.C. or even earlier), Mao became a master in stratagems and "indirect tactics."

[238] Payne, *op. cit.,* p. 91. This book was finished when Lt. Colonel Robert B. Rigg's excellent *Red China's Fighting Hordes* (Harrisburg, Pa., Military Service Publishing Co., 1951), appeared in print. At the present time, this is the best discussion of modern Chinese warfare.

[239] *Op. cit.,* Chap. 8, entitled "Five Books," pp. 171–99.

According to the old Chinese sage the highest form of generalship is to frustrate the enemy's plan. Sun Tsu considered the fighting of battles, particularly against an entrenched enemy, as bad strategy. The skillful leader should subdue the enemy without fighting and capture his cities without laying siege. Only in this manner can he maintain strong and morally intact forces throughout a long war. Sun Tsu pointed out that if the enemy should strengthen his front, he must weaken his rear; by strengthening his left, he must weaken his right; and so on.[240] The skillful tactician must take advantage of these weak points.

Mao described his tactics by saying that an enemy advance should be countered by retreat; enemy retreat by harrassment, pursuit, and reoccupation of previously abandoned territory; and the exhaustion of the hostile force should be followed by attack. In short, one always should act as the enemy least desires.

Mao's tactical concepts were permeated by dialectic thinking:

A revolutionary war is on the offensive, yet it has its defensive and retreat. To defend in order to attack, to retreat in order to advance, to take a flanking position in order to take a frontal position, and to follow a corkscrew path in order to go directly to the objective—these are inevitable phenomena in the development of all events, and why should we suppose that military events are otherwise?

Tactics of this kind require first-class operational intelligence. Mao fully accepted Sun Tsu's idea that reliable intelligence is an indispensable condition of operational mobility.

Flexibility in tactical concepts is also characteristic of Mao's military leadership. Mao made it his usual practice to attack the enemy at his weakest point. Yet, whenever there was a possibility to gain complete and long-lasting victory, he was more than willing to attack the opponent at his strongest point.

One of Mao's specialties was a decided skill in the "strategy of luring": he would induce his opponent to campaign in territory disadvantageous to his forces but suitable for the communists and, also, in areas outside of the effective range of the enemy's logistics.

Great attention was paid to the art of concealment and guerrilla

[240] Sun Tsu, "On the Art of War," in *Roots of Strategy,* ed. by Thomas R. Phillips (Harrisburg, Pa., Military Service Publishing Co., 1940), pp. 21–63.

tactics of "evaporation." In case of defeat, communist forces were told to scatter, disappear, and disguise themselves, and to reassemble in a previously selected area or "terminus of withdrawal."

Mao violently opposed the concept of "big rearism,"[241] the paralyzing idea that one cannot fight without a large and productive support base. Although big rearism was very close to Stalin's heart, Mao considered war as a method of accumulating strength rather than as an activity requiring previously accumulated stockpiles upon which to draw. Mao seemed to think that war is not only the father but the creator of all things. He carried the old Marxian concept of the creative role of violence forward from the social sphere into the military field. In contrast to current western thinking which considers war as destructive, debilitating, and detrimental to the social and political cohesion of society, Mao maintained (with earlier western mercantilists) that war can and should support itself—and make the warrior stronger.

Mao Tse-tung led one of history's most remarkable retreats, the so-called "long march" from Kiangsi-Fukien via Yunnan and the Tibetan border to Shensi and the upper Yellow river. This march of 6,000 miles lasted almost two years. The remarkable thing about it is not so much the accomplishment of a most difficult retreat but the almost complete lack of defeatism. Mao and his men refused to give up the fight even though the communist armies almost had been wiped out. To survive, this beaten army had to conquer a new hinterland. Mao showed that armies do not always need support bases. Sometimes armies must conquer the territory required for survival and growth. It is true that armies live on their stomach. But to fill the stomach, armies may have to live temporarily on their legs. *Strategic mobility may be a substitute for logistic weakness.*

Mao did not believe that war should necessarily be of short duration: "Those who believe we can win a speedy victory are as incorrect as those who say we cannot win."[242]

He emphasized the need for a prolonged war: There was no other reliable way to weaken and exhaust a stronger opponent. This idea had been voiced before him by Tukhachevsky and Frunze. It was patterned after the lessons of Napoleon's campaign against Russia,

[241] Payne, *op. cit.,* pp. 114, 125.
[242] *Ibid.,* p. 176.

and Japan's war against China. While Mao was speaking specifically of the Chinese-Japanese war, the concept of deliberately prolonged war naturally has far broader application.

According to Mao, prolonged war is fought in three phases. During the first state the "aggressor" gains considerable advantage, but at a high price, and eventually is stalled. During the second phase a stalemate is reached, involving total mobilization on both sides and a progressive weakening of the over-extended supply system of the aggressor. The third stage is introduced by a counteroffensive launched to coincide with the enemy's economic fatigue and internal disorientation. It should lead to military defeat and revolution and should culminate in the aggressor's collapse.

From the standpoint of the defender, the first phase would be a defensive mobile war. The second phase would be fought as a stationary war of position with emphasis on partisan operations, operating against the aggressor's communication and supply lines, while the third phase would again be mobile war but fought offensively.

The technique of defeating superior forces is an art which, according to Mao, holds "no mystery whatsoever." In addition to protracting the war beyond the point of the enemy's endurance, there are three major tactics. First, the inferior forces should capture spoils. Second, they should carry out centripetal withdrawals and should scatter in case of necessity. Third, if striking offensively, they should rely on disguise, concealment, mobility, and quick thrusts. "Our strategy is one against ten, while our tactics is ten against one—such contradictions provide the laws by which we overcome the enemy."[243]

Mao's over-all strategy was to win the Chinese revolution militarily through guerrilla and partisan warfare and revolutionary war, and politically through the moral disintegration of the government armies, winning over the peasants, and neutralizing the rest of the population.

Mao's formula can be described as follows:[244]

(1) Form a regular army with proper headquarters and a supreme command in addition to guerrilla or partisan forces. This

[243] *Ibid.*, p. 192.
[244] See "Foreign Report," *The Economist*, London, June 29, 1950.

army must be trained according to modern principles, and its morale must be kept at high pitch.

(2) Recruit a strong revolutionary army from the mass of peasantry who, won over by promises of land, can supply the numbers required. (This idea obviously is more applicable in Asia, Africa, and Latin America than in "capitalist" countries.)

(3) Avoid fighting battles against superior enemies. Revolutionary forces should accumulate strength by occupying remote areas: Conquest is a method of mobilization.

(4) Conquered areas must be turned into "progressive strong bases" and "great military, political, economic and cultural revolutionary strongholds." They should be set up as bases of revolutionary armies fighting a prolonged war. The army should be supplemented by a self-defense corps in charge of local defense. While fulfilling its military duties, members of this corps should not discontinue economic production.

(5) Provide the revolutionary army with modern equipment, partly through help from abroad and partly through spoils warfare.

(6) Organize sporadic actions in the cities held by the counter-revolutionaries.

(7) Continue expansion when and wherever possible through attacks on weakly held areas (expansion along the line of least resistance), through truces, and through the coalition government device. Once the revolutionary army has grown so strong that it can challenge its opponent, expansion should take the form of offensive revolutionary warfare.

(8) Armed expansion must exploit disunity and conflict within the antirevolutionary camp and must be supported by mass unrest in the territory controlled by the anticommunists.

Mao formulated ten principles which stand a good chance of becoming a classic in military literature. They read as follows:[245]

1. First strike scattered and isolated groups of the enemy, and later strike concentrated, powerful groups.
2. First take small and middle-sized towns and cities and the broad countryside, and later take big cities.
3. The major objective is the annihilation of the enemy fighting strength, and not the holding or taking of cities and places. The holding

[245] Mao Tse-tung, *Turning Point in China* (New York, New Century, 1949), pp. 7 f.

or taking of cities and places is the result of the annihilation of the enemy's fighting strength, which often has to be repeated many times before they can be finally held or taken.

4. In every battle, concentrate absolutely superior forces—double, triple, quadruple, and sometimes even five or six times those of the enemy—to encircle the enemy on all sides, and strive for his annihilation, with none escaping from the net. Under specific conditions, adopt the method of dealing the enemy smashing blows, that is, the concentration of all forces to strike the enemy's center and one or both of the enemy's flank, aiming at the destruction of a part of the enemy and the routing of another part so that our troops can swiftly transfer forces to smash another enemy group. Avoid battles of attrition in which gains are not sufficient to make up for the losses, or in which the gains merely balance the losses. Thus we are inferior taken as a whole—numerically speaking—but our absolute superiority in every section and in every specific campaign guarantees the victory of each campaign. As time goes by, we will become superior, taken as a whole, until the enemy is totally destroyed.

5. Fight no unprepared engagements; fight no engagements in which there is no assurance of victory. Strive for preparation and assurance of victory in every engagement based on the relative conditions of our forces and those of the enemy.

6. Promote and exemplify valor in combat; fear no sacrifice or fatigue nor continuous actions—that is, fighting several engagements in succession within a short period without respite.

7. Strive to destroy the enemy while in movement. At the same time, emphasize the tactics of attacking positions, wresting strong points and bases from the enemy.

8. With regard to assaults on cities, resolutely wrest from the enemy all strong points and cities which are weakly defended. At favorable opportunities, wrest all the enemy's strong points and cities which are defended to a medium degree and where the circumstances permit. Wait until conditions mature, and then wrest all enemy strong points and cities which are powerfully defended.

9. Replenish yourselves by the capture of all enemy arms and most of his personnel. The source of men and matériel for our army is mainly at the front.

10. Skilfully utilize the intervals between two campaigns for resting, regrouping and training troops. The period of rest and regrouping should in general not be too long. As far as possible do not let the enemy have breathing space.

Principle (1) is the essence of infiltration; (2) prescribes a safe line of advance (rather than a safe line of communications); (3) tells of the need to destroy the life force; (4) and (5) are principles of caution; (9) is the principle of cannibalization and the cheap war; and (10) is a principle with which the United States became familiar in Korea. Summarized, these principles can be reduced to three:

Don't hurry; be certain.
Capitalize on enemy weaknesses.
Insure everything; mass everything and attack with superiority and violence.[246]

There is actually an additional principle: that these simple rules of warfare be remembered by all commissioned and noncommissioned officers. This is not the least important aspect of the matter.[247]

Everything has a past. Some of Mao's ideas belong to the oldest military traditions of Oriental warfare. Yet, for the twentieth century, Mao is an original military thinker. His greatest novelty is the idea that war should be a paying business and that one should not hesitate to fight wars of attrition against superior forces. This is a philosophy of guts which sometimes seems to have disappeared from western military and political thinking. If Mao or one of his disciples were to influence strongly the leadership of international communism, the world could witness the boldest and most ambitious aggression of history. This aggression would not be launched for the sake of agrarian reform, but for world domination.

LUCRATIVE WAR

STALIN'S military policy has always been based on the assumption that war was not only possible but inevitable. He consistently opposed pacifist armament policies which, in his opinion, would leave the Soviet Union "toothless and unarmed" and ultimately force it to capitulate to its enemies. "If there has to be some bleeding, we shall strain all our forces so that the bleeding will be done by some bourgeois state but not by the U.S.S.R."[248]

In 1934, Stalin adopted the policy that the Red army must be stronger than any possible armed combination against the U.S.S.R.

---

[246] This summary is in Colonel Rigg's words, see, *op. cit.,* p. 182.

[247] *Ibid.,* p. 180. Consult also "Principles of Combat," more popularly known as "Principles of Short Attack" by Lin Piao, translated by Rigg, *op. cit.,* pp. 202–6.

[248] *Sochineniya, op. cit.,* X, 46.

—a communist variation of the nineteenth-century British naval policy of the two-power standard.[249]

Stalin also took precautions to avoid entanglements in conflicts that would involve a large fraction of his forces in the endless expanses of Asia. In 1929, Marshal Chang Tso-lin seized the Russian-owned Chinese Eastern Railroad in Manchuria. The soviets apparently assumed, perhaps not without reason, that this coup, engineered by Japanese-supported Russian émigrés, was designed to draw Russia into a prolonged war with China. Although the Red army punished Chang Tso-lin's forces, the soviets avoided war and did not hesitate to reveal weakness to the point of cutting their commitments in Manchuria, then, as now, the key to China.[250]

In 1938 and 1939 the Japanese twice resorted to diversionary open attack against soviet military units in order to help the nazis during the Munich and Polish crises, prevent an offensive Russian attitude against Germany, and put a high price on Japanese "peacefulness" in Asia. Stalin realized the dangers of a two-front war and adopted his peculiar type of "offensive caution," which consists not in appeasing but in diverting a threat.

In his report to the seventeenth congress of the Russian communist party (1934), Stalin reiterated his conviction that war "is sure to unleash revolution and jeopardize the very existence of capitalism in a number of countries." If, nevertheless, the bourgeois politicians force war, it is because "they have gotten into a hopeless mess, have reached an impasse, and are ready to rush headlong over the precipice." "Let not Messieurs the bourgeoisie blame us if some of the governments . . . which today rule happily 'by the grace of God,' are missing on the morrow after such a war." "It can hardly be doubted that a second war against the U.S.S.R. will lead to the complete defeat of the aggressor, to revolution in a number of countries in Europe and Asia, and to the destruction of the bourgeois-landlord governments in those countries."[251]

Stalin predicted that China would emerge from a second world war no longer an "unorganized territory" but an "independent state."[252]

[249] White, *loc. cit.*, p. 362.
[250] Minz, *op. cit.*, p. 95.
[251] *Problems of Leninism, op. cit.*, p. 481.
[252] *Ibid.*, pp. 478 f.

Stalin emphasized that a revolutionary crisis would develop as a result of war and "bourgeois terrorism." Yet, simply because there is a revolutionary situation, defeat of the bourgeoisie would not be assured. "The victory of the revolution never comes by itself. It must be prepared for and won." Revolution can come only if the revolutionary situation is exploited by a "revolutionary party of the proletariat sufficiently strong and influential to lead the masses and take power." However, although the bourgeoisie may lose its head and commit blunder after blunder, yet it could find a way out since, as Lenin used to say, "there is no such thing as an absolutely hopeless situation." Whether or not a situation is hopeless is subject to proof by "practical action" brought about by intelligence, organization, skill, and determination.[253] In other words: don't eat the capitalist before you have killed him.

At the eighteenth party congress, which convened in March 1939, shortly before the outbreak of the second world war, the chief political commissar of the Red army, L. Mekhlis, reverted to the old line that if the Soviet Union should be attacked, the Russian armed forces would carry military operations into enemy territory, "fulfill their internationalist obligations and increase the number of soviet republics." The audience received this sentence with applause. Mekhlis continued, saying that the Russian army, "internationalist according to the ideology prevailing within it, would help the working classes of the aggressor nations" to liberate themselves from the yoke of fascism and "capitalist slavery." It also would liquidate "capitalist encirclement."[254]

This was interpreted widely as a promise that the Red army would fight the war offensively, outside Russia. However, Mekhlis had stated clearly that the Red army would carry its operations abroad only after an attack on the Soviet Union. He described a comprehensive strategy of counteroffensive and enunciated an idea which later was emphasized strongly by Stalin. The strategy of the simple military counteroffensive has been traditional in Russia since the days of Peter the Great and Marshal Kutusov, but Mekhlis advocated much more: the combination of military defensive political offensive, to be followed in the last stage of hostilities

---

[253] *Ibid.,* pp. 481 f.

[254] Fedotoff White, *The Growth of the Red Army* (Princeton, N. J., Princeton University Press, 1944), p. 414.

by a military counteroffensive and a political cover operation.[255]

As already pointed out, Stalin believed in the inevitability of war and also assumed that Russia could not stay neutral indefinitely. In 1925 he suggested that Russia should enter a future war last, at a moment when the other belligerents would have weakened each other critically. By avoiding early participation in the war, Russia would become the relatively strongest power, win the last battles with comparative ease, and impose its will at the peace conference.

During the thirties, Stalin refined this doctrine and produced the idea of the concealed, cheap and easy war.

World War II, Stalin explained in 1939, has already begun "stealthily, without any declaration of war,"[256] by all kinds of minor actions on allegedly secondary fronts such as Abyssinia, Spain, Austria, and China. The fascist states were waging war against the democracies. The democracies did not resist, however, because they did not realize that the war was being fought against them.

How was it possible that the democracies failed to identify this attack? "The fascist rulers decided, before plunging into war, to frame public opinion to suit their ends, that is, to mislead it, to deceive it."[257] The democratic governments feared war because they were pacifists and were afraid of revolutionary developments. They adopted a dual policy of halfhearted resistance and uneasy non-resistance. Thus, the "imperceptible" war was a "one-sided" affair.

---

[255] The paternity of the counteroffensive concept within communist thinking is not altogether clear. In 1936, Mao wrote a military textbook entitled *Strategic Problems of China's Revolutionary War* where he discussed counteroffensive at length: "The object of strategic withdrawal is to preserve the forces and prepare for counter-attack.

The preparation for a counter-offensive requires the selection and creation of a number of conditions favorable to us but unfavorable to the enemy. To alter . . . relative strength . . . we should generally secure at least two of (these) conditions . . . so that we can shift to the offensive. These conditions are:

(1) A people who actively assist the Red Army;
(2) Terrain favorable to the operation;
(3) Complete concentration of [our] main forces;
(4) Discovery of weak spots of the enemy;
(5) An enemy fatigued and demoralized;
(6) An enemy made to commit mistakes.
The last three can be created." Quoted from Rigg, *op. cit.*, p. 187.

[256] *History of the Communist Party, op. cit.*, p. 333.

[257] *The Land of Socialism, Today and Tomorrow, Reports and Speeches at the 18th Congress of the Communist Party of the Soviet Union (Bolsheviks)* (Moscow, 1939), p. 13.

Stalin expected that history would exact heavy retribution from the democracies.

Stalin also interpreted democratic policy as "conniving at aggression." The democracies allegedly intended to embroil Japan in a war with Russia. If this policy were successful, the belligerents would weaken and exhaust each other. When the warring nations were "weak enough," the democracies would "appear on the scene with fresh strength" and "dictate conditions to the enfeebled belligerents."[258] This is the concept of the cheap and easy war which, of course, only rephrases Stalin's older principle of taking advantage of the contradictions in the enemy camp.[259]

Both the concept of the imperceptible war and that of the easy war were taken over by Stalin as part and parcel of the soviet war doctrine. The methods the democracies assertedly were employing, Stalin proposed to employ himself. Naturally enough, the soviets do not venerate war as Mussolini and Hitler were inclined to do. They consider war as a tool of expediency or an act of midwifery— the lancing of a boil that has become ripe. While war may be indispensable for their purposes, the soviets are content for somebody else, a proxy, to do the fighting, enabling the soviets to restrict their intervention to the last act and the *coup de grâce*—a strategy of the undertaker.

Stalin attempted to apply the strategy of "let-the-other-fellow-do-the-work" during World War II. By concluding a nonaggression pact with Germany (August 1939), Stalin induced Hitler to go to war against Britain, France, and Poland.[260] He pulled even more complicated tricks in Asia by encouraging Chiang Kai-shek to fight Japan, and the Chinese communists to fight both Japan and Chiang.[261] By means of another nonaggression pact, Stalin later encouraged the Japanese to fight the western powers. In the end, Russia declared war on Japan after that country had been defeated. The profit of Stalin's imperceptible and cheap wars was Manchuria, southern Sakhalin, North Korea, the Kurils, and ultimately China in Asia; and the Baltic states, Bessarabia, northern Bucovina, and eastern Poland in Europe.

Stalin had found the secret of the lucrative war.

[258] *Ibid.,* p. 15.
[259] *Ibid.*
[260] The background of the German-Russian pact is discussed in Strausz-Hupé and Possony, *op. cit.,* Chap. 14.
[261] See below, Chap. 6.

5. The Second Round of World Revolution: Eastern Europe · 1939–1948

BALANCE SHEET OF WORLD WAR II

"IT WOULD be a grave mistake," said Mao, "to underestimate the significance of the [communist] victory of the second world war." There is a widespread opinion that during World War II the Soviet Union followed a purely defensive strategy and failed to implement its doctrine of revolutionary expansion. From 1941 to 1943, Russia unquestionably was forced on the defensive. But between 1939 and 1941, and again between 1943 and 1945, the Soviet Union carried out some of the most successful offensives of history.

The chief result of World War II is frequently overlooked: While in 1939 communism ruled over Russia alone, in 1950 it controlled an area from central Germany and the Balkans to Manchuria, China, and down into Indochina. Population-wise, the communist empire expanded from 190 to almost 800 million people—one-third of humanity. In Mao's words, the war "resulted in the downfall of three great imperialist powers and the weakening of two others. Only one great imperialist power was left in the world, namely, the United States."[1]

Soviet expansion was in line with communist predictions. They always considered that war would make possible the spreading of bolshevism. An official *panegrikos,* written jointly for Stalin's seventieth birthday by the agitprop commission of the central committee of the Russian communist party and the Marx-Engels-Lenin Institute, revealed a heretofore unknown prediction by Stalin, namely, that the war of the soviet people for its freedom would merge with the struggle of other nations for their independence and "democratic freedoms"—an Aesopian statement meaning that the defensive war

[1] Mao Tse-tung, *People's Democratic Dictatorship* (London, Lawrence and Wishart, 1950), p. 9.

must be transformed into, and fought simultaneously with, revolutionary war.[2]

World War II was waged to save the world from nazi slavery. Its paradoxical result was that it strengthened communist despotism and put 600 million more people under the bolshevik yoke. True, Russian victory was unavoidable and perhaps even justified—after all, the nazis did attack the Soviet Union. Yet the sovietization of eastern Europe and China, and the enormous increase in bolshevik power, might and should have been prevented.

It would be a mistake to oversimplify the causes of western failure in World War II. The unexpected outcome of the war was due, among other things, to Hitler's criminal and insane strategy and to the impotence of the German general staff; to Japanese military megalomania; to the military and moral weakness of the continental democratic nations; to the decline of the Kuomintang; to Chamberlain's appeasement and Churchill's partial abandonment of a realistically anticommunist attitude; to general Anglo-American ignorance of soviet intentions and techniques; to Roosevelt's belief that the Russians had forsaken their plans for world revolution; to his policies of co-operation-at-any-price with the Soviet Union and unconditional surrender for Germany; to an Anglo-American military strategy which played straight into soviet hands; but also, and not in the least, to the effectiveness of communist methods of expansion. While the lessons of policy have been understood, in this field of soviet operational techniques the West still has much to learn.

Stalin as Military Leader

When Germany embarked on her second world war, it was under the leadership of a military amateur who fancied himself history's greatest strategist predestined to overthrow all established rules of sound military planning and fighting.

France and Britain were led by vacillating and incompetent defeatists who thought in terms of nineteenth-century strategy. Only in 1940 did Britain's leadership pass into competent hands.

American military leadership was competent enough, but the

[2] "Der grosse Führer und Lehrer der Kommunistischen Partei und des Sowjetvolkes," *Neues Deutschland*, December 20, 1949, p. 5.

grand strategy of the war did not compromise specific, spelled-out political objectives. That this war was in part a communist revolutionary war was not fully understood. U.S. leadership was unfortunately characterized by its lack of appreciation of the political and social aspects of modern conflict and by its lack of foresight.

By contrast, there was experienced, ruthless, and realistic leadership in the communist camp. Soviet leaders achieved an almost complete unification of military and political strategy. No one doubts Stalin's enormous, though undesirable, talents as a political leader and revolutionary strategist. When, during the war, western statesmen addressed Stalin as "marshal" or "generalissimo," it was a matter of good manners and custom. But Stalin had a right to take his military titles seriously, for, of all persons then living, Stalin possessed the most continuous and most diversified military experience, with the possible exceptions of Winston Churchill and Douglas MacArthur.

Soviet historiography is often fantastic and always propagandistic. It tries to build up Stalin far beyond his actual accomplishments. It ascribes to him feats done by others and exaggerates his influence on events. While this glorification is too apparent to require comment, it would be a grave mistake to assume the opposite and deprecate Stalin's successes as a strategist and military organizer.

In the Russian civil war—the significance of which still is underrated by western experts—Stalin occupied a prominent position. He made strategic decisions of considerable importance and acquired a great deal of battlefield experience. Like Charles XII of Sweden, he is credited with once having captured a fort from the sea, contrary to the advice of naval officers. In a letter to Lenin, Stalin explained the success of this amphibious landing. According to him, the so-called naval science was a deplorable affair. "The swift capture of Gorka was due to the grossest interference in the operations by me and by civilians generally, even to the point of countermanding orders on land and sea and imposing my own. I consider it my duty to declare that I shall continue to act in this way in future despite all my reverence for science."[3]

It is probably true that, according to Tukhachevsky, Stalin's intervention into the battle of Tsaritsyn (later Stalingrad) and his and

[3] I. Minz, *The Red Army* (New York, International Publishers, 1943), p. 84.

Voroshilov's refusal to obey orders prolonged the civil war by two years.[4] It is also true that Stalin's participation in the Polish war was unfortunate and contributed to Russia's failure. Tukhachevsky's criticism, however, does not necessarily detract from Stalin's military stature, anymore than did the failure at the Dardanelles reduce the stature of Churchill. The sign of a military leader is not that he commits no blunders but that he learns from his mistakes. Stalin showed great ability in learning: He usually accepted the criticism and frequently purged the critic.

Stalin participated in the establishment, organization, and development of the Red army. He took a hand in elaborating soviet military doctrine. He has written many professional papers on strategy and tactics including, it is said, a manual for regimental commissars.[5] Perhaps even more important, he organized the military economy and directed the expansion of the war potential of Russia. He is intimately familiar with morale problems.

In the field of non-military warfare, Stalin acquired extensive experience in industrial strikes; *coup de main* tactics (including bank robberies); revolutionary uprisings; and in large-scale revolution.

Voroshilov credited Stalin with having initiated technical changes in military equipment. The *vozhd* was often praised as the guiding spirit behind new inventions,[6] although this may be as legendary as was probably his contribution to the victory at Stalingrad in 1943. But it is fairly certain that during the entire course of World War II, Stalin paid a great deal of attention to armaments, maintained close operational control, repeatedly intervened in military decisions, and, last but not least, selected the very competent commanders of the Red army—in addition to supervising the foreign, domestic, and economic policies of the Soviet Union.

Churchill described his discussions with Stalin in 1942 on the advantages of an allied attack on North Africa. To Churchill's surprise, Stalin showed quick and full comprehension of a typically Anglo-Saxon operation. The landing in Africa would hit the German *Afrika-Korps* in the back; it would intimidate Spain; it would produce fighting between Germans and Frenchmen in France; and it

[4] E. Wollenberg, *The Red Army* (London, Secker and Warburg, 1938), p. 91.

[5] Minz, *op. cit.*, p. 73.

[6] *Ibid.*, p. 99.

would expose Italy to the whole brunt of the war. This comment is revealing for the breadth of Stalin's strategic thinking. It impressed Churchill deeply. Yet, the British prime minister was no novice in military matters. Churchill added: "Very few people alive could have comprehended in so few minutes the reasons which we had all so busily been wrestling with for months."[7]

Stalin is one of the great military captains of history. This is a matter of record, and the western nations must recognize this fact.

VULTURES OVER EUROPE

THE PACT of August 1939 between nazism and bolshevism was the most far-reaching decision made by Stalin during World War II. This pact was Stalin's, and not Hitler's, brain child. Without Stalin's promise not to attack Germany in the rear, Hitler hardly would have dared launch into the adventure of World War II. Whatever Stalin's true motives may have been, his behavior contributed nothing to the maintenance of peace and everything to make war inevitable. Without war, sovietism could not spread, and the Soviet Union could not grow.[8]

The agreement with Germany provided Russia with some machinery and technological assistance. The soviets paid the nazis rather heavily in oil and food stuffs. The pact envisaged the division of Poland and enabled the soviets to take eastern Poland by bloodless military conquest. This was an ideal application of the "cheap and easy" strategy, since the Wehrmacht had destroyed the Polish armed forces. The soviets merely took the fruits of somebody else's victory. To coin a term: "vulture strategy."

Finland was attacked on a flimsy pretext. The military attack was

[7] Winston Churchill, *The Hinge of Fate* (Boston, Houghton Mifflin, 1950), p. 482.

[8] The communists have not always avoided telling the truth about their pact with the nazis: "The mighty soviet nation, having exhausted all efforts to prevent the outbreak of imperialist war, the working class having been unable to drive out of power the Chamberlain and Daladier governments, faced with the inevitable imperialist war on a large scale, decided on new actions to protect its own interests, *strengthen the revolutionary forces, and weaken the imperialist war-makers on both sides of the conflict.* . . . The German-Soviet non-aggression pact was its first act. . . . The pact completely undermined the most immediate danger of attack against the Soviet Union. It weakened the ideological foundations of the fascist regimes." (Italics added.) *Young Communist Review,* October, 1939, p. 24.

accompanied by the establishment in Russia of a "revolutionary Finnish government," under the old Comintern wheel horse Otto Kuusinen. This was revolution from without *à la sauce tartare*. But Stalin tipped his hand too early, ignoring his own precepts stipulating the need of a revolutionary situation. He neglected the need for deception. The artificial creation of the Kuusinen government revealed that Stalin planned to take Finland in its entirety. These errors promptly stiffened the backs of the Finns who demonstrated their freedom from any "Occidental decadence." Stalin was forced to content himself with "limited objectives" obtainable by fairly cheap, though not entirely easy, war.

The three Baltic states were taken over in successive stages. The mechanics of their gradual absorption included infiltration of the government and the army, establishment by forced treaty of soviet military and naval bases, and ultimately ground attack coinciding with revolutionary seizure of power.

Bessarabia and northern Bucovina were taken over through the diplomatic blackmail of Rumania.

In western Europe the soviets acted as though they had decided on destroying France. Since France was the weakest among the main capitalist nations, such a decision would have been entirely logical for believers in the law of "uneven development of capitalism." According to this doctrine, Stalin must have reasoned that the second break-through of the revolution would occur in France. (The first break-through, it will be remembered, was the October revolution in Russia.)

For many years the communists had infiltrated successfully into the French armed forces. The antimilitarist and demoralization work of the French communists was considered a model for all communist parties. Communists also were well placed in the recently nationalized French aircraft industry and had done their worst, through strikes and perpetual slowdowns, to reduce the output of planes.

During the Munich crisis the French communists pretended to be for preparedness and war against Germany. However, the demoralization cadres were left in position. With the conclusion of the German-Russian pact and the outbreak of the war, the communist fractions became highly active. They preached immediate peace and practiced revolutionary defeatism.[9]

[9] A. Rossi, *Les Communistes français pendant la drôle de guerre* (Paris, Les Iles d'Or, 1951), passim.

A demoralization offensive was launched on a large scale with demonstrations in the chamber, open letters, distribution of leaflets, clandestine newspapers, subversion in army and factories, and high-powered propaganda in the rear of the army, especially among military personnel on leave, among *évacués,* and among wives of mobilized soldiers. A number of clandestine communist papers were printed in Germany, as Ribbentrop later admitted to Mussolini.[10] The communist propaganda campaign reached an unexpected climax when German planes dropped the text of a Molotov speech almost simultaneously with its reproduction in the clandestine *l'Humanité.*

The leader of the French communist party, Maurice Thorez, deserted from the army and, through Belgium and Germany, fled to Moscow where he was interviewed by the *Daily Worker. L'Humanité* reprinted the interview, exhibiting the communist policy of treason.

Factory workers were invited to sabotage war production. On the testimony of the then prime minister, Edouard Daladier, sabotage was particularly successful in the aircraft industry, in explosives and tank plants, and in the fortifications of the Maginot line. Sabotage of tanks resulted in considerable loss in battle, and even greater loss was caused by the sabotage of aircraft. Resulting losses and accidents were exploited for defeatist propaganda: playing two pianos with one hand.

While sabotage was widespread, the general slowdown of production induced by propaganda contributed even more to the defeat of France. "One hour less for production brings the revolution one hour earlier." Other slogans dealt with equality of sacrifice; equality of work—everybody must work in the factories, including the rich; equality of profits; and equality of wages. Equality of wages was applied to soldiers and workers, to soldiers and officers, and to French and English soldiers. (English military pay was far higher than French.)[11] When the armed clash came, the clandestine communist press invited the French soldiers to fraternize with the German troops. It was most unfortunate that the French units defending

---

[10] Galeazzo Ciano, *L'Europa verso la catastrofe* (Milan, Mondadori, 1948), p. 520.

[11] Rossi, *op. cit.,* pp. 210–13.

the Sedan gap consisted mainly of industrial workers vulnerable to propaganda infection.

Army morale undoubtedly was affected by defeatism and pacifism, and it is no wonder that, as the French commander in chief, Maurice Gamelin, expressed it, *défaillances* occurred in the French army. This demoralization resulted in large measure from the combined communist and nazi propaganda attack. Yet it was partially the result of inadequate military training, insufficient armament, equipment, and pay, and the poor political and military leadership of France.

In communist opinion, the French defeat created a revolutionary situation. Unbelievable though it may sound, communist strategy aimed at exploiting this defeat situation to seize power. The communists believed themselves to be the only French party which could deliver to Germany a reliable peace or a World War II version of Brest-Litovsk. They assumed that the strategic cover given the German-Russian pact would make this scheme acceptable to the nazis.[12]

German imperialism was specifically designated as the "temporary ally" of the French communist revolution. The objective was to overthrow the Vichy government and to establish a communist regime under the bayonets of the Wehrmacht. Had not the Prussian army in 1871 abstained from fighting the Commune? Had not the German army in 1918 assisted the Russian bolsheviks? Would not a communist France facilitate the nazi war against Britain? Would it not strengthen the alliance with Russia?

Fortunately for the world, this neat plan failed, the nazis being unwilling to co-operate. Yet there can be no doubt that this policy of the French communist party was in accord with the policies of the Soviet Union.

Did the Soviet Union consider its alliance with Germany merely a device for regional expansion, or was there a grandiose, global design?

More specifically: Did the soviets plan to use the Wehrmacht as an instrument of world revolution, a *clades revolutionis*? Did they consider the nazi movement a providential tool to destroy the "im-

---

[12] A. Rossi, *Physiologie du parti communiste français* (Paris, Self, 1948), p. 12. This book presents the evidence for this communist strategy.

perialist powers," France, Great Britain, and the United States, and which would destroy itself in the process?

The idea of a German-Russian alliance was nothing new either to influential national socialists or to important elements among the bolsheviks. There was the revolutionary tradition of 1917–18, followed by Rapallo, as well as the numerous indications that Stalin not only did not object to Hitler's seizure of power in 1933 but actually may have contributed to it. Statements by prominent bolsheviks, including Molotov, minimized the significance of the ideological differences between the Soviet Union and nazi Germany. At least temporarily, Stalin may have toyed with the idea that the nazi movement might be transmuted into a genuine revolutionary movement.

The fact remains that Stalin helped Hitler, a fact which can be explained logically only if it is assumed, for one reason or another, that the soviets considered the western powers their most dangerous opponents.

The soviets gave the nazis strong propaganda support against France and England. They stated that a strong Germany was necessary for Europe. They confirmed Hitler's claim that Germany had gone to war only to break the "chains of Versailles."[13] More significantly, the soviets did not state that Germany was fighting an imperialist war, as were France and Britain. The references to Versailles may be interpreted to mean that, in soviet opinion, Germany was fighting a war of national liberation. But even this interpretation may fall short of the mark.

The true soviet attitude was revealed by the directives given to the communist underground. The Comintern leader Klement Gottwald, now president of Czechoslovakia, reportedly made a trip from Moscow to Prague—with the permission of the nazi authorities—to order the Czech communists not to interfere with the nazi war effort. Walter Ulbricht, now second in command in eastern Germany, transmitted similar Comintern directives to the German communists insisting that the Russian people and the German workers had a common interest in wrecking the British war plan.[14] In 1940, Ulbricht spoke in Stockholm. He blamed "French and British imperialism" for the war and suggested that German workers should fight in Ger-

---

[13] A. Rossi, *Deux ans d'alliance Germano-Soviétique, Août 1939–Juin 1940* (Paris, Fayard, 1949), p. 97.

[14] *Ibid.*, pp. 112–15.

many's "defensive battle."[15] According to the communists, Germany had shown its willingness for peace while Britain and France wanted war. The German communists were instructed to abstain from applying the tactics of revolutionary defeatism against nazi Germany.

On the basis of communist theory on the types of war, it may be deduced that the soviets considered that Germany was fighting a revolutionary war. It would seem that, in Stalin's opinion, the nazi war was furthering the cause of the communist revolution. This is the only hypothesis that explains in a rational manner communist behavior during 1939 and 1940.

Once it is understood that the soviets believed the nazis were fighting a war of liberation or a revolutionary war or, in any event, a progressive or pararevolutionary war, negotiations about Russia's adherence to the German-Italian-Japanese alliance, the so-called Anti-Comintern pact, become comprehensible. This prospective alliance was directed against Britain and was concerned with the postwar distribution of the Asian and African holdings of the British empire. Actually, Britain had long been considered the archenemy of communism.

This alliance was similarly directed against the interests of the United States. In 1940, during a long conversation with Hitler, Molotov is reported to have agreed with only one statement of the Führer's: "The United States have no business in Europe, Africa or Asia."[16] The Politburo may well have estimated that Germany and Japan would not only destroy Britain but would also weaken the United States.

Speaking in purely military terms, if Stalin considered the United States and Britain to be his chief enemies and the main obstacles to the victory of communism, the alliance with Germany and Japan made sense. Stalin never would find a better chance to have somebody else do his biggest job. According to information received in 1940 by the Czech government-in-exile at London, the Czech communists were told officially that the bolshevik party central committee was planning for Russia to remain neutral until the end of the conflict and then, if possible, carry out the world revolution.[17] This strategy is easy enough to understand unless the tenuous ideologi-

[15] The New Leader, New York, April 23, 1951, p. 10.

[16] Paul Schmidt, Statist auf diplomatischer Buehne, 1923–1945 (Bonn, Athenaeum Verlag, 1949), p. 520.

[17] Rossi, op. cit., p. 116.

cal differences between nazism and communism are overstressed.

However, negotiations between Berlin and Moscow over the possibility of Russian adherence to the Anti-Comintern pact failed. Hitler was none too eager for close partnership with the soviets, especially since, in his opinion, they were asking too high a price. Actually, Stalin's price was relatively low, if compared to the profits envisaged by Germany and Japan.

But why, if they wanted to use the German army as the sword of world revolution, ask any price at all?

In the absence of reliable documentation, the answer may be hazarded that the Politburo was unable to make up its mind. They had many reasons to distrust Hitler, and were sufficiently realistic to see that Germany could emerge victorious from the conflict and put an end to communist ambitions.

The strategy of world revolution through the Wehrmacht as a transmission belt was attractive, but it also was "adventuristic." To phrase it differently, the soviets probably wanted to watch how the war would develop before they risked embarking on the hazardous course of riding the tiger. The nazi alliance offer (November 1940) came too early.

ACTIVE DEFENSE

DURING World War II the Soviet Union was compelled to fight before its military forces had reached a level of readiness which the Politburo considered adequate for offensive, revolutionary warfare. Accordingly, while the soviet war doctrine was put to a test, the test was not a conclusive one. From the doctrinal point of view, the greatest established failure was the relative ineffectiveness of subversion techniques against the nazi dictatorship.[18] Nor were the communists overly successful in their demoralization work against the Wehrmacht.

By the force of circumstances the soviets were thrown back to more conventional forms of fighting.

Actually, the remarkable thing about soviet war preparations was

[18] It must be borne in mind that this statement does not refer to soviet espionage which apparently was highly successful even in Germany. See Alexander Foote, *Handbook for Spies* (New York, Doubleday, 1949), *passim* and particularly pp. 92–115; also, W. F. Flicke, *Die Rote Kapelle* (Kreuzlingen, Neptun, 1949).

that they avoided, with much success, those ideological pitfalls which could have reduced the striking power of the Russian armed forces. Despite all doctrinal temptation they stuck to the principle "first things come first." The first thing was conventional military power. The last remnants of military "progressivism" were abandoned under the regime of Marshal Semyen Timoshenko, especially with the introduction of his *Disciplinary Code of the Red Army* (October 1940). The Russian army became the most "Prussian," most socially stratified fighting instrument in the world. It shed all pretense of being democratic and became the ruthlessly professional combat army of a militant and aggressive elite.

Stalin himself was preoccupied with the conventional combat aspects of modern war. He put great emphasis on the need for all ranks to become expert in the handling of arms. He insisted that co-ordination between all arms was the key to victory.[19] He called for improved and ever more improved intelligence, "the eyes and ears of the army," without which the enemy cannot be beaten.[20] (The corollary to this principle was formulated by Mao: "We want to take the enemy's eyes and ears and seal them as completely as possible.")[21]

Naturally, there was great stress laid on defensive problems: The Red army's most important task was to stop the nazis. "Active defense" was adopted as the standard antidote to blitzkrieg tactics, a method which frequently required defending untenable positions in order to delay and wear down the enemy and launching repeated counterattacks to interfere with his initiative and reduce his strength.

Although the soviets seemed pleased with their successes against Hitler's blitzkrieg, on close analysis they appear less impressive. Hitler thought that the soviet system was a bloated "pig's bladder" which, once pricked, would collapse completely. Only the door must be crashed, he exclaimed. Hence, Hitler risked attacking the Soviet Union with a relatively weak air force and but 2,434 tanks against a four-fold Russian tank superiority.[22] The Germans failed to discover in time the existence of the superior Russian T-34 tank,

[19] Stalin, *The Great Patriotic War of the Soviet Union* (New York, International Publishers, 1945), p. 55.

[20] *Ibid.*, p. 88.

[21] Robert Payne, *Mao Tse-tung, Ruler of Red China* (New York, Schuman, 1950), p. 177.

[22] See Walter Goerlitz, *Der Deutsche Generalstab, Geschichte und Gestalt, 1657–1945* (Frankfort on the Main, Verlag der Frankfurter Hefte, 1950), p. 549.

a failure which greatly accentuated their numerical inferiority.[23]

Magnifying the basic weakness of the Wehrmacht was Hitler's inspired operational plan, which was premised on the silly notion that the Moscow area was less important than were the Leningrad suburbs and Stalingrad. *Feldherr* Hitler attempted rapid and large-scale movements in roadless areas, and this without adequate numbers of cross-country vehicles. He halted the 1941 offensive against Moscow at the very moment when it promised success. And he refused to halt the advance when the German army had overreached itself and, without winter equipment, was surprised by severely cold weather.[24]

The sudden arrival of winter late in 1941 cost the Germans no less than 1,500 tanks, and within less than three months, 112,627 casualties to cold alone.[25] Six months after the attack on the Soviet Union, the German army had a deficit of 340,000 men—and a poor replacement potential. Yet the U.S.S.R. still possessed large and untapped man-power reserves.

The defeat at Stalingrad, also, was due in large measure to grave German errors of judgment, such as the withdrawal of armored units to the Caucasus, the simultaneous waging of two large offensives without adequate strength for either, and the refusal to withdraw in time from an untenable position.

The Germans themselves acknowledge two effective features of soviet antiblitzkrieg tactics: Russian forces usually withdrew before German tanks, and they reattacked at propitious moments. Encircled Russian units kept open what Hitler called "tubes" to the main front and repeatedly succeeded in saving themselves from destruction. These tactics were practical because the Germans were too poorly motorized for rapid movement. Moreover, the Germans lacked armored strength: While German tank production stood at 250 a month, Russian output was between 600 and 700 tanks monthly. The logistical support structure behind the German armored divisions was inadequate; in particular, there was a great lack of mobile repair shops.[26]

[23] See Heinz Guderian, *Erinnerungen eines Soldaten* (Heidelberg, Vowinckel, 1951), p. 216.

[24] See Franz Halder, *Hitler als Feldherr* (Munich, Muenchner Dom Verlag, 1949), pp. 36–44. General Halder was chief of the army general staff.

[25] Goerlitz, *op. cit.*, pp. 575 f.

[26] *Ibid.*, pp. 568, 585.

In fine, soviet military tactics played a secondary role in the defeat of the Wehrmacht. Yet the soviets compensated for their lack of full military effectiveness by economic tactics, such as the timely evacuation of industry and stock piles, and the systematic destruction of nontransportable goods. The soviets compelled the enemy to overwork his logistics while at the same time keeping their own industrial losses to a minimum. Territory was considered less important than equipment and man power, both of which were made mobile, to a degree, and removed with the retreating army.

Active defense was tied in closely with guerrilla warfare.[27] The soviets believed that mechanized armies were particularly vulnerable to attack by irregulars. Stalin ordered the guerrillas to harrass communications, destroy military stores, attack enemy rear garrisons, prevent the retreating enemy from carrying out his own scorched-earth policy and, in general, supplement the regular forces in their offensive and defensive operations.[28] By daring maneuvers the partisans were to surround and split up enemy units and capture matériel and men.[29] The guerrillas were also charged with intelligence functions.[30] In short, guerrillas handled many functions which, in western armies, were taken care of by tactical aviation.

These guerrillas were not spontaneously assembled bands of peasants or workers. In the proper sense of the word, they were organized irregular forces or partisans operating as an integral part of the soviet army. The tactical disposition and mission of these units changed with the mission of the main force.[31]

Guerrilla operations were expected to confirm a dictum by Friedrich Engels: "In the course of time the waves of popular warfare, bit by bit, destroy even the biggest army and, what is particularly important, without any evident loss to the other side."[32]

While partisan warfare did not live up to this expectation, it contributed heavily to whatever successes active defense achieved.

[27] Minz, *op. cit.*, p. 31. See also above, pp. 108 f.
[28] *The Great Patriotic War, op. cit.*, p. 82.
[29] Minz, *op. cit.*, p. 42.
[30] *Ibid.*, p. 154.
[31] Michel Berchin and Eliah Ben-Horin, *The Red Army* (New York, Norton, 1942), pp. 207 ff. The effects of partisan operations on the Germans were described by a German officer in "Russia's Hidden Army," *The Infantry Journal,* July and August 1949.
[32] Quoted in Minz, *op. cit.*, p. 155.

The war in Russia was lost by Hitler. It scarcely was won by the active defense of the Red army. Their close escape from defeat has undoubtedly been engraved indelibly in soviet military minds. To assume that communist military thinking will remain wedded to the concept of active defense as a cure-all would be most hazardous. Stalin was given credit for the idea that active defense should be linked to counteroffensive strategy. Henceforth, the bolsheviks may very well reason that a defensive, and even a counteroffensive, strategy is far more "adventuristic" than is a well-prepared and well-timed offensive. This proved to be valid in 1941 and will doubtless remain so as the world advances further into the atomic age.

People's War

STALIN's seventieth birthday in 1949 was celebrated with exaggerations and lies, but fortunately some of the birthday encomiums threw some light on the development of soviet war doctrine.

Marshal Voroshilov praised Stalin for his solution of "one of the most difficult and complicated problems of the military art, the maneuver to encircle and destroy large enemy forces." The claim that Stalin fathered the art of the *Vernichtungsschlacht* is sure to make the ghosts of the Prussian generals wince.[33] But we can deduce that the soviets have taken over the German doctrine of the battle of annihilation and that they are stressing the tactics of flank attack.

Stalin was praised for his inventions in the field of break-through operations.[34] He is said to favor a series of successive break-throughs in preference to one big push, as in the ten Red army drives of 1944. As a variant, Stalin allegedly mastered the art of simultaneous breaks through a wide front. Co-ordinated break-throughs aim to force the enemy into time-consuming regroupings and prevent him from concentrating his reserves. Successive and simultaneous break-throughs are designed to forestall hostile counterattacks and counteroffensives.

The advantages of serial attack in contrast to single attack need not be labored. The difficulty lies in gathering strength that permits

[33] "Feldherr der Freiheit," *Neues Deutschland,* Berlin, December 28, 1949.

[34] "Josef Wissarionowitsch Stalin, Kurze Lebensbeschreibung," *Tägliche Rundschau,* Berlin, December 14, 1949, p. 4.

such a strategy. The bolsheviks think that they possess the secret of maximizing strength in the full exploitation of the "constantly operating factors." Stalin defined what he meant by constantly operating factors: the strength of the rear, the morale of the army, the quantity and quality of divisions, the armament of the army, and the organizational abilities of the commanders.[35] These are contrasted with secondary factors, such as surprise and terrain.

This concept of the people's war is said to be a creative development of the Marxist-Leninist interpretation of war according to which economics, state politics, ideology, and the education and maturity of a nation's cadres decide the course and outcome of international conflict.[36]

Is this a reapplication of the industrial war potential idea, expanded by certain noneconomic, nonquantitative, and organizational factors? Such an interpretation would be misreading Stalin's mind, which is functional and operational rather than theoretical.

According to the bolsheviks, war is a contest between military and material forces as well as a struggle between the spiritual forces of nations. *War is a conflict between societies.* "The history of war teaches that only those states stood the test which proved stronger than their adversaries as regards the development and organization of their economy, as regards the experience, skill, and fighting spirit of their troops, and as regards the fortitude and unity of their people throughout the war."[37]

[35] *The Great Patriotic War, op. cit.,* p. 41.

[36] *Tägliche Rundschau, loc. cit.*

[37] *The Great Patriotic War, op. cit.,* p. 100. It seems that this thought originated with the former tsarist officer who was Stalin's chief of staff in 1941, Marshal Boris Shaposhnikov, author of a three-volume treatise entitled *Mosg Armii* (Moscow, Voyenni Vestnik, 1927). After the most extensive search, only the first volume of this work was located in the United States. This volume is a theme-and-variations treatment of Conrad von Hoetzendorf's *Aus meiner Dienstzeit, 1906–1918,* (4 vols., Vienna-Berlin, Rikola, 1921–23). It is essentially a study of the defeat of Austria-Hungary, a country which in more than one respect resembled the multinational Soviet Union. Shaposhnikov discussed the Austrian general staff and the political, personal, and organizational factors which contributed to its malfunctioning. He analyzed the role of military leadership, the relation between high command and government, and the over-all conduct of war, including the problem of the "independent soldier." In so doing, he branched out into the fields of economics, industrial mobilization, the interrelationship between economics and politics, both domestic and foreign, national sociology, and military history. His main conclusion was that social integration, organization, and leadership are the most vital

Leadership should aim constantly at increasing the strength of one's own nation and, simultaneously, at weakening the structure of the enemy. The Germans, Stalin pointed out, were strong at the beginning of the war but later grew progressively weaker. There were many reasons for the German decline. Stalin singled out Germany's shortage of officer personnel and the inadequate training given to the reserves. By contrast, the cadres of the Red army were growing and improving. Gradually, all Russian reserves would be pulled in. Ultimately, he predicted, the original force relationship would be reversed: Russia would become stronger than Germany.[38] There is no need to discuss the accuracy of this analysis. The point is that bolshevik strategy aims at increasing the relative strength of communism during war and through war.

This concept embodies a strategy of organization rather than of operations. The objective is to organize a people's war.

In 1931 the soviet general, N. S. Unschlicht described the people's war concept: "The forces of the Red army alone would not enable Soviet Russia to achieve victory. The entire population would have to take part in the next war and, accordingly, the entire population must be prepared for it."

The concept of the people's war is more than catchy propaganda. *It is a call for the complete militarization of communist society, a militarization from cradle to grave.*

And, indeed, Russia became the most thoroughly militarized country on earth. The result of this supermilitarization was that, in emergencies, so-called civilians could be drawn into combat at a moment's notice. Workers called from the bench to the trench knew their weapons, their units, and their duties. They knew the areas in which they operated, including secret roads, hiding places, and

---

elements of war, in addition to material strength. By keeping Shaposhnikov's books at his bedside (rather than Clausewitz's, as did Lenin), Stalin had an excellent guide on the mistakes to avoid. Instead of relying on a philosophical treatise and German profundity on victory in the abstract, he learned a very practical lesson on how to avert defeat—a key to bolshevik behavior. Incidentally, Shaposhnikov quoted Schlieffen's words *"Mehr sein als scheinen"*— freely translated, "be stronger than you appear to be"—saying that it should be printed over the entrance door to every general staff and should be engraved on the heart of every staff officer. He predicted dire consequences for those military leaders who do not understand the forces of modern time and who "try to appear to be more than they are." (*Op. cit.*, p. 154.)

[38] *The Great Patriotic War, op. cit.*, p. 93.

stores. Even while they remained at the bench, workers guarded factories against parachutists and partisans. They often did overtime helping out with transport, harvesting, kitchen and guard duties. Youngsters, elderly people, and women were trained to lend a hand to military units in the vicinity.[39]

When the nazis approached Moscow, the workers were organized as militia units. Women were pressed into building field fortifications. Local inhabitants transformed the suburbs into strong points. In the battle of Leningrad, the regular forces were reduced to such a point that the workers' militia, supported by companies of females and adolescents, became the city's main defenders.[40]

Stalin's people's war strategy was made possible by the deadly error in Hitler's planning: the combination of an attempt to overthrow bolshevism with "the primitive idea of reducing and enslaving the slavic race."[41]

The planned economy of the U.S.S.R. was an integral part of the people's war. The almost permanent industrial mobilization, and the unity of military and economic command, increased soviet capabilities but also induced them to overrate their strength. It still induces them to underrate the military capabilities of nations who organize their economies in a nonbureaucratic fashion and according to different principles.

In his first war speech, Stalin called upon Russia to fight a people's war. "Side by side with the Red army, the entire soviet people are rising in defense of our native land." He strove for high morale, objected to "whimperers, cowards, panic-mongers and deserters," and asked for defense to the last drop of blood. "All-round assistance for the Red army" took precedence over all other tasks. Production, the guarding of factories, air-raid, antiparachutist, and antiespionage precautions, as well as the "extermination" of elements attacking morale, were necessary. Food, machinery, fuel, and transportation equipment must be saved by evacuation. "All valuable property . . . which cannot be withdrawn must be destroyed without

[39] Mao Tse-tung carried the idea of cradle-to-grave militarization even further: He is inclined to use his soldiers for "productive purposes" whenever he does not need them for training and combat.

[40] This would not have been good enough against a determined attack, but Hitler stopped the operation because he did not want to feed the city population. Goerlitz, *op. cit.,* p. 572.

[41] *Ibid.,* pp. 566, 571, 573.

fail." "In the occupied regions conditions must be made unbearable for the enemy. . . . They must be hounded and annihilated at every step, and all their measures frustrated."

This war, Stalin concluded, was not an ordinary war between two armies. "It is also a great war of the entire soviet people against the German fascist forces." Note that, according to his careful phrasing, it was to be a people's unilateral war.[42]

The Carrot and the Stick

INTERESTS of national survival and the need to defend the base of world revolution forced the soviets into an alliance with Britain and America, the nations whose destruction they had attempted, and forced them to fight Germany, whose alliance they had sought. After the German attack, offensive revolutionary plans were shelved, temporarily. Pygmalion-like, the soviets transformed themselves into defenders of law, order, and religion. They became peace-loving champions of democracy and tried hard to make the world forget that they had just been kicked out of the nazi bed.

Basic to all soviet activities was the strengthening of their power position vis-à-vis the western nations. The *conditio sine qua non* of soviet strategy was to prevent the United States and Great Britain from winning an overwhelming victory and imposing peace terms according to democratic ideas.

The lend-lease agreement played a big role within this soviet strategy. The United States delivered weapons and equipment to help the Russians defend themselves against the nazis. So far, so good. Yet many deliveries were made at the expense of the western armies which but for lend-lease could have been significantly stronger. Also, some materials were made available which added nothing to Russian ability to fight, not to mention lend-lease equipment never used and left rotting by the soviets. Other equipment served peacetime "reconstruction," that is, the building up of the soviet posthostilities war potential. The whole operation transferred war potential and wealth from the United States and Britain to the Soviet Union.

[42] *The Great Patriotic War, op. cit.,* p. 15.

How was it possible for the soviets to operate so successfully against their western allies? How was it possible that the United States and Britain had become so gullible?

The answer is: *propaganda.*

The first basic theme of soviet propaganda took its inspiration from the nursery: "Who's afraid of the big, bad wolf?" Who can distrust communists and their motives unless he be a nazi war criminal? The allied governments, rejoicing that they had found military help for the war against nazi Germany, happily took part in the whitewashing orgy. A whole legion of sympathizers and pseudo-liberals did their best to dispel residual suspicions of the Soviet Union. The bon ton was to "trust" Stalin. It was as though Queen Victoria had locked her debutante daughter in a room with Jack the Ripper to prove the strength of her faith in humanity.

The soviets camouflaged their motives by signing the Atlantic charter, ostensibly dissolving the Comintern and emphasizing (and distorting) the alleged theory of peaceful coexistence between capitalism and sovietism. The world was made to believe that communists no longer put their faith in communism; that revolutionaries had become reformers; that the disciples of Marx and Lenin believed in Jefferson and the New Deal; that the dictatorship of the proletariat was simply "administrative discipline" or, at worst, comparable to the rule of the democratic party in the southern United States; and that the soviets had no thought of conquest or expansion but merely wanted to be left alone in Russia to build socialism in one country, and in one country alone.

It is doubtful whether this particular propaganda attack would have been so devastatingly successful if the communists and their henchmen had not been able to silence their opponents. The typical double-barreled attack: freedom of speech for soviet propaganda and the silent treatment for those who would expose communist lies.

Second, soviet psychological warfare against the western allies was built on the fear that Stalin might conclude a separate peace with Hitler. Should this occur, the West reasoned, the Anglo-American alliance would have a very costly war on its hands which, perhaps, might be impossible to win. To minimize this danger, the western powers adopted the policy of complying with Russian demands to the maximum.

Anglo-American fears were justified enough on the strength of the historical record, particularly of 1939. Far from alleviating these fears, the soviets exploited them to the fullest extent possible. They must have reasoned that the more they succeeded in frightening their allies, the greater the concessions that would be granted to world communism.

For example, after the western powers in 1942 canceled the cross-channel invasion, the soviets cut official correspondence with Britain and the United States to an absolute minimum. An allied message which promised the placing of an allied air force under Russian command, the sending of additional planes to Russia, the transfer of merchant ships to the Russian flag, the lend-leasing of an auto-mobile tire plant, the sending of large numbers of engines, and the deployment of substantial allied reinforcements to the Persian Gulf was acknowledged with a laconic "thank you."[43]

During the same period, the soviet press pretended that failure of the British authorities to try Rudolf Hess, as well as the "machina-tions" of various British politicians (including that hoary stand-by, the Cliveden set), constituted proof that Britain was working for a separate peace with Germany. Churchill told Foreign Minister Eden that "the bolsheviks have undermined so many powerful govern-ments by lying, machine-made propaganda, and they probably think they make some impression on us by these methods."

Nevertheless, allied authorities became alarmed.[44] Even Roose-velt felt it necessary to inform Churchill that the western powers must "prove to Stalin that we have carried out obligations one hun-dred per cent and we must therefore proceed vigorously with our plans for supplying them and for setting up an air force to fight on their front."

This soviet threat to make a separate peace gained greatly in force precisely because it may well not have been entirely a propaganda maneuver. If the Germans—who at that time (1942) had not yet suffered the Stalingrad defeat—had offered the Russians moderate terms, the communists would have derived considerable advantage from a separate armistice or peace, even if it had been merely a tem-porary truce.

[43] Churchill, *op. cit.,* p. 580.

[44] Robert E. Sherwood, *Roosevelt and Hopkins, An Intimate History* (re-vised ed., New York, Harper, 1950), p. 641.

We are informed today that during the period in question, the soviets themselves took the initiative in at least one attempt at negotiations with the Germans. These negotiations were begun in December 1942, that is, after the British-American attack on North Africa had weakened the German bargaining position.[45]

Similar flirtations with the possibility of a separate peace occurred time and again. After Stalingrad, the soviets established the league of German officers which, together with its mass counterpart, the free German committee, was considered by many to be a tool designed to facilitate agreement with the Wehrmacht. But again and again soviet propaganda, supplementing diplomatic tactics, accused Britain and the United States of negotiating with the Germans.

The last of these gratuitous accusations occurred early in 1945 in connection with the armistice negotiations in Italy. The communists desired to prevent allied-German contacts from taking place without their participation. The soviet insinuations and complaints aroused the ire of the otherwise patient Roosevelt, stopping this soviet attempt in its tracks, but even at that late date the soviet maneuver "thoroughly alarmed" the joint chiefs of staff because "an open break between Russia and her Anglo-Saxon allies would be the only miracle that would prevent the speedy collapse of the German army." In accordance with their views, President Roosevelt, in the last cable of his life, instructed the American ambassador at Moscow to treat this affair as a "minor incident." To Admiral Leahy, however, this minor incident demonstrated the dangerous undesirability of having "unnecessary allies." It reinforced his conviction that the United States was making a mistake "to embrace the Soviet Union as a co-partner in the final stages of the war against Japan."[46]

Clearly, then, the allied policy of placating the soviets must be regarded as founded on fear. Russian diplomatic skill in exploiting their advantage may be seen from just three examples.

Example No. 1: The aborted Italian campaign and the forestalled Balkan offensive. Had the allies pushed their 1944 spring offensive in Italy, they probably would have beaten the Red army to the Danubian plain and possibly even to Vienna and Budapest. Offen-

[45] Peter Kleist, *Zwischen Hitler und Stalin, 1939–1945* (Bonn, Athenaeum Verlag, 1950), pp. 239–41.

[46] Fleet Admiral William D. Leahy, *I Was There* (New York, McGraw-Hill, 1950), p. 336.

sive operations in Yugoslavia might have kept that country within the western sphere of influence. Moreover, a thrust against the Axis southern flank would have forced the Germans into additional dispersion and probably would have facilitated and accelerated the battle of France. For obvious reasons, the soviets did not want the allies to embark on this strategy.[47]

No one can accuse them of not making their wishes abundantly clear. At Tehran, Stalin openly opposed any deployment of allied forces through the eastern Mediterranean. Instead, he urged his allies to support their cross-channel invasion with a strike against southern France. He even suggested that they abandon the capture of Rome.

According to Stalin, "it had been the experience of the Red army that it was best to launch an offensive from two converging directions, forcing the enemy to move his reserves from one front to the other." He contended that an attack through Italy would not be of much avail since the Alps seemed to him to present "an almost insuperable barrier as the famous Russian General Suvorov discovered in his time."[48] The Balkans "were far from the heart of Germany, and the only direct way of striking at that heart was through France."

In retrospect, one would like to ask the soviets why, under the circumstances, they found it necessary to declare war on Bulgaria and to operate through the Hungarian plains; moreover, are they not themselves proponents of the strategy of indirect approach?

The British opposed the plan Stalin had outlined for the West, but the Americans, including the joint chiefs of staff, supported the soviet view. They estimated that the British proposal to operate in the Balkans and eastern Mediterranean was dictated by their desire "to acquire for the Empire post-war advantages in the Balkan states"[49] and that most of the operations suggested for the area were quite unnecessary. General Eisenhower did perceive "that an attack into the Balkans might be more productive in attaining British and American political objectives than would the attack through

[47] *Ibid.*, p. 207.
[48] Sherwood, *op. cit.*, pp. 780 f. Actually, Suvorov crossed the Alps twice. Napoleon in 1795 also showed that attacks through the Alps are entirely feasible. In 1918, Austria was knocked out of the war by an Italian offensive in the Alps.
[49] Leahy, *op. cit.*, p. 242.

southern France," yet, he felt that political decisions of this type should not be made by the military.[50] Unfortunately, allied strategy was decided according to Stalin's wishes.[51]

As it turned out, the successes of General Clark's army in Italy would have made it possible to continue the offensive into the Balkans and still invade southern France with seven French divisions. Clark proposed to General Marshall that the American Sixth Corps continue its campaign in Italy and that only French units be employed for the advance through the Rhone valley. But the American government had committed itself at Tehran, and rejected the opportunity to reevaluate its strategy in response to an entirely changed situation (spring 1944).

General Clark summed it up: By switching allied strength from Italy to France, the allies wheeled away from central Europe and charged into a "deadend street." It was one of the few examples in history where a victorious army was shifted unnecessarily from a primary to a secondary theater of operations.[52] Stalin won control over the Danubian basin and the Balkans through skillful employment of the tactics of diplomatic and psychological warfare.

Example No. 2: The loss of Prague. By early May 1945, the German army had been annihilated except for the units fighting under Field Marshal Ferdinand Schoerner against the Red army in eastern Bohemia. American forces under General Patton had penetrated into western Czechoslovakia and were pushing forward rapidly into a military vacuum. The road to the Elbe river lay open, and General Patton requested authority to liberate Prague. To his surprise, permission was denied.

What had happened? Upon receipt of Patton's request, General Eisenhower notified the Russians on May 4, 1945, that the American Third Army was ready to advance to the Elbe and the Moldau

[50] Mark W. Clark, *Calculated Risk* (New York, Harper, 1950), pp. 368 f.

[51] It is known today that the soviets were determined to prevent allied conquest of the Balkans. They went so far as to order Tito to join with the nazis in opposing an allied Balkan invasion. An offer to this effect was made officially by General Velebit, Tito's representative, to Edmund von Glaise-Horstenau, German general in Agram, but rejected by Hitler. Whether or not Tito would have carried out his orders despite Hitler's attitude is a matter of conjecture. Walter Hagen, *Die Geheime Front* (Zurich, Europa, 1950), pp. 267 f.; see also, Derek Kartun, *Tito's Plot Against Europe: The Story of the Rajk Conspiracy* (New York, International Publishers, 1950), p. 43.

[52] It compares with Hitler's strategy before Moscow in the fall of 1941.

and would occupy Prague shortly. The soviets, however, again knew exactly what they wanted the Americans not to do. In this case, they were most anxious to keep the American army out of Prague.

Accordingly, Stalin's chief of staff, General Antonov, asked that the American army not advance beyond the line Karlsbad-Pilsen-Budweis. He justified this request by submitting that otherwise a dangerous melee of American and Russian troops would be unavoidable. Actually, the American forces could have pushed ahead for a considerable distance without encountering Russian units, which still were being held up by Schoerner. Nor is it a foregone conclusion that a melee of *friendly* armies must inevitably degenerate into a shooting match. Nevertheless, General Eisenhower complied with Antonov's request, and the Russians moved in to capture Prague and gain control of Czechoslovakia. Except for eastern Germany, this was perhaps their most valuable territorial conquest in Europe. *An entire country was secured by one radio message.*[53]

Example No. 3: The Danube. The preliminary agreement in London projecting the future zones of occupation in Austria assigned to the United States the entire province of Upper Austria, part of which extends to the north of the Danube river. Under this agreement, the United States would have controlled that vital river route as far as Linz. According to General Clark, the soviets informed Washington that an "error" had been committed during the negotiations: The Russians had wished to include the north Danubian area of Upper Austria into their zone of occupation. Without further argument Washington concurred, abandoning their claim to the area in question, surrendering to the Russians partial control over navigation on the Upper Danube artery.[54]

The game of give-and-don't-take was played also for the stakes of western Saxony and Thuringia. Allied forces conquered and occupied these important areas but relinquished them, without counterpart, to the soviets (summer of 1945). This was in accordance with a previous agreement to the terms of which, however, the soviets had failed to live up.

Of course, Soviet diplomatic warfare had its failures, too. For example, during 1942 the soviets put heavy pressure on the allies

[53] Juergen Thorwald, *Das Ende an der Elbe* (Stuttgart, Steingrüben Verlag, 1950), p. 332. The capture of Czechoslovakia transferred the largest European uranium mine to soviet control.

[54] Clark, *op. cit.,* p. 454.

to launch an immediate cross-channel invasion. The Red army had been pushed back, and its cries for allied ground action were understandable enough. Yet, an attempt to establish a second front in Europe, prematurely, would have resulted in grievous defeat for the western allies, while the Russians would have benefited little. But why was this agitation continued after the Germans had fallen into the North African trap and after Stalingrad, when the Russians were no longer in serious trouble? If the Anglo-American armies had attacked Europe in 1943, at a time when they still had inadequate air power and only a handful of amphibious craft, they probably would have been defeated, albeit after prolonged and costly battle. The western powers might not have recovered for a long time. The Germans, too, would have been seriously weakened.

Yet, in this case, the relative strength of Russia would have increased. Communist "second front" agitation was inspired by the chestnut concept.

Soviet insistence on a western attack across the channel was due not to ignorance of amphibious warfare, as many supposed, but must have been the result of the soviet general staff estimate that such an attack could not succeed. Even in 1944 it was apparently assumed that the western armies would be thrown back or would be too weak to penetrate deep into the continent.

And naturally, if the allied invasion had failed, the disaster temporarily would have eliminated Britain and the United States as serious contenders for world power.[55] An allied defeat on the coasts of Normandy would have made possible soviet occupation of Germany and possibly of France.[56]

[55] Reportedly, the success of the Normandy invasion took the Kremlin by surprise. "An Exposé of Soviet Russian Plans and Policies," *Congressional Record,* July 12, 1950, p. A 5310.

[56] This interpretation is borne out by at least one soviet document, an official Stalin biography: "The successful carrying out of the Stalin strategic plan in 1944 had great military-political results. . . . The military situation which resulted meant that the Soviet Union was in a position without the aid of the allies to occupy with its own forces all of Germany and to carry out the liberation of France. This circumstance impelled . . . Churchill, who up to that time had opposed the opening of a second front in Europe, to undertake the invasion of Western Europe." This means that the soviets planned to go as far as France, but the success of the Normandy invasion was tantamount to a chestnut pulled by the allies against the soviets. *Josef Vissarionovich Stalin, kratkaya biografiya* (Moscow, 1946), quoted from, Frederick C. Barghoorn, *The Soviet Image of the United States, A Study in Distortion* (New York, Harcourt, Brace, 1950), p. 149.

To the everlasting credit of western leadership, the cross-channel invasion was launched only when its success was assured.

Failure of the soviet second-front strategy kept central and western Europe within the free world. Similarly, Russia's failure to obtain an occupation zone in Japan kept the most important Asiatic country from falling under soviet domination. At some points, thank God, the United States knew how to draw a line.

THE EUROPEAN PATTERN OF REVOLUTIONARY WARFARE

AFTER the battles of El Alamein (autumn of 1942) and Stalingrad (early 1943), two entirely different wars were being fought: The Anglo-American war to defeat nazi Germany, during which the western allies continued to assume incorrectly that the soviets were still their partners; and the soviet revolutionary war of maximum expansion.

The pattern of this revolutionary war may be exemplified by the case of Poland. The key to the conquest of Poland, of course, was the destruction of the Polish army by the Germans, which paved the way for the occupation of eastern Poland by the Russians in 1939; the nazi policy of repression; and the conquest of all of Poland by the Red army in 1944 and 1945.

Yet the non-military measures of conquest must not be forgotten. There are, in particular, four programs which deserve full attention: (1) the elimination of the opposition; (2) the establishment of a Kremlin-trained puppet government, including sham elections to legalize the authority of this puppet government; (3) purges of unreliable communists in power, to maintain control and assure political reliability; and (4) religious persecution.

Elimination of Polish leaders, potential and actual, began at the time of the initial soviet occupation of Poland in 1939. Approximately 1,500,000 Poles were deported to the U.S.S.R. between the time of the soviet occupation of Poland in 1939 and the German attack against Russia in 1941.[57] These people were placed in con-

[57] For bibliography and a thorough discussion of these events, see William Henry Chamberlin, *America's Second Crusade* (Chicago, Henry Regnery Co., 1950), p. 260.

centration camps where starvation, work, and terror took their toll. Politically conscious Poles were assigned the most degrading tasks.[58]

As a second step in the elimination of potential opposition, the soviets murdered some 15,000 Polish officers interned in three camps. Evidence assembled after the end of the war does not leave a shadow of doubt about this case of genocide. The soviet attempts to disprove the accusations were originally effective in duping allied public opinion, but in the long run failed. Mass graves of about one-third of these officers were found by the Germans near Katyn during April 1943. An exhumation of the graves revealed that all of the Poles, without exception, had been executed by a shot through the back of the head, a long-practiced method of soviet execution. Diaries and newspapers on the corpses fixed the time of the murders as April and May 1940, when the Germans did not hold this area.

The graves at Katyn explain the disappearance of approximately 5,000 of the 15,000 Polish officers interned, but another 10,000 are still to be accounted for. Fairly reliable evidence indicates that these other officers were removed from their camps, and disappeared in the vicinity of Vyazma and Kharkov. Quite probably they were executed at about the same time as those near Katyn. In any event, the soviets failed to return the captive officers to the legal Polish government as promised. The Polish officers have disappeared in Russia without leaving a trace.

The soviets also took pains to eliminate socialist and liberal opposition to communism. The clearest example is found in the murder of two Jewish socialist leaders Henryk Ehrlich and Viktor Alter. After their release from soviet prison in summer of 1941, Ehrlich and Alter were organizing an international Jewish antifascist committee. Both disappeared from Kuibyshev, temporary soviet capital, in December 1941. One year later, Litvinov assumed Russian responsibility for their execution and asserted that the two victims had collaborated with the nazis against the Red army and the soviet people. If this had been true, since the chances of socialist Jews collaborating with Hitler are considerably smaller than those of the bolsheviks concluding an alliance with the nazis, the soviets would have conducted a public trial and submitted the evidence to the

<hr>

[58] Stanislaw Mikolajczyk, *The Rape of Poland* (New York, McGraw-Hill, 1948), p. 24.

world. Ehrlich and Alter were murdered because they stood in the way of soviet plans for Poland.[59]

Early in 1944, when the Red army began overrunning Poland, the soviet secret police again began eliminating Polish patriots. As early as four months before the Warsaw uprising the Polish underground was reporting that its members were hesitant to identify themselves to the Red army.

On July 30, 1944, the radio of the Polish home army picked up a soviet appeal signed by Molotov and Osubka-Morawski, a leading Polish communist, calling the Poles to revolt:

Poles, the time of liberation is at hand! Poles, to arms! Make every Polish home a stronghold against the invader! There is not a moment to lose!

On the following day London received a similar signal.[60] Despite misgivings, the Polish home army responded to the soviet signal and rose in full, open, armed rebellion. The soviet betrayal gave proof that Polish fears had been well founded. Instead of relieving the Poles, the Red army remained aloof on the eastern bank of the Vistula while the Germans annihilated the Poles in Warsaw during sixty-three days of fierce fighting.

Approximately 250,000 residents of Warsaw, including the bulk of the insurgents, were killed. Another 350,000 were forcibly evacuated. The only land effort the Red army made to relieve the Warsaw uprising was to send the Polish Kosciusko division, which was fighting with the Russians, to its suicide. As the Polish division was pushing across the Vistula the soviets cut off artillery support, thus assuring its annihilation.[61]

This was a strategy of almost unparalleled ruthlessness; the elements which could have opposed Red domination were wiped out— by the nazis for the bolsheviks. The soviets did not hesitate to sacrifice, in addition, the Poles fighting as allies of Russia and as members of the Russian army.[62]

---

[59] For further details, see Chamberlin, *op. cit.*, p. 266.

[60] General T. Bor-Komorovski, "The Unconquerables," *The Reader's Digest,* February 1946; Chamberlin, *op. cit.*, p. 274.

[61] Mikolajczyk, *op. cit.*, p. 85.

[62] Another case of communist ruthlessness should not go unnoticed. Representative Hays of Ohio stated the following almost unbelievable fact to the House of Representatives: "The gentleman from Minnesota made a very mov-

These, then, were the essential steps by which the soviets secured control of Poland. But even soviet military occupation was camouflaged: As soviet troop strength was reduced in 1946 and Polish troop strength increased, it became a common joke that the new Polish army was remarkably fluent in Russian. Later, the virtual incorporation of the Polish armed forces into the soviet military machine was camouflaged through the appointment of fake Poles to high positions, a technique brazenly applied in the appointment of the sham Pole, Marshal Rokossovsky, as commander of the Polish forces.

When the physical control of Poland was assured, the soviets set about fulfilling their program and established, step by step, the dictatorship of the proletariat. At the command of the soviets, the Lublin committee of national liberation (a soviet-appointed body of communists and procommunists) proclaimed itself the new government of Poland on December 31, 1944. On January 5, 1945, the U.S.S.R. formally recognized this provisional government. The United States and Great Britain refused to accept this soviet *fait accompli* and continued to recognize the Polish government-in-exile, then in London. Under the terms of Yalta, however, the Big Three agreed that all Polish parties should take part in the provisional government, an agreement sabotaged by soviet insistence that the Lublin group have a majority in the new government. Without encountering serious western opposition they managed to put communists in at all levels of command. The participation of the London Poles in the government had no significance whatever, and was soon terminated.

---

ing argument here yesterday about how many people were killed in Yugoslavia during the late war and I will not question his figures. But I would like to have a little information about how many hundreds of thousands of those people were killed by Tito or Tito's men. I do know this, that on Easter Sunday in Belgrade during the last year of the war—and Easter Sunday in Belgrade does not come on Easter Sunday in the United States because they do not use the same calendar we do—Tito asked that American bombers bomb the city of Belgrade, which was not strategically important; he specified that day and he specified the hour. That day and hour happened, purely by accident I suppose, to be on Easter Sunday when the Serbs were coming out of the orthodox churches. You can still hear about that in Belgrade today and I have more than a little bit of reason to believe that he did it for a purpose, and that purpose was that he wanted the Serbs, who have a natural affinity toward the United States, to hate this country." *Congressional Record,* December 13, 1950, p. 16695.

From the moment of entering Warsaw, the Lublin puppets set about preparing for sham elections which would serve as window dressing for the removal of Mikolajczyk, chief of the anticommunist opposition. By terror, the effectiveness of his peasant party was reduced to insignificant proportions.

The secret police tormented Mikolajczyk and arrested many leaders of his party. His paper, the *Gazeta Ludowa,* was censored severely; in parliamentary sessions he was rendered impotent. Some peasant party leaders were murdered. Finally, organized opposition to the communists was destroyed and nothing was left.

The preparations for the "free and unfettered elections" promised at Yalta took nearly two years. During this period the puppet police (under the training of the soviet secret police) became very efficient. In January 1947 the puppet government felt confident enough to allow general elections to be held. The government bloc "won" by a majority of about 87 per cent, and the man selected by Stalin, Josef Cyrankiewicz, the renegade socialist, became prime minister. This was the death blow to the peasant party. Mikolajczyk was forced out of the government and fled in October 1947.

It is an established practice of the Politburo to purge key office holders periodically. By extensive elimination of communist party members, the soviets accomplish in a relatively short time complete changes of leadership for a particular region or function. This method, while demoralizing, is effective in achieving its purpose, that is, maintenance of control. Purges preclude the possibility of conspiracy and destroy the continuity of opposition.

The soviets began their application of this policy to Poland (and to other satellite countries) during 1949. On November 13, President Bierut reported that three members of the central committee of the communist party—Gomulka, Spychalski, and Kliszko—had been removed from the committee. Osubka-Morawski, former prime minister, fell into oblivion. Trusted Stalinists came to the fore.

Religious oppression appears to be one of the least fruitful of the soviet social measures. While the soviets have made major inroads on the strength of the Orthodox Church in the U.S.S.R., after thirty years of effort, the number of the faithful is still considerable. In Poland, the communist government began fighting the Roman Catholic Church almost from the start, although not intensively at first. Gradually its measures have been intensified, yet they have been forced to recognize the strength of Christianity. They must proceed slowly, using the method of infiltration and disintegration rather than that of direct assault.[63]

Soviet conquest of other nations was accomplished by methods similar to those used in Poland.

Stalin, an eminently practical man, had found an *ad hoc* solution to the vexing problems of the revolution from without. The old bolsheviks believed in revolution from below. The streamlined bolsheviks of the early twenties advocated revolution from without. In 1944, Stalin adopted the technique of combining revolution from without with revolution from above. It was a mixture of semirevolution with camouflaged conquest.

This type of conquest required the full help of the communist parties and its sympathizers. But, "the great party of the revolution . . . was the Red army."[64]

The key to revolution was military conquest. Military conquest could take the form of counteroffensive war; this was the case of Poland, Rumania, and Hungary. Or, it could take the form of aggressive and unprovoked revolutionary interference; this was the case of Bulgaria and Manchuria.

There was no valid reason to attack Bulgaria, which had been neutral in the Russo-German war and had kicked out the nazis under its own power. However, failure by the Red army to occupy would have precluded its sovietization.

Russia's attack on Japan was unprovoked aggression. This fact should not be overlooked merely because the soviets acted in agreement with the United States and Britain. Russia and Japan were signatories to a nonaggression pact. Japan was making no preparations for attack against Russia. In 1945, Japan no longer was capable of posing a threat to the Soviet Union. But without attacking Japan the soviets would not have obtained control over Manchuria. History was to reveal that soviet aggression against Japan was, in fact, an aggression against the United States.

Yet, military conquest alone was not enough. There was also the

[63] For additional details, see Chamberlin, *op. cit.*, Chap. 11.

[64] Isaac Deutscher, *Stalin, A Political Biography* (New York, Oxford University Press, 1949), p. 554. Deutscher stated that the Red army "remained in the background." Did it really? Did it not conquer Bucharest, Sofia, Budapest, Belgrade, Vienna, Warsaw, Prague, and Berlin?

need to carry out a social and political revolution. Stalin recognized that Frunze had been right and that a revolution, that is, the processes of social restructurization, cannot be imported.[65] Hence, it became necessary, after the military conquest, to organize a revolutionary movement, to bring about a revolutionary situation, and to introduce the dictatorship of the proletariat by graduated steps. To stay within the old simile, military violence was not to be the midwife of revolution, but rather its father. If the liberated country was not pregnant with revolution, the Red army produced the pregnancy.

The job of the midwife, the delivery, was entrusted to the "coalition government."

The coalition government device was nothing but open infiltration on a large scale, directed by communist members of the government.

The formula called for the communists to be invited to participate in such a government. Usually, they agreed, "in principle," but insisted on their choice of departments or ministries. They wanted the police and the judiciary, if possible the army, and, in any event, the propaganda ministry. The minimum was: the control elements of physical and psychological power. In 1917, Trotsky's detachments seized the keys to power by violent attack, but in 1945, *these keys were taken by political conquest.*

Once in partial control of the government, the communists aimed at the gradual constriction of private property. After demonstrating the inefficiency of the market economy, they developed in its stead a planned economy and allied it to that of the U.S.S.R. One by one, non-communist elements and organizations were expelled from poli-

---

[65] This may be a good opportunity to discuss the exact meaning of Stalin's interview with Roy Howard on March 3, 1936. According to Stalin, it was a misunderstanding to believe that the Soviet Union was planning to bring about world revolution.

Howard asked: "A tragic misunderstanding?"

Stalin answered: "No, a comic one. Or perhaps a tragic-comic one. It is nonsense to try to make revolution an article of export. If a country wants a revolution, it wants to make it for itself; and if it does not want one, there can be no revolution. To state that we want to bring about revolution in other countries by meddling in their manner of life is to assert something which is not true and which we never have put forward."

The deception in this statement will be understood better if it is recalled that according to soviet doctrine neither the soviet proletariat nor the Red army can make revolution in another country. The misunderstanding is neither tragic nor comic, but semantic. Stalin is talking about social transformation. This type of revolution obviously cannot be exported, but the social transformation can be stimulated from the outside.

tics or converted into transmission belts. In the end, the entire government apparatus had slipped into communist hands. Camouflaged as "popular democracy," a *de facto* dictatorship of the proletariat had emerged.[66] Cheap and easy!

Hence, the pattern of revolution as developed by Stalin at the end of World War II is this: military conquest; seizure of partial power by political means; creation of a revolutionary situation, largely by police and economic means; seizure of the power monopoly by terror and *coup d'état,* under the strategic cover of the Russian army. The "popular democracy" is a method of the gradual revolution. It is the political consummation of revolutionary warfare.[67]

[66] In the *Tägliche Rundschau,* January 25, 1949, p. 2, the Russian spokesman Sakharov identified popular democracy as a form of the dictatorship of the proletariat. According to Mao, a people's republic is a transition to socialism and communism. "Democracy for the people and dictatorship for the reactionaries, when combined, constitute the people's democratic dictatorship." Mao Tse-tung, *op. cit.,* p. 15.

[67] In an interview given on December 28, 1948, Tito accused the soviets of underrating the capabilities of the communists outside Russia. According to Tito, the soviet leaders believe that "the socialist revolution cannot be carried out without the help of the Red army." Yet, Tito commented, experience showed that military occupation, even by the Red army, entails many antisocial consequences. Equal rights disappear, and are replaced by unconditional submission to the occupying power. Such a strategy must lead to national suppression and economic exploitation. Moshe Pijade, Tito's theoretician, vituperated against exaggerating the role of the Red army and belittling that of the partisans. According to him, the Stalinists asserted that communism was able to gain power in Yugoslavia because the Red troops had created the necessary conditions there, while "unfortunately" it was not able to do so in France and Italy because of the lack of similar military assistance. Pijade asserted that if this concept were accepted, it would mean there was "no possibility for the victory of a proletarian revolution except with the aid of the weapons of the soviet army, and that the proletarians of the entire world should have no illusions that they could win their liberation by their own strength but must await the arrival of the soviet army, the liberator." Milovan Djilas, a member of the Yugoslav Politburo, in an interview in the *New York Times,* November 4, 1949, went a step further than Pijade by saying that "every people should achieve socialism by its own forces and without foreign intervention." See Hamilton Fish Armstrong, *Tito and Goliath* (New York, Macmillan, 1951), pp. 94 f., 282; also, *The Soviet-Yugoslav Dispute, Text of the Published Correspondence* (London, Royal Institute of International Affairs, 1948). These arguments cut little ice with the bolshevik technicians of world conquest who summed up their doctrine in the preamble to the new Hungarian constitution: "The armed forces of the great Soviet Union have liberated our country from the oppression of the German fascists, smashed the power of landlords and capitalists, and opened the road of democratic development to our toiling people." (*The New Leader,* September 24, 1949, p. 2.)

EUROPEAN UNDERGROUND: CAMOUFLAGED
TRANSMISSION BELT

IN THE SPOTTY record of soviet demoralization work against hostile armies, successes have been less impressive than anticipated. During the war against the Germans particularly, soviet demoralization tactics were ineffective until the Germans themselves provided wide openings. Not until the battle of Stalingrad, when German soldiers and officers, feeling that they had been betrayed by Hitler, collaborated with the soviets, did these techniques become significant. Together with German communists living in Russia, German prisoners assisted the soviet war effort within the misnamed free German committee. Morally strengthened by some of the best-known names in Germany, this committee came out for peace with Russia, for the overthrow of Hitler, and for a German foreign policy consonant with the Bismarck tradition. Veiled suggestions of a fusion between Russia and Germany, for the sake of world revolution, were made.

There were timid beginnings of an up-to-date communist ideology, Prussian style.

This propaganda was carried out by radio and through a newspaper which in its early issues had an impressive story to tell but which soon began to deteriorate. There was also a great deal of front-line propaganda.

Yet, results were very disappointing. The nazis were able to keep desertion and surrender to a minimum. The German soldier fought well to the last against the soviet.

Was this a proof that an enemy's demoralization work can be rendered ineffective even in a defeat situation? Without drawing any general conclusions, it appears that early estimates about the effectiveness and technical proficiency of soviet front-line propaganda were quite in error. The soviets apparently were not always able to avoid sectarian appeals. The committee's work was neutralized by the propaganda of the Red army which, in part, was based on the hate theme and antagonized the German soldier rather than won him over. The committee's work was done, to a large extent, by amateurs whose output often was unimaginative and ineffective. There were numerous technical deficiencies, such as inadequate numbers of leaflets, poor dissemination facilities, faulty radio equipment, and inept distribution methods.[68] The whole thing was an improvisation, and it was not handled in a very professional manner.

There were additional reasons why the soviet front-line propaganda failed: Almost till the end of the war more Russian soldiers deserted to the Germans than German soldiers to the Russians. Even at Stalingrad there were more Russian than German deserters. The Russians simply did not believe it when their own official propaganda told them that the German forces had been encircled.[69] The behavior of the Russian soldiers, especially in Germany, and the Russian treatment of prisoners were other potent reasons why the Germans preferred to fight.

Demoralization work was more successful against nazi satellite armies. The soviets made it a point to start offensives with blows against satellite forces which, in most cases, were more poorly equipped than were the Germans, and often gave way without putting up strong resistance. The Italians suffered greatly from the harsh climate and fell easy victims to disaffection. The Hungarians were unwilling belligerents and toward the end of the war surrendered in large numbers.

On the other hand, large numbers of Russians, Russian minority people, eastern Europeans, and anticommunists from all over Europe helped the nazis. Despite the character of the nazi regime, the European proletariat refused to come to the help of the soviet fatherland. Communism held no appeal. This is the basic reason why, again, the soviets had to operate through other organizations. *The national underground movements in particular became the most effective transmission belts available.*

It is not quite known at what time the soviets began organizing their underground movements, but on May 9, 1941, the executive committee of the Comintern sent instructions to the Yugoslav communist party. Since these instructions tell part of the story, we shall quote them at length:

1. The time has now come when decisive new steps must be taken along the path to world revolution. The obstacles to be overcome are still for-

[68] Heinrich Graf von Einsiedel, *Tagebuch der Versuchung* (Berlin-Stuttgart, Pontes, 1950), p. 105.

[69] *Ibid.,* p. 100.

midable, and call for a new tactical flexibility which must be carefully worked out and boldly executed along the following lines:

(a) The Communist world revolution must be presented as a series of measures to achieve true democracy, and all political and military leaders of the Communist movement must depict their activity in this light. Up to 30 per cent of the party's members may come into the open as "front-line fighters for democracy." ...

(b) The government of the Soviet Union may ... find it necessary to make temporary concessions ... in order to further the revolutionary cause. ...

(c) Until its seizure of power, the Communist party of [every] country in which the revolution is being prepared must be careful to maintain good relations with patriotic and religious circles. ... Where necessary, and with the authorization of the central committee of the party, representatives of the churches may be allowed to assist in preparing and carrying through the revolution. Their numerical strength shall determine the rate at which the influence of the churches is later to be eliminated from state affairs.

(d) The press should be used to publicize the new line among the masses. ... Secret circulars [will] keep all active revolutionaries informed of the real situation.

(e) Once [a given] party has seized power, its foreign policy will be laid down by the diplomatic representatives of the USSR, who will receive the necessary directives from the Comintern. [These] representatives will maintain liaison between the central committee of the Communist party of the USSR and [the central committee of the country] in which the party has newly taken power. ...

(f) Immediately after seizing power, the central committee will [form] a new government [which] shall be representative of the broad masses of the people and preserve every appearance of democracy. ... [Internally], the central committee will remain the supreme executive authority, while foreign policy will be controlled by the executive committee of the Comintern.

(g) Opponents of the new administration, especially those who still enjoy prestige among the people and those whose participation in the revolution may have given them access to the secret records of the Communist movement, shall be removed as soon as possible, but in democratic fashion—i. e. by being brought to trial before a regular court or a people's court. The latter should comprise one known member of the party and two secret members or reliable sympathizers. Important trials should be conducted by larger courts of a correspondingly democratic nature.

.   .   .   .

3. Until a country has been included in the Soviet Union, at least 50 per cent of the members of the Communist party must remain in under-

ground conspiratorial work and act as the administration's chief allies in the government of the country.

. . . .

5. The frontiers of countries geographically remote from the Soviet Union are not to be closed immediately after the revolution. [On the contrary], everything should . . . be done to induce all refugees, exiles, etc., to return home under democratic safeguards. Only then shall the frontiers be closed. Members of all central committees are reminded that the Comintern was once obliged . . . to hold up its plans for the world revolution owing to the large number of Russian emigrants who succeeded in stirring up the democracies against the Communist movement. The fewer the emigrants today, the more certain will be the success of the revolution. . . .[70]

Yet the underground sprang into action only after Germany had attacked the Soviet Union. The order which Tito issued on June 22, 1941, probably was typical of the orders given communists all over the world:

Proletarians from all parts of Yugoslavia—to arms! Rally round your vanguard, the communist party of Yugoslavia. Fulfil your proletarian duty without fear or faltering. Prepare for the final struggle. You cannot stand idly by while the precious blood of the heroic peoples of Soviet Russia is being shed. Mobilize all your strength to prevent our country from becoming a base to supply the fascist hordes who have unleashed their fury on the Soviet Union, our beloved socialist fatherland, our hope, the beacon to which the eyes of workers throughout the world are turned in longing.[71]

Despite the big words, Russia was unable (and unwilling) to deliver supplies to Tito and to other communist underground movements. Hence, the western powers were persuaded that these partisans were trustworthy allies of the United Nations and that they should benefit from lend-lease help (which gradually was withdrawn from movements not following the communist line, such as General Mikhailovitch's *chetniks*).[72] Tito's partisans became materially

---

[70] Stephen Clissold, *Whirlwind: An Account of Marshal Tito's Rise to Power* (New York, Philosophical Library, 1949), pp. 238–40; also, Leigh White, *Balkan Caesar, Tito versus Stalin* (New York, Scribner's, 1951), pp. 41 ff.

[71] White, *op. cit.*, pp. 38 f.

[72] For the details of how the West was induced to supply Tito, see *ibid.*, Chaps. 5 and 6, and Constantin Fotitch, *The War We Lost, Yugoslavia's Tragedy and the Failure of the West* (New York, Viking, 1948), Chaps. 18–20.

stronger after the Italian armistice in 1943: The Italian army was instructed to abandon its weapons to the allied forces, and the ten or more divisions stationed in Yugoslavia surrendered their arms to Tito. An old communist trick used in 1918 when the bolsheviks acquired weapons from the Germans forced by the Entente to evacuate Russia, it was in line with Stalin's pet idea that the capitalists should be made to pay for the revolution.

In Greece, the communists set up a united front organization, the EAM, which formed a people's liberation army, the ELAS. Mistakenly assisted by soldiers and non-communists, ELAS did not fight the Germans but organized itself to take over Greece at the time of the German retreat and before an allied landing. A plan for the seizure of Greece was worked out in August 1943.[73] This plan envisaged the destruction of all rival guerrilla organizations; communist infiltration into the Greek armed forces fighting with the allies; the establishment of a popular government which would take power before the return of the government-in-exile; and, finally, a *modus vivendi* with the Germans.

The plan failed. The nationalist guerrillas were not destroyed. Communist fractions were established in the Greek armed forces, but they tipped their hand in premature mutiny, and were rendered harmless. The trick with the popular government did not work, partly through the vigilance of the British, partly because ELAS had failed to eliminate its military competitors.

A communist agreement with the Germans provided that the communists were not to attack the Wehrmacht and were to fight all forces "determined to continue the fight against the Germans." In return, the Germans promised weapons, obligating themselves in case of retreat to turn over territory, including the city of Salonika, to the communists.[74]

Despite the failure of the original plan, the communists did not give up the idea of seizing power. Taking advantage of the interregnum after the German evacuation, ELAS attempted to capture the country by a combination of partisan attack and revolutionary

[73] "The December Revolution," *Hellinikon Aima,* Athens, January 14, 1945, quoted from Dennis Menos, *The Greek Guerrilla Movement, 1941–1944* (thesis, Georgetown University, 1951).

[74] Agreement of Leivadi, September 1, 1944. See, Greece, Under-Secretariat for Press and Information, *The Conspiracy against Greece* (Athens, Pyrsos, 1947), p. 16.

uprising. Frustrated by the intervention of Winston Churchill and the British General Scobie, the communists were driven back into the mountains, but, supplied from Yugoslavia, Albania, and Bulgaria, they continued fighting for about five years.

During the summer of 1944 the soviets organized a guerrilla uprising in Slovakia. The minister of war and the director of economics of that province, ostensibly two nazi creatures, had been won over to the communist cause. In control of the deployment of Slovakian troops and in a position to supply the insurrectionists with money, materials, and information, they created and directed an uprising against the rear of the German army. It was of considerable scope. Its suppression required several months of costly fighting. And, although the soviets failed to come to the support of the Slovak partisans, they showed their appreciation for the help received by shooting the same Slovak war minister who had directed the operation.[75]

Similarly, the maquis movement in France was not originally of communist making. During the German-Russian honeymoon, the French communist party had been discredited. The resistance movement, or what there was of it, was in the hands of nationalists. Upon the German attack on Russia, the communists saw their opportunity, sprang into action, and propagated a people's liberation war against the occupant.

The communists created a semimilitary organization having a national command, regional subcommands, and local action groups. Weapons used included propaganda, wage demands, labor unrest, and agricultural strikes. The communists organized paramilitary units and gave training to young people and soldiers. Frequently they resorted to direct action, including terrorism and sabotage. They tried their best to stimulate mass action. Guerrilla forces waged partisan warfare.

Great emphasis was laid on defense against government repression.[76] Provocation was considered one of the most powerful weapons of the anticommunists. Infiltration of *agents provocateurs* was to be prevented by guarding against corruption and demoralization, including demoralization in a political and ideological form.[77]

At first, the communists worked independently, but later, remem-

[75] Hagen, *op. cit.,* pp. 187–90.
[76] Rossi, *Physiologie, op. cit.,* pp. 128–31, 168.
[77] *Ibid.,* p. 256.

bering the advice of the Seventh World Congress, they wrapped themselves in a coat of rabid nationalism and called for the united front of all resisters. Without too much difficulty, the communist party made an arrangement with General de Gaulle and joined his underground organization. Since the communists had many people trained in irregular warfare, they quickly merited key positions in the maquis, which they exploited for the systematic infiltration of that mosaic of organizations. By the end of the war the communists had acquired very considerable strength. Numerous maquis units were openly communist, and an even larger number of units was covertly controlled by the communist party.

In October 1943 the central committee of the resistance movement at Algiers drafted an interesting insurrectional plan. This plan was sent to the regional chiefs of the resistance movement in continental France.[78] It laid down the strategy and tactics of an insurrection to be launched during the interregnum between the departure of the Germans and the arrival of the Anglo-Saxon armies.[79]

The stated purposes of the plan were to prevent Marshal Pétain's "return to power" and to carry out the "revolutionary repression" of traitors. Through manifestations of force and mass demonstrations, the provisional French government was to be given a "popular" and "democratic" basis and to be enabled to start measures of social, economic, and political "reform."

This ostensibly de Gaullist plan was fully in line with the ideas developed by Lange and Neuberg. The insurrection was to be undertaken in conjunction with regular military operations. Hence, emphasis was laid upon the cutting of railroads and the destruction of other means of transportation. Communications and public utilities, especially electric power, were designated as additional targets. But the ultimate target was the postwar political control of France.

The insurgents were told to prepare for the occupation of government buildings in order to install *de facto* administrations, taking over radio stations and newspapers, capturing police detachments, eliminating hostile political elements, and occupying key control centers. The following measures were to be employed: fake docu-

[78] "Les Consignes gaullistes pour l'insurrection de 1944," *Les Ecrits de Paris,* August 1950, pp. 104–23. This plan was drawn up at approximately the same time as the plan of the Greek communists.

[79] This similarity with the Greek plan should not go unnoticed.

ments including false orders and identification papers; deception telephone calls and ruses; infiltration into, and capture of, government and industrial organizations; isolation of rebellious cities; general strike; and the intimidation of antirevolutionary forces by mass action. Insurgents who could not be equipped were told to attack without weapons.

It is possible that this plan was drawn up by patriotic Frenchmen with good knowledge of revolution techniques.[80] It is more probable, however, that these instructions were drafted by French communists or cryptocommunists who had infiltrated into the resistance movement.[81] If the plan had been carried out, it would have opened the way to communist revolution in western Europe. The French committee of national liberation would have played a role similar to that of the Petrograd soviet in 1917. The central committee of the French resistance movement would have been the equivalent of the revolutionary military committee. The unexpected speed of the allied army's armored divisions probably spiked the party wheels.

On May 5, 1945, Prague became the scene of a communist uprising. The communists were supported by nationalist, democratic, and socialist groups intent on destroying the waning German hold on Czechoslovakia. From a military, as well as from any other, point of view, this act of violence was completely unnecessary. The Germans were in full flight. There was no doubt that Prague would be liberated within a few days. The communists had even been informed that the city would be occupied by the Red army. And yet they organized the insurrection.

One of the few rational explanations for this gratuitous blood bath is this: The communists wanted to prevent the Germans from transferring their power to the legal Czech authorities and to noncommunist organizations which could have reconstituted the prewar state and could have prevented the communists from infiltrating and taking over government administrations. Another explanation is that the communists wanted to unleash the violent passions of the

[80] Louis Rougier, "Les Origines d'une insurrection," *Les Ecrits de Paris,* April 1951, pp. 97 f.

[81] The author of the instructions was apparently Emmanuel d'Astier de la Vigerie whose postwar policies closely followed the communist party line. A short while after the instructions were issued, d'Astier was appointed de Gaulle's commissar of the interior. Thus, the instructions were given highest official sanction.

crowds as a prelude to social warfare and economic expropriation.

The insurrection started with a rumor that American tanks were approaching Prague. As a result, the masses went into the streets to greet the Americans. Czech and Red paramilitary units made their appearances. Incidents occured when German police and SS tried to break up the demonstrations. However, the communists captured the Prague radio station and immediately began radical and bloodthirsty agitation, inflaming the masses and calling upon them to commit acts of violence against the Germans. The communists seized German arsenals and captured the barracks of the secret police. German resistance was spotty, though occasionally ferocious. In the process, the communists installed themselves in all control points of Prague. This capture of the keys to Prague was the starting point of their ultimate seizure of power. Otherwise, this revolution ended in a cruel mass murder of German soldiers and civilians.[82]

The European underground movement has been given a great propaganda build-up. The underground asked for many sacrifices. It produced many heroes. Unfortunately, its military usefulness is debatable. In retrospect, it would seem that the underground cost numerous lives and caused a great deal of devastation—much of it unnecessarily. Yet, in many cases the underground helped the communists in their designs and operations. The historical function of the European underground was that it rehabilitated the discredited communist party. A sad return for a heavy investment in patriotism and selflessness.

PREPARING THE NEXT ROUND

THE SOVIETS did not believe that the end of World War II meant peace. Nor were they inclined to stop their permanent offensive against capitalism.

In 1945 it may have looked to the West as though communism had not derived much advantage from the war. The Soviet Union had suffered heavily. The Red armed forces were exhausted and in no position to continue offensive warfare. It appeared that Germany and Italy were finished as major powers, although a sort of compromise peace had been arranged with Japan. There was a good

[82] Thorwald, *op. cit.*, pp. 337 ff.

chance that France would stage a comeback. In the occupied countries there was strong resistance against communism, apparently precluding any introduction of the soviet system. Most important of all, the United States had acquired the atomic bomb and a large fleet of long-range bombers—overwhelming obstacles to revolutionary ambitions.

The soviets were undismayed. They realized that the United States, which Stalin once had called the "citadel of capitalism,"[83] had become their main enemy. They acknowledged that the capitalist enemy was still strong, yet were convinced that capitalism had become rotten and panicky in the face of impending doom. According to Mao Tse-tung, who, after Stalin, is *the* communist theoretician:

The enemy has weak foundations. Internally it [sic] is disintegrating. It is estranged from the people and is faced with inescapable economic crisis. Hence, it can be defeated. It would be a grave mistake to over-estimate the enemy's strength or under-estimate the strength of the revolution.[84]

The revolutionary forces within each country must unite, and the revolutionary forces of all countries must also unite, Mao continued. Then revolutionary victory can be achieved.

The immediate postwar phase is one of the least understood periods of modern history. In that period world strength relationships were changed to the detriment of the United States, at least temporarily.

The foremost problems of the Soviet Union were economic recovery and the consolidation of eastern Europe. Economically, these objectives were achieved by hard work and by becoming parasitic on western economic strength. Programs such as the exploitation of UNRRA, the dismantling of industrial installations in Germany, Austria and Manchuria, and the imposition of very heavy reparations on the defeated nations siphoned economic power from the West into the soviet orbit. More ambitious projects aiming at the creation of German slave labor armies from the German population were partially thwarted, although the Russians thoroughly exploited the prisoners of war and, to a degree, organized the people of the soviet zone in Germany.

[83] Stalin, *Sochineniya* (Moscow, Orgis, 1946), XII, 26.
[84] Mao Tse-tung, *op. cit.,* pp. 38 f.

Militarily, the armies of the satellite nations were re-created under strict soviet control. Even in eastern Germany there were beginnings of a people's police recruited from cadres of the former free German committee, the communist party, and graduates of the so-called *Antifa-Schulen* (antifascist schools). Quite a number of former high-ranking officers obtained key positions in this new combat organization.

Concurrently, an attempt was made to render the allied position in Europe untenable. Large numbers of refugees from East Germany and Czechoslovakia were permitted to push into the western zones of occupied Germany. Members of the free German committee and other communist-trained prisoners of war returned to western Germany to obtain positions in industry and administration. Measures of economic reconstruction were undermined. Ultimately, economic pressure was applied to push the allies out of Berlin and Germany. This particular strategy, however, had only indifferent success.

By contrast, the communists were highly successful in loosening the social cohesion and shaking the political stability of the liberated countries, particularly of France. Communist members of the maquis were integrated into the French armed forces which, at the same time, were being purged of their conservative elements. About 24,000 officers and 35,000 noncommissioned officers were dismissed from the army and air force,[85] according to a former minister of national defense, M. Michelet. There was an effective purge in the air force, while more than 90 per cent of the senior officers were eliminated from the navy. As in prewar times, the air force and the nationalized aircraft industry were riddled with communists. Concurrently, semimilitary and police organizations were infiltrated, and extralegal communist militant units were established. The French atomic energy commission for a while also passed under communist leadership.

Under the guise of a purge of alleged collaborationists, anticommunist elements were eliminated from the French administrative system, law courts, schools, and universities.

When the special courts stopped operating on January 31, 1951,

[85] For details, see L'Union pour la restauration et de la Défense du Service Public, *Requête aux Nations Unies sur les violations des droits de l'homme* (Paris, André Bonne, 1951), p. 166.

that is, more than seven years after the liberation of Paris, a minimum of 320,000 Frenchmen had been killed, purged, or otherwise eliminated from public life. A large additional number had been subjected to loss of property, economic hardship, and terroristic acts. It was estimated that during 1944 close to one million persons were arrested or ordered into forced residence.[86] Altogether, an estimated 120,000 officers and officials were dismissed. A near civil war was hidden behind terrorism and "legal" purge trials which cost the lives of an estimated 112,000 persons.[87] Events followed a similar course in Italy, except that the near civil war there reportedly cost the lives of at least 360,000 persons.[88]

Many French newspapers passed under direct or indirect communist control or were rendered unable to take a resolute anticommunist stand. Radio stations suffered a similar fate. It was some time before the situation was even partially remedied.

Politicians who could be expected to fight communism were described as "fascists" and "traitors" and were in many cases deprived of position or influence. In consequence, even some of the non-communist parties of France were run by people either acceptable to the communists or incapable of harming them.

Through coalition governments, communists were infiltrated into all parts of the governmental machine.[89] Economic, political, and military recovery was sabotaged or delayed. The adoption of a workable constitution was prevented. Help received from the United States was partially subverted. General de Gaulle, who cannot be relieved fully of responsibility for these events, tried to stop further communist encroachments but eventually was forced to resign.

Two years after the end of the war, the communists were at last kicked out of the government of France (and Italy). They countered with strikes in transportation, coal mining, public utilities, and government administration, and, finally, with abortive attempts at gen-

[86] *Ibid.*, p. 177.

[87] The instructions about insurrection in France established precise rules for summary executions. See *ibid.*, pp. 226 f.

[88] *Bulletin de l'association d'études et d'informations politiques internationales,* Paris, April 15, 1951, p. 8.

[89] Maurice Thorez, the deserter of 1939, had become vice-premier of the French government. He had been amnestied by General de Gaulle who showed less leniency to many patriotic Frenchmen convicted by kangaroo courts of the resistance movement.

eral strike. This threat was subdued. The communist revolutionary capability was reduced greatly. France began to put its house in order.

Nevertheless, a communist semirevolution had taken place. Many anticommunists had been killed. The forces of recovery were dispersed. The country's powers of resistance had been weakened dangerously.[90]

In the postwar period, soviet strategy probably did not consider the conquest of western Europe feasible. It focused rather on preventing the resurgence of European military power. By carrying out a cryptorevolution in France, the communists deprived the United States of strong European allies. Remedial action was taken hesitatingly—and only against one aspect of the threat, in the form of the Atlantic pact.

Soviet ambitions were not restricted to the old continent. A very determined psychological warfare effort was directed against the new world, especially against the United States.

The atomic bomb was attacked by an all-out propaganda campaign, culminating in demands to "share the secret." Its aim was to reduce American reliance on atomic air power as the strongest block to soviet ambitions and to give many Americans a bad conscience about this "weapon of mass destruction."

While this incidental music was played fortissimo, the soviets proceded, pianissimo, to spy out the American atomic industry, to incorporate German scientific and technological skills, and to harness their own resources to a successful atomic program. Simultaneously, American progress in the field was kept at a slow pace, partly by difficulties with scientists and the public, but mainly by obliviousness to the crucial significance of atomic power in the hands of democracy.

Late in 1945, conventional American strength was of great concern to the soviets. The American armed forces had to be persuaded or be pushed out of Europe and Asia lest they interfere with soviet "peacemaking." This was done by harping on the bring-the-boys-

---

[90] It must be remembered that the communists got into the act via the maquis and that the maquis was assisted by the western powers because of its alleged military importance. However, that importance was greatly exaggerated. For example, the allied plan called for the mobilization of 9,000 maquis in fifteen departments in central France; but only 1,700 men responded to the call. See *Requête aux Nations Unies, op. cit.*, pp. 183 f.

home sentiment. Originally, the bring-the-boys-home movement was not very strong. But when the government revealed willingness to yield to pressure, the movement grew, stimulated by rivalry between the services which were hoping to find popularity through a demobilization race.

Communist propaganda aiming at fast U.S. disarmament began rather late, on September 4, 1945, with an editorial in the *Daily Worker* calling for immediate demobilization. The *Daily Worker* criticized the plan of keeping 400,000 American soldiers in Germany and 1,000,000 in the Pacific and opposed the suggestion that by July 1946 the United States should find a peacetime army of 2,500,000 and a navy of 550,000 men. America did not need such military power. This line was hammered home in the weeks to come, in print as well as by demonstrations, for example, of GI wives in Washington (October 27, 1945). It was spiced by howls over alleged discrimination against Negro troops who "are now being sent to the Pacific because they lack the number of points necessary for demobilization."

The official announcement that shipping was inadequate for fast demobilization was countered by statements from officers of a communist-controlled maritime union according to which 400 ships were idle and 55 ships were being used "for profit." Leaflets and post cards advocating the end of American intervention in China and calling on the government to bring the boys home were distributed in large numbers. As in all successful propaganda, the effort snowballed. Congress was swamped with telephone calls, telegrams, and other communications. As a result, several bills advocating accelerated demobilization were introduced.

The zenith of all this activity came in the form of soldier protest demonstrations between the seventh and seventeenth of January 1946 in Manila, Guam, Japan, Korea, Okinawa, Honolulu, Frankfurt, Vienna, Paris, London, Reims, Le Havre, and Fürstenfeldbruck. The largest demonstrations were in Manila where, on January 7, 1946, 25,000 soldiers "protested." Obviously, military discipline was weakening.

Demobilization was put into high gear. For all practical purposes, the American armed forces disintegrated as a combat corps. While substantial numbers of men remained in the armed forces, most of the key personnel and experienced technicians went home. Few units remained capable of combat operations. Nothing of the kind happened in the soviet armed forces. Hence, the Russo-American strength relationship changed. The soviets fell into possession of marked military superiority.

GOLIATH AND TWO TYPES OF DAVIDS

THE CZECH coup was the masterpiece of soviet postwar technique. In broad outline, Czechoslovakia fell in the following fashion:

Overture: The government-in-exile of President Beneš negotiated a mutual-assistance pact with Russia (1945), returned to Prague via Moscow, and oriented their foreign policy in accordance with the alliance with Russia. For this "protection" the Czechs paid a substantial territorial price, ceding Ruthenia to the USSR, and, in their domestic policies, adopted a prosoviet course.

First Act: The Red army overran large parts of Czechoslovakia (1944–45), gave local communists full material and financial support, and helped them to establish themselves in local governments. Armies of the western powers also occupied a part of Czechoslovakia but decided not to push on to Prague. The United States determined not to leave any troops in Czechoslovakia.[91] This gave little encouragement to local democratic leaders. A provisional coalition government was created with a cryptocommunist prime minister. The communists obtained key cabinet posts, including the ministries of the interior (police) and information. A pro-Russian general became head of the army; officers with Russian training were given key commands and staff posts. The conservative parties were outlawed as collaborators.

Second Act: In elections during May 1946 the communists polled 38 per cent of the vote but, together with the social democrats whom they came to control through infiltration, obtained a workable parliamentary majority. A new cabinet was created under a communist prime minister; 12 out of 25 cabinet ministers were communists, social democrats, or communist-controlled "technicians." All key jobs fell into communist hands; their agents were placed in all minis-

[91] *The Forrestal Diaries,* ed. by Walter Millis (New York, Viking, 1951), pp. 98, 101.

tries, nationalized industries, and in the armed forces. Political opposition to the coalition was eliminated, and energetic, hostile politicians were prosecuted for alleged war crimes. A communist-oriented police force was organized under the minister of the interior. As the party's authority was established, the Red army gradually withdrew from the country.

Third Act: By November 1947, however, those elements in opposition to the communist regime began to recover and regroup. Elections scheduled for spring 1948 were expected to show a decline in communist strength. The social democrats kicked out their cryptocommunist leadership, thus foreshadowing a day when they might join the other non-communist parties, establish a strong parliamentary majority of anticommunists, and displace the commuist government. To preclude defeat, the communists decided to mount a coup; this decision probably was made late in 1947. But to prevent the break with the communists which he saw coming, President Beneš stated that the communist party should not be excluded "from anything" (November 21, 1947). Instead of helping the anticommunists, he discouraged them. The communists began discovering all kinds of espionage plots, linking some of the non-communist parties to western powers in order to provoke dissension in the non-communist camp.

Fourth Act: Vaclav Nošek, the communist minister of the interior, exercising his power of personnel appointment in the government police, quite brazenly transformed the organization into an arm of the party. When the communists attacked the parliamentary system as such, the social democrats, for the first time and very timidly, joined the anticommunist vote. The crisis was mounting rapidly when Valerian Zorin, deputy foreign minister of Russia, suddenly appeared in Prague. The non-communists, believing that they could force the issue, resigned, except for the social democrats, who assumed an ambiguous attitude (February 20, 1948). Beneš took the position—apparently after some "persuasion"—that the next government should again be headed by a communist. Klement Gottwald, prime minister and communist party leader, asserted that he would not take any of the resigning ministers back into his government. He would continue working with the other parties, but only with those of their members who were acceptable to his party. A deadlock ensued.

Fifth Act: The communists staged street demonstrations. The trade unions, safely under control, announced their support of Gottwald, called a one-hour protest strike, and began preparations for a general strike. Rifles were issued to the Prague police, which complied with all communist orders, while the army did not budge. Headquarters of non-communist parties were searched, and hostile politicians were terrorized and arrested. The socialists were compelled to submit again to cryptocommunist leadership. Gottwald called for the establishment of "action committees," or soviets, in all phases of Czech life. A central action committee was chosen to prepare the way for a new government. The minister of the interior accorded supreme authority to these committees, which barred non-communists from their public offices and took over ministries, factories, newspapers, radio stations, and combat organizations. The social democrats then announced that they were ready to form a government with the communists. The list of the new government was announced, but when Beneš apparently refused to approve it, Gottwald simply asserted that Beneš had accepted the ministerial list. On February 27, 1948, the ailing, vacillating, and isolated Beneš was forced to swear in the new cabinet. Valerian Zorin, his work done, departed for Moscow.

Thus, the communists were able to take Czechoslovakia because (1) the Red army provided strategic cover; (2) the party controlled virtually all the levers of power within Czechoslovakia except the army, which it was able to neutralize; (3) the social democrats collaborated fully until the last moment; (4) the non-socialists were split and lacked courage as well as energy; (5) the opposition tried to beat the communists with parliamentary means and made an improper use of power by resigning instead of using ministerial authority; (6) President Beneš failed to support the non-communists; and (7) the western powers remained entirely aloof.[92]

The Czech coup represents a peak of the communist art, an ideal performance which the soviets will use as a model when they can. The only blemish on the record is that the prior military occupation

[92] *House Committee on Foreign Affairs, The Strategy and Tactics of World Communism, Supplement III, The Coup d'Etat in Prague* [U. S. Congress, 81st, 1st sess., House. (Washington, D. C., Govt. Print. Off., 1949)]; and Ivo Ducháček, *The Strategy of Communist Infiltration: The Case of Czechoslovakia* (research paper, New Haven, Conn., Yale Institute of International Studies, 1949).

by the Red army was the key to the ultimate success of the communist party.

Can the communists dispense with this military phase of the operation in the face of substantial opposition? The Finnish example suggests that this is not possible.

By 1944–45 the foundation for the development of a revolutionary situation was laid in Finland. The nation was suffering grievously from two recent wars and defeats. There were social tensions, partly due to the fact that about 10 per cent of the population was forced to move away from soviet-annexed Karelia. The soviets had acquired naval- and air-base rights. But, there was no military occupation of Finland, and the Russian forces were kept in isolation from the country. Despite soviet pressure, the non-communists were neither intimidated nor eliminated from political life, and even war-crimes trials, a favorite device of demoralizing and discrediting non-communist parties, could be applied only in a token fashion against a few high officials.

Long students of communism, the Finns understood the soviet game and were familiar with the soviet technique. They were unwilling to give up their country, and had not the slightest illusion about soviet intentions. They identified most of the communists and soviet sympathizers living in their midst. They took precautions in time and on a scale commensurate with the danger.

The population at large showed remarkable stamina and, unlike the Czechs, did not vote to please the conqueror. In 1945 the communists polled barely 25 per cent of the vote. All the leftist parties combined had a somewhat smaller popular vote than did the liberals and conservatives. The Finnish social democrats, unlike their colleagues in other European countries, from the outset took a firm stand against communism. Nevertheless, the communists were given 4 of 19 seats in the cabinet, including the critical ministry of the interior, obtained for Yrjo Leino.

Fortunately for Finland, the interior ministry did not control the police in its entirety. The Helsinki police, as well as local and municipal police units, were to a degree free of Leino's supervision. Naturally, true to the communist pattern, Leino proceeded to build up the ministry's mobile police as a communist force, but the army general staff, anticipating military occupation, had, before the armistice, recruited clandestine counterrevolutionary cells and set up secret weapons caches. Occasionally some of these caches were turned up by Leino's police. Several dozen officers, including the onetime chief of staff, were indicted for illegal possession of arms, but trials were delayed and the officers were let off with light punishment. Leino's forces proved quite incapable of destroying the military strength of the non-communists.

In March 1946, however, the wind seemed to be blowing in their direction. Communist participation in the cabinet was enlarged to 6 out of 17 ministerial posts. But the anticommunists strongly opposed communist policies and successfully attacked doubtful personnel appointments. The communists were kept under constant political pressure. Since their subversive schemes rarely went unnoticed, they were compelled to operate in the open.

Early in 1948, Stalin asked Finland to enter into a mutual-assistance pact with Russia. As the Czechoslovakian coup was being staged, a Russian general was appointed minister to Finland. Finnish independence was obviously menaced.

The Finns reacted. First, they negotiated an innocuous pact with Russia which satisfied Russian stipulations but which in practice turned out to mean relatively little.

Second, the non-communists, especially the social democrats, revealed the weakness of Finnish communism by forcing votes in unions, municipalities, and in the parliament. The communists invariably lost and, in the process, had to yield a number of key positions.

Third, and most important, the communist civil-war machine was destroyed. Leino was indicted for malfeasance in office and was forced out of the government. The Helsinki police confiscated the machine guns and other weapons of Leino's mobile police. The staff officers guilty of hiding weapons were released from prison. Militant groups made ready to suppress any bolshevik uprising.

Having been deprived of their insurrectional capability, the communists resorted to their last weapon: the general strike. Again, they failed dismally. The workers obeyed the socialists, and continued working.

Elections following these events revealed a serious reduction in communist strength (July 1948). The communist vote was reduced to a manageable 19 per cent. An exclusively social democratic government was formed which, with the concurrence of all non-communist parties, maintained itself in office.

The communists were outmaneuvered and isolated, yet in August 1949 they saw another chance. They were able to launch strikes in the basic industries, but the major unions rejected their lead and expelled the communist-controlled unions and union locals. Troops were deployed to quash unrest. In protest, the communists made another attempt at general strike (September 1, 1949), but again they failed.[93] The Finnish workers were too well informed and the Finnish people too courageous for the communist game to succeed. As a result, the Finnish communists have adopted a policy of co-existence. They are waiting for better opportunities to come along.

The Finnish performance is unique. The Finns are the only people who succeeded in maintaining their freedom while, for all practical purposes, being behind the iron curtain. True, the Scandinavian countries sided with Finland and gave the country considerable support. True, the soviets did not want to drive Sweden, with its considerable military strength, into the arms of the Atlantic treaty organization. True, that while the Russian army was poised on the Finnish border, it would have been costly and difficult to invade this subarctic lake country.

If the Red army had been able to occupy Finland, as it temporarily occupied Czechoslovakia, Finland's fate would probably have been sealed. As it was, Finland could have fallen, but the attitude of the Finnish majority, the courage of the Finnish government, and the foresight of the Finnish army and police have so far saved the country.

It is interesting to speculate about what would have happened in Czechoslovakia if the Czechs had reacted differently, if they had fallen less for the communist lure, and if they had shown greater skill and a stronger will to resist. In any event, the Finns have proved to the world that the soviets can be beaten at their own game. They also demonstrated that a small nation need not give up hope and independence in the face of the soviet threat.

[93] For more details on Finland's fight, see Franklin D. Scott, *The United States and Scandinavia* (Cambridge, Mass., Harvard University Press, 1950); and Dr. Scott's excellent articles on Finland in the consecutive issues of the *Britannica Book of the Year.*

6. The Third Round of World Revolution: China · 1937–1949

"Today's generation of generals in China will have more life and death impact on the world than any Chinese of the past or near future. . . . There will be no real compromise with these jingoists, who individually are more anti-American than any group of soviet generals. The red generals of China are graveyard fillers. . . . These men . . . are the world's most authentic communists. The soviets may bend them partially to Russian will and design—but in the end these Chinese militarists will prove to be communists first, Chinese second, and soviet puppets last."

ROBERT B. RIGG,
Red China's Fighting Hordes, pages 20 and 56.

"Communists learn many fundamental lessons from the socialist experience of the soviet people. . . . Communists are also learning much from the experience of the Chinese people."

WILLIAM Z. FOSTER, 1949

THE WAR waged by the communists under Mao Tse-tung against nationalist China under Chiang Kai-shek must rank as one of the classics of communist warfare. Communists all over the world evaluate Mao's victory in line with a statement made by Lenin and quoted by Malenkov in 1949: "The outcome of the world struggle between capitalism and communism [depends] in the long run on the fact that Russia, India and China comprise the gigantic majority of the population" of the globe and are now being drawn "with exceptional rapidity into a struggle for liberation."[1]

The grand strategy of the Chinese war was outlined in 1926 by Stalin:

The revolutionary army of China is a supreme factor in the struggle of the Chinese workers and peasants for their liberation. In China it is not a defenseless people that is resisting the armies of the old government but an armed people which is represented by its revolutionary armies. In China the armed revolution is fighting an armed counter-revolution. This is one of the peculiarities and one of the advantages of the Chinese revolution. And in this also lies the particular importance of China's revolutionary army.[2]

Stalin admonished the Chinese communists that the revolutionary army must be fully indoctrinated with the precepts of communism. The communists were told to peruse military science texts closely: The "military factor" was the key to the Chinese revolution.[3] At the same time, Stalin warned that it was impossible to overcome imperialism and feudalism by military force alone. To win, communists also must consider social factors. In the particular case of China, they must carry out the agrarian revolution, solving the agrarian question through the army, "under the leadership of the proletariat."[4]

The proper relationship between the Chinese proletariat and the Chinese peasantry, however, was never fully clarified. Obviously, a strictly proletarian revolution was not possible in China. Some light is thrown on the solution to this difficulty by Mao Tse-tung's statement that communist successes were due to three factors: a disciplined party; an army led by such a party; and a united front of all revolutionary strata and revolutionary parties, also led by such a party. In sociological terms: The revolution was made not by one class—least of all by the proletariat—but by an elite of

[1] The *New York Times,* November 7, 1949, p. 15. The statement is quoted rather frequently by lesser bolshevik luminaries such as Pospelov, editor of *Pravda.* See the section *"The Oriental Flank,"* pp. 148–66.

[2] Stalin, *Sochineniya* (Moscow, Orgis, 1946), VIII, 362.

[3] *Ibid.,* p. 364.

[4] *Ibid.,* p. 371. Western policy-makers often toy with the idea of stopping communism in Asia by means of agrarian reform. Under certain conditions such a policy may play into the communist hands.

professional revolutionaries in control of an army supported by the peasants and public opinion.

OVERTURE

THE COMMUNIST seizure of China took about fifteen years. It started in 1934, when the remnants of the communist guerrillas who had escaped destruction in Kiangsi and Fukien established a small soviet state in northern Shensi beyond the effective range of the Chinese army. Originally, this state covered about 30,000 square miles and was inhabited by two million people, roughly comparable to South Carolina.

The national Chinese government under Chiang Kai-shek was unwilling to tolerate this communist state and was prepared for an anticommunist military campaign. These preparations coincided with substantial nationalist reforms in economic, social, and administrative fields. China was making considerable progress, a fact which induced Japan to prepare for military action designed to assure the latter's control of the Far East. However, Chiang Kai-shek, quite wisely, had determined to avoid war with Japan at all costs and to arm China against future conflicts by completing the program of internal reform, including the elimination of the communist "state."

In December 1936, Chiang Kai-shek was kidnapped at Sian by one of his subordinate officers. Communist leaders were present at the resultant talks.[5] Although the entire background of this affair has never been clarified, the generalissimo, negotiating under pressure, promised to abandon his plans for a campaign against the communists and committed himself to fight Japan even before completion of his internal reform program. In return, he was assured the support of the united front of the Chinese people and communist assistance in the war against Japan.[6]

[5] See, *House Committee on Foreign Affairs, The Strategy and Tactics of World Communism, Supplement III, Communism in China* [U. S. Congress, 81st, 1st sess., House. (Washington, D. C., Govt. Print. Off., 1949), pp. 22 ff.]. (Hereafter referred to as *Communism in China.*)

[6] The united-front agreement was formalized in September 1937, see *ibid.*, p. 23. According to Robert B. Rigg, *Red China's Fighting Hordes* (Harrisburg, Pa., Military Service Publishing Co., 1951), p. 47, Chou En-lai persuaded the

The coup of Sian was carried out with extraordinary skill and boldness.[7] There is no proof that the soviets were implicated in the affair directly, but it seems unlikely that a decision of this magnitude—to wage full-fledged war against Japan—was arrived at by the Chinese communists without consultation with Moscow. There is no question that the pledge of united-front support was in full harmony with the current decisions of the Seventh World Congress. Nor can there be any doubt that the war between Japan and China served Russia's strategic interests.[8] The marooning of Japan in the Asiatic continent prevented an effective military alliance between Japan and Germany, thus obviating any serious danger of a complete encirclement of Russia.

The Sian coup did indeed produce a war between China and Japan. Chiang refused to compromise further with the Japanese and opposed them with his full military power when they resorted to one of their periodic acts of aggression in July 1937.

As promised, the Chinese communists participated in the war

---

young marshal Chang Hsueh-liang, Chiang's kidnapper, to ally himself with the communists. The presence of Agnes Smedley at Sian at the precise moment when Chiang was captured is an interesting and unexplained fact. Did she have telepathic vision or information?

[7] Chiang had made the mistake of sending Manchurian troops against the communists. These troops were, perhaps, the most vulnerable to communist propaganda and, furthermore, did not think much of the idea of fighting in Shensi against other Chinese when their own country was occupied by the Japanese. Why did Chiang commit such an obvious error? He wanted to reduce the power of the Manchurian military leaders. Hence, he sent the Manchurian units into battle, or so he thought, while he kept his loyal forces behind the front. Time and again, Chiang kept his most trustworthy units out of battle, apparently without realizing that this was the surest way to destroy their combat skill and morale. Chestnut strategy has its difficulties.

[8] "The new line . . . was in all probability prompted by the Kremlin's realistic appraisal of the Soviet Union's position in the Far East. Russia was threatened by Japan. The Japanese army . . . apparently decided upon a policy of continental expansion. . . . The Japanese seemed to be intent upon outflanking the Russians through China. China could not be expected to offer strong resistance to Japanese expansion so long as it was torn by internal dissension." This was good political analysis by an American diplomat in China (1943). He also stated correctly that the Chinese communists "embraced in 1935, in compliance with Moscow directives, the policy of the united front." But he erred when he stated that this new line was an abandonment by the Comintern and the Chinese communists of the "program of world revolution." *U. S. Relations with China, With Special Reference to the Period 1944–49*, Department of State, Publication 3573 (Washington, D. C., Govt. Print. Off., 1949), p. 565.

against Japan. Yet, their strategy was not designed to liberate China from the Japanese yoke, let alone help Chiang in his struggle. Mao Tse-tung followed the strategy he is said to have outlined in 1937: "Our determined policy is 70 per cent self-development, 20 per cent compromise, and 10 per cent fight the Japanese."[9]

The communists fought the common enemy in such a fashion that the Japanese never felt compelled to destroy them. Gradually, the communists and the Japanese arrived at a *modus vivendi*[10] which left the Japanese troops free to fight the nationalist forces almost exclusively and also made it possible for the communists continuously to seize territory from the nationalists, thus forcing Chiang to maintain a second front against them.

When World War II was over, the communists had acquired a territory of about 300,000 square miles inhabited by roughly 116,-000,000 people. This area was as large as France and Algeria put together; its population almost equalled that of France and Germany combined. The communists had used the Japanese as a sword of revolution to beat down the nationalist armies. At the same time Chiang was used to check the Japanese. It was "triangular warfare" —all according to the book.

The First Act

THE SINO-JAPANESE conflict lasted from July 1937 until August 1945. It was preceded by a period of about twenty-five years of revolution and local, civil, and foreign wars. Although it left China an ostensible victor, rarely has a higher price been paid for victory.

The outbreak of the war found China in the midst of social and economic transformation. Industry was in its early growing pains; the transportation system, though somewhat improved, was still totally inadequate for the civilian needs of the country and even less able to bear the military requirements of a major war. The reform of the army had not been completed.

[9] See *Communism in China, op. cit.,* p. 24.

[10] As will appear from the next section, there may be more to the Japanese willingness to adhere to such a *modus vivendi* than would appear at first glance.

The Japanese limited themselves to seizing the economically most valuable parts of China, particularly the sea ports and the food-producing river valleys. By October 1938 all major ports, including Canton, were in Japanese hands, cutting off China from the rest of the world, except for the caravan route to Russia through Mongolia and Turkestan; the so-called Burma road connecting the Burmese railroads with the valley of the upper Yangtze and an inland railroad in southern China; and finally the railroad connecting Indochina with the city of Kunming.

In March 1938 the Japanese installed a puppet government in Nanking which took over the various administrative and economic organs along with most of the civil service personnel. China was politically split into four major parts: the nationalist, the communist, the puppet areas, and Manchuria, controlled through a separate set of puppets by the Japanese.

After the fall of Canton, the western nations continued to send limited supplies to Chiang. However, in 1940, after the fall of France, they stopped deliveries through Burma and Indochina. Russia reportedly went on supplying some equipment: The soviets ensured Chiang's continuing to fight the Japanese. But whether they sent equipment to the communists in Shensi is conjectural.

In April 1941, Russia and Japan concluded a nonaggression pact which secured the eastern flank of Russia, precluded the danger of a co-ordinated German-Japanese attack, and released Japan to fight Britain and the United States. It is not certain whether the Russians, to obtain Japan's connivance, promised them a free hand in China, but, whatever their pledges, the soviets were primarily interested in involving Japan in a maximum number of wars.

Japan's decision to fight the West rather than Russia originally found full German agreement; in fact, the Germans informed the Japanese foreign minister, Yosuke Matsuoka, that they would protect Japan's rear against the Soviet Union if the Japanese should go against Singapore.[11] Nevertheless, the Germans—at least in April 1941—were opposed to drawing the United States into the war, and while undoubtedly the world situation favored a chestnut strategy for Japan in Southeast Asia, it hardly justified the foolhardiness of

[11] *Nazi-Soviet Relations 1939–1941, Documents from the Archives of the German Foreign Office,* Department of State, Publication 3023 (Washington, D. C., Govt. Print. Off., 1948), p. 299.

the Pearl Harbor attack. There is no doubt that the Germans were in favor of Japan's war against Britain. Yet, despite their reverses in Russia, they never seem to have pressed Japan to attack Siberia.

What had happened? Let us see what Prince Fumimaro Konoye, three-time Japanese prime minister, had to say. In retrospect, Konoye came to doubt seriously "whether the whole series of events from the Manchurian incident [1931] to the present war have not been what they [the communists] have purposefully planned." He spoke of the "disguised activities of the communists behind both the military and bureaucrats" and intimated that some young officers (presumably of the Kwantung army) had been flirting with communism. In his opinion, these men brought about the Manchurian war to achieve their purposes.[12]

Hallucinations? Perhaps, but the following facts are known:

(1) A prominent soviet agent, the German Richard Sorge, before and during the war lived in Tokyo where he held a semiofficial position with the German embassy and maintained a close relationship with the German ambassador, Eugen Ott. He was very close to a secret communist, Hozumi Ozaki, a key member of Konoye's brain trust and an individual in a position to influence Japanese policy. Ozaki had two friends, also in high and influential positions (for example, secretaries to the cabinet) who collaborated with him and Sorge. All these persons were later tried for espionage in favor of Russia; Sorge and Ozaki were executed.[13]

(2) Sorge requested Moscow's permission to influence and sabotage Japanese policy. In his own words, Sorge told the following story:[14]

[12] *Japan's Struggle to End the War, U. S. Strategic Bombing Survey* (Washington, D. C., Govt. Print. Off., 1946), p. 22.

[13] *Hearings before the Subcommittee to Investigate the Administration of the Internal Security Act and Other Internal Security Laws of the Committee on the Judiciary, on the Institute of Pacific Relations, Part II, Testimony of Mitsusada Yoshikawa, Director, Special Investigation Bureau, Attorney General's Office, Japanese Government* [U. S. Congress, 82nd, 1st sess., Senate. (Washington, D. C., Govt. Print. Off., 1951), p. 504]. (Hereafter referred to as *IPR Hearings*.)

[14] *Hearings before the Committee on Un-American Activities on American Aspects of the Richard Sorge Spy Case* [U. S. Congress, 82nd, 1st sess., House. (Washington, D. C., Govt. Print. Off., 1951), pp. 1202 f.]. (Italics added. Hereafter referred to as *Sorge Spy Case*.)

I was strictly forbidden by Moscow to engage in any nonintelligence activity, that is, to undertake any propaganda or organized functions of a political nature.

This ban meant that my group and I were not allowed to make the least attempt to exercise any political influence on any persons or group of persons. We obeyed it faithfully, with one exception, that we worked actively on other people to influence their opinions of soviet national strength. It was utterly impossible not to violate a general restriction which made no special provision for such cases. If Ozaki and myself as advisers, political experts and experienced advisers, had endorsed the prevailing derogatory opinion and underestimation of soviet strength, our positions would have been directly endangered. It was for this reason that our group took a special stand in connection with the evaluation of soviet strength. In doing so, we did not engage in propaganda on behalf of the Soviet Union, but endeavored to teach various persons and classes of society to evaluate soviet strength with due caution. We encouraged individuals and groups not to underestimate Russian strength and to strive for a peaceful solution of the pending Soviet-Japanese problems.

Ozaki, Voukelitch, and I maintained this attitude for a number of years. When the cry for war with the Soviet Union became urgent, in 1941, I sent an inquiry to Moscow, prompted by conversations with Ozaki, in which he expressed the belief that he could successfully exceed the limits mentioned above and influence members of his group in favor of a positive peace policy toward the Soviet Union. *He was confident that if he took a strong stand against a Soviet-Japanese war in the Konoye group he could turn Japan's expansion policy south.*

The inquiry was very general, outlining the possibilities of positive action by Ozaki, myself, and other members of the group. The reply was negative, not forbidding such activities outright but labelling them unnecessary.

With tension ever mounting over the outbreak of the Soviet-German war in 1941, I felt that it was within my authority not to interpret the reply as a clear-cut prohibition. I imparted a wider and more discretionary meaning to the word "unnecessary," refusing to construe it as an explicit ban on our participation in such activities. Accordingly, I did not restrict Ozaki's positive maneuvers within the Konoye group, *nor did I hesitate to work on the Germans,* particularly in view of the fact that my attitude had remained unchanged over the past several years. The maneuvers that my group and I attempted were confined to the scope and the political problems described on the two preceding pages. No one of our members exceeded this restriction, because to have done so would have been to endanger our original and principal mission. I would like to emphasize this point thoroughly. What we did was not propaganda by any means. . . .

The argument which [Ozaki] employed was briefly as follows: The Soviet Union has no intention whatsoever of fighting Japan, and even if Japan should invade Siberia would simply defend herself. It would be a short-sighted and mistaken view for Japan to attack Russia, since she cannot expect to gain anything in eastern Siberia or to wrest any sizable political or economic benefits from such a war. The United States and Britain would very likely welcome such a Japanese embroilment with open arms and seize the opportunity to strike at the nation after her oil and iron reserves were depleted. Moreover, if Germany should succeed in defeating the Soviet Union, Siberia might fall into Japan's lap without her raising a finger. Should Japan aspire to further expansion elsewhere than in China, the southern area alone would be worth going into, for there Japan would find the critical resources so essential to her wartime economy, and there she would confront the true enemy blocking her bid for a place in the sun.

(3) Ambassador Ott, who was strongly influenced by Sorge's thinking, participated in Matsuoka's Berlin conferences. Ott made strenuous efforts to induce the Japanese to attack in a southern direction and especially to go to Singapore.[15]

(4) Matsuoka's attitude toward Soviet Russia was not entirely free of ambiguity; for example, he told Stalin that "the Japanese were moral communists,"[16] and there are unconfirmed statements that he went much farther in his declarations.

(5) Nevertheless, on May 9, Matsuoka informed the emperor that in case of a German-Soviet war, "Japan would have to abrogate the neutrality treaty, stand by Germany, and advance at least as far as Irkutsk."[17] However, gradually the idea to attack Russia disappeared from Japanese deliberations, and there are no convincing strategic reasons to explain this disappearance.[18] Quite obviously, the question was sidetracked.

(6) Prince Konoye came to the conclusion that a group of Japanese "bureaucrats and civilians . . . who are in close collaboration with the military are definitely intending to bring about . . . a revolution. . . . I now realize that I have, during the last ten years, come across many events the meaning of which I did not then fully appreciate. . . . I failed to perceive the true intentions hidden behind" the arguments of the "radical elements."[19]

15 *Ibid.*, p. 1142.

16 *Nazi-Soviet Relations, op. cit.*, p. 297.

17 *Hearings before the Joint Committee on the Investigation of the Pearl Harbor Attack, Part XX*, "Memoirs of Prince Konoye" [U. S. Congress, 79th, 2nd sess. (Washington, D. C., Govt. Print. Off., 1946), p. 3989].

18 See *ibid.*, pp. 3993 f., 3999 f., 4004.

19 *Japan's Struggle to End the War, op. cit.*, p. 22.

These are all the facts known today. *Sapienti sat.*

With the Japanese attack on Pearl Harbor, pressure on China abated. At the same time China became formally the ally of the western powers and Russia, a political change carrying little military meaning. The Japanese navy still controlled the sea routes to China, and the Japanese army had taken over control of the Indochina and Burmese approaches. Whether or not the Russians wanted to send equipment, they could spare none. The isolation of nationalist China was therefore complete, except for a tenuous air transport route from India.

Continued Japanese possession of the richest parts of China led to a steady economic and social deterioration and to considerable military attrition. The United States, recognizing that China needed substantial help, believed that the opening of a good supply route into China should take precedence over all other operations in the Asiatic theater. Chiang Kai-shek met President Roosevelt and Prime Minister Churchill at Cairo (November–December 1943) and found agreement to the launching of an amphibious offensive against southern Burma. Within a few days, however, this decision was reversed at Tehran: Not enough amphibious equipment was available. Actually, with the exception of the United States, no one seems to have been interested in the Burma operation. Ironically, the attack required just twenty-seven landing craft, but these ships were recalled on British insistence after they had set sail.[20] The supply route into China remained closed.

General Joseph Stilwell, ranking American officer in the Chinese theater, insisted, despite his lack of amphibious equipment, on a campaign in Burma, the operations to be restricted to the northern part of the country. Although this campaign could not possibly improve the Chinese supply situation, Stilwell won his point. Strategically useless territorial gains were made at the cost of some of the best-trained and best-equipped Chinese forces, including divisions which had been trained in India.

The results of the futile Burma campaign were far-reaching. Supplies destined for China were diverted into the Burmese "rathole."

[20] *Hearings before the Committee on Armed Services and the Committee on Foreign Relations, Military Situation in the Far East, Part I* [U. S. Congress, 82nd, 1st sess., Senate. (Washington, D. C., Govt. Print. Off., 1951), pp. 551 f.]. (Hereafter referred to as *Far East Hearings.*)

The military strength available in China was significantly reduced. Taking advantage of the situation, the Japanese launched an offensive in eastern China, inflicting a heavy defeat on the Chinese, seizing a number of airfields used by the American air force, forcing the evacuation of additional fields, and denying to the Chinese nationalists one of their few remaining rice-producing areas.

As a result of the heavy fighting, the Chinese fell short of combat divisions. By the fall of 1944 the Japanese were advancing toward Chungking, the Chinese wartime capital, and Kunming, the main supply base. General Albert C. Wedemeyer, Stilwell's successor, asked Chiang to redeploy against the Japanese five divisions which had been containing the Chinese communists. These divisions stopped the Japanese, but at the cost of increasing the relative capabilities of the communists.[21]

The plight of the Chinese armies was extreme. Prior to June 1944 the entire Chinese army (with the exception of the expeditionary forces in India and Burma) had received not "one single rifle or piece of artillery from American lend-lease." The United States made strenuous efforts to improve the situation, yet, up to the end of the war, the entire lend-lease effort for China totaled but $1,247,-000,000.[22] This actually represented only a moderate amount of weapons and ammunition, since most of the investment was eaten up by high transportation costs and medical and food supplies. Even after arrival, most of the military supplies were used by the American air forces fighting in the Chinese theater.[23]

While the political, economic, and military structure of nationalist China was receiving one blow after the other, the communist problem remained unsolved, becoming, if anything, rather more complicated because of the intimate collaboration between the West and the Soviet Union. American diplomats and soldiers were anxious to bring the Chinese communists into the fighting, and they considered all kinds of schemes by which the communists could be armed and used in conjunction with other Chinese military forces. This led to visits by American representatives to the communist state

21 *Ibid., Part III*, p. 2229.

22 Not all of this help reached China; portions of it were used by Chinese troops in India and Burma.

23 *Far East Hearings, Part I, op. cit.*, p. 541; *Part IV*, pp. 2870 f. It must be remembered that all the supplies were air-lifted into China across the Himalayas.

and to negotiations with the communists. It led also to the conviction of some American observers that the communists were better organized, more efficient, and more popular than the nationalists, who, as time progressed, were beginning to come apart at the seams. Many Americans predicted that the nationalists would fall. Some felt strongly that "the communists are in China to stay."[24] But proposals for an energetic policy to reverse the trend were not considered favorably. Instead, a line that the United States "make a determined effort to capture politically the Chinese communists rather than allow them to go by default wholly to the Russians" was accepted as more realistic. It was estimated that a coalition government "in which the communists find a satisfactory place is the solution . . . most desirable" to the United States.[25] Insufficient weight was given to the possibility that the communists would embrace their partners in the coalition not to love but to strangle them.

Actually, the prospect of a communist China did not seem to have worried all American officials in 1944 and 1945. There was a widespread belief that the Chinese communists, although they had "a background of subservience to the U.S.S.R.," were subject to "new influences—principally nationalism" which were "modifying their outlook."[26] The communists were reported to have carried out a "moderate and democratic" revolution in their own area which had improved "the economic condition of the peasants by rent and interest reduction, tax reform and good government." The people in the communist area had "democratic self-government, political consciousness" and had been freed from "feudalistic bonds."[27] The implication was that the United States had nothing to fear from a communist China.

The United States government, anxious for military co-operation from the Chinese communists, hoping to avoid disagreement with the Soviet Union over China, estimating that the Chinese communists were too strong to be liquidated, and desirous of revitalizing

---

[24] U. S. Relations with China, op. cit., p. 573.

[25] Ibid., p. 574; see also, Far East Hearings, Part IV, op. cit., p. 2905.

[26] U. S. Relations with China, op. cit., p. 565.

[27] Ibid., p. 566. On the widespread illusion that the Chinese communists were agrarian reformers, see Far East Hearings, Part I, op. cit., pp. 392, 569; Part III, pp. 2401, 2543; Part IV, pp. 2905, 2912, 2914, 2928; Part V, p. 3219; IPR Hearings, op. cit., p. 565.

the war in the Chinese theater, decided that the best solution would lie in a reconciliation between Chiang Kai-shek and Mao Tse-tung.

The really interesting speculation is where the concept of the agreement between the Kuomintang and the communists originated. Obviously, this idea dovetailed both with the resolutions of the Seventh World Congress and with Mao's dissertation on coalition government. The idea may have been borne, quite spontaneously, in American brains intent on using the communist armies in the same fashion as Tito's partisans were used in Europe. Or there may have been some secret prompter. Whether or not Chiang really believed that a true and honest coalition with the communists was possible, or whether he simply wanted to humor his American allies, is also conjectural. In any event, by the end of 1944 a superficial agreement existed between the American and the Chinese governments that it was imperative to forestall civil war through agreement with the Chinese communists and the Russians.[28]

Meanwhile, greatly impressed by the difficulties of the war against Japan, the United States government was striving to involve the Soviet Union in the far-eastern war so that the Red army could eliminate the Japanese on the Asiatic mainland. As early as 1943 the Russians had promised their participation, but the United States wanted a firm commitment. This desire was the basic underlying factor at the Yalta conference (February 1945), where decisions were made that influenced the course of events in China considerably.

Why American military leaders overrated the residual defensive powers of Japan is a mystery; and certainly not all of them did. Nevertheless, the opinion of the foot soldiers prevailed.[29] It was concluded that Russia's participation was of "the utmost importance," to use Secretary Acheson's words.[30] According to Mr. Ache-

[28] *Far East Hearings, Part I, op. cit.,* p. 552; *Part IV,* pp. 2909 f.

[29] For the U. S. navy's estimate that Japan could be defeated by blockade and bombardment alone, see Fleet Admiral Ernest J. King's letter, *ibid., Part IV,* pp. 3055 f. Admiral King was in favor of Russia's participation which in his opinion would hasten Japan's capitulation, but he wanted to pay only a minor price for it. Fleet Admiral William D. Leahy, *I Was There* (New York, McGraw-Hill, 1950), p. 318, was against Russia's participation. He revealed that the "military" wanted Russia in the war and that the President accepted their view.

[30] *Far East Hearings, Part III, op. cit.,* p. 1845.

son, "there was very little doubt that they [the soviets] would come in. But the great danger was that they would really wait until the war was over, and until we had expanded our effort and blood to win the war, and they would come in and do what they wished."[31]

The American attitude must have puzzled the soviets. What could the United States gain from soviet influence over Manchuria and North China, with the implication of a Russian junction with the Chinese communists, at the very moment when, in the words of an American diplomat, "power in China [was] on the verge of shifting from Chiang to the communists?"[32]

Never loath to take advantage of an opportunity, the soviets asked a stiff price for their participation: the restoration of the "former rights of Russia, violated by the treacherous attack of Japan in 1904." Although these pretended rights had been acquired by tsarist Russia through imperialist aggression against China; although the restoration involved a penalty on allied China rather than on hostile Japan; and although the demand was in violation of the Atlantic charter, the United States and Britain met the Russian condition. While, in its text, the Yalta agreement merely internationalized the port of Dairen, ceded to the Soviet Union a naval base in Port Arthur, and established joint Russo-Chinese operation of the Manchurian railroad, it predictably operated to transfer Manchuria, the key to China and to much of the entire Far East, to soviet control.

The agreement was made without the knowledge of China, a procedure unprecedented in American diplomacy.

The irony of all this is that the American joint chiefs of staff originally had opposed Russia's participation in the war against Japan, estimating that Russia was logistically so weak in the Far East that it barely would be able to sustain its defensive forces. But the United States helped overcome this soviet handicap. For a considerable period of time 100 to 150 American vessels carried war supplies from Seattle and Vancouver to Vladivostok.[33] Without this traffic, soviet capabilities in the Asian theater would have been greatly reduced; the Russians might have been hard put to enter the war at all.

[31] *Ibid.*
[32] *U. S. Relations with China, op. cit.,* p. 574.
[33] *Far East Hearings, Part IV, op. cit.,* p. 2731.

In April 1945 an American intelligence report pointed out that Russia's participation in the war would save but few American lives. Yet, it would destroy China and "injure the material and moral position of the United States in Asia."[34] The American ambassador to China, on his part, voiced objections to the agreements made in Yalta. He suggested revision of the terms, yet the American government refused to reconsider the Yalta agreement and forced Chiang to abide by the commitments made for him and enter into a pact with the Soviet Union.[35]

There might have been a chance to obtain peace with Japan immediately after the German collapse and before August 1945, the earliest date for soviet entry into the war. Prince Konoye had advised the emperor on February 14, 1945, that the war should be stopped as soon as possible.[36] Some time in the summer the Japanese informed Moscow of their "strong desire to secure a termination of the war."[37]

Yet the soviets did not inform the United States of this Japanese overture. Apparently they were not oblivious to the fact that prolongation of the war between the United States and Japan would rebound to their interest.

It is not surprising, therefore, that communist propaganda in the United States went all out against reasonable conditions to Japan. The communists were yelling, at the top of their voices, that the "modification of the unconditional surrender policy . . . is only prolonging the war. . . . Instead of shortening the war, this is literally

34 *Ibid.*, p. 2916; *Part V*, p. 3668.

35 According to Mr. Acheson, the Chinese regarded the treaty with Russia which they concluded on August 14, 1945, as "very valuable" because it "carried with it the obligation of the Russians to evacuate Manchuria, to recognize the Chinese nationalist government, and to aid in the re-establishment of Chinese sovereignty in Manchuria." *Ibid., Part III*, p. 1846. The treaty and the subsidiary agreements concerning Dairen, Port Arthur, and so forth, are printed in *U. S. Relations with China, op. cit.*, pp. 585–96. Other sources, including General Patrick J. Hurley, then American ambassador to China, had a different impression of Chiang's attitude. He believed that Chiang submitted only to American pressure. However that may be, the treaty was not carried out according to its stipulations.

36 *Japan's Struggle to End the War, op. cit.*, p. 22.

37 *The Forrestal Diaries*, ed. by Walter Millis (New York, Viking, 1951), pp. 98, 101.

costing American lives."[38] The emperor had to be eliminated as the prerequisite of a "democratic" peace in Asia.

Unfortunately, the American government was in no hurry to give its peace terms to Japan, although they knew on July 13, 1945, at the very latest, that the unconditional surrender terms were "about the only thing in the way of termination of the war."[39] Clarification of these terms had been initiated on May 8 by a presidential declaration, but full clarification was delayed till July 26 when the Potsdam ultimatum was issued, too late to end the war before Russia's participation.

American policy at that time was described most aptly by Harry Hopkins, returning from his last trip to Moscow where he had put the finishing touches on the U.S.-Russian understanding concerning China. According to this *éminence grise* of American dealings with communism, "the world was now definitely swinging toward the Left." It was "in the middle of the revolution" which "it would be unwise to try to oppose."[40]

THE SECOND ACT

WHEN the war ended, the nationalists were in control of only the southwestern segment of China. The structure of the Kuomintang regime was neither firm nor efficient. The privations and disappointments of the war had isolated the government from the people and had drained its spiritual and material resources. The pressure of war was relieved, but, if anything, the letdown accelerated the process of disintegration.

Upon the cessation of hostilities the weakened nationalist government was confronted by gigantic tasks. The Japanese and puppet

[38] *IPR Hearings, op. cit.,* p. 614. The quote is from the *Daily Worker,* July 24, 1945.

[39] Millis, *op. cit.,* p. 74.

[40] *Ibid.,* p. 72. Upon Forrestal's objections, including "that it was not inconceivable that the real reactionaries . . . would be those who now call themselves revolutionaries, because the dynamics of their philosophy all tended toward the concentration of power in the state, with the inevitable result of exploitation of the common man by the masses," Hopkins terminated the conversation. Forrestal suspected that "he did not want to be driven to the position that he was advocating either revolution or communism for this country."

armies had to be disarmed. The administration of areas previously controlled by the Japanese had to be assumed. The Kuomintang found that it had to establish its authority very rapidly in order to prevent disorder and forestall communist capture of vital territories.[41]

The collapse of Japan led to the disbandment of the Japanese-controlled civil service. While many officials continued in their jobs, others fled or were removed. Chiang's administrative machine had been adequate, perhaps, to manage the territory controlled by him during the war, but by extending his limited administrative force over the whole of China, he spread it entirely too thin. Since the change of regime in itself created serious administrative problems, especially in regard to food supply, the nationalists were compelled to enlarge their civil service hastily. Large numbers of untrained, unqualified, and untrustworthy individuals entered the administration.

The military occupation of the liberated territories presented even more complex problems. For all practical purposes, the Chinese armies had no supply facilities. They possessed virtually no strategy mobility, being unable to mount large movements over long distance. American transport aircraft carried three nationalist armies to key points in eastern and northern China, including Shanghai, Nanking, and Peiping.[42] Additional Chinese forces were subsequently moved by water.[43] Considering the size of the areas involved, Chinese forces were excessively diluted, with the main body still concentrated in the Southwest.

On the other hand, 50,000 U.S. marines were landed in China to permit the nationalists to establish themselves in the vital parts of their country.[44] The marines occupied the principal seaports, guarded the coastal rail lines, and protected the coal mines.

By the end of 1945 it became obvious that the limited transportation facilities available in China were inadequate to complete the redeployment of the Chinese forces and at the same time evacuate

[41] No attempt was made to establish government authority over communist-controlled areas in Northwest China.

[42] A nationalist "army" was about the equivalent of an American division.

[43] *Far East Hearings, Part IV, op. cit.*, p. 2814.

[44] *Ibid., Part III*, p. 1847.

about 3,000,000 Japanese. When additional ships and transport aircraft were requested but not forthcoming, the American forces concentrated more and more on the evacuation of the Japanese, leaving the Chinese to do their own redeployment. Since the Chinese had obtained a few ships from the United States and had gradually coaxed better service from their railroads, redeployment to the North continued, but not on a large enough scale.

In the hope that logistical support ultimately would be made available from the United States, the Chinese continued to overextend militarily. While the nationalists picked up considerable military equipment from the disbanding Japanese and puppet forces,[45] they attempted to occupy and defend too much territory with too few troops, too little equipment, and barely any tactical or strategic mobility. This overextension of the nationalist army, to a great degree a function of the poor transport system of China, was one of the fundamental causes of the eventual downfall of the Kuomintang.[46]

On their part, the Chinese communists, too, went on the march. As early as January 1945 they had started to move toward the coast.[47] After the Japanese collapse, this movement gained momentum, carrying them into Manchuria (early 1946). The predominant objective for the communists was linkage with the soviets who, in turn, rendered them considerable assistance. The soviets prevented the nationalists from taking over several key rail points in Manchuria and restricted their use of the port of Dairen, denying them this point of entry without which the nationalists could never hope to achieve a strong position in the Manchurian provinces. In other cases Russian forces actually disarmed nationalist forces on

[45] During the war against Japan, nationalist units several times deserted to the enemy army and particularly to Chinese puppet forces. This was done in cases when resistance was hopeless and also in the expectation that surrenders *en bloc* would preserve nationalist strength for the postwar period. In fact, some of the deserting units were left intact by the Japanese and puppets, and later reverted to nationalist control. It goes without saying that similar practices while, perhaps, occasionally justified, must sap the moral cohesion and the fighting spirit of an army.

[46] On Chiang's overextension, see *Far East Hearings, Part I, op. cit.*, pp. 549, 688, 698; *Part III*, p. 1840.

[47] *Ibid., Part IV*, p. 2928.

flimsy pretexts, such as alleged violations of the armistice agreement. This happened, for example, in Changchun.[48]

Most important was the cession by the soviets to the communists of a considerable portion of Japanese army equipment and stores.[49] Two hundred thousand communists under General Lin Piao alledg-ly entered Manchuria unarmed and returned fully equipped with Japanese matériel.[50]

There are indications that soviet material help at first was given only on a small scale, but as American policy in China was better understood and as the Russian armies prepared to evacuate Man-churia, this help was stepped up rapidly.[51] The move into Man-churia enabled the communists to transform their forces from guer-rilla or partisan units into something closely resembling a regular field army.[52]

Thus by early 1946 the Chinese nationalists had a fair measure of control over southern and central China but were weak and over-

[48] For further details, see, *China Presents Her Case to the United Nations, Statement by Dr. T. F. Tsiang before the First Committee*, Chinese Delegation to the United Nations, November 25, 1949, New York, 1939, *passim*.

[49] Confirmed by General Marshall. See *Far East Hearings, Part 1, op. cit.*, p. 548.

[50] According to *Communism in China, op. cit.*, p. 36, the communists may have gotten matériel for more than one million men. This figure may be too high, but the stocks of the Kwantung army were very considerable according to a table reproduced by Lieutenant Colonel Rigg, *op. cit.*, p. 277. There were, in round figures, 300,000 rifles, almost 14,000 machine guns, 2,600 guns, 11,000 mortars, a sizeable number of tanks, motor vehicles, supply cars, and aircraft, as well as more than 700 munitions and supply depots.

[51] *Far East Hearings, Part I, op. cit.*, p. 696. According to Rigg, *op. cit.*, p. 245, discussions about soviet help to the communists "consistently missed the forest for the trees. In the first six months of soviet occupation the Chinese reds gained entry to the cities, obtained arms, and secured their biggest meas-ure of soviet assistance. So firmly entrenched were the Chinese reds thereafter that there was no need for the soviets to supply any advisors on the battalion, or even division, level. Many observers have failed to grasp these facts."

[52] *Ibid., Part III*, p. 2302. "The Chinese communists built up their military and political power on three interrelated levels. First there were the regular armies. . . . Second, there were the guerrilla forces which were organized on a local basis but which had considerable mobility. They could be employed away from home in close coordination with the regular armies. They could be transferred into regular army units almost at will. Third, there were the self-defense corps of the villages and towns. These were essentially local in char-acter and were not usually called upon to do any fighting away from home." See George E. Taylor, "The Hegemony of the Chinese Communists, 1945–1950," *The Annals*, CCLXXVII (Philadelphia, September 1951), p. 17.

committed in northern China and especially in Manchuria. Their relative military striking power was reduced due to the dilution of their armed and administrative strength. In contrast, the Chinese communists had increased their military power greatly. They had linked up with soviet forces, secured large quantities of modern weapons, and assumed control over key points in North China and Manchuria.[53]

ENTR'ACTE: THE AMERICAN POINT OF DECISION

I. Alternatives

THE AMERICAN government influenced Chinese events in a decisive manner. There is evidence that as early as 1943 the soviets properly evaluated the importance of the United States for China and that, in true Stalinist fashion, they assumed that Washington was a decisive link in the chain of the Chinese revolution. Ever since 1927 the American communist party was a sort of a parent organization for communist parties in the Far East.[54]

Back in 1937, at the time of the Sian coup, American communists ceased praising their Chinese comrades as champions of sovietism. They began emphasizing their democratic character, bringing out the "full democratic content of the communist movement," and tried to paint them as sort of "North Dakota non-partisan leaguers."[55] This was a parallel effort to that initiated by Earl Browder, who wanted to represent communism to the American people as "twentieth century Americanism."

The Chinese communists were being made popular in the United States at the same time that Chiang was being supported in his fight against Japan. In 1942 the American communists put pressure on

[53] The achievement of the communists in extending their control over large areas and, unlike the nationalists, not overextending their forces, must be attributed to their better training, organization, and morale. Moreover, they showed greater determination and ruthlessness. An up-and-coming political movement can do many things which are beyond the resources of an aging and decadent regime which, to make things worse, imposes restraints on the ruthlessness of its actions. It is the ancient tale of the new broom.

[54] *IPR Hearings, op. cit.,* p. 511, 593. Frequent travel of American communists to China is a significant indicator for the role of the CPUSA. For additional documentation, see, *Sorge Spy Case, op. cit.,* p. 1225 and *passim.*

[55] *IPR Hearings, op. cit.,* p. 521.

the State Department and extracted from it a pledge that the U.S. would not oppose the Chinese communists, that it would not support Chiang in civil war, and that it would work for unity in China. This pledge was given, in written form, by Undersecretary of State Sumner Welles to Earl Browder, general secretary of the communist party, after Browder had attacked the State Department. It was published by Browder in the *Daily Worker*,[56] one of the rare cases when American policy was made public through the columns of that paper.[57] Browder was quoted as having commented within party circles that this agreement between the American communist party and the State Department "was as important as an agreement between nations."[58] This was hardly the State Department's interpretation of it, but it is revealing for an understanding of communist practice.

Gradually, during the years, the communists had become ever more lukewarm about Chiang Kai-shek and had adopted an attitude of passive opposition. In 1943 they switched over to an attitude of very active opposition against the Kuomintang. The united-front times were over.

This change from the defensive to the offensive coincided with a change of soviet strategy in Europe. It had been made possible by the series of German defeats at Stalingrad and in North Africa. The official signal of the change in party line was given by a piece in the soviet trade-union periodical *The War and the Working Class*. On August 12, 1943, this article was reprinted in the *Daily Worker*.[59]

The themes of this propaganda do not need to concern us here. Suffice it to say that henceforth communist propaganda aimed at organizing a people's war. A second propaganda line was that the existence of two Chinas should be recognized and that it should be considered a task of statesmanship to merge these "two Chinas into one." Chiang's China was called "feudal China," and Mao's was described as "democratic China."[60]

---

[56] October 16, 1942.

[57] The amazing story of this transaction is found in *IPR Hearings, op. cit.*, pp. 594–601.

[58] *Ibid.*, p. 600.

[59] *Ibid., Part I*, pp. 128–30; *Part II*, pp. 531–33; for the reactions of the Chinese government on anti-Kuomintang propaganda in the U. S., see *ibid.*, pp. 535–40.

[60] *Ibid., Part I*, pp. 165, 168.

By summer of 1944 the military situation in China had deteriorated due to Japanese military successes on the mainland. Vice-President Henry A. Wallace was sent to China with a view to reviving China's war effort. China's weakness was due largely to shortages in supplies, general exhaustion, and moral fatigue. The United States could do little to alleviate these weaknesses, but pressure was exerted on Chiang to come to an agreement with the communists, the only other potentially "friendly" force on the mainland.

Mr. Wallace referred to the patriotic attitude of the communists in the United States and said that he could not understand the attitude of the Chinese communists as described by President Chiang. President Chiang said that the difference in the attitudes of the American and Chinese communists might be explained by the fact that there was no possibility of the American communists seizing power, whereas the Chinese communists definitely desired to do so in China. He then said that the United States was far removed from the U.S.S.R., but that the U.S.S.R. would not feel safe if the communists were not in power in China. He then laughingly remarked that the Chinese communists were more communistic than the Russian communists.[61]

Nevertheless, Chiang was ready to settle with the communists, provided they would support his government and the war effort, incorporate their military forces into the Chinese nationalist army, and agree that the communist-controlled territories ought to be an integral part of China. In the meantime, Chiang advised the United States to adopt an attitude of coolness toward the communists. He implored the United States to understand the threat "which the communists constituted to the Chinese government" and cease overestimating the "utility of the communists against the Japanese." He complained that "much pressure has been brought to bear by the United States government to have the Chinese government reach a settlement with the communists but the United States government has exerted no pressure upon the communists."[62] The United States did not follow Chiang's advice. On the contrary, it continued working toward a settlement which, in practice, meant that it tried to needle Chiang into substantial concessions in the interests of coalition.

As the nationalists proved adamant, and as the Japanese danger

[61] *U. S. Relations with China, op. cit.,* p. 553.
[62] *Ibid.,* pp. 553–55.

faded, communist propaganda in the United States became more and more intensified. With increasing frankness it spoke of withdrawing American support from Chiang and transferring it to the communists, in emulation of the transfer of western help from Mikhailovitch to Tito.[63] This propaganda reiterated three main contentions: the corruption and inefficiency of the Chiang regime; the assertion that "the only real democracy in China is found in the communist areas"; and the theory (or implied threat) that a policy aiming at suppressing the communists would lead to a conflict between the Soviet Union and the United States.

At the end of the war in Asia the United States had reached the pinnacle of its military power and moral reputation. It was within American capabilities to prevent the emergence of a situation contrary to U.S. interests.

What were American security interests in the Far East? On July 5, 1945, a few days before the cessation of hostilities, the military intelligence division of the army general staff produced an estimate of the situation in China. According to this estimate, the Chinese communist were not a democratic group but were part of an international communist movement "sponsored and guided by Moscow." The estimate warned that the soviets probably planned "to create Russian-dominated areas in Manchuria, Korea and probably North China," but that China could not exist without the natural resources of Manchuria and North China. The report pointed out, quite rightly, that the communists were the "best led and most vigorous of present-day organizations in China," with a high morale, sharply defined policies, and fanatical devotion to their cause.[64]

The report emphasized that there were three alternatives for a settlement of the internal situation in China: (1) civil war between the Kuomintang and the communists; (2) the establishment of a national assembly to inaugurate a democratic and constitutional form of government in which all parties would find representation; and (3) the division of China into two or more parts united in a loose federation presided over by a coalition government of all parties.

According to the report, the first solution, although it would de-

[63] *IPR Hearings, Part I, op. cit.,* pp. 213 f., p. 169.
[64] *Far East Hearings, Part III, op. cit.,* p. 2268.

cide the question of power in China, would prove disastrous and ruinous to the Chinese people.

The second solution, proposed by Chiang, assumed the dissolution of the partisan army, the subordination of the communists to the national government, and a moral and political transformation of the communists. Yet, even then it was reasonable to estimate that the communists would not consent to the disbanding of their armies. Nor would they ever become a conventional political party. Even if they would have done so, the establishment of a national assembly and a constitutional party system in China would have required many years of social and political readjustment. It was, essentially, a parodoxical proposal to solve the communist problem by parliamentary means in a nation which had never known parliamentary government.

The third solution was championed by the communists themselves. According to this blueprint, the decisions of the coalition government would be carried out independently by communist and Kuomintang regional governments. The two parties would continue to maintain their separate armies and administration. The intelligence report stated that

... the plan for a coalition government might be workable if the communists would accept a clear demarcation of Kuomintang and communist areas. But throughout the war the Kuomintang has vainly tried to obtain an agreement with the communists for a demarcation of defense areas, and there is no indication that the communists would accept any demarcation of Kuomintang and communist areas if a coalition government were to be established. In view of this, the coalition government, were it to be established without the communists being committed to a specific demarcation of their areas, would only serve the interests of the communists in that their present areas would obtain legal status by consent of the Kuomintang and other parties, while leaving the Kuomintang part of the country open to further communist infiltration through legal and illegal means.[65]

It was also pointed out that if this communist solution were adopted, North China and Manchuria would probably come under direct or indirect Russian control. In the event that these areas would fall into communist hands, the communists would acquire a position of such power that ultimately they would be able to seize

[65] *Ibid., Part III,* p. 2271.

China in its entirety. The communist solution had the advantage that it was based on a recognition of the *status quo*. It offered possibilities for short-range arrangements, and it might have been practical if it had been less of a coalition government and more of a partition of China. But, in the long run, the communist solution was unacceptable.

Thus, there was but one solution left—civil war—or, to phrase it differently, a war bent on destroying the Chinese communists. While this solution was most unattractive and indeed would have entailed great hardships and sacrifices, it was the only one which could have prevented the ultimate communist seizure of China.[66]

If it is granted that the first mission of the United States in its China problem was the containment of communism in that country, the only remaining alternative for the United States was to strengthen nationalist China to the maximum extent possible, militarily, socially, and economically, and to be ready if necessary to support the nationalists in battle. The course of the Chinese revolution cannot be grasped unless it is understood that no short cut and no easy solution was at hand. There was no alternative for the United States but to accept this last disagreeable and painful alternative or to consent, ultimately, to communist victory.

II. Choices

WHAT was needed to make the nationalists strong?

It has often been asserted that the nationalists could have been upheld only by unlimited help from the United States, the implication being that an incredible amount of military strength would have been required to subdue their opponents. There has been a consistent overrating of the military power of the Chinese communists. Before 1946 the Chinese communists were very poorly equipped. They had no aircraft, tanks, motorized vehicles, or heavy artillery. They made the best of partisan warfare, and, in comparison with other existing Chinese forces, they undoubtedly were

[66] The intelligence report stated: "Cooperation or a united front between the Kuomintang and the Chinese communists has always favored the communists against the nationalists, no matter what political shading the latter represent, whether reactionary or liberal. By contrast, the communist cause in China has suffered whenever the Kuomintang has fought the communists in an all-out civil war." *Ibid.*, p. 2272.

strong. Yet, against a properly trained, well-equipped, and adequately commanded modern military force of even inferior numerical strength, they would have cut a poor figure. Had the morale of the communist armies been as high as enthusiastic observers asserted, it could not have compensated for their material and numerical weakness, logistic handicaps, and poor technical-military training. Militarily speaking, neither the Chinese communists nor a war in China posed problems fundamentally different from any other military operation.[67]

The American command in China wanted to put seven American divisions into Manchuria, the most exposed area, and assign 10,000 American officers and noncommissioned officers to the nationalist army for training and tactical assistance. These American cadres would have been distributed throughout the Chinese army down to the regimental level and, according to contemporary estimates, probably would have transformed the nationalist armies into an effective combat weapon.[68]

It is quite likely that additional American divisions would have been needed for the defense of the rest of China: perhaps three divisions in northern China; two or three divisions in the seaports, and three divisions as general reserve—a maximum of fifteen divisions. This would have been more than adequate to pacify and reorganize China, permit a degree of social and economic recovery, and simultaneously re-train the nationalist army. Expensive, but cheaper than the loss of China.

The communists, on their part, apparently reasoned that the United States could and would protect China. Accordingly, their propaganda concentrated on pointing out that the American communists had a "special responsibility" for the development of Chinese communism, this responsibility being that the American communists should avert civil war and forestall the execution of an "imperialist policy" in China.[69]

The communists used their propaganda facilities to considerable

---

[67] The alleged "invincibility" of guerrilla forces is one of the most powerful pieces of communist propaganda. Poorly equipped, slow, inadequately trained, and stupidly led regular forces cannot overcome efficient and mobile communist guerrillas. Yet a modern force, equipped with mobile weapons, flexible and superior fire power, and adequate tactical air power is capable of defeating and destroying guerrillas.

[68] *Far East Hearings, Part III, op. cit.,* pp. 2415, 2526.

[69] *IPR Hearings, Part I, op. cit.,* p. 126.

advantage. Charged with providing the Chinese communists with strategic protection, the communists directly or indirectly succeeded in influencing some decisions of the American government. At the present time it is impossible to examine fully the policy sabotage practiced against the United States and Chinese governments. Suffice it to give a few examples of specifically communist propaganda.

On June 2, 1945, the national board of the communist political association (the then American counterpart of the Russian Politburo) adopted, among others, the following "slogans of action":

Guarantee a free, democratic Asia with the right of national independence for all colonial and dependent peoples. Curb those who seek American imperialist control in the Far East. Press for a united and free China based upon the unity of the communists and all other democratic and anti-Japanese forces so as to speed victory. Full military aid to the Chinese guerrillas led by the heroic eighth and fourth armies.[70]

To implement these resolutions of the national board, a special front organization, the committee for a democratic far-eastern policy, was established to convince the United States that it should abandon the nationalists and not hamper the development of the communists.[71]

On August 16, 1945, twenty-one "prominent Americans" urged President Truman to prevent any turning over of American equipment to the nationalists and recommended that Japanese troops be ordered to surrender "to patriotic Chinese troops on the spot." The Japanese were to be instructed not to delay surrender until the nationalist forces arrived.[72]

At the same time, strong opposition was voiced against nationalist reoccupation of China and American efforts to help the nationalists retake their country. "For Chiang to attempt to possess these areas," such as key ports and places allegedly liberated by the communists,

[70] *Daily Worker*, New York, June 4, 1945, p. 4. See *IPR Hearings, Part II, op. cit.*, p. 607. For a communist policy directive of 1949, see *Far East Hearings, Part III, op. cit.*, pp. 2266 f. In this directive we read, *inter alia:* "Demand . . . an end to all forms of American intervention in China. . . . The Chinese people are defeating the American reactionaries. So can we. . . . China shows up the weak spot in our reactionaries' program. Let's fight on China policy and take advantage of the blow the Chinese people have dealt the American reactionaries."

[71] *Ibid.,* p. 581.

[72] *IPR Hearings, Part II, op. cit.,* p. 622.

"would mean to oust the liberation armies and declare war upon the people," exclaimed the *Daily Worker*.[73]

The prospects of peace "in the Pacific and in the world" were being endangered, and the American people, especially the labor movement, were invited to "intervene directly, and at this very moment, when the end of the war is at hand." The nationalists were to be prevented from getting "possession of enemy arms,"[74] and Chiang was to be hindered from flying his troops into Shanghai and Nanking.[75]

On November 19, 1945, the *Daily Worker* printed this headline: "Communists launch drive for withdrawal from China." The paper revealed that at a session of the national committee presided over by William Z. Foster, the party had decided on a "crusade for peace" directed against American intervention in China. Five hundred "get-out-of-China" mass meetings were called to promote the slogans: "Stop the reactionary intervention of the U.S.A. in China's internal affairs" and "withdraw American troops from China and the Philippines."

Finally, on December 2, 1945, William Z. Foster stated that the communist "key concentration" was on the China question. And he wrote down this significant sentence: *"The war in China is the key to all problems of the international front and it is here, above all else, where we have to deal the hardest blow to reaction."*[76]

Another example. In 1947 an edition of Chiang Kai-shek's book *China's Destiny and Chinese Economic Theory*,[77] commented upon and footnoted by Philip Jaffe, former editor of *Amerasia*, made its appearance. The gist of Jaffe's comments may be gleaned from this sentence: "Honest students of the Chinese political and social scene recognized that communism is not the issue in China, and that no human power can convert today's backward Chinese economy into the basis for a communist state."[78]

Jaffe then proceeded to quote Mao Tse-tung's ideas on coalition

---

[73] August 15, 1945, p. 2.

[74] *Daily Worker*, August 18, 1945, p. 2.

[75] *IPR Hearings, Part II, op. cit.*, pp. 612–17.

[76] *Daily Worker*, December 2, 1945, quoted from *Communism in China, op. cit.*, p. 5. (Italics added.)

[77] New York, Roy Publishers, 1947.

[78] *Ibid.*, p. 329.

government and distorted them by suppressing their revolutionary meaning. Instead of honestly emphasizing that coalition is a strategy of transition and therefore temporary in nature, he suggested that the Chinese communists actually wanted to introduce capitalism. The impression was created that communism could well be a capitalist blessing for China. Far from constituting a danger to the security of the United States, it would be an excellent thing for American commerce.

Perhaps the clearest picture emerges from a brief analysis of books dealing with China, published between 1945 and 1950.[79] Of forty-one American books sufficiently important to merit published reviews, only five (or 12.2 per cent) took a clear anticommunist stand; ten (or 24.4 per cent) were neutral in varying degrees or did not deal primarily with current political questions; and twenty-six (or 63.4 per cent) were strongly hostile to the nationalists or openly procommunist or both. Of sixty-seven reviews of books on China published in two leading book magazines, forty-seven, or 70 per cent, were written by critics hostile to the Kuomintang or friendly to the communists or both. On the basis of these figures, it can be inferred that the American mind was subjected to a concerted campaign of "reorientation."

Two events, partly stimulated by communist propaganda, played right into communist hands: a change in American personnel dealing with China, and the "tumultuous" demobilization of the American armed forces.

Immediately upon cessation of hostilities State Department personnel conscious of the communist threat and long under propaganda attack resigned in large numbers or were reassigned to other areas of the world. They were replaced by people whom the communists, rightly or wrongly, had praised as liberals. Whatever the attitudes of these new men, few were intensely anticommunist or well informed about communism.[80] Virtually all of them were opposed to Chiang and the nationalists; most of them believed that the Kuomintang was through and that the communists were bound to take over China.

The communist outcry for demobilization, previously discussed,

[79] For the list of these books, see *Far East Hearings, Part V, op. cit.,* p. 3225.

[80] For examples, see *IPR Hearings, Part II, op. cit.,* pp. 617, 633.

was clearly linked to the China issue.[81] This antimilitarist propaganda was assisted by the poorly conceived "point system" of demobilizing soldiers. According to the testimony of former Secretary of Defense Louis Johnson, the point system

. . . reduced an army which had been a splendid organization into an aggregation of individuals looking for the quickest way home. . . . Under that system an air squadron would suddenly find itself without pilots or a tropical base without malaria-control officers, or a tank corps without gunners or a regiment without officers. . . . We now know that this was not the right system and we are paying a diplomatic price for it.[82]

This was also the opinion of General Marshall, who stated that the "confused and tumultous demobilization was very injurious, and . . . the failure to establish a very definite procedure for maintaining our defensive posture was a very serious error."[83]

The demobilization quickly reduced the American capability of maintaining strong military forces in China. Valid though it is, this point should not be overstressed. However tumultuous the demobilization may have been, the United States retained enough forces for the occupation of Germany and Japan. It sent large military missions and enormous amounts of weapons to many countries. When it became necessary to fight a full-fledged war in Korea, it mobilized, within a few short weeks, adequate forces which, incidentally, under the worst tactical conditions held at bay vastly superior numbers of morally stimulated communists.

The point therefore is not that American forces were being demobilized, although premature and excessive demobilization presented a very grave complication. The point is rather this: *The American government did not make a decision to oppose the Chinese communists by military strength.* At no time did the U.S. find it advisable to deploy strong military forces into China. If the estimate had been made and a decision arrived at accordingly—that the

[81] The clamor for demobilization was accompanied by clamor for "hard peace" in Germany and Japan. It is easy to see how the military situation of the United States would have become untenable if it had tried to impose really drastic measures with a completely dismantled armed force. The ultimate objective probably was to get the United States to evacuate Germany and Japan within a short time and to leave behind undying hatred.

[82] *Far East Hearings, Part IV, op. cit.,* p. 2660.

[83] *Ibid., Part I,* p. 627.

United States, in protection of its own interests, should send a given number of divisions into China—the required forces could, and would, have been found.

III. The Fundamental Decision

BY NOVEMBER 1945 it became apparent that the United States had to take some action in regard to its China policy. Even to help Chiang evacuate the Japanese would have resulted "in some collateral aid . . . in favor of the nationalist government vis-à-vis the communists." On the other hand, it was recognized that withdrawal of American troops "may seem substantial frustration of a policy we have long supported which contemplated unifying China and Manchuria under Chinese national forces." The State Department decided that the United States would transport no more nationalist troops into Manchuria and would "not support the national government vis-à-vis the communists except insofar as necessary to get the Japanese disarmed and out of China."[84]

On November 20, 1945, General Wedemeyer recommended that all troops either be withdrawn at once or that Chiang receive stepped-up military and economic support. While the secretaries of war and navy took a more ambiguous stand, they nevertheless recommended the support of Chiang, because the passing of Manchuria and North China to soviet control would "in the long run, probably be at least as grave militarily as any situation likely to arise due to continued U.S. support of the national government."[85]

On November 27 there was a state-war-navy meeting in which Secretary of State James F. Byrnes made the American decision:

The wise course would be to try to force the Chinese government and the Chinese communists to get together on a compromise basis, perhaps telling Generalissimo Chiang Kai-shek that we will stop the aid to his government unless he goes along with this. . . . Mr. Patterson [secretary of war] stated that it is in his opinion clearly in our interests to see China united under Generalissimo Chiang Kai-shek if that is possible.[86]

From this fundamental decision stemmed the directive that the United States would never support the nationalist government in

84 Millis, *op. cit.,* p. 109.
85 *Ibid.,* p. 112.
86 *Ibid.,* p. 123.

"fratricidal warfare."[87] The first objective of American policy in China henceforth was to stop the fighting.[88] The second objective was to settle the Chinese problem by negotiation.[89]

This course was predicated on the assumption, later expressed by Secretary Acheson, that "it was quite impossible to solve the problems in China by military force" and that "there was no available force in China to settle these problems by force."[90] Assertedly, for the United States to put into China "unlimited resources and all the necessary military power to try and defeat the communists, remove the Japanese, and remove the Russians from Manchuria . . . was a task so great and so repugnant to the American people that the government could not undertake it, and it was one which was not in accord with American interests."[91] This was Secretary Acheson's explanation of why the United States elected to give to the national government of China merely "important assistance of all sorts."

There is no evidence available to show that the American government adopted this course of circumscribed action while simultaneously considering practical alternatives to guard against the possibility of failure of this policy.

The adoption of what was, essentially, defeatism as the American government's China policy could not fail to have far-reaching repercussions. The average Chinese was given the impression that so far as the Americans were concerned there was nothing basically wrong with the communists. In any event, the differences between the corrupt nationalists and the reform movement of the communists were not substantial enough to merit a fight to death. The most important thing for China, evidently, was to terminate the war. Communist victory was the only practical way to end the fighting at an early time. Under the circumstances, the nationalist soldier saw no particular reason to sacrifice himself for a cause of doubtful value. It is surprising that he fought as well and as long as he did, but not surprising that the communist soldier fought even better than before. American defeatism was a main condition, and a par-

[87] *Far East Hearings, Part II, op. cit.,* p. 1605.
[88] *Ibid., Part I,* p. 458.
[89] *Ibid., Part III,* p. 1897.
[90] *Ibid.*
[91] *Ibid., Part III,* p. 1842.

tial cause, of the communist conquest of the biggest country in the world.

THE THIRD ACT

FOLLOWING the decision to settle the Chinese problem by political means, General Marshall was appointed the president's special representative to China. His mission was to achieve the unification of China by "peaceful and democratic" methods and to urge the solutions which the United States deemed desirable. Concurrently, he was to bring about the cessation of hostilities, speed the evacuation of the Japanese troops, and see to the withdrawal of American armed forces "as soon as possible." He was authorized to tell Chiang Kai-shek and other Chinese leaders that a disunited China torn by civil strife "could not be considered realistically as the proper place" for American economic, technical, and military assistance.[92]

But what political solution was General Marshall supposed to advocate? According to the instructions from the president, he was to seek unification of China along the lines suggested by Chiang, that is, work toward establishment of a national assembly. Yet, a memorandum sent by Secretary of State Byrnes to the war department stated that while the government of Chiang afforded "the most satisfactory base for a developing democracy, . . . it must be broadened to include the representatives of those large and well-organized groups who are now without any voice in the government of China."[93] This, fundamentally, was the solution propounded by the communists.

That these two instructions were in contradiction does not seem to have been clearly understood or even discussed, and General Marshall proceeded to China with the double mission of bringing about elements of both the Chinese and the communist solution.

Arriving in China at the end of December 1945, General Marshall found that the Chinese government and the communists had concluded an agreement on general principles. During January and February 1946, three other agreements were concluded. General

92 *U. S. Relations with China, op. cit.,* p. 606.
93 *Ibid.*

Marshall participated in the drafting of one of these, stipulating the conditions of a military truce. The second agreement under negotiation envisaged the setting up of an interim state council. The council was to comprise forty members, twenty of whom were to belong to Kuomintang and twenty divided among the communist and various other smaller parties and nonpolitical organizations. Chiang, as president of China, was to appoint all forty members. This state council was a compromise between the previously proposed national assembly and a coalition government, and it was to function both as a provisional government and as a constituent assembly until a constitution was drafted.

While the practicality of such a scheme was dubious, negotiations broke down on a dispute about the number of communist representatives. It had been agreed that one-third of the council members could veto decisions made by simple majority. Hence, the communists demanded fourteen seats, while the nationalists, knowing well the use the communists would make of their veto power, were willing to accord them only thirteen seats. This type of discussion proved highly frustrating to Americans on the scene, who did not always grasp the implications of what appeared to them to be chicanery by both sides.

The third agreement was to provide for the amalgamation of the military forces of the nationalists and communists. Both sides were to reduce and combine their military strength. The Chinese army was to consist of sixty divisions, including fifty nationalist and ten communist divisions. It was agreed that fifteen of these divisions should be stationed in Manchuria, of which only one was to be communist.

The United States was willing to help in the amalgamation of the Chinese forces. According to General Marshall, the communists were set up in a rather informal way and could not be amalgamated with the nationalists without being first organized. Moreover, they could not co-operate in the planned *quid pro quo* demobilization of the Chinese forces because "they had no organized units of that character as the basis of such a procedure."[94]

Hence, to amalgamate and demobilize the Chinese armies, there first had to be created a proper communist army, but in order to do so, American personnel and equipment were necessary. Legal au-

[94] *Far East Hearings, Part I, op. cit.,* p. 603.

thority had to be procured from Congress. As is well known, Congress is sometimes hard of hearing, and regarded the argument in favor of this arrangement as specious. General Marshall returned to China in April 1946 to find that the agreements between the nationalists and the communists had been violated by both sides, that negotiations had all but broken down, and that fighting had been resumed on a fairly large scale.[95]

In retrospect, the question arises why the communists ever consented to some of these agreements which, if taken at face value, would have given considerable advantage to Chiang. In the first place, the communists used these negotiations to gain time and drive a wedge between the United States and the Kuomintang. Furthermore, the second agreement would have given them political advantages which they did not enjoy before. Only the third agreement might have hurt them—if analyzed superficially. Actually, it was predicated on previous American military assistance. Once the U.S. had brought the communist army into shape, the agreement might have lapsed. Moreover, no parallel American military assistance was contemplated for the nationalists. Hence, this agreement, too, in the end would have increased the relative power of the communists. As soon as the communists realized that American help was not forthcoming and that the United States was not willing to back up the Kuomintang, they reversed their policy, abandoned their attempts to reach Trojan horse agreements, and adopted a strategy of direct approach.

With the purpose of stopping fraticidal war, General Marshall repeatedly put pressure on Chiang to conclude truces and armistices. In many instances the communists succeeded in exploiting these armistices to their advantage, either by extricating themselves from an unfavorable military position or by seizing important territorial objectives, especially in Manchuria.[96] In the course of these truces the communists gained control of some key passes in North China and were able to obtain weapons from Manchuria and increase their territorial holdings from an estimated sixty to three hundred coun-

[95] *Ibid.*, p. 637.

[96] *Ibid., Part III,* pp. 2230 f., 2460; see also, Freda Utley, *The China Story* (Chicago, Regnery, 1951), pp. 11–13, and the Preface to General Claire L. Chennault, *Way of a Fighter* (New York, Putnam, 1949).

ties.[97] By contrast to this substantial strengthening of the communists, military victory slipped from nationalist hands in various instances. The moral and material effects of such interference can be imagined easily, although it is true that at the time under discussion the nationalists greatly reduced communist holdings in central and southern China.

Despite the fact that the nationalists permitted themselves several times to be persuaded to discontinue military operations, they did not do so in every instance. General Marshall concluded that "quite evidently" there was an attempt by Chiang Kai-shek "to defeat the communist effort by military action."[98] Hence, he ordered an embargo on military equipment from the United States to the nationalists. This embargo, in which Britain and most arms-producing countries participated, was enforced from early August 1946 to the end of May 1947, but, with the exception of one ammunition shipment and a transfer of equipment from the U.S. marines, no military supplies were sent to China until the beginning of 1948.[99]

Pressure on Chiang was thus extremely severe. It was avowedly exerted to bring about a coalition government and to achieve the entry of communists into the government of China.[100] Halfway through the embargo, in November 1946, Chiang declared himself ready to accept communists into his cabinet. The communists now refused to participate in a coalition. Yet the embargo was not lifted.

While the general situation of Chiang went from bad to worse, his specifically military problems continued to plague him very severely. American pressure and economic difficulties had forced him to demobilize part of his army. By 1947 the nationalist army had been reduced by about one million men. Demobilized soldiers were not easily absorbed into the economy, and they became either elements of social unrest or joined the communists. As Chiang's force grew weaker, the communists increased their military numbers.[101] At the same time, the U.S. marines who had been guarding

[97] *Communism in China, op. cit.,* p. 40. This figure was given by the communist General Chu Teh.

[98] *Far East Hearings, Part I, op. cit.,* p. 699.

[99] *Ibid., Part III,* pp. 1929, 1949.

[100] See the State Department letter of October 2, 1946, *ibid., Part I,* p. 553.

[101] *Ibid., Part III,* p. 1852.

vital communication lines no longer provided effective military support.

By January 1947, General Marshall reached the conclusion that his mission could not be successful. As he explained it in a public statement, both the nationalists and the communists had been responsible for his failure. Yet, while he was calling for a "plague on both houses," he was more severe with the Kuomintang than with the communists. In the Kuomintang, he stated:

There is a dominant group of reactionaries who have been opposed, in my opinion, to almost every effort I have made to influence the formation of a genuine coalition government. . . . They were quite frank in publicly stating their belief that cooperation by the Chinese communist party in the government was inconceivable and that only a policy of force could definitely settle the issue. . . . Between this dominant reactionary group in the government and the irreconcilable communists . . . lies the problem of how peace and well-being are to be brought to the long-suffering and presently inarticulate mass of the people of China. The reactionaries in the government have evidently counted on substantial American support regardless of their actions. The communists by their unwillingness to compromise in the national interest are evidently counting on an economic collapse to bring about the fall of the government, accelerated by extensive guerrilla action against the long lines of rail communications—regardless of the cost in suffering to the Chinese people.[102]

What was the solution? General Marshall saw only the possibility of assumption of leadership by the liberals in the government and minority parties. He did not mention the possibility that a few trustworthy and effective soldiers might have taken over the job, although he himself stressed that these liberals as yet were lacking "the political power to exercise a controlling influence." Nevertheless, General Marshall professed to believe that "successful action on their part under the leadership of Generalissimo Chiang Kai-shek would . . . lead to unity through good government."[103]

Actually, General Marshall did not know how to solve the problem. As he stated later: "When I came back I was hard put to find a long-view conclusion in the matter because of the failing structure of the Kuomintang and the determination, organization and discipline of the communist group and their undoubted advice and

102 U. S. Relations with China, op. cit., pp. 687 f.
103 Ibid., p. 688.

possible support that would occur later from the soviet government."[104] He did not want the communists to take over nor did he want the Kuomintang to remain. Yet, there was no third force available.

Marshall did not think that the Kuomintang could be maintained without massive American intervention. Yet, he was opposed even to small-scale military help in the form of weapons assistance and military advisers.[105] He was already in the state of mind which Secretary of State Acheson reached in 1950 when the latter explained that an American policy in China could not be formulated "until the dust settles," a phrase which he used to describe his "own inability to see very far in this situation."[106]

Despite all the pessimism and defeatism, the American government apparently was not convinced that the Chiang government would collapse. On March 20, 1947, Mr. Acheson, then undersecretary of state, explained the difference between the situations in China and Greece. "The Chinese government is not in the position at the present time that the Greek government is in. It is not approaching collapse. It is not threatened by defeat by the communists. The war with the communists is going on much as it has for the last 20 years."[107]

THE FOURTH ACT

DURING the summer of 1947, General Wedemeyer was sent to China to analyze the situation and to formulate recommendations for action. While in China, he made a speech to the state council and ministers of the national government giving them his estimate.

According to Wedemeyer, the growing weakness of the government was due to various military and economic factors, but above all it was a function of its own administrative inefficiency. General Wedemeyer pointed out that the communist threat could have been overcome if the government had not merely occupied the areas evacuated by the Japanese but had also appointed efficient and

[104] *Far East Hearings, Part I, op. cit.,* p. 397.
[105] *Ibid., Part III,* p. 1854; Millis, *op. cit.,* pp. 285–87, 373.
[106] *Far East Hearings, Part III, op. cit.,* p. 1766.
[107] *Ibid., Part IV,* p. 2811.

honest officials and had established conditions of economic and political stability. General Wedemeyer's criticism was to a considerable degree valid, and no analysis of the Chinese revolution would be complete which did not take it into account.

The army was in bad shape. The officers showed little interest in the welfare of their men, and the relationship between the two groups was poor. The soldiers had little sense of mission and had never been told what they were fighting for. Promotion was not by merit; there were too many overaged generals with little military education.

Conscription was applied in an arbitrary fashion: Rich men's sons and city dwellers were passed over, while poor peasants were drafted. The relationship between the military and civilians was deplorable because the soldiers indulged in a great deal of looting and unnecessary violence.

Economically, taxation was heavy and unjustly distributed, while the use made of available national resources was completely inadequate. Administrative organization and functioning was reduced to a low level by corruption, ill-defined and overlapping responsibilities, competing agencies, and badly trained personnel. Last, but not least, the secret police was operating widely and through arbitrary action, was undermining popular confidence in the government.[108]

These shortcomings existed. But the real question was: How was the Kuomintang to overcome them? There is no doubt that the Chinese government, fully cognizant of all these problems, neither pulled its full weight nor took the steps necessary to improve its own efficiency. Yet, its capabilities to cure its own diseases actually were quite limited. It is easier to talk about reforms than to lift up a gigantic, tradition-minded, and war-weary country by its bootstraps.

The remaining strength of the government was gradually eaten away by the monetary inflation which Chiang's government proved completely unable to control. Various efforts were made to prop up the Chinese currency, and American support was not entirely lacking. Yet, how can a government which is not in possession of an up-to-date financial and administrative machine ever control inflation effectively? How can a government which has to spend more than its revenue on the army, and which cannot reduce this army

108 *Ibid., Part V,* pp. 3238–41.

substantially, stop inflation? The Chinese tried, but corruption cut down the efficiency of their halting measures, and the dwindling confidence of the Chinese people continually undercut the value of the money. Actually, there was no way of controlling inflation except by ending the war or by having the United States pay the military expenses of China.

The middle strata of Chinese society, the only group from which Chiang could draw support for any liberal reform policy, was hit hardest by the inflation. Their disaffection and political impotence drove Chiang into the arms of the conservative and reactionary wings of the Kuomintang, which remained strenuously opposed to reform.

The communists exploited Chiang's deterioration to the hilt. They specialized in propaganda designed to accelerate the inflation. They also concentrated on the character assassination of individuals whose coming to power they wanted to prevent. This communist propaganda was often picked up by American newspapers and then repeated as well-informed American opinion.[109] At the same time, of course, there was a great deal of anti-American propaganda designed to exploit the feelings of xenophobia and war fatigue.

Most important, however, was the propaganda directed to the nationalist soldiers. Privates had a monthly allotment of $1.00, corporals $2.00, and sergeants $3.00. Officers' salaries ranged from $4.00 for the lieutenant to $9.00 for the colonel. General officers received $20.00 and commanding generals $30.00. However, even these token salaries were paid only rarely. Nor were the soldiers properly fed, clothed, or looked after when wounded or sick. Care for dependents barely existed.[110]

Under the circumstances, communist propagandists found it relatively easy to disaffect nationalist soldiers. According to General Wedemeyer, the troops became dispirited and were no longer anxious to fight.[111] Ever more often they withdrew without orders and permitted the communists to capture ammunition and equipment.[112] As this equipment was lost, and as the nationalists became less able to replenish their armaments, their military position weak-

[109] *Ibid., Part IV*, pp. 2792 f.
[110] *Ibid.*, pp. 2968, 3023.
[111] *Ibid., Part III*, p. 2318.
[112] *Ibid., Part IV*, pp. 2986, 3039.

ened at an even faster rate than the military capabilities of the communists increased. Revolutionary antimilitarism demonstrated the full measure of its effectiveness.

C'est par la tête que le poisson pourrit. Nowhere did this proverb apply more forcefully than to the nationalist army. Chinese military leaders occasionally were honest, brave, and semiefficient. But more often than not they were cronies of political leaders, party wheel horses, old-fashioned war lords, and men for whom sham war was a business proposition. Their actions were dictated by personal rivalries and ambitions, economic considerations, traditions of surrendering back and forth, misconceptions about the communists, and lack of the will to resist. There were so many men of this type in key positions, and they were removed so rarely, that the good officers were unable to exert real influence on events. The reader will remember the situation in the Russian army command of 1917. Conditions in the Chinese army were infinitely worse. There were a few reliable generals, to be sure, but the majority of the Chinese military leaders were officers of the Cheremisov type, or worse.

The business-as-usual attitude was not restricted to the Chinese generals. It also embraced the Chinese upper classes and the foreign business community. The westerners should have known better, but the fact is that they greatly underrated the danger, assuming that the communists would not have the administrative talent and trained personnel necessary to rule China. The communists, of course, did not beat the drum for communism but simply promised much-needed reforms. Hence, parts of the Chinese elite and middle strata anticipated that a communist victory would not amount to much more than an overdue change in government. The parallel to the 1917 events in Russia is again striking: In both countries the victims doubted that the executioner could, or would, swing the axe; in both countries the executioner posed as the doctor.

Still, the communists played the game cautiously. During the no-war-no-peace period (1946–48), they contented themselves with seizing key areas, augmenting their arms and equipment, and training and indoctrinating their forces. Limited offensive operations were combined with their customary "sociological warfare." As they advanced, they redistributed farm land so that the poor peasants came to anticipate, with something approaching pleasure, the arrival of the communist army. Quite consistently, the communists paid for requisitioned food, while the nationalists despoiled the population ruthlessly. But the communists were not averse to utilizing terror, too, and frequently exterminated the inhabitants of entire villages on the pretext of collaboration with the nationalists. Since the peasants did not rate the staying power of the nationalist forces very highly, they tended to collaborate with the communists and to sabotage the nationalists. Even the middle-class peasants were subjected to communist appeals: Mao promised that he would protect them against "exaggerated land reform."

"Railroad warfare," however, proved the most devastating form of attack. The communists believed that railroads were the key to the control of China and concentrated on cutting rail communications. The disruption of transportation accentuated China's economic plight. The railroad war ruined the tenuous logistics of the nationalists in North China and Manchuria and forced them to disperse their units in order to guard the rail lines defensively. In the course of this phase of the war, the communists time and again encircled outnumbered nationalist detachments, talked them into surrender, and recruited them into their own units.[113]

The vain attempts to counter this type of warfare made the Chinese command increasingly defensive-minded. It exhausted the nationalist troops who were trying vainly, with inadequate transport, to catch flying communist units.[114] It was a vicious circle which drained the nationalists of men and weapons, and, as time went on, the nationalist forces became increasingly immobile. The Chinese government officially summed up the situation as follows:

The armed opposition of the communists was the greatest single destructive force against all the effort of the government in carrying out rehabilitation and in restoring law and order, particularly in areas formerly held by the Japanese. When every possible effort was being made, for instance, to restore the main communication lines, mobile communist squads were actively engaged in demolition work disrupting newly repaired railways, cutting telegraph and telephone lines, and causing havoc in the countryside. . . . The communist issue remained unsettled, the

[113] The communists were masters in a series of tactical tricks which the very conventionally led nationalist armies found extremely difficult to oppose. These tricks include "sparrow tactics," "jointed worm tactics," "tunnel tactics," attacks on the "tail," "rice patrol," and psychological warfare with gongs, bugles, and pyrotechnics. See Rigg, *op. cit.*, pp. 213 ff.

[114] *Far East Hearings, Part IV*, *op. cit.*, p. 2812.

plans for army reorganization could not materialize owing to communist obstruction thus hampering the reduction of the armed forces. As a result, a policy of retrenchment in national budget could not be put into effect, and inflation developed to such an extent as to threaten every fabric of our political and economic life. It lead to the lowering of the efficiency of the government administration and the undermining of the morale of the army. The bulk of the civil servants were not paid enough to meet anew the requirement of a bare subsistence.[115]

Nationalist China was thus weakened from within and from without. It had been abandoned by its erstwhile friends. And when these friends came to their senses, it was too late. The cancer had progressed too far.

AMERICAN POLICY OF NONASSISTANCE

ON JUNE 4, 1951, an interesting exchange occurred between Senator Bourke B. Hickenlooper, of Iowa, and Secretary of State Dean Acheson. If the Chinese nationalists, Senator Hickenlooper asked,

... were on a diminishing supply of ammunition and equipment, which was being used up all the time and they could not replenish it, and their opponents, the communists, were on an increasing supply of ammunition and equipment, which they could replenish, and did apparently replenish, is it going beyond reason to say that the Chinese nationalists under those circumstances would eventually have to succumb?

Secretary Acheson answered: "Well, if those two facts were true, it would tend in the direction you say."[116] He added that he knew nothing to show that these facts were true.

We have seen that between August 1946 and January 1948 the nationalists received but two small consignments of military equipment from the United States. Acheson stated that 1948 was the last chance to make effective help available to the nationalists. Any later assistance would have been pointless: After mid-1949 the communists were in possession of the Chinese mainland.

In 1948, Congress enacted the China aid act, approved on April

[115] *U. S. Relations with China, op. cit.,* p. 818 f.
[116] *Far East Hearings, Part III, op. cit.,* p. 1888.

3, which included an allocation of $125,000,000 for military assistance to China.[117] During 1948, $60,700,000 were shipped under this program, and during 1949 an additional $55,000,000 were made available, or a total of $115,700,000 of military equipment under this grant.[118]

Thus, the military help which the nationalists received between the summer of 1946 and their expulsion from the mainland was $115,700,000 (to which, perhaps, may be added minor amounts of abandoned matériel and military purchases in various countries). The bulk of this help came *after* the military situation of the nationalists had degenerated almost to the point of no return, *after mid-1948*. True, the United States may have helped in a few earlier instances and, on nationalist testimony, did so in two cases; true, there was indirect and invisible help. But the conclusion that U.S. military assistance was not only very small, but also very late, is still valid.

Total military help to China after VJ-day has been calculated officially at $781,000,000, of which $335,000,000 went for overhead in the form of transportation, services, and other expenses. There must also be deducted $102,000,000 for allotments of surplus property which was "not suitable for civil war"[119]—making a total of $344,000,000 to represent delivered military assistance to China during the period 1945–49. Since $115,700,000 were appropriated after April 1948, when the time for arms subsidies probably had passed, aid delivered during the period the Kuomintang was in a position to use it effectively is seen to be in the neighborhood of $228,000,000. The Chinese themselves put this net figure at only $110,000,000 of effective military assistance.[120] Whatever figure is chosen as the most valid, American military aid—in terms of the problem—must be considered almost negligible. China after 1946 appears to have received only one-third of the military equipment that went to Greece—a small country with an army of less than 200,000 men.[121]

No army can fight effectively if it does not receive the matériel it needs. Most of all, the nationalists needed small ammunition. Of

[117] *Ibid.*, p. 1869.
[118] *Ibid.*, p. 1929.
[119] Figures from *U. S. Relations with China, op. cit.*, p. 969 f.
[120] Utley, *op. cit.*, p. 34.
[121] *Far East Hearings, Part III, op. cit.*, p. 2253.

this precious commodity they got very little. It was almost easier for them to get warships and transport planes than cartridges. There is ample evidence that the nationalist troops had virtually no ammunition for training purposes and, time and again, were sent into battle with just a few rounds of ammunition, barely any signal equipment, and at best a few run-down trucks. Many battles were lost because the nationalists ran out of ammunition.[122]

These shortages, which occurred unevenly and in sensitive supply items, compounded logistic problems. For example, according to General Wedemeyer there were 16,500 non-serviceable trucks in nationalist hands. The cost of providing spare parts for these vehicles might not have exceeded $10,000,000, yet this small investment greatly would have increased Chinese military mobility. Large numbers of troops required to guard the railroads would have been freed for combat. Even more important, it would have worked to reduce the communist capability of railroad warfare.

The *White Paper* lists numerous instances where equipment was given to the Chinese only in a demilitarized status. This was in line with the policy that the United States would not support fraticidal war. For whatever reasons these supplies were given, demilitarized weapons can hardly be considered military assistance. The delivery of non-operable equipment was continued right through the last days of the nationalist regime. For example, between January 1948 and March 1949, fifty-three P-51's and forty-two P-47D's were delivered, but not one of these planes was usable.[123] Obviously, the Chinese did not have the facilities to make these planes combat ready. In other cases automatic rifles were delivered without magazines.[124]

The Greek aid program, which provides a useful comparison, was carried out in accordance with a specific military plan. Implemented through specially established channels, the program was supervised by military advisers, training groups, and supply experts. Such adherence to the basic rules of effective military support is not found in the Chinese example. The United States "did not support plans

[122] For some of the data, consult *ibid., Part III,* pp. 2025, 2557; *Part V,* pp. 2746, 2762, 2812.

[123] *U. S. Relations with China, op. cit.,* pp. 945 f. There also were delivered during the same period seventy P-47's in "combat operational condition."

[124] *Far East Hearings, Part III, op. cit.,* p. 2054.

as to timing or as to quantity or as to objective."[125] In fact *there never was a broad strategic plan to solve the Chinese problem and stop the Chinese communists*.[126] It was mostly improvisation and, more often than not, despairing helplessness.

The Chinese, like the Greeks, lacked the technicians and the administrative apparatus to handle the supplies. Nor could they, by themselves, make proper use of the weapons given to them. Therefore, the equipment transferred without proper American supervision, administration, training, and staff assistance was for all practical purposes wasted. Instead of unloading the material in Chinese ports, American skippers might almost as well have dumped it into the sea. American failure to give staff and logistics assistance to the nationalists perhaps constituted the most serious deficiency of American operations in China.

Nevertheless, in quite a few battles the nationalists were defeated despite a fairly adequate supply of matériel and ammunition. Frequently their morale was sagging, and their fighting spirit was lost. Partly due to the lack of support from the United States, this faltering morale must in large measure be ascribed to the decadence of the Kuomintang.

American disinclination to help the nationalists in a truly effective manner was evidenced by the fact that personalities who believed in the nationalist cause were kept away from China. For example, General Wedemeyer was appointed ambassador to China, but, upon communist objections, the appointment was withdrawn.[127] Former Secretary of Defense Louis Johnson testified that the State Department, according to his impression, "really wanted to have nothing to do with the nationalist government" and that it was not their policy always to regard the national government as the government of China.[128]

One of the most interesting stories in this respect was the presentation to Congress of a telegram received from a chamber of commerce in a Chinese city advising the United States government to withhold help from the nationalists. This telegram played a signifi-

---

[125] *Far East Hearings, Part IV, Testimony of Admiral Oscar C. Badger, op. cit.*, p. 2748.

[126] *Ibid.*, p. 2759.

[127] *Ibid., Part III*, p. 2311.

[128] *Ibid., Part IV*, pp. 2579, 2593.

cant part in discouraging Congress from giving further aid to the Kuomintang, and yet it turned out that the telegram had been sent from a city in communist hands.[129] There was no evidence that it reflected the true judgment of the Americans living in that city.

Even the economic help given China was not so large as is commonly assumed. According to official figures, $800,000,000 were given for economic assistance plus $474,000,000 in UNRRA supplies. If we postulate that only $74,000,000 of this sum were turned over to communist hands, $1,200,000,000 were given to the nationalist areas populated by about 350,000,000 Chinese. Prorated over four years, this help amounted to less than 2c per head, per week. And yet China was the country which had fought longest and which needed economic help most.

It is true that the cost of helping China properly would have been large. Yet many things could have been done cheaply. For example, military equipment captured in Germany, Italy, and Japan could have been given to China. The transfer of German arms was initiated, but later, for unexplained reasons, called off. American equipment which was dumped in the ocean, destroyed, and left rotting, might also have been sent in U. S. liberty ships which then were being laid up in American rivers. Not only was this not done, but the help which was given to China was doled out slowly, grudgingly, in piecemeal fashion, and very often fell into the wrong categories. There were only a few shining exceptions, such as the work done by ECA.

All over the world, surplus equipment was sold for a few pennies on the dollar. In many instances surplus equipment was not sold to the Chinese or was sold at considerably higher prices than materials transferred to Greece and Turkey. Much of the surplus equipment already in China was sold only after it had been demilitarized.

By contrast, the soviets did support the Chinese communists. Whether or not they delivered Russian weapons is a matter of conjecture and, in any event, not significant because non-Russian types of equipment including American lend-lease were available in abundance. The soviets made Manchuria and many of its arsenals and factories available to the communists, furnished them technical assistance and training, and, perhaps most important, gave moral sup-

[129] *Ibid., Part V*, p. 3599 and the references given there.

port and guidance.[130] Chinese and Koreans who had served with the Red army transferred in fairly large numbers to the Chinese communists.

The average Chinese believed that, for all practical purposes, the United States had abandoned the nationalist government. He also believed that the soviets were helping the Chinese communists. He could not fail to perceive that the communists enjoyed international support while the nationalists were completely isolated. The conclusion for him must have been obvious.

It cannot be asserted that China would have been saved if the United States had given adequate material and moral help and military staff support. It is not unreasonable to argue that the United States would have strained its resources to the utmost if, in addition to its help to Europe, it also would have extended full assistance to China. No one can deny that the Kuomintang had become a disastrous failure. The fact remains, however, that the military, economic, and moral help given by the United States to the nationalists was insufficient to stop the communists.

THE FIFTH ACT

EARLY in 1948 the Chinese government made one last effort to stop inflation, but the attempt failed rapidly and catastrophically. Deeply discouraged, the nation as a whole withdrew even residual support from the Kuomintang. When the final collapse in nationalist morale became obvious, the communists decided to launch offensive revolutionary warfare.[131]

[130] For some details, see Utley, *op. cit.*, pp. 50 ff., and *China Presents Her Case to the United Nations, op. cit., passim.*

[131] On communist methods to avoid inflation within their territory, see Rigg, *op. cit.*, p. 267: "The Reds caught the backwash of inflation, but they guarded their soldiers from its impact. Noticing that even their currency trailed, to some extent, the spiraling of deflated nationalist dollars, the reds were clever enough not to pay their troops in cash that might show a visible depreciation. Red army units bought the food and small luxuries and issued them to the troops. There were usually sufficient supplies to give the communist soldiers a feeling of consistent support. They did not know that their units' funds were often inadequate, that even in red territory certain prices doubled—they simply saw consistency of food, under most conditions (except

At the beginning of this last campaign, the nationalist army had an estimated strength of 2,700,000. While communist strength is not accurately known, according to the best evidence it was between 1,200,000 and 1,600,000 soldiers. Thus, the nationalists outnumbered the communists in a ratio of about 2:1, yet this conventional comparison of over-all strength proved to be a meaningless piece of intelligence.[132]

About 300,000 of the best-equipped nationalist forces were stationed in Manchuria, principally around Mukden and in three other isolated areas. Approximately 150,000 moderately well-equipped soldiers stood in North China around Peiping, and another 200,000 nationalist troops may have been scattered over the northern theater of operations. The poorly equipped bulk of the nationalist army, over 2,000,000 men, was located in central and southern China, far removed from the decisive battlefields.

By contrast, the communists had concentrated most of their strength in the decisive northern theater. Communist guerrilla pockets existed throughout the whole of China, but at least 1,000,000 communist troops were brought to bear against 500,000 nationalists in the key areas of Mukden and Peiping. This 2:1 numerical superiority of the communists at the decisive front was enhanced by their better training, indoctrination, and morale and by more plentiful arms and supplies.

The best elements of the nationalist army, including seven of the thirteen remaining American-trained divisions,[133] were stationed around Mukden, where they were supplied by air lift and from local resources. These nationalist forces entertained poor relations with

---

certain days of combat), and they gained the impression that their leaders had a firm hold on the situation. The communist key lay in not letting the soldiers fumble with currency 'lettuce.' As the reds learned from reading Lawrence's *Seven Pillars of Wisdom,* soldiers' money is meant for frivolous items if the troops are at all well cared for."

[132] For strength figures see *Far East Hearings, Part III, op. cit.,* p. 1855.

[133] Colonel Rigg wrote, *op. cit.,* p. 303: "Before the US China theater closed up, it made a careful evaluation of the weakness of the sprawling nationalist army. Lieutenant General Albert C. Wedemeyer and his staff visualized an eventual 60 Chinese nationalist divisions organized along US lines. (By the end of 1945, nationalist China had about 252 divisions of varying strengths, with an army of 3,800,000.) However, this US army vision was a distant one and the 'Alpha' program was aimed at 39 divisions, of which only 12 were realized before the exodus of the nationalists from the mainland."

the local Manchurian population. Southern Chinese in origin, they spoke another language and, in general, behaved as foreign conquerors rather than as friends and liberators.

Perceiving that the Manchurian position was untenable, General David G. Barr, chief of the American advisory commission in Nanking, advised Chiang in March 1948 to withdraw his forces from Manchuria and to redeploy them for the defense of North China. This was sound advice, but Chiang refused to accept it.[134]

The American military advisers therefore investigated what could be done with the armies which, under the command of General Fu Tso-yi, were holding the Peiping area. They found that General Fu had a total of eleven armies (divisions); of these, four were well equipped, three were poorly supplied, and four armies had no equipment at all. General Fu's troops averaged three to five cartridges per man (July 1948). His four unequipped armies had to be kept in reserve; whenever reserve forces were sent to the front they received the weapons and equipment of the units they were relieving. Fu's armies were able to do little more than keep the communists out of their area. Amazingly enough, these forces were still in good spirits. General Fu stated that if he "could obtain equipment for the 4 additional trained armies he then would be able to set up an offensive to the north-east," stabilize the supply lines into Manchuria, and prepare for the relief of Mukden.

The American officers under the leadership of Admiral Oscar C. Badger estimated that General Fu needed supplies costing about $16,000,000. This was not a great sum of money, and the requirement was presented after the enactment of the China aid act; hence, the supplies could be made available. The American officers believed that General Fu had better than a 50-50 chance of success.[135] In contrast to Manchuria, General Fu's armies were not unpopular with the local population. The Kuomintang administration of North China was more honest and efficient than that of other nationalist-held territories. "The situation there was as strong all around as any situation that we have seen in China for three or four years."[136] A victory in the strategic North might have changed the entire situation. Fu's victory might have qualified him as the long-sought and

[134] *Far East Hearings, Part IV, op. cit.*, p. 2961.
[135] *Ibid.*, p. 2763.
[136] *Ibid., Testimony of Admiral Badger*, p. 2776.

never-found successor to Chiang. Hence the American officers recommended that the requested help be given forthwith.

Within three or four days this recommendation was approved by the joint chiefs of staff. Chiang also decided to support General Fu with Chinese supplies to the maximum extent possible.[137] Thus, the Peiping area was selected as the critical spot for the defense against the communist offensive. Although General Fu's army was not strong enough and had an inadequately protected rear, this decision was sound, geographically and militarily. It was the best solution that could be adopted under the circumstances. The decision was accepted by all the American agencies in China.

In view of the urgency of the situation, it was expected that American supplies would arrive within a few weeks. However, nothing happened for almost five months. On November 30, the first supply ship entered Tientsin. It carried about 10 per cent of the equipment requested, but most of this cargo was deficient, lacking in parts and spares. Many machine guns, for example, were unusable for lack of mounts, loading machinery, magazines, and clips.[138] Some of these deficiencies were made good within a short time from Japan,[139] but it was too late: The morale of General Fu and of his command had received a terrific blow from which it did not recover. They felt betrayed. Insofar as they were concerned, they no longer saw any point in risking their lives in futile gestures of unappreciated heroism.

A few weeks before these events the communists had launched their offensive and had won two decisive victories, at Tsinan (September 25) and in Manchuria (fall of Changchun and Mukden, end of October).

Tsinan, the provincial capital of Shantung, is an important rail junction connecting North China with Manchuria. By selecting Tsinan as their first strategic objective in North China, the communists aimed at severing permanently the communications between the Manchurian and Peiping armies. The Tsinan forces were attacked by superior communist strength. In the midst of the battle the best nationalist troops, under the trusted General Wu Hua-wen, deserted to the enemy: The Reds had captured General Wu's family and solicitously transmitted to him their letters, the contents of which can be left to the reader's imagination.

---

137 *Ibid.*, p. 2746.
138 *Ibid.*, p. 2747.
139 *Ibid.*, p. 2964.

The fall of Mukden came after seven unsuccessful communist attacks. The American-trained divisions gave an excellent account of themselves, but were defeated when a strong nationalist unit turned traitor and attacked them on the battlefield. Only a small part of the garrison was able to escape, but a very few were able to make their way back to the nationalist lines. It was complete annihilation.

Shortly after General Fu's unfortunate experience, the communists attacked Hsuchow (December 4), the key junction linking China's most important North-South and East-West rail lines. This battle was won by the communists through superior combat tactics.[140] The nationalists lost very heavily. With the subsequent loss of Kalgan (December 26), the main communication centers of North China were in communist hands.

After these battles General Fu's army was greatly outnumbered. The communists now controlled 1,000,000 square miles of territory inhabited by 200,000,000 people. There was not much choice but to withdraw the remnants of Fu's forces in the hope that they might still be used in battles farther to the South. But Chiang instructed Fu to defend Peiping to the last.[141]

Fu made up his mind that further resistance was hopeless and pointless. Taking his divisions on a cross-country march, he left them in the towns from which the men had been recruited, thus demobilizing his forces and protecting the lives of his men. Tientsin fell on January 15. On January 22, 1949, Fu surrendered Peiping. It is believed that, totally disgusted, he ultimately joined communist service. Thus ended the career of a man who could have been one of China's most effective leaders.

By that time the total strength of the nationalists had fallen to a point well below that of the communist armies. Barely any first-class troops were left. The communists had reached clear-cut superiority in all aspects of military power. Each victory was making them stronger.

---

[140] The Chinese communists had developed three tactical devices. The "fast end run," a rapid and unexpected movement on the battlefield to achieve surprise and attack from a flanking position against the enemy's weak spots; the "short attack," a Chinese modification through full use of terrain, darkness, mobility, and surprise, of the old principle of "git there firstest with the mostest"; and the "human sea," the swamping of the enemy by vastly superior numbers, attacking from all sides and, if necessary, in several waves, in total disregard of losses.

[141] *Far East Hearings, Part IV, op. cit.,* p. 3042.

The much-publicized crossing of the Yangtze (April 20, 1940), for all practical purposes, terminated the war on the mainland. The nationalists hoped that the communists would be unable to cross the gigantic river. But these hopes for an Asiatic miracle on the Marne were shattered when the Eighty-eighth nationalist army defected and the garrison in a key fortress mutinied. Once the communists were across the Yangtze, entire nationalist armies went over to the Reds, complete with equipment.

The military decision had fallen. Mopping-up operations were directed against Shanghai, Tsingtao, Canton, and Chungking, which fell on May 25, June 2, October 15, and November 30, respectively. During December, the nationalists abandoned the mainland and went to Formosa.

The communist conquest of China was made possible by four factors: the effectiveness of communist strategy, antimilitarist techniques, and combat tactics; the ineffectiveness, demoralization, and military ineptness of the nationalists, accentuated by communist infiltration; the foreign assistance given to the communists; and the lack of adequate assistance from abroad to the nationalists.

According to Mao, the following external factors applied: the strength of the Soviet Union; the defeat of Germany and Japan; the sovietization of eastern Europe; the nationalist struggle of the Asiatic peoples; and the "struggle inside the United States, Great Britain, France, Germany, Italy, Japan and other capitalist countries between the popular masses and the reactionaries who rule over them." If there had been no such external assistance, Mao asserted, the Chinese communists could not have been victorious.[142] This is another way of saying that the chancelleries of the West were one of the battlefields on which the communists conquered China.

Proud of victory, Mao boasted: "Communists everywhere in the world are more competent than the bourgeoisie. They understand the laws governing the existence and development of things. They understand dialectics and can see further ahead."[143]

Contrary to the book of Stalinist rules, Mao must have been dizzy with success when he penned these words. The fact remains that when the time came for China, the communist midwives were pre-

[142] Mao Tse-tung, *People's Democratic Dictatorship* (London, Lawrence and Wishart, 1950), p. 13.
[143] *Ibid.*, p. 6.

pared for it. They had thousands of trained experts experienced in the arts of revolutionary warfare and fully versed in Chinese affairs. This, in part, was the result of the work done at the University of the Peoples of the East created in Moscow, with enviable foresight, on May 18, 1921.

The western powers had no qualified technicians to defend their interests in Asia and protect the Chinese people against communist enslavement. Nor was there a strong western will to prevent the fall of China or carry out the announced policy of containment.

The communists helped each other; the non-communists did not—they helped the communists. The soviets won by commission; the United States lost by omission. The communist flood was not contained, but broke through the dams that never had been built.

7. Toward the Fourth Round of World Revolution

> *"A communist war which lasts ten years may be surprising to other countries, but for us this is only the preface. Historical experience is written in blood and iron."*
>
> MAO TSE-TUNG

> *"We are living in an age in which all roads lead to communism."*
>
> MOLOTOV,
> November 6, 1947

INDICATIONS OF PRESENT DOCTRINE

THE SOVIETS find themselves confronted with the problem of eliminating America as the last serious obstacle to the establishment of communist world rule. The United States is a far more dangerous and difficult opponent than any ever before faced by the communists. With an industrial war potential far superior to anything the soviets can muster now or in the foreseeable future, the American system, time and again, has proved its vitality and, despite communist predictions to the contrary, has developed techniques effective enough to avoid economic crises of revolutionary significance. By and large, the American people are loyal to their institutions and show little vulnerability to disintegration tactics. Even if the United States were in the throes of an economic or political crisis, a war against it would entail heavy risks. Consequently, from the soviet point of view, the task of undermining this country requires the development of some highly effective techniques. Whether the soviets have made any appreciable progress in the elaboration of an up-to-date doctrine which would be applicable against the United States is not known, but there are a few straws in the wind which may be indicative of the general soviet approach to the problem.

First of all, it is noteworthy that both Marshal N. A. Bulganin, member of the Politburo supervising the armed forces, and Marshal Alexander Vasilyevsky, chief of staff and perhaps the most important professional soldier in the Soviet Union, are both intimately concerned with doctrinal problems. Vasilyevsky reputedly was one of the commissars of the military revolutionary committee in 1917, took a prominent part in World War II, and seems to be well versed in the arts of political warfare. He is said to consider himself the spiritual heir to Frunze and to have written at the staff academy a dissertation on the "new doctrine of war."

Marshal Bulganin has not always been a professional soldier but came to prominence as president of the state bank. In a little book published in 1948 he pleaded that the planning of war should not be limited to the drawing up of operational military plans but should take fully into account the economic and psychological elements as well.[1] According to him, the principal mistake of bourgeois military leaders lies in their overstress of the strictly military aspects of war; at best, they are able to extend their thinking to a consideration of war potentials. Actually, according to him, war planning must cover the military, the economic, and the psychological fields, and operations must be correspondingly undertaken in all three spheres.

Bulganin is in favor of replacing the ill-defined German concept of total war with that of the politico-military war. Modern war, he believes, is both a national and a social conflict. Propaganda is a weapon as effective as conventional military measures. Political techniques can paralyze an army through destructive propaganda aiming at the annulment (rather than the annihilation) of hostile forces.[2] Psychological warfare can be the major factor leading to the overthrow of the defeated nation's government and its replacement by a new regime socially and politically acceptable to the victor.

On the basis of soviet strategy during the postwar era, it can be

[1] *Tridzat let sovyetskikh vooruzhennykh sil* (Moscow, Ogis, 1948), pp. 12 f.

[2] Cyrille D. Kalinov, *Les maréchaux soviétiques vous parlent* (Paris, Stock, 1950), p. 272. While the authenticity of this book has not been established, the term "annulment" seems an excellent description of soviet thinking.

deduced that the soviets consider that the socialist encirclement of the United States is one of their foremost objectives. Steps that appear to have been directed toward the isolation of the United States were: (1) the seizure of China, (2) the various attempts to get control of France, Italy, and western Germany, and (3) the maintenance of small wars in peripheral countries such as Greece, Indochina, Burma, and Malaya.

This strategy is built upon the theorem that the antisoviet front "must, as a rule, give way where the links are weaker."[3] It is also tied in with an idea Stalin formulated in 1924 that "in the remote future, if the proletariat is victorious in the most important capitalist countries, and if the present capitalist encirclement is replaced by a socialist encirclement, a 'peaceful' path of development is quite possible for certain capitalist countries, whose capitalists, in view of the 'unfavorable' international situation, will consider it expedient 'voluntarily' to make substantial concessions to the proletariat."[4] Hence, according to theory, socialist encirclement might lead to a "peaceful" defeat of the United States.

However, this strategy has not yielded any very impressive results. Despite their weakness and irresolution, the western powers have managed to contain and reduce communist depredations and, far from becoming isolated, have joined one another in a union which, granted its imperfections and hesitations, still promises a greater degree of unity than any previous coalition of western nations.

Under the circumstances, the soviets apparently have considered that other methods must be evolved. Seizing the idea that peace might prove a most powerful weapon of communist advance, they have reoriented their entire propaganda effort toward revolutionary pacifism. The Cominform has been pushed into the background in favor of the *partisans of peace* movement. This ideological reorientation has reached a point where the traditional slogans of class warfare are being replaced by the concept of a struggle between peace lovers and warmongers.[5]

The objective of this pseudo-pacifist movement is to prevent the

[3] Stalin, *Problems of Leninism* (Moscow, Foreign Languages Publishing House, 1940), p. 21.

[4] *Ibid.*, p. 35.

[5] The origins of this reorientation are to be found in France where these ideas were formulated during the thirties.

emergence of a strong western alliance, reduce armaments in the West, and prevent the rise of a positive policy against the Soviet Union. More specifically, the partisans of peace are presently the most significant element within the communist program of revolutionary antimilitarism. Even if this effort is unsuccessful in reducing armaments, western morale can be hurt sufficiently to render American and European soldiers reluctant to fight in a war against the Soviet Union. Communist leaders in the component states of the North Atlantic treaty organization have gone on record that the comrades under their command will never bear weapons against their soviet fatherland.

The partisans of peace have organized world-wide agitation and signature campaigns in order to commit people individually to the slogan of peace and to create some sort of organization to that end. According to a soviet mastermind of the movement, M. Suslov, peace partisan organizations are created on a local, national, and international scale.[6] For American conditions, this was spelled out to denote movements, campaigns, organizations, or committees "in every union, church, block, neighborhood, shop, department, shift, industry, city, county, state."[7]

The term "partisan," of course, has not been selected accidentally: The "peace lovers" are supposed to become partisans in the proper meaning of the word and to be able, in case of war, to engage in sabotage and rear area warfare, that is, to destroy military equipment, disorganize logistics and traffic, call industrial strikes, blow up ammunition dumps and warehouses, and so forth.[8] As an indication of soviet plans, we need merely to remember the communist effort during 1949 and 1950 to block the dispatch of military equipment from the United States to western Europe.[9]

Great emphasis is laid on work "in decisive factories and unions."[10] Religious, women, youth, student, sport, and cultural or-

[6] *Report on the Communist "Peace" Offensive, a Campaign to Disarm and Defeat the United States,* U. S. House of Representatives, Committee on Un-American Activities (Washington, D. C., Govt. Print. Off., April 1951), p. 5.

[7] *Ibid.,* p. 39.

[8] See *Manifesto to All Slavs,* issued by the Second All-Slavonic Congress (Moscow, 1942), *ibid.,* p. 7.

[9] For a few details, see *ibid.,* p. 30.

[10] *Ibid.,* p. 41.

ganizations,[11] as well as national minority groups, are principal targets.[12] There are attempts to set up foreign-policy fronts designed to change the policy of the United States. The purpose of it all is "to sap American morale and secure converts to treason."[13]

However, there is an even more sinister purpose: The peace partisans have been making systematic attempts to induce scientists, a key group in modern war, to civil disobedience. This stratagem has the triple purpose of supplying secret information to the Soviet Union, of reducing and sabotaging American production of modern weapons, and of turning the influence of the scientists "in a direction advantageous to the Soviet Union."[14] Concurrently, the partisans try to negate the effectiveness of atomic weapons in the American arsenal by demanding that "any government which first uses atomic weapons against any other country . . . should be dealt with as a war criminal."[15]

The ultimate of the soviet peace strategy would be to provoke, if and when advantageous to the Soviet Union, western predemoralized armies into offensive attacks, destroy the fighting spirit among western soldiers, induce the defeat and surrender of western forces on forward battlefields, and accomplish the destruction of units not yet demoralized or defeated. This would be in line with Stalin's ideas on the great value of the counteroffensive.[16]

In accordance with the Stalinist idea that propaganda alone is not effective but must be accompanied by real struggle, the soviets have engaged in peripheral war in Korea. No operative contradiction exists between pacifist propaganda and the launching of aggressive war. In soviet thinking, pacifist propaganda cannot hit home unless the targets of that propaganda are actively engaged in fighting and unless, by their physical sufferings and psychological experiences, they are convinced of the absolute necessity for peace.

The concept of peripheral war has assumed a significant place

[11] *Ibid.*, p. 6.

[12] *Ibid.*, p. 41.

[13] *Ibid.*, p. 2.

[14] *Ibid.*, pp. 82 f.

[15] *The Communist "Peace Petition" Campaign,* U. S. House of Representatives, Committee on Un-American Activities, Interim Statement (Washington, D. C., Govt. Print. Off., July 1950), p. 2.

[16] Stalin's Letter to Colonel Razin, *Military Affairs,* XIII, No. 2 (Summer 1949), p. 77.

in the soviet scheme of things. Such wars disperse western strength and prevent a concentrated build-up of real striking power. They create dissensions among allies and offer an excellent chance of splitting the Atlantic union. By pitting second-class satellite forces against first-class western armies, they give the soviets an opportunity to keep abreast of western military developments while, precisely because of that war, they are in a position to consolidate their hold over the satellite areas.

The Korean war showed the emergence of a novel type of non-military attack. This attack can be described best as the "freezing of strategy" or the concept of the artificially "fixed war." It is a concept which seems to be applicable when war is waged without intense public support and without a clearly defined strategic purpose. Obviously, it is feasible to influence an opponent's strategy if his war depends upon a coalition of nations whose various interests are neither harmonious nor congruent and who intend to fight only to arrive at a poor compromise.

The mechanics of fixed war are simple: The opponent is to be restrained from using his strongest weapons and from using to their best advantage the weapons which he does employ. For example, a nation controlling the seas may be dissuaded from imposing a naval blockade, or a nation controlling the air may be restrained from bombing industrial targets of significance.

There is also the new concept of the "sanctuary," established by threatening further aggression. In the Korean war, the Chinese communists operate from bases in Manchuria which have been made safe from United Nations attack exactly as the partisan bases in Yugoslavia, Albania, and Bulgaria were never touched during the guerrilla war in Greece.[17]

The idea of fighting a war from a safe haven is indeed highly attractive and will probably be developed much further. Its most important application for the future possibly lies in the neutralization of technical superiority. While this tactic does favor an aggressor by eliminating many of the risks inherent in seizing the military initia-

---

[17] For other examples of restrictions on United States forces in Korea, see, *Hearings before the Committee on Armed Services and the Committee on Foreign Relations, Military Situation in the Far East, Part IV* [U. S. Congress, 82nd, 1st sess., Senate. (Washington, D. C., Govt. Print. Off., 1951), pp. 3076, 3090]. (Hereafter referred to as *Far East Hearings*.)

tive, some disadvantages, especially those relating to the requirement for reciprocity in allowing sanctuary, are apparent. The Japanese sanctuary for U. S. aircraft must have annoyed the communist fighters on the Korean front, just as the safety of central Greece for those Americans directing and underwriting the Greek war effort undoubtedly posed some exasperating problems for communist guerrillas. The sanctuary tactic cuts both ways, but it works, nevertheless, to the advantage of the party on the offensive.

Unquestionably the soviets are working on a technique which would make an all-out shooting war unnecessary and still provide them with the coveted world success.

Marxism teaches that capitalism inevitably breeds imperialistic wars. This is a true proposition. But the talmudists draw the false conclusion from this about the impossibility of avoiding a new world war. They do not take into consideration the fact that in contemporary conditions— because of the increased strength of the USSR, because of the presence of the countries of people's democracy, because of the colossal extent of the organized mass movement for peace, because of the basic change in the relationship between the camp of peace, socialism, and democracy and the camp of war and imperialistic reaction—a new war can be avoided, if the peoples take the fate of peace into their own hands. To deny this possibility means to play into the hands of the warmongers, to sow abroad a feeling of hopelessness, despair, and fatalism, instead of inspiring the masses to struggle against the warmongers.[18]

The meaning of this is simple: If the partisans of peace succeed in getting into power or if they persuade the democratic nations to surrender to communism, revolutionary war would be superfluous. Democratic capitulation is a more satisfactory alternative to the Kremlin than a third world war which sovietism has a lesser chance to survive or win than capitalism. The soviets must reason that the peaceful method is worth a try.

[18] *Bolshevik,* No. 11, June 15, 1951, p. 23.

Communist Doctrine in World War III

> *"Only after we overthrow, completely defeat and ex-*
> *propriate the bourgeoisie in the entire world, and not*
> *only in one country, will wars become impossible."*
>
> LENIN,
> The Military Program of the Proletarian Revolution.

IT OFTEN is asserted that atomic weapons do not fit into the soviet operational concept, that the soviets evaluate atomic weapons as relatively unimportant, and that even if they wanted to employ them they would not be able to use them effectively. Moreover, why should they utilize atomic aerial weapons if conventional methods prove adequate?

In the first place, the soviets, so long as they remain realistic, cannot believe that, however effectively they may employ their non-military weapons, the United States will inevitably be eliminated without the application of military force and without the infliction of decisive military defeat. Whatever stratagems they may try out, they cannot afford realistically ever to plan on any other basis. To establish world communism, a soviet war with the United States is prerequisite.[19]

In the second place, how can Russia defeat the United States? Ground defeat overseas would scarcely have decisive significance. In any event, it would not destroy the American capability of waging atomic air war against the Soviet Union. However severe American defeats overseas might be, American industry would stay intact, while the Russian industry would suffer from devastating air attacks. But how to attack the United States?

---

[19] The tactics of the partisans-of-peace movement can be compared to early socialist tactics of "utilizing all paths of legal development for the purpose of forming and training the proletarian armies, to utilizing parliamentarism in conformity with the conditions under which the status of the proletariat was . . . that of an opposition." According to Stalin, the mortal sin of this tactic was not that the parliamentary (or propagandistic) forms of struggle were used but that their importance was overestimated. These "forms of struggle" were succeeded by a "period of open revolutionary battles" and "extra-parliamentary forms of struggle." *Problems of Leninism, op. cit.*, p. 58.

Surface invasion is hardly possible, for obvious reasons. An airborne invasion on the scale necessary to defeat the United States is likewise impossible: There are simply not enough planes to make such an assault feasible. Consequently, strategic air power is the only military method presently in sight which could be used effectively against the United States.

We need not belabor the fact that atomic air power is far more powerful than conventional air power. Actually, there are not eonugh airplanes in the world to bomb the United States into submission with conventional bombs. Thus, if the soviets are preparing for war against the United States, they must plan for atomic warfare. They have no other choice in the matter, except to forego military conflict.

Is atomic warfare in contradiction to communist doctrine? Of course, even if the soviets did not like the idea of atomic air war, they still would be compelled to adjust their thinking to reality. However, a decision to wage atomic warfare would actually be fully in accord with communist doctrine. Stalin has always been a firm believer in "master weapons." In the course of his long military career he repeatedly singled out the weapon which he considered the most important or, as he once spoke of artillery, the "God of War." This belief in master weapons is not metaphysical but is simply an acknowledgment of the fact that, at a given time and within a given situation, some weapons have a predominant influence on military operations.

Stalin has never stuck to one particular master weapon but has acted on what might be called a theory of variable or succeeding master weapons. This is not only in line with dialectic reasoning but lends support to the contention that, in Stalin's thinking, the master weapon of the next war will be different from the master weapon of the last war.

According to Stalin, World War II was "a war of motors." He anticipated, quite rightly, that those powers with "overwhelming superiority in the production of motors" would win the war.[20] Thus, Stalin is fully aware of the value of mobility. His concern of more than thirty years with artillery also shows that he is fully cognizant of the value of fire power. He is enough of a military expert, as are

[20] Stalin, *The Great Patriotic War of the Soviet Union* (New York, International Publishers, 1945), p. 32.

most of his advisers, to realize that an airplane carrying atomic bombs is the one weapon which at present combines maximum fire power with maximum mobility.

True, there is no record that, prior to World War II, Stalin considered aviation a master weapon. Yet, both he and Frunze noted the importance of air power at a very early stage and assigned to it vital tactical roles. Tukhachevsky developed the concept of strategic air-borne operations. This concept was not put into practice, despite three costly attempts, because it exceeded soviet capabilities.[21] Voroshilov pointed out that aviation is the best weapon for surprise attacks and the only one with which to wage war against a distant enemy.[22]

During World War II, Stalin is said to have developed the idea that air power must be used in a concentrated fashion and in massive strength.[23] According to a Russian analysis of Stalin's thinking, air power must support ground operations, execute strategic bombing missions, and aim at achieving air control. Aviation is the weapon of the heavy blow, which aspires to full destruction and defeat of the enemy.[24] While not couched in familiar terms, this broad concept is not essentially at variance with western ideas of strategic air power.

Still, Stalin may not be an air enthusiast. It is known, however, that G. M. Malenkov and V. M. Molotov, two of the likely successors to Stalin, are great believers in air power. Malenkov presently bosses Russian aviation.[25] As Stalin's influence wanes and the importance of these younger men grows, the Soviet Union more and more will be oriented toward strategic air warfare.

[21] Asher Lee, *The Soviet Air Force* (London, Duckworth, 1950), pp. 96–116. The soviets are confident that the importance of air-borne operations will increase. See *Voyennaya Mysl*, Moscow, August 1946, pp. 29–39. The soviets, incidentally, did use strategic air-borne forces for the occupation of Bessarabia and, less successfully, in Finland (1940). According to Kalinov, *op. cit.*, p. 285, a Russian marshal is said to have advocated "three dimensional" tactical break-throughs with air-borne forces: "The acceleration of the tempo of war remains the supreme objective of military operations."

[22] Stalin and Voroshilov, *L'Armée rouge est prête, suivi d'un précis populaire de l'histoire de l'armée rouge* (Paris, Bureau d'Editions, 1938), p. 31.

[23] Colonel A. G. Ordin, *Moguchaya stalinskaya aviatsiya* (Moscow, 1950), pp. 22–25.

[24] Colonel A. G. Ordin, *Vozdushnyi flot strany sovyetov* (Moscow, 1949), p. 38.

[25] *Military Review*, XXXI (December 1951), 73, Ft. Leavenworth, Kansas.

So much for the theory which, obviously, was being altered and developed along with technological changes. Soviet operations seem to be in line with doctrinal changes. The fundamental fact is that the soviets are in possession of atomic bombs. They acquired their atomic capability, contrary to western expectations, within a time span of less than four years. They needed just a few months more than the United States for the production of their first bomb. While their espionage and cannibalization of German and other foreign technicians and scientists unquestionably were of great help, it must be remembered that the soviets carried out their atomic program (bossed by Marshal L. Beriya) in a country which had suffered greatly from the war and which possessed a far smaller industrial plant than did the United States. They could not have acquired the bomb in such a short time unless they assigned highest priority to the atomic program. If this is true, atomic weapons must play a major role in soviet war preparations.

The same argument can be made with respect to their rapid and all-out production of jet fighters. This program similarly indicates, in its defensive connotation, the very realistic soviet appreciation of atomic weapons.

Characteristically, the Russian anti-air defense force is headed by Lieutenant General Vassily Stalin, son of the dictator.[26]

The soviets established a long-range air force as an equivalent to the U. S. strategic air command. Organized in 1942 on Stalin's initiative, it was assigned the mission of attacking German morale and bombing the Rumanian oil fields. Before 1945, the long-range air force was small, but its build-up never suffered interference even during the darkest hours of the war.[27] After the war, the soviets duplicated, in record time, American B-29 bombers which had fallen into their hands. About what enemy was Stalin really thinking when he withdrew strength from the battlefield to invest it in a force that could not become effective before a lapse of at least ten years?

Summarizing the argument to this point, we can say:

(1) To achieve true world control, a soviet war against the United States is necessary.

[26] *Military Review, loc. cit.*
[27] Lee, *op. cit., passim.*

(2) Aerial atomic weapons are the most effective, and probably the only effective, military means of fighting the United States.

(3) The use of atomic air power is fully in line with soviet doctrine.

These three arguments are supported by three facts: (1) Russia's stress on the speedy development of atomic weapons; (2) the hurried acquisition of a strong air defense system; and (3) the urgent creation of a long-range strategic air force. Moreover, we have the most influential men in the Soviet Union directly interested in atomic or aerial warfare: Molotov, Malenkov, Beriya, young Stalin, and possibly also Bulganin.

Thus, all signs point to the high probability that in case of war the soviets would use atomic weapons against the United States. In what fashion would they employ the master weapon of the future?

A massive atomic attack on the United States would, as far as possible, be timed to coincide with a moment of extreme weakness of the American armed forces and with a period when exhaustion, frustration, and demoralization were rampant among the American people, preferably as a result of a profound economic or political crisis.

Other factors bearing on the timing of attack include: large-scale infiltration into the government apparatus, disaffection of loyalties among wide strata of the population, and an advanced stage of socialist encirclement. While the simultaneous occurrence of these factors would be sought, they would not be prerequisite for the attack. However, to the extent that human action can be anticipated at all, it is unlikely that a soviet attack would come at a moment when the United States was strong.

The atomic strike would be launched according to the principle of the inverted golden rule:[28] The soviets would do their utmost to neutralize the life force, that is, the military forces of the United States. This could be done by achieving tactical and timing surprise in attacks on military installations, through paramilitary and local insurrectional attacks. These would be aimed at destroying the American capability of retaliating and attacking the Soviet Union in great strength.

[28] See section on "Specific Soviet Principles," pp. 377–83.

A soviet atomic attack would not be launched as a one-strike affair. The initial blow would be executed with force and rapidity, followed by additional attacks. According to soviet doctrine, there would be at least three attack waves, with a third blow possibly launched with maximum power. The first and second waves would strike at the military forces in being; subsequent attacks would be directed at strategic targets—the military reserves, political, administrative, and economic centers.[29]

Specific strategic targets would be selected in accordance with the doctrine that there are "keys to a country" and "decisive links" which hold the politico-military structure together. Soviet writings do not enlighten us about what are considered the keys and links of the United States, but communist party activities have paid particular attention to the auto, steel, electrical, textile, mining, rubber, and transport industries.[30]

The soviets would never rely on atomic air strikes alone. First, they would co-ordinate atomic air attacks with all other delivery systems which can put atomic explosives on American targets, and with support techniques, such as revolutionary antimilitarism, defeatist propaganda, policy perversion, mass sabotage, subversive terror attacks (perhaps with atomic and biological weapons),[31] local uprisings, and partisan warfare, perhaps supported by limited air-borne landings in the western hemisphere.[32] Second, they would launch surface and submarine attacks to maroon American forces overseas, deprive American air power of forward bases, and isolate the United States from its allies. Third, once American military

[29] The concept of successive waves has been defined by Colonel N. Pavlenko, in *Voyennaya Mysl,* Moscow, September 1946, pp. 3–18.

[30] *Report on the Communist "Peace" Offensive, op. cit.,* p. 41. For a discussion of aerial target selection, see Stefan T. Possony, *Strategic Air Power* (Washington, D. C., Infantry Journal Press [now Armed Forces Journal Press], 1949), Chapts. 5–9.

[31] Biological weapons are the fulfillment of the *saboteur's* dreams. Not unexpectedly, the soviets have shown exceptional interest in biological weapons—and in the water-supply system of American cities. See *Materials on the Trial of Former Servicemen of the Japanese Army Charged with Manufacturing and Employing Bacteriological Weapons* (Moscow, Foreign Languages Publishing House, 1950); Fendall Yerxa and Ogden R. Reid, *The Threat of Red Sabotage* (reprinted from the *New York Herald Tribune,* 1950), pp. 7, 9.

[32] It is significant that the long-range air force includes large transport aircraft. Therefore, according to soviet organization, air-borne and bombing attacks would seem to be of a single piece. *Military Review, loc. cit.*

power was severely reduced or broken, the communists would foment armed insurrection or organize an American coalition government which would sue for peace and surrender to communism.[33]

In emulation of Stalin's strategic and tactical principles, we can set down the bare outline of a soviet attack against the United States:[34]

The main force of the revolution:	atomic air power and other forms of atomic power.
The most vulnerable spot of the United States and its allies:	fear of atomic war and chaos created by war.
Favorable factors:	protracted international crisis and high expenditures.
Reserves in United States:	pacifists, leftists, specific national minorities, economic dissatisfaction, infiltrated labor unions, infiltration in government, demoralization of the nation as a whole.
Reserves outside:	the same categories, plus strong communist parties, semicommunist parties, guerrillas, and partisans.
Indirect reserves:	conflicts within allied camp, subsidiary wars, local political and economic crises, unrest in underdeveloped areas.
Direction of main blows:	atomic attack on American armed forces.

[33] On the applicability in the United States of the coalition government device, see William Z. Foster, *In Defense of the Communist Party and the Indicted Leaders* (New York, New Century, 1949), p. 93.

[34] For the pattern of this scheme, see *Problems of Leninism, op. cit.*, pp. 62 f.

atomic attack on American economic and social structure, and population.

social fission attacks aiming at isolation of American government and high command from popular and allied support, disaffection of armed forces, and war-weariness of population at large.

ultimately, open or camouflaged revolutionary attacks to replace the U.S. government by a communist regime.

Disposition of forces:

long-range air force to attack United States and main allies.

Red army to take main forward bases and individual, populated areas.

submarines to cut supply lines and attack coastal cities.

satellite armies for subsidiary attacks to disperse allied strength.

air-borne forces for seizure of key points and support to uprisings.

communist parties in western countries and Latin America.

national independence parties in Asia, Africa, and Latin America.

partisans of peace and genuine pacifist movements wherever they can be placed.

infiltrators to practice policy sabotage in United States and allied countries.

infiltrated labor organizations to call strikes, slowdowns, and carry out mass sabotage.

infiltrators into scientific circles to enhance soviet and obstruct American military technology.

> paramilitary forces to practice terror-
> ism and stage uprisings and partisan
> warfare.
>
> saboteurs and "wet squads" (assassins)
> for specific missions of violence.
>
> spies and agents to procure intelligence
> coverage and accomplish acts of de-
> ception, diversion, and provocation.

In short, *social fission would be the strategic weapons system which the soviets would apply against the United States. Atomic fire power would be the tactical master weapon of this system.*

Such a concept may not prove practical. There may be no encirclement, no serious subversive capability, no demoralizing crisis.
War may come at a moment when soviet preparations are as yet incomplete. The soviets never may obtain a military capability of such
superiority that they can rely on their ability to defeat the United
States. There may never be a time really propitious for attack on the
United States: It lies within the hands of American statesmanship to
avoid debilitating crises, demoralization, and disarmament.

Moreover, the soviets cannot possibly overlook the brutal fact
that atomic bombs would not only have a cataclysmic effect on the
United States but on the Soviet Union as well. The atomic bomb is
unsurpassed as a weapon of chaos to develop a revolutionary situation where none existed. The atomic bomb can produce economic
crises of unparalleled dimensions, give rise to mass unemployment,
and cause mass demoralization. It can destroy the machinery of
state and disrupt society. Thus, the atomic instrument of Armagged-
don may redeem Marx's faulty predictions about the future of capitalism. But, at the same time, it can rescue the hopes of freedom-
loving people and destroy the communist dictatorship.

Will the soviets take up the challenge or, in the face of atomic destruction and perhaps self-destruction, reconsider their plans for
world conquest? The soviets think that World War II has altered the
relationship of strength. The "forces of peace" (read: the communists) have become superior to the "forces of war" (read: the western nations). The communists appear to be assuming that they have
accumulated sufficient strength to keep the "aggressors" in check.

Translated from Aesopian language, this means they seem to believe that they can best their opponents.

The organ of the central committee of the Russian communist party—which speaks authoritatively for the entire communist world movement—greeted the arrival of the second part of the twentieth century with these words: "The era of stability of capitalism—comrade Stalin points out—is over, taking with it the legend of the indestructibility of the bourgeois system. The era of the downfall of capitalism has begun."[35]

If the free nations of the world do not heed this warning, the bolsheviks may be proved right. If the free nations of the world live up to their historic responsibility and to the duties of freedom, communism will suffer the oblivion of all oppressors and tyrants.

[35] *Bolshevik*, No. 1, January 1950, p. 6. According to Stalin, an article printed in *Bolshevik* is to be taken "as a directive or at least deeply informative for our party workers." See Historicus, "Stalin on Revolution," *Foreign Affairs*, January 1949, p. 175, quoting *Bolshevik*, May 1941.

8. Soviet Conflict Management: A Synthesis

FROM CANNAE FORWARD

DURING the twentieth century the Germans usually lost their wars. However, before being beaten by superior strategy and strength, the Germans usually won their battles and showed themselves past masters of military tactics. Twice within one generation they were able to hold at bay enemies with crushing numerical and material superiority and to inflict defeats of extraordinary proportions on potentially stronger opponents. These defeats might well have proved decisive had the Germans had better strategic sense.

The tactical excellence of the German army was not due to the martial talents of the Teutonic race. It is true that Germany disposed of brave, well-trained, well-disciplined, and well-equipped armies. But the German superiority in what may be called the "field military virtues" was not great enough to make it possible for them to win the battles of 1914–18 and again of 1939–41. The chief reason for Germany's tactical excellence was a creative military doctrine.

This doctrine was developed, shortly after the turn of the century, by von Schlieffen, chief of staff of the German army. Schlieffen's doctrine, which, incidentally, was not studied in the United States before 1916, was patterned after the battle of Cannae won in 216 B. C. by Hannibal over the Romans under Terentius Varro.

In Schlieffen's interpretation, Hannibal's battle concept was as follows:

The hostile front is not the objective of the principal attack. It is not against that point that the troops should be massed and the reserves disposed; the essential thing is to crush the flanks. They ought not to be sought merely in front but along the entire depth and extension of the hostile formation. The extermination is completed by an attack against the rear of the enemy.[1]

[1] General Field Marshal Count Alfred von Schlieffen, *Cannae* (rev. ed., Ft. Leavenworth, Kan., The Command and General Staff School Press, 1936), p. 4.

At Cannae, Hannibal succeeded in winning a battle of complete annihilation. "In spite of all theories, it had been won by a numerical inferiority." Schlieffen criticized Clausewitz and Napoleon for their opposition to "concentric action" and flank attacks by a weaker force. "The weaker Hannibal had . . . acted concentrially contrary to all tradition and not only enveloped both flanks, but even encircled the hostile rear."[2] Schlieffen firmly believed that Cannae was the masterpiece of battle tactics and that it should serve as a model of all war planning.

But under twentieth-century conditions, attack on both flanks was found to be very difficult technically. Attack against the rear was virtually impossible, partly because of the logistic requirements of mass armies, and partly because fronts extended over entire continents with the flanks leaning on the sea or on neutral frontiers. It was entirely impractical to plan to win a twentieth-century Cannae with inferior forces.

The Germans drew the practical conclusion that it was best to concentrate attacks against one flank, thus shifting the main attack away from the center. They won their initial victories in 1914 through the envelopment of the French left flank.

Subsequently, it became necessary to achieve break-throughs of the enemy front before flanking tactics could be applied. During World War II the Germans developed the tactic of *Keil und Kessel* (wedge and kettle). This tactic consisted in an armored break-through at two points, with the two attack forces, or *Keile*, joining up in the rear of the enemy, encircling a segment of the enemy forces to form a *Kessel*, and then destroying the encircled units from a reversed front.

Keil und Kessel tactics required great superiority of strength at the points of attack. In general, they were found successful only if and when surprise was achieved. Surprise must bear on one or more of the following factors: timing, location of attack, direction of strategic blow, weapons employment, tactical procedures, and new weapons and equipment. However, once the enemy has been surprised successfully, battle tactics do not matter too much. Hence, the ultimate German concept was to rely predominantly on surprise in all its aspects and to be highly eclectic in the choice of tactical and

[2] *Ibid.*

strategic combinations.[3] But the ultimate objective remained the enemy rear.

The concept of attack against the enemy rear thus became an integral part of modern tactics. But, more importantly, the term "rear" also assumed strategic meaning. It no longer denoted the back flank of an army but the entire hinterland: economy, society, population.

During World War I allied sea power attacked the rear of the German army by naval blockade. The ensuing reduction of German industrial output, coupled with its psychological effect on the German nation, sapped the strength of the Kaiser's armed forces. During World War II the newly developed techniques of amphibious and air-borne assault made possible flank attacks of a scope never anticipated by Hannibal, Schlieffen, and Ludendorff.

The modern doctrine of strategic bombing is nothing but a variant of the concept of rear attack. It is the most formidable type of such an attack because it can be launched against the rear as a whole and against each of its elements: military forces, military logistics, armament industries, civilian industries, transportation, the governmental control apparatus, morale, food, people, and social and political cohesion.

Naval, air-borne, and bombing warfare became the foremost western applications of the rear-attack concept. These techniques aim at the disarming of enemy nations predominantly by material and economic destruction.

What is the soviet version of Cannae or rear-warfare thinking?

The Russians were close students of German military thought. In fact, it would seem that the soviets made a more thorough study of Cannae than did the Germans. They realized that this battle could not be understood properly by concentrating attention on battlefield developments and troop movements.

A more detailed study of Cannae disclosed that Schlieffen's analysis was incomplete. It reflected the narrow professional preoccupation of a tactician and overlooked that Cannae was merely the military pay-off of an entire campaign. The really significant question was: How could Hannibal's hazardous tactics possibly have been successful?

[3] General Waldemar Erfurth, *Surprise* (Harrisburg, Pa., Military Service Publishing Co., 1943).

The Roman defeat at Cannae was preceded by Hannibal's psychological warfare against Fabius Maximus Cunctator, the Roman commander in chief who avoided battle in order to wear down the Carthaginians by a strategy of attrition. This strategy scored against Hannibal's overextended army. According to Plutarch, Hannibal, turning to political means, contrived the overthrow of Fabius while covertly stimulating the Roman public and senate to demand the immediate expulsion of the Carthaginians from Italy. The induced political crisis forced the Roman army into an "adventuristic" strategy. Terentius Varro, one of the two alternating commanders, inexperienced, vainglorious, and politically ambitious, sought battle prematurely, before the Romans had developed the military capability to fight their enemy successfully. Hannibal had "sucked" the Romans into defeat.[4]

Hannibal also made effective use of a ruse of war: Shortly before the battle, he instructed a Numidian cavalry unit to surrender to the Romans. Having no time to investigate and no troops to guard the alleged defectors, the Roman general placed the Numidian horsemen behind a hill, taking away only their swords. When the battle reached its peak, the Numidians pulled out short swords hidden under their burnooses, picked up shields from the dead, and charged the Romans from the rear.[5] Hence, the critical rear attack was not caused by conventional battle tactics but by "unconventional warfare."

Thus, the battle of Cannae was brought about by what Hitler called "extended strategy" (*erweiterte Strategie*). This strategy made full use of non-military weapons in addition to surprise battle tactics.

It is this broadened version of warfare which is at the bottom of soviet military thinking.

The fundamental principles of war are applied not only to the limited military sphere but to society and its war-making powers, neglecting none of the innumerable factors which contribute to victory or defeat. All elements of human activity must be harnessed for war, offensively as well as defensively.

---

[4] Cannae would have been the fate of Anglo-American armies if the Stalin-produced clamor for a second front had led to an invasion of Europe in 1942 or 1943.

[5] Sextus Julius Frontinus, *The Stratagems of War* (London, Coxhead, 1816), p. 170.

The communists were the first to reinterpret social and political life from the point of view of war and to expand military techniques to the full range of their applicability. They adopted the fundamental principles taught at military academies, in particular the hallowed principles of the safety of base, economy of force, concentration of effort, importance of the offensive, surprise, adequacy of logistics, adequacy of intelligence, co-ordination of all weapons, singleness of purpose, unity of command, and the will to win.[6] But to the communist mind these principles are only a first approximation to a true doctrine of war—a subject for middle-school teaching rather than for Lenin Institute treatment.

The soviets have not seen fit to publish their doctrine of conquest except in fragments. It may be advisable, therefore, to reconstruct this doctrine synthetically. There is enough documentation available to give a reasonable hope that such an undertaking will not be entirely unrealistic.

Since it is impossible to document each step of such a reconstruction, but since it is even more impossible to forsake the advantages that can be derived from insight and intuition, errors of interpretation are unavoidable. There is no foolproof system by which all the pertinent points can be discovered and the exact meaning of each identified doctrinal element be determined. The choice lies between reconstruction on incomplete evidence or abandonment of any effort to understand the inner springs of the soviet expansion technique.

History does not wait for the time when college professors will be able to footnote every noun and comma of their analyses. Hence, I opted for the first alternative, although I realize that my travels into the *terra incognita* of the soviet mind may reserve for me the unenviable fate of that celebrated explorer Captain Cook.

THE BASIC STRATEGIC CONCEPT

THE OVER-ALL *objective of communist strategy is to bring about the cataclysm predicted by Marx.* According to communist

[6] William R. Kintner, *The Front Is Everywhere, Militant Communism in Action* (Norman, Okla., University of Oklahoma Press, 1950), pp. 153 f. and *passim.*

doctrine, the struggle between capitalism and communism must be directed according to the dialectic development of world society. To achieve the ultimate objective, communist strategy must take advantage of all subsidiary conflicts, exploiting both leaps and lulls in the historical process. The final victory of communism cannot be brought about prematurely. The time must be ripe. However, this consideration in no way mitigates against accelerating the course of events or introducing communism wherever and whenever the situation permits.

After eighty-five years of empirical observation since the publication of the first volume of *Das Kapital,* the soviets certainly have realized that Marx's prophecies will never come true if capitalism be left to work out its problems and contradictions. When undisturbed by socialist planning and war, the market economy shows little sign of leading to cataclysm but, on the contrary, seems steadily to create new wealth and raise the standard of the workers. This development tends to kill the "will to revolution."

Stalin cannot prescribe the holy scriptures of Marxism without destroying the communist movement. Yet, it is scarcely conceivable that a realist like the Russian dictator still bases his strategy on predictions demonstrated as false.

What remains true is a hypothetical syllogism: *If* there were insufferable and continuing misery and unemployment, *if* the economic system were to benefit only a very small number of profiteers and harm the overwhelming majority of the people, *then* the process predicted by Marx would probably occur: A revolution of the miserable and the dispossessed would ensue.

Marx's conclusion was valid, provided his premises were correct. Since they have proved false, the objective of soviet strategy is to validate them. Once the economic cataclysm, or any type of cataclysm, has been created, the historical process can develop as predicted.

If he were to put words into Stalin's mouth, he would say: "All right, Marx's predictions did not come true. Let us make them true. Let us ruin the capitalist political and economic system. Let us force and forge that big and prolonged cataclysmic crisis. Then the people will have no choice but to rise and to support the soviet liberators."

Thus, the strategy of modern communism depends not upon

Marx's original construction but upon the following variant: The capitalist society with its democratic political structure is subject to the artificial induction of severe crises. Where Marx was inclined to expect spontaneous and natural developments, the modern communists act to infect capitalism artificially. Communism is seen not as the product of relatively uncontrolled historical processes but as the consequence of sociological warfare. The destruction of capitalism must be accomplished, not by historical or economic erosion, but by the strategy and tactics of power. The communist movement must not be pulled by the locomotive of history but must act as engineer of its own success.

COMMUNIST ATTITUDES TO ACTION

ENTHUSIASM and efficiency are the keys to communist success. Revolutionary enthusiasm involves a strong will to win the conflict with capitalism. This will to win must permeate and vitalize all communist activities, be they strategic, tactical, or organizational. Persons subject to vacillation or imbued with defeatism do not qualify as professional communists.

Efficiency is, first of all, tenacity and endurance. It is an "indomitable force which neither knows nor recognizes obstacles; which with its business-like perseverance brushes aside all obstacles; which continues at a task once started until it is finished, even if it is a minor task; and without which serious constructive work is inconceivable."[7]

Second, efficiency is organization. The struggle between capitalism and communism is a conflict between organized societies and classes which may or may not mean conflict between armed forces but which must necessarily involve a struggle between organized units of power. As power embraces all phases of human life, so must it be organized in all its manifestations.

All other factors being equal, a struggle for total power will be won by the society or class whose strength is best organized, the class which is unified and not paralyzed by serious cleavages.

[7] Stalin, *Problems of Leninism* (Moscow, Foreign Languages Publishing House, 1940), p. 85.

Communist organizations are characterized by the following general factors:

(1) Political leadership is supreme, taking precedence over all others. The operative basis for a decision must always be political rather than technical.

(2) Political leadership is always held by the communist party and, internally, in the hands of the controlling elements within that party.

(3) Communist organizations are all-inclusive, extending to all phases of human activity.

(4) There are communist, semicommunist, sympathizing and cryptocommunist organizations.

Efficiency is achieved when component organizations are run in a military fashion and the rules of military discipline are observed.[8] Communist organizations are not debating societies but are military and paramilitary staffs and cadres.

Efficiency depends, third, on proper decision-making.

Decisions must be made rationally, with full regard to expediency and opportunity: In a given situation, which strategy and which tactics yield the best results in return for the least investment and least risk? The term "rational" does not mean the same in the Marxist as in the western context.[9] The assumption underlying the Marxist rationale is that the non-communist world is decaying.

In making decisions, care must be taken to anticipate the future. The future should be constructed according to the dialectic scheme. The basic decision must fit the thesis situation. It should be supplemented by tentative decisions fitting the anticipated antithesis situation. A new strategy must be prepared for the expected synthesis.

Each situation must be met with a maximum and a minimum program. If possible, there should be alternate solutions to each maximum and minimum decision.

Each decision should consist of two parts: What is to be done to the enemy? What is to be done to the communist forces?

Decision-making should not be rendered difficult by moral or

[8] This point was fully developed by Kintner, *op. cit., passim.*

[9] While Stalinists try to be rational, they are prone to interpret and decide in rigid patterns. In the past they have proved quite unable to understand the workings of American society. They may discover weak points but often fail to perceive elements of strength.

ideological inhibitions nor by infatuation with doctrinal points developed a long time ago. The basic assumption is, in Molotov's words, that "all paths can lead to communism."

While decisions must be prepared with great care and made with scientific (Marxist) objectivity and personal detachment, errors can occur.[10] Therefore, efficiency depends, fourth, on unity of command. Communist and semicommunist organizations everywhere must follow the line as laid down by the highest communist authority.

There must be no deviations or modifications, unless they have been calculated carefully and are deliberately parts of the over-all plan. Obviously, this emphasis on unity of command necessarily entails a reduction of tactical flexibility and initiative in lower echelons.

The communists put great emphasis on "style in work." The principles of will to win, singleness of purpose, and unity of command play a more central role in communist doctrine than in any other doctrine of war.

SPECIFIC SOVIET PRINCIPLES

IN ADDITON to the standard military principles, the soviets make use of several of their own. Unknown in the West, they are substantial modifications of conventional principles or are entirely novel communist inventions.

The "life force" principle is perhaps the most important of these soviet novelties.[11] It covers three different ideas.

The life force is, first, the main offensive striking element of a power organization, the force that can most damage the opponent. Usually, this type of life force will comprise the armed forces or vital parts of it, for example, the plane-tank-engineer team of the Wehr-

---

[10] Nathan Leites, *The Operational Code of the Politburo* (New York, McGraw-Hill, 1951), Chap. 4, "The Calculus of the General Line," gives additional points on communist techniques of decision-making.

[11] In the strictly literal sense, the term "life force" (*zhivaya sila*) refers to human beings. It is used to describe man power *per se* or key personnel or key organizations. There is also the term "vital points" (*zhivyye* or *zhiznennye punkty*) which denotes both points with a great deal of activity and material points of focal importance. If the teachings at the Lenin Institute are taken as a guide, the operational usage of the term "life force" refers to all elements, human or otherwise, which are of key or vital importance in a given situation and, above all, to those which possess offensive striking power.

macht in 1941. But the main striking arm could also be of a non-military nature, for example, a very effective political warfare program.

From the offensive viewpoint, the enemy life force is the primary target of attack. Defensively, one's own life force must be protected against enemy attack and against exhaustion. Once the enemy striking arm has been destroyed, forces can hit or occupy any target they like.

Life force is, second, the key element or elements by which a society or organization is held together. This cohesive or cementing force can be a political party or ideology, a quasimilitary organization like the secret police, or an economic factor, such as transportation. Upon removal of this keystone element, the society loses its cohesion and combat capabilities.

Under certain conditions, there may be but one key element, for example, Hitler in 1941; or sea transport for British society. Usually, however, there are many key elements. In this case, any vital element which is both vulnerable and subject to attack should be regarded as a life-force target.

Offensively, the main strategic attack should be directed against the cohesive life force, although the attack on this element will usually follow the destruction of the offensive striking force. Defensively, attack on the cohesion force must be prevented, deflected, or rendered harmless. The principle applies to all echelons of cementing organizations, from local tactics to grand strategy.

To clarify the relationship between these two kinds of life force, let us use an example from aerial warfare. To carry out an effective bombing campaign, one must select a target system the destruction of which will collapse the war-making capability of the enemy. Let us assume that two basic industries, for example, transportation and food, are the target system selected; they correspond to the cohesive life force.

To attack these targets effectively, it is necessary to knock out first the offensive life force, the enemy air force. Leaving the air force untouched would preclude attack on the target industries, at least if the two competing air forces were substantially equal in strength. Once the enemy air force is destroyed or grounded, the target system can be destroyed in a systematic fashion. The significant fact is that the destruction of the air force per se would leave the enemy society more or less intact. Yet the subsequent destruction of the cohesive force targets would disintegrate that society.

Third, there is in any strategic situation a "decisive link," or a factor of overriding importance.[12] For example, the decisive link in the world situation of 1936 was Hitler's intention to go to war, but not the Italo-Abyssinian war, the Spanish civil war, the French popular-front election, or the American economic situation (which was the link in 1929). Within France, the controlling factor was the anti-militarist and pacifist sentiment, and within the antimilitarist movement the key strategic factor was the social program of the popular front, and so forth. The problem is to grasp which of the numerous power factors is the decisive link at a given place and time and to act accordingly. Defensively, the enemy must be prevented, perhaps by deception, from identifying and perceiving the decisive link.

Next in importance to that of the life force, the principle of most significance is that of the "balloon squeeze." Children have a toy: Two balloons are connected by a tube. If one balloon is squeezed the other balloon increases in size.

This principle, which also could be called the "inverted golden rule," is fundamental to virtually every communist action.[13] For example, if the soviets set about improving the morale of the soviet military forces, they will at the same time try to deteriorate the morale of the enemy. If they want to produce an economic crisis in an enemy country, they will at the same time attempt to guarantee the Soviet orbit against economic disturbances. If they concentrate for an offensive strike, they will aim at dispersing the enemy's military forces.

What is the significance of the principle? In most cases, communist disintegration work will have only moderate success. Most communist short-range efforts at building up their own forces likewise will yield limited results. Taken singly and projected over short periods, neither effort makes much difference. Yet in conjunction, the two limited successes may yield rapidly very formidable results.

Let us assume that demoralization work reduces the effective

[12] The "decisive link" is not a "life force" in the proper sense. Since the two terms often are confused, they are treated here together.

[13] Despite its importance, I have been unable to discover the soviet name of this principle which, incidentally, is but an application of the dialectic scheme.

striking power of an enemy from 100 to 90. Let us assume, further-more, that concurrent morale-building in the communist organization increases the striking power from 100 to 110. Neither operation, by itself, is too significant, but the theoretical difference achieved by the combined operation is one of 22 per cent.

The principle of "parasitation" states that elements of enemy strength ought to be detached from the hostile force and added to the communist organization. For example, deserters should be re-trained and incorporated into the communist armed forces; or in-dustrial facilities situated in the enemy country should work for the communists or, if possible, be bodily transferred into soviet-con-trolled territory (lend-lease, dismantling); or wealth produced by non-communists should, if possible, be transferred to communists through gifts, loans, patent grants, and so forth.

Balloon squeeze and parasitation can be employed concurrently. Assume a non-communist power has a potential of 100, while the communist power's potential stands merely at 80. Parasitation trans-fers 10 points from the non-communists to the communists. The po-tential of both now stands equal at 90. Application of the balloon squeeze, for instance in the form of demoralization and morale-building, reduces the non-communist potential by another 10 points and increases that of the communists by the same amount. The orig-inal non-communist superiority of 100:80 has been replaced by a non-communist inferiority of 80:100.

Whenever possible the communists will not limit their efforts to one specific problem but will tackle several problems at once. Such an approach does not lead to dispersal of their strength but enables them to withdraw when and where they are unsuccessful in order to concentrate where conditions are better. There should be simul-taneous offensives and a mixture of offensive and defensive tactics. Parallel operations make it more difficult for the enemy to identify the main thrust and to take proper and timely countermeasures. Whenever enemy countermeasures prove effective, the center of op-eration gravity is shifted.

Parallel and successive operation methods are closely correlated with the technique of variable attack. In general, no action should ever be undertaken without confusing the opponent on intent and method. If simple deception cannot be relied upon, double deception must be resorted to: One actually must carry out what one appears to be doing, on the theory that the enemy will assume that one does something else.

Deception is facilitated by continuous feints, series of unrelated actions, alternations of tension and relaxation, alternations between weapons systems, and by activity of such diversity and scope that the span of the enemy's attention is not adequate to cover the pattern of operations. This latter might be called the "razzle-dazzle" principle.

Reserves are considered to be of great importance; the soviets have done more thinking about reserves, and value them much higher than most western strategists. (A major factor in the French defeat of 1940 was the failure of the French general staff, though preparing for a defensive, to keep an adequate strategic reserve.)

Reserves are of a triple character: There are, first, the forces which the soviets use in addition to their regular forces. Second, the regular forces are divided into strike and reserve units. Reserves should be relatively large and should be weakened only in extreme emergencies. They are needed to follow up offensives, to provide security in defensive operations, as well as for tactics of multiple blows and for counteroffensives.

Third, there are stock-pile reserves. It is considered adventurist not to maintain ample reserves of ammunition, weapons, food, raw materials, and so forth, especially if the enemy possesses strong air power.

Soviet thinking on the factor of surprise varies somewhat from that of western strategists, who aim to achieve maximum surprise in all fields. The soviets believe that total or strategic surprise usually is not practical and frequently is undesirable. The masses must be prepared for the impending attack; subversive forces must be alerted, for otherwise the soviets would renounce the use of that part of their strength. However, tactical, technological, and surprise in timing are essential in virtually all cases.

This principle, of course, should be interpreted with a few grains of salt. While it is possible that a major conflict might arise out of a prolonged international crisis, during which communist forces inside and outside Russia are mobilized and warning given to all the world, the soviets cannot always afford to forego the advantages of strategic surprise. There was warning before the attack on Finland; none, or at any rate very little, before the attack in Korea. If the soviets initiate a major war in the future by air attack, the odds are that they will opt for strategic *and* tactical surprise.

WESTERN AND COMMUNIST MILITARY PRINCIPLES

A COMPARISON

Western Military Principles	*Communist Conflict Principles*
1. Selection and maintenance of aim	Same
2. Unity of command	Complete political control plus triple structure of operational commands
3. Co-operation	Extends to non-military warfare (rear and front warfare)
4. Superiority of force	Same, plus inverted golden rule
5. Concentration of force	Force concept much broader: multiplicity of military and social forces
6. Economy of force	Use forces which cost nothing: Use them even if success is indifferent
7. Maintenance of morale	Simultaneous destruction of enemy morale
8. Center of gravity	Also emphasis on enforcing dispersal
9. Surprise	Deception; double-deception Disinformation; misinformation Maximum intelligence cover Maximum secrecy on technology and cannibalization of opponents' technological progress
10. Offensive	Greater stress on counteroffensive; first blows against life force, subsequent blows against "links"; target selection based on sociopolitical and economic considerations
11. Indirect approach	Same
12. Maneuver	Simultaneous and successive strikes Double and echeloned pincers
13. Initiative	Same, with injunction always to do something, even on the defensive
14. Flexibility	Not only in tactics but also in weapons and strategic systems
15. Simplicity	Discarded, except for tactics
16. Security	Applies to information; base; and rear
17. Administration	Same, plus militarization from cradle to grave. Greatest emphasis on organization which is considered the main force.

Western strategy has taken its cue from a shallow interpretation of the least valid rule of Aristotelian logic: the insistence on simplicity. Western military academies teach that a battle plan should be simple. The communists do not accept this idea. They follow the opposite doctrine, that a war or battle plan should be made undecipherable to the opponent. Although the basic plan may be simple in its broad outline, it should be complex and contrapuntal in execution.

FORCES

THE STRUGGLE between the communist and the non-communist world is predominantly a power struggle. The ultimately stronger of the two competing groups is going to win; the weaker group is going to lose. The nonsurvival of the less fit is a natural and unavoidable law of politics as understood by the communists.

Power is not a constant or static element. It is dynamic and subject to manipulation. Hence, the foremost requirement the communists place upon themselves is to compete for power positions and to increase their strength as it relates to that of their opponents.

Efforts at power accumulation must be made during any given phase of the struggle regardless of whether the objective strength relationship favors the communists.

Whenever possible, communists must demonstrate their strength and create an exaggerated picture of it. The purpose is to influence the morale and political resolution of competing groups and paralyze their will to act.

The activities of the communists are meant to be guided by the precept that temporary successes or setbacks, while requiring more attention and absorbing most of the day-to-day work, are less important than major showdowns. Every communist effort must aim explicitly at the optimum preparation for the decisive battles.

The material strength relationship between opposing forces should influence the choice of organization, strategy, and tactics. If the communists are strong, they should employ offensive tactics. If they are weak, their choice should center on active defense and camouflaged organizations.

However, they should not be blind to the nonmaterial factors of power but should rather consider strength *in toto*. Strong material force combined with weak moral strength results in relatively weak power. High morale may compensate for material weakness, but not vice versa. Decisions should be responsive both to material strength and morale. Bold decisions may change the moral strength relationship to the over-all advantage of the materially weaker contestant.

Power is a multisided and complex phenomenon, subject to grave errors of interpretation. A nation or class may consider itself powerful even though its power is merely of a temporary nature; or it may underrate the power at its disposal. Errors of this type must be avoided among communists and must be induced among non-communists.

Power is composed of permanent and temporary factors of strength. The temporary factors of strength may give temporary advantages. These advantages should be integrated into an over-all plan of action to enhance the permanent factors of strength.

Mobilized forces, tactical deployment, surprise in all its forms, and morale are the most important temporary or variable factors of military strength. Large-scale industrial production of technologically advanced equipment and man power are the most significant permanent elements of power.

Man power is broken down into the two main categories of organized and unorganized groups of people. Unorganized people, once captured, must be organized. Organized groups of people are either communist or non-communist. Those consisting of, or controlled by, "oppressor" classes must be neutralized, defeated, and ultimately destroyed. Groups consisting of members of the oppressed classes—peasants, racial minorities, colonial peoples, the poor and disenchanted, enlisted soldiers, and so forth—as well as "progressive" groups, are considered as the reserves of the revolution and must be transformed into regular and controlled allies. The proletariat and, to a point, the uprooted intelligentsia of non-communist nations are considered the natural and permanent allies of communist states. Among strictly communist groups, states and parties are the most important factors of revolutionary strength.

Groups of the in-between classes, especially of the petty bourgeoisie, cannot be made into reliable and stable allies. Only in crisis situations can they be induced to withdraw their support from the ruling class and, occasionally, to side with the revolutionaries. However, their attitude to the revolutionary movement is of crucial importance. Hence, every effort must be made to destroy the cohesion of the middle class and to compromise its members through economic insecurity and impoverishment.

Communism concludes long-lasting or short-lasting alliances. Long-lasting alliances are concluded with oppressed classes and groups indispensable to communist operations, for example, soldiers. Prospects for temporary alliances are: groups which, at a given time, oppose the enemies of communism; forces whose interests coincide partially and temporarily with those of the communists; nonpolitical groups which happen to help the communist movement (for example, businessmen who want to make profits); power-hungry groups of any kind; and groups which are the victims of a severe political, psychological, and economic depression.

In the last analysis, according to the doctrine, there are no organized forces in the world which can stay out of the conflict between communism and "capitalism." One of the two camps must ultimately establish control over every existing force. Communists must see to it that they establish control over a maximum number of the as yet uncommitted forces.[14]

Alliances with non-communist forces can be arranged in many ways: by negotiation, deals for specific purposes, parallel courses of political action, economic pressure, intimidation, provocation, propagandistic and ideological orientation, infiltration, and so forth.

It is a basic principle that any non-genuinely communist force must be infiltrated and subverted. Negotiated arrangements are unreliable. The "allied" force must be steered, checked, and commandeered by secret control. It is unwise to enter into alliances with forces that are inadequately infiltrated or which cannot be guided by indirect means. At a given time, it may be necessary to establish direct and open control over non-communist forces. However, communist purposes usually are better served by maintaining secret control over seemingly anticommunist organizations. Invisible strength is a great asset in power conflict.

WEAPONS AND WEAPONS SYSTEMS

COMMUNIST weapons of *violence* include all types of fire power and are used in regular and irregular military operations,

[14] Leites, *op. cit.*, pp. 40 f.

seizure of power, uprisings, sabotage, unrest, and terrorism. They are handled by military and paramilitary organizations and by special operations units.

The weapons of *non-violence* comprise all the tools of propaganda and agitation, parliamentary subversion, antimilitarism, defeatism, political and economic warfare, diplomacy, negotiation, intimidation, and so forth. They are applied by communist political organizations, paracommunist units, transmission belts, and by communist state organs, including the armed forces.

The weapon of *infiltration* is designed to reduce the opponent's efficiency, suborn decisions made by the enemies of communism, neutralize and capture hostile organizations from the inside, and control allies. Infiltration is carried out partly by direction, partly spontaneously as the opportunity arises, and partly by the in-place conversion to communism of persons holding positions in non-communist organizations.

Deception is employed to achieve surprise, disperse enemy forces, facilitate the employment of military and non-violent weapons, and render operations of all types cheap, easy, and effective. Deception is achieved by military feints, secrecy, camouflage, release of partial information, misinformation, disinformation (the neutralization or disproving of correct information), disorientation (the gradual imposition of a wrong framework of categories and alternatives), distortion (false-to-fact emphases), and simple falsification and false-flag propaganda.

Areas in which deception is applied systematically include education, publications, mass communications, diplomacy, technology, intelligence, and all kinds of military and paramilitary operations. Deception is practiced by communist organizations of all types, including the Russian state, cryptocommunist organizations, and transmission belts, as well as by secret communists infiltrated into the armed forces, government, communications channels, educational agencies, and so forth. The main purposes of deception include: hiding of the true strength of communism; distorting the true strength of the anticommunist camp; covering vulnerabilities in both camps; concealing infiltration; hiding communist intentions; preventing proper evaluation of the politico-military situation; and, in general, forestalling and paralyzing effective action.

The weapons of violence, non-violence, infiltration, and deception can be combined to form the additional weapon of *provocation*, which is designed to incite the opponent to action under conditions of strength, place, and timing unfavorable to him and favorable to the communists. Rash and ill-considered hostile action is the pre-condition of counteroffensive strategy.

Provocation presupposes successful propaganda, deception, and infiltration of non-communist organizations. It will yield maximum results if used in conjunction with violent means: Military maneu-vering and threats are the most effective method of forcing the en-emy into action. The counteroffensive hurts most if it takes a mili-tary form.

Communists can choose from three strategic weapons systems: revolution from within; revolution from without; and revolution from above through coalition government. None of these weapons systems has dogmatic precedence; they can be used singly or in com-bination so long as each strategic problem is solved in the most ex-peditious and economical manner.

The technique of revolution from above will rarely be successful if used singly, although unexpected opportunities may present them-selves and must be grasped. The device can always prove useful as transition method to reduce the cost of violence.

Violent revolutions from the inside, possibly followed by civil war, may occur in countries which are poorly armed, have inade-quate internal security, or are in the throes of a severe political or economic crisis.

Revolution from without must be employed against strong and intact countries. They can be conquered by war only. If there is simultaneous combination, these systems stand in a dialectic or re-versible relationship to each other:

War is a weapon of revolution: Military conflict produces the revolutionary situation, facilitates the organizing of revolutionary forces and uprisings, and, through conquest, may install a revolu-tionary or coalition government.

Revolution is a weapon of war: Paramilitary forces support regu-lar armies. Uprisings constitute an integral part of military strategy. Successful revolutions from within shorten war and install a revolu-tionary or coalition government.

Revolution is a military operation: Uprisings must be organized and run like military undertakings. By the same token, *war—revo-*

lution from without—is a revolutionary operation. It should be conducted to bring about social and political transformations in the enemy nation.

Revolution from within makes revolution from without unnecessary. Absence or failure of internal revolution makes war inevitable.

It has become axiomatic in the western world that "war does not pay." No doubt, war destroys goods and human lives, damaging a communist society as much as any other. Yet, communists do not think that war must necessarily be a deficit proposition. While there is always a price to pay, war may be profitable. The communists reason that successful revolution from without will prevent further suffering from "oppression" and, on balance, will pay for itself.

More important, war increases the power of the victorious belligerent. War should be used in such a fashion that the fighting forces taken as a whole are not being weakened but strengthened. War, in other words, is an effective method of accumulating both capital and power.

The soviets put much emphasis on the principle of the security of base which, in all orthodox military thinking, primes the principle of the offensive. Disinclined to gamble with what they have, they shun unnecessary risks. They do not make major offensive decisions without allowing for insurance factors. While not afraid to lose face, they are careful not to fall for provocation. They abhor rash action. However, once a decision has been made, action never should be timid. Offensive blows should be bold and even reckless. The soviets have a cautious strategy but use audacious tactics.

In line with this insistence on strategic security and tactical boldness, they put great emphasis on intelligence. They make no important decisions without previously obtaining a maximum of information.

RULES OF OFFENSIVE ACTION

COMMUNISTS "do not play with revolution or war." They rely neither upon violence nor war *alone*. Offensive military action is to be undertaken only if conditions and the concurrent employment of non-military weapons make success highly probable and significant.

The objective of offensive action is to eliminate the life force of the enemy. A determination of the decisive link in the conflict situation is the first step of the offensive action; the second, the identification of, and attack against, the enemy's offensive life force. The third step is the identification of, and attack against, the enemy's cohesive force. Offensive action should not be undertaken unless a relatively assured capability to neutralize or destroy, as a minimum, the enemy's offensive life force exists.

The first blows of the offensive must concentrate against the enemy striking force. Other targets, however attractive, must be neglected initially. If communists plan an uprising and if the target city is protected by, let us say, an armored battalion, this battalion is the initial target of the uprising rather than the police or the municipal government. Once the enemy striking force has been eliminated, all other elements of enemy strength can then be attacked at will.

The enemy cannot be overthrown except by the use of offensive means. Within the limits set by the principle of security, which must be applied both to territorial bases and to the communist movement, it is advantageous to make the offensive as permanent as possible. Initiative should be retained constantly in communist hands. Continuous action strengthens and trains the forces of communism, gives them self-confidence, and tends to demoralize their enemies. Occasionally, it provokes the opponent into ill-considered retaliation.

If the enemy should engage in offensive action, the possibilities of counteroffensive operations should be explored fully. Counteroffensives can be more effective than straight offensives because they hit an extended enemy. Hence, an enemy counteroffensive must be avoided by restricting each phase of the offensive to limited objectives and to alternate advances with periods of consolidation.

No engagement should be fought without striking at the enemy's rear and flank and, if at all practical, at both flanks: Double envelopment is preferable to single-flank attack. This principle is valid in ground warfare as well as in all other types of action, including aerial operations. Rear and flank attack should be carried out with great strength, if possible by regular forces, but in any event, by irregular forces. If the over-all capability for offensive action is small, the main effort should be concentrated against flank and rear rather than against the front.

The direction of the blow must be considered very thoroughly. A blow may be directed along the geographically shortest line, but often it may be more advantageous to detour and exploit vulnerabilities existing at various locations.

Usually the blow should be preceded and accompanied by maneuvers to induce enemy movements and to camouflage the direction of main attack.

Whenever practical, the main blow should be accompanied and followed by subsidiary attacks. Blows should be multiple, echeloned in time and space without neglecting the concentration principle. The main attack force should be supported by any force that can participate in battle, regardless of its strength.

The main effort must be designed in such a fashion that effective follow-up attacks will be facilitated. The basic criticism of the concept of blitzkrieg is that the Germans had an excellent plan for the first blow but were not clear as to how to develop an initial success. It may be that the soviet estimate of atomic blitzkrieg is precisely that the atomic strikes must be co-ordinated with other types of action, concurrently and successively.

Offensive operations should aim at multiple purposes. Occupation of territory per se is not an adequate justification for attack. Territory must be taken, not in order to control real estate, but to increase power. The new lands must add raw materials, facilities, industrial and man-power resources, and improve communist morale and organizational capabilities. At the same time, conquest must withdraw strength from the enemy. However, even objectively unimportant territorial positions can be useful as gateways to significant areas. The capture of almost any position, as well as the development of vacuum positions like polar areas, causes redeployment and sometimes dispersal of enemy forces. Conquest also engenders confusion and demoralization in the non-communist camp.

In the long run, territorial advance should aim at the encirclement of the main opponent or opponents of communism. In the present circumstances, this implies that communist territorial conquests should culminate in the socialist encirclement of the United States.

Offensive action should be mounted as frequently as possible, but care must be taken to apply that type of offensive action which is most appropriate. Offensive military action should be essayed only if a favorable strength relationship exists or absolute necessity demands.

The pros and cons of offensive action should be considered in great detail. While the future must be plotted dialectically, it is impossible to plan concretely beyond the first stages of the offensive action. The offensive must be adapted to the enemy counteraction whose nature and results are unpredictable. There should be neither definite timetables nor preconceived, never-to-be-abandoned notions on future steps. Strategic action should be developed in line with Napoleon's dictum: *"On s'engage, et puis on voit."*

If effective enemy counteraction is likely, advances may have to be broken down into short steps, but if no serious counteraction is expected, advances may be considerable in scope. Interval periods may be long or short, depending on the resolution of the enemy. Regardless of apparent success, safe and open lines of retreat should never be jeopardized. This rule applies to military as well as to non-military action.

One of the most effective and least risky types of offensive action is to take advantage of conflicts in the enemy camp. If anticommunist powers fight each other, communist strength will increase relatively. If the communists can put the burden of creating revolutionary situations on enemy shoulders, so much the better.

Since it is impossible to anticipate the results of military action, infiltration must be practiced on maximum scale. By having agents in non-communist organizations, the soviets may be able to steer developments according to their intentions and interests.

Offensive action may or may not be successful. If it fails, communists should not be discouraged but should try and try again. If it works, communists should never get dizzy with success. New offensives remain to be launched.

TIMING OF OFFENSIVE ACTION

ORIGINALLY, the communist movement did not plan to operate on a strategic or long-range timetable. The coming of communism was considered inevitable. Since it was believed that the transition to communism would require a whole historical era, most bolsheviks thought in terms of generations.

The idea was that decisions should not be made on the basis of calendars. Offensive action should be geared to the situation. The rule of thumb was that if and when a revolutionary situation occured, an attack could be launched. Care must be taken not to overrate the "revolutionariness" of a situation: There should be no putschism with improvised or ill-prepared forces. An offensive push should be risked only if it could achieve more than ordinary success.[15] Only the possibility of contributing fundamentally to the advance of communism could warrant a major risk, but, given a favorable situation, there should be no hesitation to launch a bold strike.

Disdain for calendar strategy may still be characteristic of communist thinking about the ultimate battles.

But as masters of a system of states, the communists must time their current and proximate strategy. They are forced to draw up mobilization and armament schedules. Since modern conditions put narrow limits on improvisation, and since modern war heavily punishes the improviser, the soviets cannot rely exclusively on situation thinking. They are compelled to operate on timetables.

There are other reasons. Offensively, the bolsheviks can produce, or contribute to the emergence of, a revolutionary crisis and adjust their action to the maturity of the situation. Defensively, they must take into account the timetables of their opponents and prevent consolidation and strengthening of hostile power groups.

Ideologically, they do not believe that capitalism must fall automatically. They are no longer convinced that communism must be its inevitable successor. Politically, they cannot help being responsive to the erosion of their own system. The faithful must be expected to wish that the most decisive battles will be fought before the vigor of the original bolshevik elite lessens and before the life span of the old guard, and perhaps of the first generation leadership, ends.

However, the soviets hardly operate on a tight strategic time schedule. It is not unreasonable to assume that they have something like five-year plans of expansion, to be executed only if and when circumstances warrant the risk. Such time planning supplements, but does not supersede, the principles of opportunity, expediency, and "no putschism." Timing of offensive action should coincide with demoralization and weakness of the enemy. The termites must have done their work before the hammer falls.

Timing should be flexible enough to take full advantage of revo-

---

[15] The difference between ordinary success and significant victory was also stressed by Schlieffen.

lutionary incidents and unforeseen events. It is desirable that offensive attacks are in the nature of a *coup de grâce*.

No offensive action should be risked at a time when communist forces suffer from material weaknesses, demoralization, lack of enthusiasm, faltering political support, or some other "disease of strength." Offensive attacks should be launched only when strength is at a peak and when the masses are eager for action.

If it is impossible to determine the exact relative position of strength, an approximation of proper timing must be sought through probing actions and, occasionally, full-fledged battle tests.

In tactical operations the communists usually act according to strict timetables. Once the strategic decision has been made, the main attack and all subsidiary operations must be launched according to predetermined schedules, with little regard for the local situation. Intervals between attacks are calculated beforehand: The next blow is to fall at the moment when the enemy has not yet recovered from the previous blow or when the first blow's results are at a maximum. Intervals should be timed to force the enemy into costly and time-consuming redeployment.

The timing of tactical operations should surprise the enemy.

RULES OF DEFENSIVE ACTION

THE FUNDAMENTAL rule of defensive action is to protect the life force of communist power. While the enemies of communism will inevitably win victories and even force the communists into retreat,[16] space and time are expendable as long as the life force of communism is preserved for future counteroffensives.

While expansion is not possible without offensive operations, the soviets must operate defensively at a time or place of an adverse strength relationship. The defensive is meant to compensate for temporary weakness and should provide the opportunity for power accumulation.

By definition, the defensive is only a temporary or local strategy designed to prepare or support offensive action. Soviet grand strategy is not, and never has been, defensive in nature. But it employs the defensive as a supplementary technique. And it attempts to camouflage offensive action as defense.

[16] Leites, *op. cit.*, p. 61.

Soviet military power is the main striking force of communism. The cohesive or cementing life force of the proletarian dictatorship is contained within the police, higher echelons of the party, the political and possibly the military and technological cadres, and, as in any other modern state, the key industries.

The life force of the communist movements abroad are the cadres of the communist parties and the infiltrators into the opponent's administrative, economic, and military structure.

The historial process follows a rhythm similar to that of the sea. There are high and low tides.[17] There are situations during which revolutionary expansion is easy and those in which it is difficult; vice versa, the capabilities of the non-soviet world change according to circumstances.

The communist movement never should swim against the trend of the historic cycle. During revolutionary ebbs and non-communist tides it should avoid risk and protect its position while simultaneously accumulating strength.[18]

In the case of enemy success, the enemy must be prevented from deriving substantial advantage from his victory. Scorched-earth tactics indicate the pattern to be adopted. Active defense must exact from the enemy a high price for no return.[19]

Active defense must employ incessant maneuvers and resort to frequent counterattacks even with small forces, preferably against the enemy's flank or rear. Propaganda and political warfare must conceal from the enemy his successes and prevent him from pushing on with his offensive. Communist weakness must be camouflaged by a smoke screen of military and non-military activity.

Occasionally forces may have to be withdrawn to avoid overexpansion. Loss of face or diminished prestige is less important than the preservation of the life force. So long as the defensive forces retreat in order, they can resume battle once the force relationship has been altered. However, if retreat becomes flight, a serious defeat may ensue.

The prevention of routs cannot be left to chance. It is a matter of planning and organization. Special units, such as the military arm of the MVD, must be available to stop flight and panic, if necessary

[17] See *ibid.*, pp. 62 f., for further data on the ebb-and-flow concept.

[18] This is a traditional Russian concept expressed after the Crimean war by Gorchakov: *"La Russie ne boude pas, elle se recueille."*

[19] Leites, *op. cit.*, p. 86.

by force. Procedures must be worked out beforehand to rescue units that cannot be salvaged in a normal military fashion. If a military unit cannot be saved, it must change its character. It may transform itself into a guerrilla band; or a guerrilla outfit may disperse into several sabotage units.

Whatever the type of operation, one defensive principle must always be observed: The rear must be safe. No major operation should be started under conditions of a vacillating rear. There must be no enemy guerrillas operating in back of the army. There must be no indigenous sabotage and propaganda directed against the communist war effort.

If offensive strikes for conquest are undertaken, they should be launched in the direction of areas which, once secured, can be trusted not to germinate resistance, rather than against areas whose population sympathizes with the anticommunists. The longer the conflict lasts, the harder the fighting becomes and the greater the need for the protection of the rear.

Retreats should be undertaken when it would seem most advantageous from the purely military point of view, yet premature retreat must be avoided. If retreat is delayed, the enemy may be induced to believe that his attack was a failure.

Occasionally there are advantages in abandoning territory to the enemy: The evacuated territory can be "seeded" with agents, spies, *saboteurs,* and guerrillas. If properly employed, these forces can create disturbances in the enemy's rear. Hence it may be advisable to feign a retreat to lure the enemy into an ill-considered advance. If an attack against the enemy flanks is not possible, flanks can be created artificially by opening up pockets and weakening the enemy inside the pockets through irregular warfare.

Mao went furthest in this thinking aimed at wresting success from failure. He holds that retreats "should be executed so that tactically they will possess the same military value as advances."[20]

RULES ON CHANGING STRATEGY

WITH a change in a strategic situation, a new line of action may become necessary. There are two types of changes of course:

[20] From an official Chinese communist document, quoted by Robert B. Rigg, *Red China's Fighting Hordes* (Harrisburg, Pa., Military Service Publishing Co., 1951), p. 51.

those which the communists can carry out on their own volition, and those which require a "deal" with the opponent.

In the former case, the change of course should be made without hesitation. There is no need for cover-up, no need for concern over inconsistency or betrayal, and no hesitancy in saying or doing exactly the contrary of what one did before. It is better not to use any alibi than to employ an unconvincing one. There should be no concessions to former commitments and alliances. In other words, the way to change the course is to change it.

When the decision cannot be made unilaterally, deals are made in order to negate defeat or exploit victory. The purpose of a defeat deal is to cut losses and to save the life force. If an unsatisfactory deal or surrender cannot be avoided, it may have to be signed but should not be honored.

Negotiations and deals are weapons. The communists utilize this device in a defeat situation to recover maneuverability and strength. The enemies of communism usually are pacifist-minded. Hence, discussions induce premature rejoicing which, in case of unsuccessful negotiations, makes it difficult for the anticommunists to resume battle. Negotiations per se compel non-communists to make concessions.

Negotiations should be undertaken whenever the non-communists show eagerness to talk. Negotiations should be preceded by discussions about the agenda or by preliminary agreements on some fundamental points. This is a method of securing success beforehand. Properly handled, preliminary agreements can predetermine the outcome of the formal negotiations themselves.

Negotiations should be conducted in such a fashion that in case of failure the blame can be put on the non-communists. The communists always should appear as champions of peace, justice, and progress, enabling them to strengthen their concurrent psychological warfare and put their opponents under pressure.

Deception is an important negotiation technique. Communist objectives should be camouflaged, the opponent deceived as to true communist objectives. He should be led into error on this point in order that he may be induced to yield on the important issue and be adamant about the trifle.

In the case of exploiting victory, negotiations should be employed if non-military means are adequate; or if further use of military means would be disproportionately costly and reduce communist freedom of action; or if continuation of hostilities would entail undesired complications. Victory deals are a method to make war cheap and easy.

By camouflaging communist objectives, weakening the enemy life force, undermining the will to resist, and making a show of conciliatoriness, negotiations can transform limited military successes into politico-military victories of considerable scope.

Communists, of course, never consider any deals permanent. "Agreements" are the phase lines of strategy, sooner or later to be violated or rendered inoperable.[21]

Some Notes on Communist Organization

I. Organizational Purposes

THE FIRST and foremost purpose of communist organization is to insure party leadership under all circumstances; more particularly to insure the leadership of the chiefs of the Russian party.

Organization is needed to direct the struggle according to the criteria posited, to forestall spontaneous action, and to prevent conflicts from degenerating into battles fought for their own sake: Competition for power must not detract the communist fighters from their goals.

Organization must keep the movement from being split into local endeavors guided by subordinate or secondary interests not in line with over-all strategy. The struggle is conceived as global conflict and must be conducted according to the global interests of communism. The danger of national communist parties adopting their action to local requirements must be obviated. Organization must enable the communists to fight efficiently, to use their strength to the maximum, and to insure the optimum utilization of the nations and movements under their control. The combined use of military and non-military weapons and a multi-approach to conflict situations with variegated weapons systems is the responsibility of organization.

The life force must be organized with the greatest acumen and

---

[21] For further discussion of deals, see Leites, *op. cit.*, pp. 88 f.

efficiency. The striking force and the cohesive forces command priority on organizational effort.

Over-all organization must be responsive to the decisive elements, or "links," in the situation: Its character must reflect the predominantly military or non-military character of a given conflict.

II. Organizational Ground Rules

UNLESS organized, ideas are inconsequential and forces inert. According to communist thinking, *organization per se is a force, perhaps the most vital of all.*

The increasing complexity of modern conflict has rendered simple organizations ineffective. The more complicated the character of modern conflict becomes, the more complex organization should be. Conflict organizations must be diversified to handle each phase of the struggle in an individual and appropriate manner. At the same time, tight control must be maintained and the danger of organizational independence averted.

All conflict problems are predominantly organizational in nature. Psychological warfare is as much an organizational problem as industrial production. No activity should ever be undertaken in a spontaneous fashion, although an existing organization must be able to improvise action. Co-ordination of all activities has become a crucial organizational problem in itself.

Leadership is only partly a matter of genius. Not even the greatest genius can guide events unless he has an effective organization at his disposal and unless he can impose his will on his subordinates everywhere. Admittedly, military and political events are partially spontaneous and unpredictable and can never be controlled entirely. Yet, in the last analysis, conflict is a matter of strength. In turn, strength is an organizational problem: Only organization can apply it.

This rule applies to all spheres of conflict, including non-military warfare. Propaganda is partly a matter of appeals and ideologies the creation of which depends on intuition. Once created, however, appeals and ideologies can be brought on the target only through organization.

Since organization problems must be reexamined continuously, and since effective solutions cannot be found by amateurs, there is a need for professional staffs specializing in organization. Like experts in charge of ordnance or logistics, these staffs should devote their full time and apply scientific knowledge to the task of devising and improving organizational procedures. Since organization permeates the entire power structure, the organization staffs must have a great deal of authority. They should be at the top of the hierarchy, one notch below political leadership.

The communists have developed a set of organizational rules to which they stick almost without exception. These rules are:

(1) Political leadership is the supreme authority and decides all broad questions, including questions of strategy, tactics, production, and organization.

(2) Organizational solutions are worked out by the organizational bureau.[21A]

(3) Organizational effectiveness is dependent upon the setting up of specific organizations for specific tasks.

Together with the organizational bureau, a control apparatus must see to it that all echelons and units operate efficiently and that the members of all organizations are imbued with enthusiasm and eagerness for success. The theoretically most efficient organization cannot function properly without co-operation from its personnel. Personnel that does not conform to the high standards of "revolutionary sweep" must be eliminated.

In addition to efficiency and enthusiasm, organization is also a matter of cadres, the officers in the middle echelons. The proper execution of orders depends on their zeal and competence.

Regardless of their enthusiasm, cadres can be effective only as a result of extensive training and experience in all facets of their jobs. Cadre training should not be given in accelerated courses, but requires several years of study and all-round experience. The student must be made familiar with the practical aspects of his trade and be given a thorough theoretical foundation. From there on, study, training, and experience are continuing requirements of the professional communist.

[21A] The draft for the new statute of the Russian communist party makes no mention of the organizational bureau. However, it appears that the secretariat which is charged with "the organization or verification of the party decisions and the selection of cadres" has taken over the organizational functions. See, New York *Times*, August 21, 1952, p. 4.

III. Organizational Patterns

COMMUNIST power is usually transmitted through three parallel chains of command. The triple chain is the first of the communist organizational patterns. (*See* Chart I)

The primary chain of command is the political one, usually identical with the communist party hierarchy.

The second chain of command is the conventional state structure: the government bureaucracy and the armed forces. Its duty is to carry out the missions assigned to it. In communist parties outside the soviet orbit the secondary chain is found in the secret "apparatus."

The third chain of command exerts control over communist organizations and their members. It enforces orders; eliminates unqualified, disloyal, or oppositional individuals; and watches over ideological integrity.

Both the second and third chains of command are under the orders of the political leadership. Control over the second chain is maintained through the appointment of leading communists to cabinet and ministerial posts. The control chain is under the supervision of the committee of party control which is attached to the central committee of the communist party but which, *de facto,* seems to be under the orders of the politburo (or presidium) and perhaps also of the secretariat.

Within the primary chain of command the political bureau or, as it was renamed in 1952, the presidium, rules supreme. Theoretically, it is an organ of the central committee of the communist party which in turn is dependent upon the party congress. Practically, the politburo, or presidium, makes the main decisions while the central committee functions as its staff; the party congress has very little importance. Organizational implementation of the political decisions and supervision of their execution was formerly the mission of the organizational bureau. In 1952 it apparently became, within the structure of the Russian communist party, the function of the secretariat. In practice, the secretariat makes all the routine decisions while the presidium concerns itself almost exclusively with the major issues.

Stalin has had a controlling influence over all these establishments.[22]

These bureaus direct all party activities, which in turn, break down into two types, military and non-military. Sometimes, as in the French communist party, or in the case of the Greek guerrillas, one group handles all military and another all non-military activities. The political leaders always retain full command authority.

If no military or paramilitary capability is at hand, the national or regional top echelon is concerned only with non-military activities.

Below this senior echelon various "commissions" are charged with specific functions and tasks. Their jobs depend on the requirements laid on them. For example, while the French party has a commission specially created to deal with communist members of parliament, the American party has no such commission, for obvious reasons. By contrast, the American party has a "national groups commission" for which there is no need in France.

Virtually all communist parties have commissions dealing with labor, farmers, education, defense, veterans, women, youth, culture, public relations, propaganda, and so forth. In many national parties, there are commissions dealing with paramilitary activities, infiltration, sabotage, and the like.[23] Lately, communist parties all over the world have been acquiring "peace" commissions.

Co-ordination with political leadership is assured by making the commissioners interlocking members of the political or organizational bureau.

Like other politico-military establishments, the communists are organized pyramidally. However, a great deal of interlocking occurs: The same individual may appear on several levels or may hold several positions on the same level. Moreover, one function may be

[22] For the pre-1952 Russian pattern, see, Julian Towster, *Political Power in the U.S.S.R., 1917–1947* (New York, Oxford, 1948), Chaps. 7, 8. Formerly the politburo and the orgburo had interlocking membership and secured close co-ordination in this manner. Whether the new secretariat will take over the administrative functions of government and leave fundamental policy and strategy to the presidium as a supergovernment and, at the same time, ruler over the communist world movement remains to be seen. The full implications of the organizational changes announced during August 1952 cannot be assessed at the time of this writing.

[23] The current organization of the CPUSA is given in *National Republic, a Magazine of Fundamental Americanism,* Washington, D. C., December 1950.

distributed among several commissions: For example, antimilitarist work may be handled concurrently by the defense, youth (students), peace, national groups, and minority commissions. Depending on circumstances, a commission may change its assignments. At one time the veteran commission may be in charge of antimilitarist work, but at another period it may concentrate on the establishment of paramilitary organizations.

Stepping down to the next echelon, the commissions each run a variety of auxiliary organizations, such as the youth movement. Such organizations often acknowledge to be communist; sometimes they admit, but do not advertise, the fact; and in other instances the connection with the party is concealed. These organizations are designed to make direct contact with the masses, which the echelons above them are not meant to do. By taking over these functions, they enable the party to concentrate on leadership and to preserve its elite character.

The second type of organization performs the function of a transmission belt or, in Lenin's own image, of a system of cogwheels. The affiliation of front organization with the revolutionary movement is kept secret. The front organizations use communist and cryptocommunist appeals, but in a camouflaged version. They present them in their most acceptable form. The technique is that of the roué inviting a young lady to see his etchings.

Transmission belts are themselves divided into several categories. There may be, first, a front "which substitutes for the communist party."[24] Such a front may be used to parallel party activities. It may reach those potential and philosophical communists who are reluctant to join an outfit they know to be foreign-controlled. Or, it may substitute for the party if the latter must go underground. The wolf in sheep's clothing is the model of such a camouflage organization.

Second, a front may be designed "to gobble up other groups, such as socialists, so-called progressives or 'liberals' with Marxist confusions in their head."[25] This type of front "represents the extension

[24] Joseph Z. Kornfeder, *Communist Fronts, Their Order and Purpose* (unpublished manuscript, 1950). I am grateful to Mr. Kornfeder for his help in analyzing the various types of transmission belts.

[25] *Ibid.*

of communist political influence into the ranks of others." Example: any leftist party controlled by communists, putting forth communist policies but disclaiming its communist character.[26]

Third, there is the specific-issue front. It organizes people, mostly non-communists, who *on one* specific problem side with the bolsheviks, for example, antifascism, antiwar, antidiscrimination, labor and civil rights, a current election, opposition to a specific policy, and so forth. Organizations of this type may be quite innocuous, like consumers' associations. There are educational fronts to further the success of communist propaganda and labor fronts to give the communists influence over segments of the industrial war potential. Foreign and military policy fronts clamor for help to Russia, create opposition to Russia's enemies, oppose military training, advocate pacifism, and, in general, attempt to influence the nation's over-all policy.

If an issue cannot be exploited effectively, fronts may be created to "sterilize" the issue against its anticommunist impact and to deflect an anticommunist effort.

Fourth, there are operational fronts functioning as part of the party's support structure, for example, commercial concerns whose profits go into the party chest or organizations which give military training to young communists, such as sports clubs or flying schools.

Last, there are espionage fronts. This type may assume a variety of forms: political organizations, credit investigation bureaus, private detective firms, professional and scientific associations, patent law firms, business firms, newspapers and magazines, school, clubs, canteen, and so forth.

Fronts, particularly of the third, or specific-issue types, change their names and appeals. They come and go with the issues. While the objective remains immutable, the front technique swings flexibly with the situation.

The organizational principle underlying the system of front organizations has often been symbolized by the iceberg, where one-eighth is visible while seven-eighths are submerged. The flower perhaps may give a more appropriate image: The concentric circles represent the communist party with its auxiliary organizations, while

[26] The Nenni socialists of Italy are an extreme example.

the eccentric circles represent the fronts. The pollen disseminated by the flower represents the secret agents.[27] (*See* Chart II)

The third basic organizational pattern cannot be represented graphically but must be visualized through the image of biological process.

Communist organizations are handled according to the principle of "organizational vitality."[28] An effort is made to maintain efficiency at its highest peak and to prevent the organization from degenerating into a routine machine.

Organizational vitality is obtained through experienced leadership, careful selection of members, full discipline, and absolute obedience. Compliance with orders is achieved by continuous indoctrination and severe sanctions.

Members mutually supervise one another's ideological purity. Efficiency is subject to constant inspection and control. Supervision is maintained through secret agents and the requirement on each member to report. The intention is to make every communist feel that in all his activities he is being watched by numerous invisible eyes.

Punishment for inefficiency and error range from "self-criticism," demotion, and temporary expulsion to purges and liquidations. Purges are carried out periodically, whether or not there is reason for drastic action. It is believed that unless there is the eternal purge threat, the organization would tend to slacken.

Communist organizations are given the "biotic treatment," with agents and informers playing the role, for example, of penicillin.

With respect to hostile establishments, the obverse principle of organizational disease is applied. The purpose is to undermine confidence, dispell obedience, destroy enthusiasm, disorient thinking, and misdirect effort.

Hostile organizations are disintegrated through misdirection, misinformation, infiltration, and policy sabotage. (*See* Chart III)

Once the hostile organization has been infiltrated and misdirected, an attempt must be made to capture it. Individual infiltrators

[27] Adolf Ehrt, *Communism in Germany* (Berlin, Eckart, 1933), p. 27.

[28] The practical use by materialists of Bergson's *élan vital* is an amusing illustration for Engels's contention that history takes place "behind the heads of the participants."

and small fractions form large units. The chief mission of the small fractions was to delay and procrastinate. The large units may assume control of the organization and employ the captive body, openly or stealthily, for communist purposes.

Infiltration takes its cue from the termite or the cancer. Organizational capture imitates the parasite.[29]

THE MISSIONS OF THE COMMUNIST PARTIES

CONVENTIONAL political parties are loose organizations designed to win elections. Communist parties are revolutionary, paramilitary, or military machines, designed for conflict, violence, and social fission. While communist parties, like other political organizations, have patronage and election functions, they are primarily what Selznick calls "combat parties" or "organizational weapons." Whether communist parties are operating singly or in conjunction with other parties of a similar type, whether they operate openly or clandestinely, they are an integral part of the world-wide communist military and non-military effort.

The primary mission of the communist armed forces is to defeat the armed forces of the non-communist powers. The primary mission of communist parties is to weaken and disorganize the rear of anticommunist armed forces and to destroy their inner cohesion. While the specific mission of the communist armed force, like that of any other armed force, is physical and military destruction, the broad mission of communist parties (and their subsidiary organizations) is the political, social, economical, and psychological paralysis and fission of anticommunist states and coalitions.

The specific functions of communist parties can be divided into three broad categories: organization, deployment, and operations.

(1) As the organizers of *rear attack forces,* communist parties carry out the following assignments:

[29] This book was completed when Philip Selznick published his excellent treatise *The Organizational Weapon, A Study of Bolshevik Strategy and Tactics* (New York, The Rand Corporation, McGraw-Hill, 1952). Selznick's book is highly recommended to anyone who intends a further study of the "combat party" and of induced organizational disease.

(*a*) *Membership and Training*

recruitment of members
enlistment of sympathizers
individual training ⎫
unit training   ⎬ disciplining, weapons, tactics
ideological indoctrination ⎭

(*b*) *Personnel Assignments*

promotions and demotions
assignments for special missions and schools
development of staffs and cadres for:
    mass organizations
    propaganda and agitation units
    secret combat units
    secret cells
    subsidiary and front organizations
    communications units, and so forth
selection of command personnel
dispatch of personnel abroad
contacts with foreign personnel

Logistics is another organizational function of communist parties.
It consists of the following:

(*c*) *Logistics*

Finances:

dues collection
subventions and inheritances
international money transfers, both open and secret
business ventures, for example, publishing, insurance,
    real estate, specific types of trade, and so forth
"expropriations" by violence
counterfeiting

Armaments:

purchase of weapons on open market
weapons procurement by illegal and violent means
weapons transfer from abroad
weapons storage

weapons maintenance
weapons distribution

Equipment:
purchase, procurement, operation, and distribution of:
printing presses
paper and printed matter
communications equipment
uniforms, flags
food
means of transport, including passports, and so forth

Installations:
buildings
secret meeting places
training grounds
"letter boxes"
signal sites
lookouts
sites useful for penetration and attack, and so forth

(2) Deployment is the second broad function of communist parties. Unless the communist party is outlawed, there is an open deployment of communist forces as well as a clandestine one. The secret deployment is undertaken always and, except in revolutionary situations, is considered the more important.

The deployment functions of communist parties may be summarized as follows:

(*a*) *Geographic:*
house or hamlet
house blocks
city or village sectors
groups of sectors
village, town, city
county
province or state
region
nation
groups of nations

(*b*) *Functional:*

>   factory of one type
>   industry of one type
>   factories within geographical area
>   groups of industries
>   similarly for transport, public utilities, and governmental
>   administrations

(*c*) *Specialized party units:*

>   professional organizations
>   sports clubs
>   party or front newspapers
>   party business organizations
>   subsidiary organizations
>   general purpose front organizations
>   special purpose fronts
>   staff, command, liaison units

The general principle is that individual communists join together in cells, fractions, or units and that these cells be integrated into units of a higher order. However, in some countries communist trade unions may be able to organize the entire crew of a given factory; in this case there is no cell formation. In other instances, the communist cell may be formed not in the factory but in the trade union controlling the factory's labor force.

Each individual may belong to the cell in whose area he lives or to the cell within whose jurisdiction he works. Depending on time, place, and tactics, he may participate in the work of both cells or even of more units (for example, if he also belongs to a professional organization) or in only one. Generally speaking, the place of work takes precedence over the domicile, while specialized party units take precedence over the place of work.

Military deployment:

>   cells in field units
>   staffs
>   supply, maintenance, and communication units
>
>   large combat units:

division
corps   (similarly for navy
army   and air force)
army group
special corps (artillery, tanks, and so forth)

higher headquarters
reserve and national guard units
organizations and meeting places of recruits and draftees

Under certain conditions there will be no formation of cells, but individuals will operate on their own, although (in most cases) under supervision by communist superiors.

Indirect military deployment:
civilians serving with armed forces
restaurants frequented by service personnel
military magazines and newspapers
civilians living close to military camps
workers in armament factories
entertainers
veterans' organizations

Combined direct and indirect military development:
regional:
all units in vicinity of military or other installations
all units in cities, provinces, and so forth

functional:
cells in military aircraft maintenance units combined with cells in aircraft factories
cells in military newspapers and morale support units combined with cells in civilian publishing enterprises, and so forth

Cells consist usually of five to ten members; if membership is larger, they usually are split.

The fundamental objective is to have a cell in every block and in every industrial and military establishment. When this proves impossible, in the absence of enough communists, cells are created at the next highest practical echelon. Areas and organizations without communist cells are meant to be visited and worked over by party organizers. Strategically important areas and organizations with insufficient numbers of communists are to be "colonized" by professional communists who, like the military, are subject to "changes of station."

Clandestine deployment supplements, or if necessary takes the place of, open deployment. If the latter, it follows closely and often parallels the pattern of open deployment, except that additional activities are carried on secretly, with a minimum of meetings and propaganda and with a maximum of camouflage and front tactics.

Clandestine deployment must supplement open deployment in the fields of finance and business, communist schools, infiltration, direction and key membership of front organizations, neutralization and capture of hostile organizations, intelligence, and the establishment and training of terror groups and paramilitary forces.[30]

(3) The operations of communist parties may be divided into four broad categories: Intelligence, non-military, paramilitary, and military activities.

(a) Intelligence operations:

collection of information
transmission to local collection points
transmission to the political and military command posts of
    international communism
dissemination of misinformation and disinformation
deception and double-deception

---

[30] The communists claim that they are opposed to individual terror. Actually, they are opposed to it only if terror is improperly related to the main effort or becomes the chief weapon of revolutionary tactics. The party line was defined by Lenin in 1916, shortly after the assassination of the Austrian prime minister Count Stürghk by the socialist Friedrich Adler: " 'Killing is no murder,' our old 'Iskra' [No. 20] said about terroristic acts. We *do not at all oppose* political killing (in this sense, the servile written statements of the opportunists in *Vorwaerts* and the Vienna *Arbeiter Zeitung* are simply revolting), but as revolutionary tactics, individual attempts are both impractical and harmful. It is only a mass movement that can be considered to be a real political struggle. Individual terroristic acts can be, and must be, helpful, only when they are directly linked with the mass movement." See *The Letters of Lenin*, trans. and ed. by Elisabeth Hill and Doris Mudie (London, Chapman and Hall, 1937), p. 401. [Italics in original.]

(*b*) *Non-military operations:*

agitation and propaganda
character assassination and building up of individuals
antimilitarism and defeatism
economic warfare, inclusive slowdowns, strikes
political warfare, inclusive elections and diplomacy
policy sabotage
subversion
disintegration of hostile organizations
provocation

(*c*) *Paramilitary operations:*

retail sabotage
mass sabotage
individual terror
mass terror
demonstrations
coups de main
riots
guerilla undertakings

(*d*) *Military operations:*

auxiliary military missions, for example, scouts, couriers,
    signalmen
disobedience
desertion
rebellion
mutiny
breakoff of military units and their incorporation into revo-
    lutionary forces
attacks by revolutionary forces
partisan and irregular warfare
uprisings $\begin{cases} \text{local} \\ \text{nationwide} \end{cases} \begin{cases} \text{independently, or in} \\ \text{support of Red army} \end{cases}$
civil war

In addition to their main functions, communist parties devote
great attention to the control of their members and their operations.
In fine, then, just as the navy is the force waging naval warfare,

the communist party is the force waging social fission warfare.[31] To phrase it differently: The armed forces wage *front warfare,* the communist party, *rear warfare.* Together with the conventional military force, the communist parties are integral parts of the soviet conflict machine, components of a machine responsive to the nature and needs of modern total war, which consists of front and rear warfare. Not only with atomic weapons is this war fought but with military forces and social fission organizations. Modern war is a conflict between political structures and organized societies. The communist party is a machine designed for use in a war in which "the front is everywhere." (*See* Chart IV)

SUMMATION: ALL IS WAR, AND PEACE IS ITS PROPHET

SOVIET strategic doctrine is based on the theory of the class struggle: The bourgeoisie and the proletariat are locked in deadly conflict. The fate of all other classes, regardless of the subsidiary struggles in which they may be engaged, is dependent upon this central conflict.

The class struggle takes place within each nation. It is also fought between nations. According to communist doctrine, domestic and international conflict are but two sides of one coin.

In a struggle between nations controlled by the bourgeoisie, the proletariat of both hostile camps have identical interests: the overthrow of bourgeois class rule. Wars between imperialist powers do not interrupt or end the class struggle, but rather accentuate it. Class struggle is an integral part of every war, and vice versa.

In Marxist interpretation, the struggle between proletarian-led and bourgeoisie-led nations is a form of class struggle. The local class struggle within the bourgeois nation must be linked to the ex-

[31] This description applies only to communist parties which are not in control of a state. As part of the preparation for the seizure of power, the communists organize in such a fashion that, upon success, they can immediately begin operating as a government and take over, or substitute for, the state apparatus. In a state controlled by communists, the communist party supervises or exercises all government functions, controls and indoctrinates the population, exploits the material and spiritual resources of the nation, and, in general, acts as a defensive force against organizations aiming at social fission within the communist state.

ternal struggle. By definition, there can be no class struggle within the fully developed proletarian nation; but should it occur, in residual form, any linking to the external struggle must be prevented.

Sooner or later domestic class struggle expands into the international arena. The contrary is also true, since international class struggle must similarly transform itself into domestic class struggle, even in nonbelligerent nations.

Peace, as defined by the communists, is the terminal point of class struggle to be reached only after the destruction of the last vestige of bourgeois power and the universal establishment of the proletarian power monopoly. Prior to this distant date, there can be no peace.

In communist terminology, the word "peace" has a double meaning. It can denote the non-conflict type of political relationship in a classless society; but whenever the term carries this meaning in communist writings, it is spelled out clearly. Peace usually connotes a conflict situation in which non-military weapons and methods short of full-fledged war are employed.

War is considered to be the most significant form of political intercourse in the era of class society. All other forms of conflict are subordinated to war, the highest expression of class struggle.

Before the establishment of final peace, the communists contend that the world must pass through a series of major collisions in the form of world wars fought with the utmost intensity and with a minimum of restraint. There also will be periods of "consolidation" and "peaceful" penetration.

Soviet strategic thinking can be summarized in a series of dialectic propositions.

The fundamental proposition is based on Clausewitz: *"War is the continuation of politics."* Since the employment of political weapons can normally yield only limited results, political tactics of carrying forward this class struggle must be supplemented, at the right moment, by military action.

War is the instrument of politics: Military war is the strongest tool in the hands of the statesman, including the proletarian ruler. Second, the political orientation of a nation or a class influences its strategy in times of war or civil war.

The inverse statement, *politics is the continuation of war,* also holds true. As the military profit returns begin to diminish, the war must be terminated and the struggle continued by political and non-military rather than military means. Furthermore, the political strategy of nations and classes will be influenced greatly by the outcome of the preceding war.

The conduct of war is the continuation of the conduct of politics, and vice versa. The political objectives of belligerent nations or classes remain identical whether they are sought by military or by non-military means. Basic political objectives change only if the class structure of a nation is changed.

The proposition that *revolution is a continuation of war* signifies that fundamental social changes are most likely to occur during and after a major war. In the course of war, conditions are created in which armed uprisings can be mounted to install a regime acceptable to the victor.

The inverse of this proposition, that *war is a continuation of revolution,* means that revolution may create a change in the class structure of a nation which (as in the case of the French revolutionary wars) leads to war. A revolution may be exportable to other countries by means of a revolutionary war, or revolution may lead to the intervention of an antirevolutionary power.

The same general meaning is attached by the communists to the proposition that *civil war is the continuation of international war.* War may lead to revolution. Revolutionary seizure of power may be followed by civil war, or civil war may follow international war without an intermediate revolutionary uprising.

Conversely, a civil war may lead to foreign intervention both by revolutionary and antirevolutionary powers. It may be terminated through seizure of power by one of the belligerent classes, or it may lead to war between the interventionist powers. An international war fought between nations led respectively by the proletariat or the bourgeoisie takes the form of civil war.

War is the continuation of peace. Periods of struggle with relatively non-violent means must always be followed by periods in which violent means are employed, and vice versa. The relatively non-violent weapons must be employed as preparation for a coming conflict.

The armed forces are the continuation of society. Strong and weak points of a society will find their counterpart in the military establishment, since the class structure of a given society must be reflected within conscript armies. Conversely, *society is the continuation of the armed forces.* Major victories or defeats will be reflected in the cohesion of society. Strategic requirements may force reorganization of the social structure. Military necessities may impose obligations on society.

Both society and the armed forces are interacting parts of one whole. Without a strong backing of society, the armed forces cannot be strong. Without strong armed forces, the integrity of society cannot be protected. A weak society will germinate defeat, just as defeat will lead to social disintegration.

The conflict is fought in gradations; war occurs at different "temperatures." There never is all-out war without an admixture of peace nor is there ever a total non-war without the admixture of violence. The struggle may be dormant or very intense. It may be fought for limited objectives or for objectives of major importance.

The temperature of war, cold or hot, must be regulated according to expediency and opportunity. This choice is essentially one in tactics and weapons systems.

War is fought both with military and with non-military weapons. Both types of weapons are applied against the enemy as a country, that is, externally, and against the enemy as a nation, that is, internally.

There is a scale of violence. The main categories of violence in ascending order are: unrest, sabotage, intermittent terrorism, class-against-class terrorism, uprisings, seizure of power, civil war, war of national liberation, defensive revolutionary war, and offensive revolutionary war. Likewise, *there is a scale of non-violent techniques* which range from agitation and propaganda via demonstrations and antimilitarism to demoralization, revolutionary defeatism, policy sabotage, and coalition devices. In ascending fashion, these non-violent techniques advance from a reorientation of individual minds to the influencing of class and mass *behavior* which may be activated, paralyzed, or neutralized. These various forms of violence and non-violence can be used either singly; or successively, whether crescendolike or not; or simultaneously; or in multiple combinations. The non-violent scale can be run up by itself. If the intensity of the violence is being increased, non-violent techniques must follow suit and by direct-action appeals facilitate and enhance the application of violence.

A revolutionary war can be of three types: a war imposed on countries in which revolution has been victorious; a war conducted to stimulate and defend revolution abroad; and a war initiated for the purpose of exporting the revolution.

Revolutionary wars play the role of midwife to a new society or of undertaker to lay the old society to rest.

To a western mind, there is no moral difference between an offensive and a defensive *during a war*—whether or not to campaign offensively is essentially a matter of military strategy at a given time. Once it is stipulated, as the communists do, that a permanent conflict exists between two hostile camps, there is likewise little difference between "aggression" or "defense." Within the framework of the permanent conflict concept, aggression to start war is not different from an offensive during a war already in progress.

The soviets always label their enemies "aggressors" for the propaganda profit, but for themselves, they are unconcerned over the moral problem attached to aggression. To them, war is inevitable and must result from the ever sharpening world crisis. The soviets are convinced that sooner or later, for reasons of self-preservation, the capitalist powers must attack. Therefore, the war will be forced upon the soviets ultimately.

Assertions by western statesmen that they are eager to preserve peace are meaningless to the communists. The soviets firmly believe that class affiliations prevent the capitalist statesmen from seeing the truth; whether or not they may be intellectually honest is beside the point. The class structure of the bourgeois society must drive capitalism into aggression, even though its leaders may be sincere pacifists. According to Lenin, "our enemies themselves do not realize what they are capable of in this respect," for example, aggression.

Communists make a distinction between just and unjust wars. The only criterion of a just war is: Who is waging it? If the war is waged by the revolutionary class or its temporary allies, it is a just war; or, more crudely, any war waged by the communists is just, and any war against the communists is unjust.

Taken by categories, just wars are defined as (1) wars of liberation fought to defend nations from attempts to enslave them; (2) wars undertaken to liberate the people from capitalist slavery; and (3) wars to liberate colonies and dependent countries from the yoke of imperialism. Unjust wars are defined by Stalin as those "of

conquest waged to conquer and enslave foreign countries and foreign nations."

Hence, an aggressive war can be a just war, while a defensive
war waged by a capitalist nation must be an unjust war.[32]

Soviet doctrine definitely does not call for aggressive war at all
times. Communists are not militarists and do not fight for the sake
of glory. War is simply an extension of politics and must not be more
costly and risky than necessary. According to Lenin, "the soundest
strategy in war is to postpone operations until the moral disintegration of the enemy renders the delivery of the moral blow both possible and easy."[33]

Thus, a most fundamental rule of communist strategy is that *the
use of violence must be preceded, accompanied, and followed by
techniques aiming at demoralization and at preventing the enemy
from using violence.*

Violent means must be camouflaged to the greatest extent possible. The enemy has to be convinced that his own use of violent
means would be inadvisable; or, failing this, he must be prevented
from employing weapons successfully.

Communist strategy can be expressed in a dialectic sequence. The
thesis reads: The establishment of world communism is dependent
upon the use of force. Therefore, communist forces must be strengthened systematically, to the maximum point.

The *antithesis* reads: The destruction of the old society will be
most conclusive if the bourgeois forces put up only weak resistance.
Their material power and their will to use power must be reduced
to the minimum.

The *synthesis* of these two concurrent processes will be reached

---

[32] Late in 1950, Senator Henry Cabot Lodge, Jr., American delegate to the
United Nations, discussed the role of "just war" in soviet thinking and ascribed
the theory discussed above to Vyshinsky. Actually, this "Vyshinsky doctrine"
dates back to Lenin and was subsequently incorporated as an integral part of
Stalinism.

[33] This concept also interested Hitler, who stated that war must be initiated
long before actual military operations begin. "How to achieve the moral
breakdown of the enemy before the war has started—that is the problem that
interests me," Hitler told Rauschning. Liddell Hart rephrased Lenin's principle: "The soundest strategy in any campaign is to postpone battle, and the
soundest tactics to postpone attack, until the moral dislocation of the enemy
renders the delivery of a decisive blow practicable." See *The Strategy of Indirect Approach* (London, Faber and Faber, 1946), p. 155.

through tearing away elements of strength from bourgeois control and adding them to communist power.

The political victory of communism requires the moral destruction and the physical defeat of the bourgeoisie. The strength of communism must be increased physically and morally, while the weaknesses of the bourgeoisie are to be accentuated, physically and morally. To their own defeat, the bourgeoisie must contribute partial self-destruction. Bourgeois self-destruction will result from demoralization. Demoralization will be stimulated by "pacifism." The war for communism must use peace as one of its most powerful weapons. The idea is simple indeed: degenerative peace for the bourgeoisie and a strong war for the communists.

Conclusions

What are the errors and shortcomings of the communist doctrine of conflict management?

The fact that it was the communists who put together this doctrine, combining their own ideas in a creative manner with the best operational thinking in world history, should not blind us to the realization that this doctrine, while cynical and unethical, is in general sound and effective.

A fundamental rule in logic stipulates that the personal characteristics of an individual do not prove or disprove the validity of a proposition enunciated by him. Whether a person is a scientist or a criminal does not necessarily have a bearing on the accuracy of his mental processes. A scientist may advance a poor argument while a criminal may propound a factually and logically accurate syllogism. *Argumenta ad hominem* are inadmissible.

While one may disagree wholeheartedly with the objectives of communism, as does the author, it cannot be denied that the communists are fighting with great skill and that, technically speaking, their strategy and tactics are better finished and show far greater craftsmanship and virtuosity than do the strategy and tactics of their opponents. Nothing can be gained by belittling the communist conflict doctrine. Superficial arguments designed to show imaginary loopholes in soviet operational thinking would be highly dangerous.

Only fools refuse to learn from their enemies. There is no reason why we should not pick up some of the communist tricks and use them if and when they fit into the framework of our own requirements and morality. If only for defensive purposes, we must understand soviet procedures. The western world must urgently develop a new synthesis of the operational art (which however must be the subject of another discussion).

But despite these undoubted accomplishments of communist conflict thinking, we should not make the error of assuming that the soviets are able to apply their doctrine always and everywhere; that their doctrine requires no further creative development; and that the communists always possess the skills and brains to apply it in a masterly fashion.

Soviet strategy is subject to the personal limitations of communist decision-makers. The present rulers of the Kremlin, most of whom are no longer the products of revolutionary struggles but of intra-bureaucratic competition, are suffering from a gradual hardening of the categories. Soviet strategy often stems from faulty intelligence and erroneous assumptions. Frequently it appears as a pale compromise between opposing concepts. Their strategy is not formulated on the basis of doctrine alone but is required to take into account the military, economic, social, psychological, and political capabilities and vulnerabilities both of the soviet and of the American orbits. *The fundamental fact is that the United States is more powerful and less vulnerable than the Soviet Union.* We often tend to overlook this detail. Yet, we should never forget that up to the present time soviet doctrine has served the soviets as a compensating crutch to weakness.

Once the United States learns and applies the arts of extended strategy, the Soviet Union will be shown as extremely vulnerable. The soldiers of the Red army, and particularly of the satellite armies, are highly susceptible to techniques of revolutionary antimilitarism. The communist state has all the characteristic deficiencies of overly centralized government, overconcentration of responsibility, rule by clique, excessive controls, and of arbitrary and personalized power.

The soviet rulers have to work with a fundamentally disloyal population. Working from an insecure position, they have become frustrated. As their early ideology proved inapplicable and their actions stood in contrast to their professed beliefs, they also became highly cynical. Originally, some of them dreamed of a classless society and of equal distribution of wealth. Today, there is a highly stratified class society in Russia, with an almost hereditary aristocracy, extreme economic disparity, unmitigated poverty, and a most uneven distribution of privilege. Lo and behold! Even profits are making their reappearance, upon official invitation. Discrimination of the worst kind, forced labor, and the most blatant belief in the mission of the Great Russians as the leading nation are commonplace. The old believers have the choice only between cynicism, desertion, suicide, or liquidation. The new rulers are but power-hungry bureaucrats, an elite of yes-men and meek followers of a deified leader, a group of men mortally afraid of each other, of the political police, and of the people with whom they have lost contact.[34]

Whatever the weaknesses of the United States, it does not suffer from decisive cleavages and pronounced economic inequalities. However incompetent some of its statesmen may be, they will be changed in due time, and meanwhile their decisions are subject to congressional and public control. American faith in democracy has matured, but it has not become cynical. The United States government enjoys the full and loyal support of its entire people—even in its blunders. If there is an American weakness, it is to be found in our lackadaisical attitudes, in our political verbalism, and in the slowness of our reactions—all penalties we are paying for our innermost and semiconscious conviction that we are leading from overwhelming strength. Fundamentally, the difference is this: *the American way of life is a success; the soviet is a failure.*

The record of recent history shows that as long as the West is on guard, the danger of communist success is limited. The first series of soviet conquests occurred after World War I, when the western powers concentrated too intently on the war against Germany. The second series of soviet conquests grew out of the nazi-soviet pact of 1939, which was brought about by western military impotence and the resultant need to depend on soviet support against Germany. From 1943 until 1945, Britain and the United States believed that

[34] There is a plentiful literature on this subject. See, for example, Manya Gordon, *Workers before and after Lenin* (New York, Dutton, 1941); Nicholas S. Timasheff, *The Great Retreat, The Growth and Decline of Communism in Russia* (New York, Dutton, 1946); Jules Monnerot, *Sociologie du communism* (Paris, Gallimard, 1949); and the concise, moderate, but devastating history by Waldemar Gurian, *Bolshevism, Introduction to Soviet Communism* (Notre Dame, Ind., University of Notre Dame Press, 1952).

they needed the help of the Soviet Union against Germany. And from 1945 to 1947 the western powers were chasing ideological butterflies hoping that the soviets had forsaken their dreams of world conquest and were eager to collaborate for genuine world peace. But since 1948 the soviet threat has come to be recognized for what it is, and, with the notable exception of China, the soviets have collected more failures than successes.

In order to keep our sense of proportion, we never should look at soviet successes alone. By overlooking the enemy's failures, we overrate communist power and skill. Before World War II the soviets suffered heavy defeats in Hungary, Bavaria, Poland, Finland, Germany, China, Spain, and in dozens of insurrectional attempts all over the world. During the war their plans for France, Germany, Finland, and Greece were frustrated, and they escaped destruction only by the skin of their teeth. After World War II the soviets were prevented from getting control over western Germany and Berlin. They were unsuccessful in Italy, France, Indonesia, Finland, and Japan. The soviets were compelled to withdraw from northern Iran. They failed to intimidate Turkey and to get control of the Dardanelles. They were defeated in the undeclared war against Greece and, at the time of this writing, are a long way from success in Indochina, Malaya, Burma, and India. Their revolutionary war against southern Korea was a military disappointment and a political disaster in that it sparked a massive rearmament of the United States.

No less important than these defeats was the failure of the soviet scheme to seize control of the world labor movement. At the time of this writing, world labor is more anticommunist and antisoviet than ever before. Despite frantic soviet countermeasures, the western nations have prevented the occurrence of economic chaos, and, ignoring soviet threats, they established friendship with Germany and Japan, and concluded the Atlantic pact, which spells the ultimate neutralization of the communist danger.

The defection of Tito was not caused by superior western tactics but represents a breakdown of soviet control and ideological strength. The retention of Yugoslavia outside the field of soviet coercion was due to western strength and flexibility.

None of these soviet failures need to be permanent. New opportunities will arise for new encroachments. But it is also true that postwar soviet successes need not prove to be permanent. Opportunities will arise for the western nations to roll back the soviet orbit. It is within the capabilities of a courageous and imaginative western policy to transform the iron curtain into a straw mat.

In 1920, Bertrand Russell anticipated three possible outcomes from the bolshevik revolution: "The first is the ultimate defeat of bolshevism by the forces of capitalism. The second is the victory of the bolshevists accompanied by a complete loss of their ideals and a regime of napoleonic imperialism. The third is a prolonged war, in which civilization will go under, and all its manifestations (including socialism) will be forgotten.[35]

This forecast is still valid today. Since we do not desire the second or third alternatives, we must prepare for the first—the ultimate defeat of bolshevism.

Whoever would deduce from this statement that war is inevitable has not grasped the meaning of this book. Communism and anti-communism are now locked in deadly conflict. This conflict is being fought with many weapons and techniques, of which an all-out shooting war is only the most extreme. The chances to avoid this sort of war are the greater, the lesser the relative military power of the Soviet Union; the more we succeed in undermining the domestic strength and controls of the soviets; the more hostile the Russian and satellites peoples become toward their rulers and the more they become convinced that the western nations are their friends and allies. If we do not adopt an extended strategy of our own, if we do too little and do it too late, we may be confronted by Russell's second or third alternative. The objective of our strategy should be to make all-out war an *extreme risk* for the soviets and to work toward a gradual modification, contraction, and replacement of soviet rule.

Predictions are the province of prophets but not of normal human beings. We do not and cannot possibly know what the future will bring. Hope is a bad counselor, but lack of courage and faith is the greatest plight of modern politics. Civilization and freedom cannot survive in fear. God did not create man after the image of a squirming worm. He created him as a *Man*.

[35] Bertrand Russell, *The Practice and Theory of Bolshevism* (2nd ed., London, Allen and Unwin, 1949), p. 8.

Index

Index